The Private Press

Cuala Press. Miss Elizabeth Yeats and her companions

The Private Press

RODERICK CAVE

WATSON-GUPTILL PUBLICATIONS
New York

First published in 1971
by Faber and Faber Limited
3 Queen Square, London, W.C.1
Printed in Great Britain
Published in 1971
by Watson-Guptill Publications
165 West 46 Street, New York, N.Y. 10036
Library of Congress
Catalog Card Number: 78-118669
ISBN 0-8230-4400-9

Contents

PART I: PRIVATE PRESSES

Contents

PART II: PRIVATE PRESS TYPEFACES

Illustrations

PLATES

FIGURES IN TEXT

FIGURES

FIGURES

TO MY PARENTS

Plate 1. The Printing Office at Strawberry Hill, c. 1785

Preface

'The possession of a private printing press is, no doubt, a very appalling type
of bibliomania. Much as has been told us of the awful scale on which drunkards
consume their favoured poison, one is not accustomed to hear of their setting
up private stills for their own individual consumption. There is a Sardanapalitan
excess in this bibliographical luxuriousness which refuses to partake with other
vulgar mortals in the common harvest of the public press, but must itself
minister to its own tastes and demands. The owner of such an establishment is
subject to no extraneous caprices about breadth of margins, size of type,
quarto or folio, leaded or unleaded lines: he dictates his own terms; he is
master of the situation, as the French say, and is *the true autocrat of literature.*'

When John Hill Burton wrote this comment a century ago, printing was
one of the few manual trades in which the amateur had played much part.
Today we wonder less at the 'Sardanapalitan excess' of the amateur printer:
the impact of the Arts and Crafts Movement and more recently of 'Do it
yourself' has accustomed us to the idea of people making their own pottery,
operating their ham radio, running their narrow-gauge railway or building
their own small hovercraft for the sheer pleasure of it. As anyone who has ever
set and printed a line of type knows, to achieve the authority of the printed
word, however badly it is done, gives a rare sense of satisfaction, even in these
McLuhanatic days. It is in the end-product that amateur printing remains
different from most of these other hobbies; in the books and pamphlets which
the private presses produce.

Many of the publications of amateur printers are utterly negligible by any
standards. But many are worth reading and collecting; at times the existence
of these presses outside the commercial field of printing and publishing has
produced books of very real literary or artistic importance. Indeed their work
has at times powerfully affected commercial book design, though as the
printing trade becomes more highly automated and more remote from its
traditional craft methods this influence is not likely to recur.

15

There are probably more amateur printers at work in the English-speaking world today than ever before, and a good many articles on the work of these little presses and exhibitions of the books they print have appeared in the past few years. But despite this current interest, there has been no extensive account of amateur printing since Will Ransom's *Private presses and their books* published forty years ago; nor any detailed study of pre-Victorian private presses for over a century.

'What is a private press?' is a question which has never been answered altogether satisfactorily. The fact is that no simple or concise definition is possible; it is almost as hard to explain as the word 'democracy'. Every writer on private printing has produced his own definition. For the French bibliographer Anatole Claudin, writing on early private presses in France, it was one 'set up in a monastery, a palace, a residence or a private house, not the residence of a professional printer'; in other words a printing establishment which did not exist for commercial gain. For the period of which Claudin was writing this is a useful definition, but when one is considering later periods in which state printing offices, university presses and printing departments in every type of organization exist, his definition becomes far too wide to be of use. Other writers, particularly on the continent where strict regulation of the printing trade continued far longer than in England, have often regarded as private any presses which were set up over and above the usual number permitted. Edmond Werdet, for example, in his *Histoire du livre en France* (1862), included in his list of pre-revolutionary private presses in France those of the typefounder Pierre-Simon Fournier (who had in 1762 been named *Imprimeur surnuméraire* and allowed to install a press on which his *Manuel typographique* was printed) and of the Department of War, set up by government decree in 1768. Neither was in the least an amateur affair, and Werdet's English contemporaries would unhesitatingly have rejected them as 'private presses'. What constituted a private press seemed a simple enough matter to them; it was a press owned by a private individual who used it to print whatever he chose, with no thought of making it pay its way. But so narrow a definition excluded William Morris's work at the Kelmscott Press, and with it many later presses such as the Doves or Golden Cockerel, which to the twentieth-century book-collector are still private presses although operated on an increasingly commercial scale. For these modern presses a more suitable definition of a private press would be that of C. R. Ashbee, as one 'whose objective is an aesthetic one, a press that, if it is to have real worth, challenges support on a basis of standard, caters for a limited market, and is not concerned with the commercial development of printing by machinery.' An excellent contemporary explanation is that of John Carter, who in his introduction to the Times Bookshop's catalogue of an exhibition of *English private presses 1757 to 1961* (1961) wrote of 'the fundamental principle of private press printing; the principle that, whether or not the press has to pay its way, the printer is more interested in making a good book than a fat profit. He prints what he likes, how he likes, not what someone else has paid him to print. If now and then he produces something more apt for looking at and handling than for the mundane purpose of reading, remember he is concerned as much with his own pleasure and education as with yours.'

In this book I have attempted to show some of the different sorts of press which have been owned or operated by amateurs who have worked outside the conventional book trade channels in the past five hundred years. Some of those I have described fit uneasily into the section in which I have dealt with them; any classification for such eccentric and often irrational undertakings can be little better than a Procrustean bed. By no means all private presses have been included, nor has it been possible to deal at length with the work of all those mentioned: the selection is necessarily a personal one, and if it proves eccentric it will be in the traditions of the material.

It is always a pleasant duty to thank those who have given help. In the present case, if formal acknowledgement were to be made to all those libraries and individuals who have assisted me there would be little room in the volume for the text, and to all those contemporary private printers whose work is mentioned I am very grateful; to those I lacked space to include I owe apologies as well as thanks. Particular thanks for advice, encouragement and assistance are due to Iain Bain, Leonard F. Bahr, John S. Carroll, Sebastian Carter, David Chambers, J. Rives Childs, Dra. Elly Cockx-Indestege, Brooke Crutchley, Miss Jennifer Daish, John Dreyfus, W. E. Gocking, Rigby Graham, Loyd Haberly, B. Fairfax Hall, Mrs. Dora Herbert-Jones, Trevor Hickman, Miss S. M. Hoskins, Mrs. Schuyler B. Jackson (Laura Riding), Roger Levenson, Ben Lieberman, George McLeish, Sir Francis Meynell, James Mosley, Ray Nash, G. W. Ovink, John Peters, Miss Eiluned Rees, Peter Reid, Christopher Sandford, Roy Stokes, Geoffrey Wakeman, the late Mrs. Beatrice Warde, James M. Wells, Thomas Yoseloff, John Cashman, Wilmarth S. Lewis, John Walton and Kenneth Padley. To my wife, who has lived with it all patiently for twelve years, I am even more heavily indebted.

Loughborough   R.C.

PART ONE

PRIVATE PRESSES

1

The manuscript book and the
development of printing

M ost of us have a fairly clear mental picture of the production of books before the invention of printing in the middle of the fifteenth century. It is a picture we will have acquired in our more junior years in school of a monastic scriptorium, with two or three monks busily engaged in writing or illuminating manuscripts to the greater glory of God. For some of us, the beautiful simplicity of this picture will be disturbed by the half-realization that many medieval manuscripts can never have been anywhere near a monastery (Domesday Book? the work of the Archpoet?) and that there must also have been a good number of scribes working outside the religious houses. But few of us will think of there being the regular production and sale of books in the sense that there is a book trade today.

As with all these hazy half forgotten images acquired at school, our picture is very far from being an accurate one. It is commonplace that the production of books was a well-established and flourishing business long before printing. The length of time needed to produce manuscript volumes must have been a limiting factor in their availability, and there is plenty of evidence to show that they were very expensive. But books were certainly readily available for purchase in fifteenth-century Italy, as is shown by the purchases made by Duke Humphrey of Gloucester, by John Tiptoft of Worcester and by other English humanists.

Naturally enough, the scarcity and cost of manuscripts meant that nearly all libraries were very small (Cambridge University Library in 1424 possessed only 122 volumes) and individuals were unlikely to own more than one or two books. It was the dream of the Clerk of Oxenford to possess twenty books, but Chaucer certainly does not tell us that this was more than an unfulfilled dream. Undoubtedly scholars consulted many manuscripts in the course of their studies, and sometimes acquired copies.

21

There were several methods available to the would-be purchaser of books, as can be seen from the example of the monk Thorirus Andreae. While attending the Council of Constance he wrote out some manuscripts himself, had others transcribed for him by scriveners, bought on the spot and gathered still more through purchases from a number of booksellers. The professional production of manuscripts was undertaken in the monastic scriptoria (some of which were very large: there were over thirty scribes working for the Dominicans in Basle in the 1430s); by lay scribes like those working for Vespasiano da Bisticci, Diebold Lauber or John Shirley. There were also the semi-professional scribes; the university students who worked their way through college by copying texts for others. But—as Curt Bühler has pointed out in his penetrating study *The fifteenth century book: the scribes, the printers, the decorators* (Philadelphia, 1960)—this professional copying was almost certainly dwarfed by the number of manuscripts which scholars copied out for their own use, as Petrarch, Chaucer and many others are known to have done. Some of these men managed to build up very respectable collections in this way: in 1444 Johann Sintram of Würzburg presented sixty-one manuscripts to a Franciscan library in his native city—manuscripts he had copied in libraries as widely scattered as Ulm and Oxford, Strasbourg and Reutlingen. Many of his volumes were *Sammelbände* containing many short texts by different authors collected together to suit his own personal tastes—precisely the sort of work that Marshall McLuhan has suggested that the modern reader can do with a xerox copier, in fact.

In the years before the introduction of printing, the nature of authorship and of publication was totally different from what it was to become in later centuries. A writer might quote a passage here, garner an idea there, mixing what he had read with his own original text with a glorious disregard for the source of his material. When he published his completed book, he did so by permitting his friends to read the manuscript he had written. (It is precisely in this sense that today a librarian will in law be regarded as publishing a book by issuing it to a reader, which accounts for the difficulty one encounters if wishing to consult potentially actionable books in the 'private case' at the British Museum or other great libraries.) If the author's friends liked the book, copies of the manuscript would be made and the work would circulate to a wider audience.

It is scarcely exaggeration to say that in the production of books before Gutenberg's invention of printing from movable types one can see the foundations for the development of the private press quite as clearly as one can those for the growth of commercial printing and publishing. In a sense the monastic scriptoria, with their duty to preserve and transmit works of lasting importance, were the ancestors not only of the modern university press but also of the many private presses which have been maintained for the production of scholarly books at different times during the past five hundred years. In the work of some of the professional scribes, producing calligraphic manuscripts of outstanding beauty but often appalling texts, like those of Vespasiano da Bisticci,[1] we can find the true ancestors of some of the modern private presses producing 'the Book Beautiful', intended to be looked at and admired but not read. And in the production of a copy or two of a manuscript for circulation among friends of the author we have the origin of a great deal of private publishing.

It is by no means unreasonable to regard the first printing in France and in England as being of a private nature. When in 1469–70 Johann Heynlin, who had been Rector and Librarian of the Sorbonne, together with Guillaume Fichet the Professor of Philosophy and Rhetoric (and also a former Rector and Librarian) invited three German printers to come to the Sorbonne to set up a press, one may regard their enterprise as an early instance of academic publishing—and certainly in the following two years the printers produced a good many books of academic interest. But undoubtedly some of their work was of a more purely private nature: of the edition of Cardinal Bessarion's orations in favour of a crusade against the Turks printed in 1471, at least forty-five copies are known to have been presented to various potentates and dignitaries entirely at Fichet's expense. Very much the same thing happened, though on a less lavish scale, with Fichet's own *Rhetoric*.

To regard the first English printing as being of an equally private, non-commercial nature, is just as reasonable. The reason that Caxton has not been more widely recognized as the father of the private press can be found in William Blades' masterly *Life and typography of William Caxton* published a century ago. 'Himself a practical printer, Blades saw in his hero only Britain's prototypographer', wrote G. P. Winship in his study of the literature of printing (*The Dolphin*, vol. 3, 1938). '. . . His conception of his subject as a man who set type and worked a press is indelibly fixed in the mind of the

---

[1] 'From the textual point of view Vespasiano's admirable masterpieces of calligraphy are written with extraordinary slovenliness. Whole lines are left out, mistakes abound, repetitions are left uncorrected rather than spoil the beautiful page. Vespasiano's manuscripts are written for people who wanted to possess these books, not to read them, and the scribes knew it and were much more attentive to the evenness of their letters than to the sense of what they were writing.' E. Ph. Goldschmidt, 'Preserved for posterity' in *The New Colophon* vol. 2, 1950.

reading public. It is unlikely that it will ever be displaced by the realization that the man who introduced economical bookmaking into England was a well-to-do retired wool merchant who enjoyed translating French romances and who provided himself with a private press because this was cheaper than having copies made by hand for the many friends who asked him to give them his translations.'

Winship was probably overstating the case, but what is the evidence either way? Caxton had been 'Governor of the English nation' in Utrecht and Bruges in the 1460s. In 1469 he had undertaken a translation into English of Raoul le Fèvre's *Recueil des histoires de Troies* in order 'to eschew sloth and idleness and to put myself into virtuous occupation and business' as he expressed it in the untruthful formula of the times. But the translation did not go well, and was laid aside. About 1470 Caxton relinquished his post as Governor—perhaps in order to marry—and in 1471 he entered the service of Margaret of York, Duchess of Burgundy. In due course he showed his work to the Duchess, who ordered him to complete it. So the translation was resumed; Caxton taking the book with him on a journey he was making to Ghent and to Cologne. While at Cologne 'having good leisure and none other thing to do at this time' he completed his version of the *Recueil*. Word of his translation must have spread as a result of the Duchess's interest, and a single manuscript copy was not enough. Caxton's own words on his solution to the problem are clear enough: 'For as much as in the writing of the same my pen is worn, mine hand weary and not steadfast, mine eyes dimmed with overmuch looking on the white paper . . . *and also because I have promised to diverse gentlemen and to my friends to address to them as hastily as I might this said book.* Therefore I have practiced and learned to my great charge and dispense to ordain this said book in print after the manner and form as ye may see here . . . to the end that every man may have them at once.'

The invention of printing brought no immediate or sudden change in the normal pattern of book production. As Curt Bühler has shown, the scribe continued to flourish for many years in competition or in collaboration with the printer. To set up as printer demanded considerable capital, as the record of Gutenberg's lawsuit with Fust shows. The demand for books in the first few years after the invention of printing was not such that printers could earn a tolerable living for any length of time unless they were working in university towns or important trading centres. Even in such centres they did not always find life easy. 'We first among the Germans brought the art of printing to

Rome, at great labour and expense. We struggled against difficulties which others refused to face, and in consequence our house is filled with unsold books, but empty of the means of subsistence. Broken in strength we crave your gracious help . . .'—this is the gist of the plea which Sweynheym and Pannartz addressed (not unsuccessfully) to Pope Sixtus IV in 1472. Even in Rome the market had become saturated very rapidly.

The history of printing in the fifteenth century is full of competent printers who were unsuccessful in business: Johann Zainer, Ulrich Zell, Johann Neumeister—the list could be lengthened almost indefinitely. The cut-throat competition in the larger cities and the dire threat of bankruptcy (nothing to view with equanimity in those days) compelled many of these printers to take to the roads, settling in a place for a few months to produce books in local demand before moving on. Work of this sort was seldom of a normal commercial nature, undertaken as a speculation. Instead, the printer contracted to print a book or books at the order and expense of a patron.

The commonest work of this sort was probably in the field of missals and breviaries for church use. During the first twenty years of printing bishops seem often to have looked askance at printed books and it was not until 1474 that a printed missal was placed on an altar. But when the new method had become acceptable, several different methods of commissioning the printing developed. The policy of the German bishops was to commission the best printer they could find to undertake the work; they permitted him to charge an agreed price, and they required each church in their diocese to provide itself with a copy before a certain date. This method was to be followed very closely with the printing of Bibles in England.

In France there were several instances in the fifteenth century of an approach which cuts across normal commercial printing to a very much greater extent. About 1478, for example, a wealthy Canon of St. Hilaire, Poitiers, named Bertrand de Brossa, installed Stephen des Grez, a printer from Paris, in his own house. Stephen printed a *Breviarum historiale*, a quarto of some 326 leaves, in 1479; another book printed at the Canon's orders, Cardinal Torquemada's *Expositio brevis . . . super toto psalterio*, was completed two years later. Similarly in 1482 Pierre Plumé, Canon of Chartres, invited the Paris printer Jean du Pré to produce a missal for use in the Cathedral, and installed his equipment and lodged him in the Canon-house while it was being printed. A breviary for Chartres use followed in 1483. Perhaps these were not true private presses, and we should think of the Canons as amateur publishers rather than amateur printers with hired men to do the heavy or tedious work.

It would certainly be a mistake to regard them only as customers who took printers into their households for want of a better alternative. They knew what they wanted, and by having the work done under their immediate supervision they were able to ensure that they got it.

France was by no means the only country in which such patronage was employed. Shortly after Granada had been taken from the Moors, for instance, Juan Varela de Salamanca is known to have been summoned there from Seville by the energetic archbishop Hernando de Talavera. Between 1504 and 1508 he printed several books at the order and expense of the archbishop. They included a breviary, a gradual, an antiphoner, and an Arabic grammar and dictionary which the archbishop had instructed to be prepared as an aid to those engaged in the conversion of the recently conquered Moors. That these books were special commissions and not produced by way of trade is sufficiently shown by the fact that when Varela left Granada soon after his patron's death in 1508 he handed over the stocks of the books he had printed to the cathedral authorities.

2

The quasi-official or patron's press

W hen a wealthy man wished to have particular books printed in the manner he chose, he might very well take a printer into his employ for a while, as Bertrand de Brossa had done at Poitiers. By no means all such ventures were for the production of church books. Towards the end of 1484, for example, Robert Fouquet and Jean Cres set up a press in the little town of Brehan-Loudéac in the Duchy of Brittany. The town was on the estates of Jean de Rohan, and in all save the last of the books they printed they stated that they worked under his protection. It seems very likely, if not certain, that the work was done at his expense as well, for the publications were of a sort which one would not have expected: books of poetry instead of the devotional works which would have been the natural choice for printers in such a religious country. When they had printed their seventh book in 1485, Fouquet departed —war had broken out between France and Brittany—and the Breton Cres continued to print alone, having prudently removed himself to the greater safety of the Benedictine Abbey of Lantenac three leagues away. There he printed an edition of Mandeville's *Travels* in 1488, and is believed to have followed it with a number of liturgical works for the Abbey, of which only *Le doctrinale des nouvelles mariées* (1491) has survived.

Jean Cres was still a peripatetic printer. But when such printers settled in one place to work wholly on work ordered by a particular patron, we have the first main group of private presses, those semi-official or court presses which were at once private and the forerunners of the modern government printing offices. The earliest printer to receive official recognition, by virtue of his appointment as court printer to the Emperor Maximilian I, was Johann Schönsperger the elder (1481–1523); and in the works printed for the Emperor—the Emperor's prayer book (1512–13) of which only ten copies were pulled, and the *Theuerdank* completed in 1517—no expense was spared in

27

the quest for magnificence. Similarly, the splendid Complutensian Polyglot which was printed by Arnaõ Guillen de Brocar at Alcalá in Spain at almost exactly the same time is said to have cost Arnaõ's patron Cardinal Ximenes the sum of fifty thousand gold ducats to produce; a figure which half a century ago Updike regarded as being the equivalent of 'considerably over a million dollars'.

Such presses as these are far too princely to be regarded as private presses; they had evolved into something far less humble: Guillen de Brocar was in effect running a university press. Nevertheless the continuity was there in the involvement and interest of the patrons in the work that was done for them; an involvement that one can find more easily and frequently in the field of the fine arts.

In the sixteenth century, as A. W. Pollard has said, 'the enthusiasm with which the new art had at first been received died out. Printers were no longer in palaces, monasteries and colleges; Church and State, which had at first fostered and protected them, were now jealous and suspicious, even actively hostile . . . Printing had sunk to the level of a mere craft . . .' The appointment of court printers and the work which they produced became very much less the personal concern of the monarch. But this was in the typographically developed countries of western Europe; in the less settled territories of eastern Europe they survived very much longer. In Transylvania, for example, the Prince Johann Sigismund Zapoly summoned the printer Raphael Hofhalter to Carlsberg in 1566 to take charge of his private press, a press which continued to be run by Hofhalter's widow and children after his death the following year. When their patron died they were unable to support themselves by commercial printing but had perforce to leave the country. Subsequently in 1637 George Rakotsky re-established a private press; the celebrated *Officium Ragotzianum* written by his son after he had succeeded to the throne was (according to Brunet) printed under his personal supervision.

A far more romantic story is told by Brunet of another of these semi-official presses in Transylvania, that of Count Wolfgang Bethlen at the castle of Kreisch. The Count's printer, Michael Székesi, was in 1687 engaged in printing a large folio *History of Transylvania* written by the Count. Some eight hundred pages had been printed when the Turkish army arrived; the castle was besieged and taken, and the Count and his men taken and sold into slavery. A century later, when the castle was being rebuilt after the territory had been recaptured from the Turks, the workmen uncovered a cellar which had been bricked up; when it was opened it was found to contain a mass of rotting paper which turned out to be the sheets of the book abandoned so hastily. Only two nearly complete copies of this *liber rarissimus rarior* could be made up . . .

To an even greater extent than in eastern Europe the spread of printing overseas in the wake of European expansion was at first usually of a non-commercial nature. Printers might be called to undertake official printing, or for missionary purposes; in more than a few cases mission presses were operated by priests with no training as printers, like the Jesuits' press in Paraguay described in Chapter 22. The introduction of printing into Iceland, to give one example, followed the fifteenth-century French pattern closely: in 1530 the Bishop of Hoolum, the ancient capital of the island, organized the establishment of a press which was operated under his direction by a Swede named Jon Matthiesen. In 1531 Matthiesen printed a *Breviarium Nidarosiense* of which no copies now survive; after the death of the Bishop his printer continued to work for his Lutheran successor.

It is perhaps stretching a point to regard this early Icelandic printing as private, however representative it is of the non-commercial nature of printing as it spread from Europe. But there can be no doubt at all about the private nature of the earliest printing in another Danish colony, Greenland. The modern settlement of the country from Europe came relatively late; it was not until 1721 that a post was established at Godthaab. A few years later Herrn-huter missionaries from Saxony started evangelizing the Greenlanders, and it was one of these missionaries, Jesper Broderson, who was responsible for the introduction of the printing press.

Only one work printed by Broderson has survived: a collection of choral songs in Greenlandic published in Nongme (Godthaab) in 1793. For many years the authenticity of the book, of which only a single copy is known, was the subject of considerable suspicion among scholars, as it was printed over half a century before printing was believed to have been introduced into Greenland. But recent research by a former Director of the Government of Greenland, Knud Oldenow, has shown the suspicion was unfounded.

While attending a synod in his own country it appears that Broderson on his own initiative equipped himself with a small 'Handbuchdruckerey' which he took back with him to Greenland. There he set himself to learn how to print, and painfully produced his little sixty-eight-page book using a very small type. It seems that it was not his intention to use the press for any extensive work (or perhaps he found the results did not justify the labour involved) and the headquarters of the Mission in Saxony knew nothing of it. In the year follow-ing the publication he had to leave Greenland because of severe illness, and his press and type were abandoned. They remained unused and forgotten for over half a century.

In the middle of the nineteenth century Hinrich Rink was appointed Crown Inspector of southern Greenland. This was a post roughly comparable with that of District Commissioner in the old British colonial service, and Rink, like so many district officers, devoted himself wholeheartedly to the service and study of the country and its people. In 1855 he discovered Broderson's printing equipment which had lain neglected for so long, and in the autumn and winter of that year he used it to good effect on a number of small publications.

The first of these was a little handbill in Greenlandic which he printed on 21 October 1855. 'Exciting news!' it proclaimed. 'The ship has arrived and will make two voyages this year. England and Russia are at war with one another, but there is no fighting in the North [i.e. Denmark]. When the King was out riding recently he had a fall and was injured, but is recovering. The reindeer hunting has been poor, but seals are plentiful. Praise God, there is little illness. The Danes in Godthaab wish you well!'

As well as this quaint news-sheet, five other pamphlets were printed. They include a note on the school syllabus, news of the Crimean war, a Christmas hymn and *Aid for the sick*, a thirty-two-page handbook on diet, hygiene, and similar topics.

Rink printed these 'Godthaab pamphlets' as they came to be known, in order to establish that it would be practicable and useful to set up a proper printing press in the country, to be run by the Greenlanders themselves. He had already used a woodcut in one of the pamphlets which had been cut by the Greenlander Rasmus Berthelsen, whom Rink taught to print and who was probably almost entirely responsible for the production of the pamphlets. Armed with his work as an example of what could be done, Rink was in a position to approach the authorities in Copenhagen for a grant to purchase equipment for his press.

While on leave in the capital in the winter of 1856–7 he managed to persuade the government that his proposals were reasonable, and with the modest allowance of 250 rix-dollars he purchased type, a small handpress and an even smaller lithographic press which he took back to Greenland and installed in his house in Godthaab in the spring of 1857.

There can be no doubt that even according to the strictest of definitions Rink's work had previously been that of a private press. From 1857 it was private no longer as it was officially financed and approved, but although an increasing number of publications came from the Inspector's press during the 1860s and 1870s as his assistants became more skilled, and though many of them are unmistakably official printing, nevertheless a good many of its productions still bore the stamp of private enthusiasm rather than of public policy. At least one of the earliest, a thirty-four-page booklet on *Hans Egede* seems from the crudity of its production not to have been printed in a press at all, and tradition has it that it was produced by pupils in the Godthaab school by impressing the paper by hand on to the inked type.

The first real book printed on the new press was *Pok; a Greenlander who has travelled abroad* which was set and printed under Rink's supervision by Rasmus Berthelsen and his assistant Lars Møller (or Arqualuk, as he became known throughout Greenland) in 1857. This little eighteen-page book which was illustrated with woodcuts by Berthelsen (and in some copies with lithographs perhaps drawn by Rink himself) tells of the adventures of the first Greenlanders to visit Denmark in 1723.

Through pressure of official duties Rink's personal involvement in the work of his press became much less during the 1860s, and by the time that ill-health forced him to leave Greenland for good in 1868 the operation of the 'South Greenland Press' as it came to be known was in the capable hands of Lars Møller, who had in the winter of 1861–2 been sent on a short training course to Denmark. With the subsequent development of this press down to the present day we are not concerned, but that it should have grown so successfully through the difficult circumstances of its early years can only make us marvel at the determination of the printers. For the press was essentially a winter occupation—the summer was spent in hunting and fishing and gathering fuel—and printing in the Greenland winter was not easy: the press was housed in an icy stone workshop in the grounds of the Inspector's house, and the dampened paper often froze stiff while being used. Supplies of ink often ran out, and fresh ink of a sort had to be made by boiling up soot and varnish . . . It was not until the turn of the century that the press was more suitably housed.

At about the time that Rink was experimenting with Broderson's old press, a Herrnhuter missionary named Samuel Kleinschmidt also became interested in printing, probably through seeing some of Rink's experimental pieces. In 1856 Kleinschmidt wrote to his half-brother in Holland asking him to send him a press. This arrived in 1857, and from then until his death in 1886 Kleinschmidt used it constantly. The books which he printed on the press at Neu Herrnhut during the first two years were *Nunalerutit*, a primer of geography completed in 1858, and an outline of world history the following year. Both volumes were produced in their entirety by Kleinschmidt who was author, compositor, pressman, binder and distributor. For the work of one entirely self-taught they are of a very high standard.

After the production of the world history there was a lull in the press's activity. Kleinschmidt broke with the Herrnhuter mission and became a teacher in the Danish school in Godthaab. He was in fact moving closer and closer to a personal identification with the Greenlanders, and adopted the Greenland costume of anorak and sealskin trousers (and the old eskimo aversion to washing) and built himself a log cabin of the traditional pattern. In this he installed his press, which the Herrnhuters had allowed him to take on condition that they received copies of anything he printed free of charge. Kleinschmidt (or Samualé as he became known to the Greenlanders) produced many books of an educational or missionary flavour from his press, entirely at

A A N T E E K E N I N G E N.

VAN

H. J. D O M I S.

RESIDENT VAN PASOEROEAN,

Lid van het Bataviasche Genootschap van kunsten
en wetenschappen, Lid van de koninklijke
Asiatische Maatschappij van groot
Brittanien en Ierland,
enz. enz. enz.

———————

2 de Stukje.

———————

GEDRUKT TE PASOEROEAN,
ten huize van den schrijver, door deszelfs inlanschen
schrijver *TJOKRO DIE WIRIO.*

1829.

Fig. 1. Title-page of H. J. Domis' *Description of Java*, printed in the author's home at Pasuruhan, Java, by his servant Tjokro die Wirio: an instance of private enterprise in colonial printing

his own expense. The most important was a translation of the Bible into Greenlandic which was issued in parts between 1864 and the late 1870s; a fantastic labour for one man to undertake. Samualé regarded his version only as a first draft to be revised and improved by other missionaries, but nevertheless his Old Testament text remains the standard to this day. Of an entirely different nature was a little book *About animals* which he wrote and printed in 1863. In this he described various animals previously unknown to the Greenlanders, and for which of course no names existed in their language. The names he invented—'he who noses around and tears things up' for the rhinoceros, 'the one without joints' for the elephant—have become the standard Greenlandic names for these creatures. But Samualé's contribution to the language was far greater than this; with a grammar and dictionary which he had published before he acquired his press he virtually created Greenlandic as a written language.

Greenland was unusual in the importance which private printing assumed in the development of the press, but it is not too exceptional to serve as an example of the importance of the amateur in spreading the craft of printing. The extent to which the self-taught missionary printer was responsible for the introduction of printing into many parts of Africa, Asia and the South Seas has not yet received the attention it merits, although many entertaining accounts can be found buried in the records of missionary societies and elsewhere. One further example, quoted from Timperley's *Dictionary of printing* (1839) is representative:

'1818. The art of printing introduced into the Society Islands at Tahiti or Otaheite, and the first books executed were the *Spelling book*, 2,600 copies; a *Tahitan catechism*, 2,300 copies; a *collection of texts or extracts from Scripture*; and the *Gospel of St Luke*, which bears for imprint, *Tahiti, printed at the Windward Mission Press*. The press was erected at Afareaitu, under the direction of their king, Pomare, who took an especial interest in the proceedings of the first work, and who requested that he might be sent for whenever the press should begin to work. "A letter having been sent to inform him," says the missionary, "that we were nearly ready, he hastened to the printing office, accompanied by a few favourite chiefs, and followed by a large concourse of people. I took the composing-stick in my hand, and observing Pomare looking with curious delight at the new and shining types, I asked him if he would like to put together the first *A.B.*, or alphabet. His countenance lighted up as he answered in the affirmative. I then placed the composing-stick in his hand; he took the capital letters, one by one, and made up the alphabet. He put the small letters together in the same manner; and the few monosyllables composing the first page of the small spelling-book, were afterwards added. The king examined, with great minuteness and pleasure, the form as it lay on the press, and prepared to take off the first sheet ever printed in his dominions. Having been told how it was done, he jocosely charged his companions not to look very particularly at him, or to laugh if he should not do it right. I put the ink-ball into his hand, and directed him to strike it two or three times upon the face of the letters; this he did, and then placing a sheet of clean paper upon the parchment, it was covered down, turned under the press, and the king was directed to pull the handle: he did so, and when the printed sheet was lifted up, the chiefs and assistants rushed towards it, to see what effect the king's pressure had produced. When they beheld the letters black and large, and well-defined, there was a simultaneous expression of wonder and delight. The king took up the sheet, and having looked first at the paper, and then at the types, with attentive admiration, handed it to one of his chiefs and expressed a wish to take another. He printed two more: and while he was so engaged, the first sheet was shown to the crowd without, who, when they saw it, raised one general shout of astonishment and joy. The king with his attendants passed by the printing office every afternoon, and seldom omitted to call, and spend some time in watching the progress of the work. The curiosity awakened in the inhabitants of Afareaitu by the establishment of the press, was soon satisfied; day after day Pomare visited the printing-office; the chiefs applied to be admitted inside, while the people thronged the windows, doors, and every crevice through which they could peep, often involuntarily exclaiming, Be-ri-ta-ni-e! *fenua paari*, O Britain! land of skill, or knowledge. The press soon became a matter of universal conversation; and the facility with which books could be multiplied, filled the minds of the people in general with wonderful delight. Multitudes arrived from every district of Eimeo, and even from other islands, to procure books and see this astonishing machine".'

Though presses of this sort were without doubt private in the sense of being completely uncommercial and operated by amateurs, their work calls for more space than can be given to them here.

3

The scholarly press

***

Scholarly books were often printed by the presses under the control of a patron or operated by missionaries, but the production of such books was not the central reason for their establishment. They were in many respects the ancestors of the modern official and religious publishing houses, and did not function as a service to scholarship in the way we have come to expect from the university press. How were scholarly books published in the early years of printing? A great many were of course produced by way of trade by the ordinary commercial printer, and the importance of the 'scholar printers'—of Aldus Manutius in Venice, of Froben in Basle and many others—cannot be stressed too highly. Nevertheless the private press also had a part to play; most particularly in the field of astronomy.

There are excellent reasons for this. Astronomy is nothing if not an exact science, and the printing of astronomical tables calls for a care and knowledge which was all too rare among commercial printers. For the astronomer who had sufficient means at his disposal a press which was operated under his constant personal supervision was an obvious solution, particularly as such an arrangement removed all risk of the loss or theft of his work.

Perhaps the first scholarly private press of any importance was that of Regiomontanus. Born in 1436 in Königsberg (from the latinized form of which his name is taken) he went to Vienna at the age of sixteen to study under George Purbach, one of the foremost astronomers of the time. After some years in Italy and Hungary he settled in Nuremberg about 1471. Among his pupils there was the wealthy citizen Bernhard Walther who assisted him financially so that he was able to build an observatory and construct astronomical instruments. This was not all: Walther provided Regiomontanus with a printing press from which he published a number of astronomical books. Its activity ceased in 1475 when Regiomontanus was called to Rome to advise

nach zesetzten figur nemen. Es gildt gleich wie du die höch des Thurns ynnen werdest. Darnach / vnd in sölher gestalt magst du zu einem Fenster auß messen / wie weyt du vber ein wasser hast zu einem Thurn / so du voz hin seine höch erkendt hast.

Das Acht Cap. wie du messen solt wie
weyt ein gebew von dem andern stehet / oder ein
Brunn von dem andern / des gleichen auch
die brayt eines Thurns.

JN diser abmessung ist nit von nötten / das ich dir ein newe regel gebe / sonder du solt in aller massen allhie brauchen / was dich das drit Capitel gelernt hat von der höch. Allein ist das die vnderschid / das du alhie den lüffer nach der seyten halten müst / vnd was dir vormals die höch geben hat / das gibt dir allhie wie weyt ein Thurn vom andern stehet. Deßhab ich dir einen leychtern verstandt geben wöllen durch dise figur.

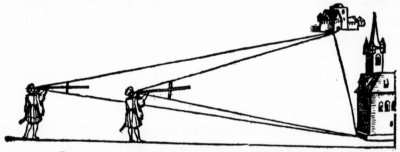

Das Neundt Cap. Wie du durch den
Stab die tieff eines Brunnen messen solt.

Fig. 2. Opening from Peter Apian's *Instrument buch*, printed at the author's press in Ingolstadt, 1533

Pope Sixtus IV on calendar reform, and was not resumed as the astronomer was murdered while in Rome.

Among the books printed at this press were an edition of Purbach's *Theoricae novae planetarum*, a series of annual almanacs and a volume of ephemerides for the years 1475 to 1506. This last was of particular importance, because it contained the method of 'lunar distances' which Regiomontanus had discovered, and which enabled mariners at sea to fix their position whenever the moon was visible. It is more than possible that Columbus navigated with these ephemerides; certainly they were used by Amerigo Vespucci on his voyage to the New World.

Two of the publications from Regiomontanus are of a different nature from his other work: editions of Vegius' *Philalethes* and of St. Basil's *Opusculum ad juvenes*. It has been suggested by Victor Scholderer that these may have been printed at the request of Regiomontanus' patron-pupil Walther, and it is possible that the astronomer had at times to adapt his programme to fit in with Walther's wishes.

The next astronomical private press, that of the Dane Tycho Brahe, was emphatically not subject to the control of anyone other than the astronomer himself. Brahe had been born into a noble family in 1546. By no means a typical member of the Danish nobility of the time, he had from a very early age been fascinated by the heavens and as young as seventeen he was, despite discouragement, making skilful observations. After studying at the university in Copenhagen he travelled to Germany and became friendly with the Landgrave William of Hesse, and had thoughts of settling in Basle. But the king of Denmark, Frederick II, had wit enough to recognize Tycho's potential, and granted him the little island of Hveen in Äresund, together with a sufficient income to build an observatory there.

In 1576 work on the observatory, Uraniburg or 'Castle of the heavens', was started. The building of his great observatory, and the construction and installation of his sextants, armillae and other instruments naturally absorbed Tycho's energies for a time. But when this work had been completed, and Tycho and his assistants were able to settle down to methodical observations— observations that were fuller and more exact than any made before—the idea of writing a book, a *Theatrum astronomicum*, which would cover his entirely new theory of astronomy, occurred to him. There were considerable difficulties in the way: Tycho doubted whether the printers in Copenhagen were competent to be entrusted with exacting work of this nature, yet to go further afield and send his book to be printed in Hamburg would be to increase the risk of loss or theft—and Tycho was throughout his life almost pathologically afraid of having his work stolen. The solution was to have the printing done under his own supervision at Uraniburg, but it was not until 1584 that his printing office came into being. Its establishment was not a simple matter, as all things necessary—printer, presses, type, paper—had to come from abroad. Tycho was fortunate enough to be able to engage Christopher Weida, a capable German printer, to manage the press for him. In a letter written to his friend Heinrich Bruceus at Rostock Tycho explained why the press was essential: he was engaged in writing two books, and because plague had broken out in Copenhagen it was impossible for him to get any work done there. He was therefore, he wrote, sending his man Joachim to Wittenberg to buy equipment. A small building to the south of the observatory was converted into a printing office, and work started in 1585. To his friend and kinsman Henrik Rantzau, Governor of Holstein, Tycho wrote enthusiastically offering to print anything he wished, and soon followed his offer with the gift of the first work from the press, some Latin poems addressed to various friends.

The equipment of the printing office was modest: a press, a few sizes of roman and italic type, to which as time went by were added some engraved blocks of astronomical instruments and of views of the observatory. Publications—such as *Diarium astrologicum et meteorologicum*, a calendar for the year 1587—appeared fairly rapidly. But from the beginning there were difficulties in obtaining sufficient supplies of paper from Germany, and although King Frederick issued instructions that 'Our man and servant Tyge Brahe of Knudstrup must be given as many *cartas cosmographicas* or as much paper as is to be found in Our library in Our castle of Copenhagen or in Our Danish or Norwegian kingdoms or in any of Our possessions in order to assist him in his undertakings' the situation did not improve. It must have seemed to Tycho that he would never get his great work printed.

Characteristically, he decided that he would build his own paper mill at Uraniburg. He was not unfamiliar with the craft, having assisted an uncle in establishing the first paper mill in Scandinavia at Herrevad in 1572. In October 1590 he recorded that 'our first book, on the most recent heavenly phenomena, is receiving its last touches from the printer. But the failure of the paper supplies has caused some delay, and prevented the work from being finished. Although I have taken the trouble to erect a papermill (at no small expense) I am without a suitable papermaker, and so this has not yet been of any use.' He invoked the assistance of the Landgrave William, who offered to try to engage assistants for him at Frankfurt, but in the end Tycho managed to find the staff for himself. The paper mill had been expensive because of the elaborate system of reservoirs necessary to ensure an adequate supply of water to the mill in summer, but it worked satisfactorily. The supply of raw materials for papermaking was ensured by Tycho's influence at court: 'rag sermons' being preached throughout Denmark exhorting the people to send their rags to his paper mill.

Tycho's book which had been held up for lack of paper, *De mundi aetherii recentioribus phaenominis*, had been started in 1588. It is a substantial quarto, and was intended to form the second volume of his *Theatrum astronomicum*, but as events turned out he did not live to complete either the first or third volumes, and it remained for his greatest pupil Kepler to finish the work.

Even before the paper mill had been completed, the end of the Uraniburg observatory was in sight. In 1588 King Frederick II died, and the court of his successor Christian IV was filled with those jealous of the special favour in which Tycho had been held. At first King Christian continued to support the observatory, but by 1597 Tycho had been so far disgraced that the whole of the royal subsidy of his work had been withdrawn. It was in great part his own fault: he was no courtier (his pride and choleric temper prevented that) and he had neglected all other duties for his beloved astronomy; but the slander of jealous rivals also played a considerable part.

So, his income gone, Tycho abandoned Uraniburg. Determined to quit Denmark he moved to Rostock, then to Wandesburg near Hamburg, and finally at the invitation of the Emperor Rudolph II to Prague.

Although Uraniburg had been abandoned, astronomy had not, and Tycho took with him all his more portable instruments and the printed sheets of his uncompleted books. According to some early accounts, he also took his printing equipment—and he was certainly soon printing again: at Henrik Rantzau's where he stayed for a little more than six months he continued his observations and had his handsome folio *Astronomiae instauratae mechanica* printed by Philip de Ohr, a printer whom he had summoned from Hamburg to work under his supervision. When Tycho moved to Prague and refounded his observatory at Benatek, the various incomplete books again followed with the baggage. After his death in 1601 many of the sheets came into the hands of a Nuremberg bookseller, G. Tambach, by whom several of the books were reissued.

Tycho Brahe's press was not the last significant private undertaking in the field of astronomy. At Danzig, the wealthy Johann Hevelius (1611–87) established an observatory in 1641 which in its time was the best equipped in

Europe. Inspired by Brahe's astronomical work, he improved on Tycho's star catalogue, made the first accurate study of the moon's surface and produced the first systematic study of all recorded comets. It was natural for one who so admired Tycho's work to imitate his methods of publication, and take a printer into his permanent employ. This printer, Simon Reininger, also served as an assistant in Hevelius's observatory and appears to have become his most accurate and valued helper. Several books of considerable importance were produced at the press, and for at least one of them, *Selenographia* (in which the chief features of the moon were named), Hevelius engraved the map himself. In 1679 the observatory, the printing house and all the instruments were destroyed by fire. Despite the disastrous losses which Hevelius suffered as a result of the fire (including the loss of most copies of the books he had printed) the observatory was rebuilt, but the printing office does not appear to have been revived.

On a similar though even grander scale than the presses of Tycho and Hevelius was that started in Sweden by Hevelius's contemporary, Count Per Brahe. Lord High Steward, Governor of Finland and the greatest landowner of the country, the Count was one of the most important figures of the Swedish Golden Age. In contrast to most continental princes of the time, he was a very benevolent magnate, and while away from his own province of Visingborg kept in constant correspondence with his officials there. In 1634 he established a high school at Visingö; ten years later he started a paper mill. In 1666 he started a printing press, a step which he had long contemplated. The printer appointed to direct it, Johann Kankel (1614–67) was a Pomeranian who had in 1663 attempted unsuccessfully to obtain the Directorship of the royal printing office in Stockholm, and was eking out a poor living in the city. He seems to have been recommended to Per Brahe by Chancellor de la Gardie. It appears that Kankel's appointment was to the staff of the school in Visingö, but he was first and foremost printer to the Count—a survival of the earlier, semi-official presses which is scarcely surprising when one considers that there were only nine printers in the whole of Sweden at that time.

The press was set up in a specially built house near the school. The equipment purchased was limited to a single press and a few small founts of type, but Kankel was a competent typefounder and was well able to supplement his slender typographical resources. The Count had appointed a bookbinder to assist him, and he had an apprentice who did much of the presswork, but fairly obviously Kankel could not have had time on his hands—nor was his marriage proving satisfactory, as the earliest surviving piece from the press shows: a letter sent to his wife (whom he was attempting to divorce) which he printed 'because I know you can never read handwritten letters'!

The records which have survived enable us to form a very good picture of the working of Per Brahe's press. The Count would give Kankel instructions on what was to be printed, or would send them to him through his secretary, and frequently corrected the proofs of the more important books himself. Kankel was left to exercise his own initiative to a considerable extent, however, and many of the slighter pieces seem to have been printed without any specific instructions from Brahe. Now and again there were difficulties over the supply of paper, but on the whole production ran very smoothly.

Rather more than fifty works from the Count's press have survived. Of the more substantial works ordered by Brahe were a number of voyages of Swedish mariners to Japan, the West Indies and other countries; a translation of Icelandic sagas, the *Norlantz Chronicles*; an old Swedish rhymed chronicle of Alexander the Great. There was a genealogy of the Brahe family; an edition of *Œconomia* (a household book for young noblemen which had been written by the Count's grandfather in 1581); and a medical manual prepared by one of the Count's army surgeons. There were probably several books printed especially for the use of the school, but of these only a song book, *Piae cantiones*, has survived.

The works printed by Kankel on his own initiative seem usually to have been ephemeral pieces: verses of homage, verses *in memoriam* and the like. The Count made it his regular practice to spend Christmastide in his castle at Visingborg among his own people, and for his arrival Kankel prepared very elaborate broadsides. Several of those which survive are in the form of maze-prints, typographical *tours de force* in the troublesome preparation of which Kankel seems to have taken special delight. In the production of these maze-prints Kankel had no rival in Sweden, though in other respects his work was little better than that of his contemporaries and like theirs shows German influence very markedly.

In 1680 Per Brahe died, and the government of his province was re-organized and taken over by the crown. The new Count, Nils Brahe, seems to have intended to pension Kankel off, but when the school was taken into the patronage of the crown he was permitted to continue in his office, where he continued printing until at least 1685. In 1686 he was offered the appointment of university printer at Uppsala, but declined the post on the grounds of age and infirmity. When he died the following summer the printing equipment was sold, and used for the first press to be established in the town of Jönköping.

Fig. 3. A maze-print by Johann Kankel, Per Brahe's printer, 1674

The presses of the two Brahes, Tycho and Per, represent the patron's press of the sixteenth and seventeen centuries in their finest form. But although private presses were seldom maintained on so lavish a scale as these, there were many of them throughout Europe. Sometimes they were used for the production of provisional texts in the way that today we would resort to the duplicator. Cardinal du Perron, for example, maintained a private press in his chateau at Bagnolet for the express purpose of printing a preliminary edition of his works, for circulation to his friends; then—having received their comments and criticisms—a revised edition would be prepared for general publication. Bossuet resorted to a similar method for his *Exposition de la doctrine de l'église catholique*, and one can indeed find a faint echo of it in the production of Sir Winston Churchill's *History of the Second World War*, for which a first draft was set in type, and the text then largely rewritten on the basis of the proofs.

In England, Archbishop Parker's *De antiquitate Britannicae ecclesiae* is sometimes said to have been the first book privately printed in this country. The basis for this tradition is to be found in a note written by the Archbishop's son John on the fly-leaf of one of the Bodleian copies: 'liber iste et collectus et impressus est propriis in aedibus Lamethiae positie' [This book was both compiled and printed in his own house at Lambeth]. There is no other evidence for the existence of a private press in Lambeth Palace, but as Parker explained in a letter to Cecil he intended to have the book always beside him so that he could amend the text whenever the need arose, and the work exists in so many 'states' that it seems possible that the Archbishop had no intention of producing a final text. It would therefore have been convenient for the printer John Day (who printed several other books at the Archbishop's expense) to have transferred one of his presses temporarily to Lambeth to carry out the printing. The edition was a small one; Parker recorded that he had not sent the book to more than four people in the kingdom, but 'some men smelling the printing of it, seem to be very desirous cravers of the same'.

The great Richelieu was another who as well as taking considerable official interest in printing—he was responsible for the establishment of the Imprimerie Royale in 1640—had a sufficient personal interest to set up his own private press at the Château de Richelieu in 1633. The press was put under the direction of Estienne Migeon (or Michon) and employed a small type, *petite sédanoise*, which is thought to have been cut by Jean Jannon at Sedan and which closely resembled the founts used by the Elzevirs. Richelieu's press had considerable virtues, the books produced there rivalling those of the Elzevirs in quality of presswork. After Richelieu's death the press seems to have been continued by his brother, and its publications to have included a Bible and a translation by J. Desmarets of extracts from Plato, Epictetus, Plutarch and other classical authors published in 1653. The later history of the press is confused, however: the type appears to have passed into the hands of Protestant printers at Charenton, who used it to print surreptitious editions of various books bearing Desmarets' name and the Elzevir press-mark. An interesting account of some of these later 'Richelieu' pieces appears in Charles Nodier's *Mélanges tirées d'une petite bibliothèque* (Paris, 1829).

Though with the rise of the learned presses at universities private scholarly presses of this sort became less common, they continued to be set up from time to time up until the eighteenth century or even later. In Casanova's *Memoirs*, for example, we find recorded a visit which Casanova paid to Count Mosca Barzi at Pescaro in 1766. When he called on the Count, he was shown his library, and presented with a four-volume set of comments on the Latin poets from Ennius to the twelfth century which the Count had printed at his own press. Casanova was not impressed with the Count's work: 'There was nothing of his own in it;' he wrote in his *Memoirs*, 'all he had done was to classify each fragment in chronological order. I should have liked to see notes, comments . . . In addition the type was not elegant, the margins were unsatisfactory, the paper of poor quality and misprints common . . . As a consequence the book was not profitable and as the Count was not wealthy his wife often reproached him with the money he had squandered on it.' G. Natali's study in his *Idee costumi uomini dell settocento* (Turin, 1926) confirms the general accuracy of Casanova's account, and adds considerable extra details on Count Mosca Barzi's life and publications. Casanova's own story of his visit, as given in the authoritative Brockhaus-Plon edition of his *Histoire de ma vie*, differs in many ways from that given in earlier editions such as that in Machen's translations.

At much the same time that Count Mosca Barzi was sqaundering his money on his Latin poets, the antiquary Edward Rowe Mores (1730–78) ran a press of very considerable interest in England. Mores, a typical antiquary of his time, a saxonist, and one of the earliest figures in the field of life insurance, seems to have bought a small press soon after taking his degree at Queen's College in 1750, and a number of slight pieces from his press which he printed after his move from Oxford to London and later to Low Leyton in Essex in 1759, are preserved in the Bodleian Library. But the chief work which he printed at his press, the principal reason for his name being remembered

A DISSERTATION UPON ENGLISH TYPOGRAPHICAL FOUNDERS AND FOUNDERIES.

BY EDWARD ROWE MORES, A. M. & A. S. S.

M, DCC, LXXVIII.

Fig. 4. Title of Rowe Mores' *Dissertation*, which the author printed at his press, 1778

by printing historians today, was his *Dissertation upon English typographical founders and founderies* (1778), the pioneer history of typefounding in Britain. Eighty copies of the book were printed, and it is evident from the quirks of style and eccentricity of arrangement that the type was set by Mores himself.

Mores died in November 1778 'of a mortification in his leg, which he suffered to reach his vitals, sitting in an arm-chair, while the workmen passed through the room to repair the next. He would not admit physician or nurse; and scarcely his own mother . . .' The copies of the *Dissertation* passed into the hands of John Nichols, who added an eight-page appendix and published it, price six shillings, in 1779. The edition prepared by Harry Carter and Christopher Ricks (Oxford, 1961) contains a considerable amount of information on Mores' press and a list of its equipment and the prices realized when it was sold by auction after Mores' death—information of a kind which is all too rare for early private presses.

4

The press as an educational toy

And Frederick William he, of Saxony the lord
A private press maintain'd, with Printers round his board.

So William Blades translated a passage written by Johann Rist in his *Depositio cornuti typographici* (1654). The Friedrich Wilhelm II, Duke of Saxe-Altenburg, of whom he was writing, certainly maintained a private press of the quasi-official kind we have already described, from which a sumptuous edition of Luther's works was published between 1661 and 1664. But even before this time rulers of Saxony had been interested in printing, another Friedrich Wilhelm having set up a press at Torgau in 1596. At this press operations were under the direction of a printer, Jakob Popperich, and a schoolmaster, Johann Wankel, and it is possible that it was an early example of many presses maintained by royalty as toys to be used in the education of their children.

Such use of the press for the education of princes did not, of course, necessarily call for the special establishment of a private press. In 1648, for example, the ten-year-old Louis XIV was taken on a visit to the Imprimerie Royale (which had been established only eight years earlier, and which because of the serious interest taken by the Bourbons in its work was to become the supreme example of a royal press) and 'helped' with the production of an edition of the *Mémoires* of Philippe de Commines. Rather similarly—though making the mountain come to Mahomet—on 15 February 1731 'a printing press and cases for composing were put up at St James's house for their majesties to see the noble art of printing' reported the *Gentleman's magazine*. 'His Royal Highness the Duke [of Cumberland] wrought at one of the cases, to compose for the press a little book of his own writing, call'd, *The laws of Dodge Hare*. The two youngest princesses likewise compos'd their names, &c., under the direction of Mr. S. Palmer, printer in this city.'

47

Nevertheless, there are more than a few instances of private presses being set up deliberately because of their usefulness in making education attractive. One can probably dismiss the toy press exhibited at the 1877 Caxton Celebration as having been used by Charles I as a child, as it seems very likely that it was made very much later than the early seventeenth century. On the other hand, a miniature printing office installed in the Tuileries in 1718 is well authenticated. The press was set up for Louis XV, and the little boy—then eight years of age—was taught the rudiments of the craft by a distinguished Paris printer, Jacques Collombat. Louis set the type and may even have printed one or two copies of some lessons in geography entitled *Cours des principaux fleuves et rivières de l'Europe. Composé & imprimé par Louis XV . . . À Paris, dans l'Imprimerie du Cabinet de S.M.* The press survived until 1730, and nearly fifty pieces were issued from it—though not many, one imagines, produced by the King's hand!

Louis XVI, when Dauphin, was also taught how to print by A. M. Lottin, and in 1776, at the age of twelve, produced an edition of *Maximes morales et politiques tirées de Télémaque, imprimées par Louis Auguste, Dauphin.* A curious and well-authenticated story is told of this book by Charles Nodier in his *Mélanges tirées d'une petite bibliothèque*: when the Dauphin had finished printing the twenty-five copies of his book, he bound them up for presentation. The first copy was naturally for his grandfather the King, who took the book, opened it and read the first maxim his eye chanced upon. For a man as preoccupied with thoughts of future revolution as Louis XV is known to have been, what he read was profoundly significant: it was a passage which stated that once rulers broke the barriers of good faith and of honour, they could not restore the confidence necessary to them, nor could they re-establish a respect for the principles of justice in their subjects; they would become tyrants, and their subjects rebels, and only through revolution would an equilibrium be restored. It was too much for the King. 'M. le Dauphin,' he observed, 'votre ouvrage est fini, *rompez la planche.*' As Nodier says, since the book was already complete the King could only have been playing on words to refer to the future.

Louis XVI never lost his interest in printing: a year or two before the revolution he was shown the new press which Philippe-Denis Pierres had devised, and was so pleased with it that he printed many sheets on it himself.

In England royal presses of this sort were less common. Despite the interest shown by Charles II in the sciences, his direct experience of printing seems to have been limited to a visit he paid shortly before his death to the 'frost fair' which was set up on the frozen Thames in January and February of

Rivieres de France. 3

LA MARNE.

CEtte Riviere a ſa ſource en Champagne, à une demie lieuë au-deſſus de Langres, d'où coulant au Septentrion elle paſſe à Vitry-le-François & à Chaalons; paſſant à l'Occident par Château-Thierry & par Meaux, elle ſe rend enfin dans la Seine près & au-deſſous de Charenton.

L'OISE.

CEtte Riviere a ſa ſource en Picardie, d'où coulant au couchant, & peu après vers le Midy, elle paſſe

Fig. 5. A page from *Cours des principaux fleuves et rivières de l'Europe*, set up by the young Louis XV under the guidance of Jacques Collombat, 1718; possibly also printed by the King

1683–4. The royal party included the Queen, the Duke of York and his wife, Princess Anne and her husband Prince George of Denmark, and a flysheet recording their visit was printed on a press on the ice. For presses producing keepsakes were regular sideshows at these frost fairs of which there were others in 1739–40, 1788–9 and 1813–14. In the words of John Evelyn's diary, in 1683–4 'the Thames before London was . . . planted with boothes in formal streetes, all sorts of trades and shops furnish'd and full of commodities, even unto a printing presse, where the people and ladyes took a fancy to have their names printed . . . The humour took so universally, that 'twas estimated the printer gain'd £5 a day for printing a line onely, at sixpence a time . . .'

There was at least one royal press in England in the nineteenth century—that at Frogmore Lodge, Windsor, which was set up during the residence there of Queen Charlotte in 1809. Her companion, Miss Ellis Cornelia Knight, was closely concerned in its operations, editing a volume of translations from the German, and contributing (with Samuel Rogers) to a volume of miscellaneous poems in 1812. But most of its work was uninteresting—abridged chronologies of the history of various European countries, evidently for the use of children—and wretchedly produced. The printer employed, E. Harding, appears to have been a jobbing printer in Windsor.

The use of the press in education was not limited to royalty, and there is plenty of evidence of small presses being used by the aristocracy in this way, particularly in eighteenth-century France. An interesting and very little-known press of this sort belonged to the last Marquis de Bercy, though it is far from typical in that it was operative at the height of the French revolution in 1791. That the press is little-known is scarcely surprising, as only one book was produced, and that is of extreme rarity: *Fables et oeuvres diverses*, by Maximilien -Emanuel-Charles Malon, Marquis de Bercy.

This book was originally issued in parts, and was never completed, printing being brought to a halt after four parts had been produced. It was printed by the eleven-year-old son of the author a year after the latter's death in 1790, from a press set up in the Château de Bercy, which then stood on the outskirts of Paris, near to the Porte de Charenton. In the Preface, addressed to his uncle and aunt, his godparents, the young printer gave this engaging account of the book: 'What! do we read the name of Charles Malon on the titlepage of a book? And has our nephew, our little cousin, turned printer? This is indeed a puzzle . . . I can well understand your surprise, my dear Godparents, and I hasten to give you the explanation.

'My good friends M de Praslin and M de Montesquiou had been given little

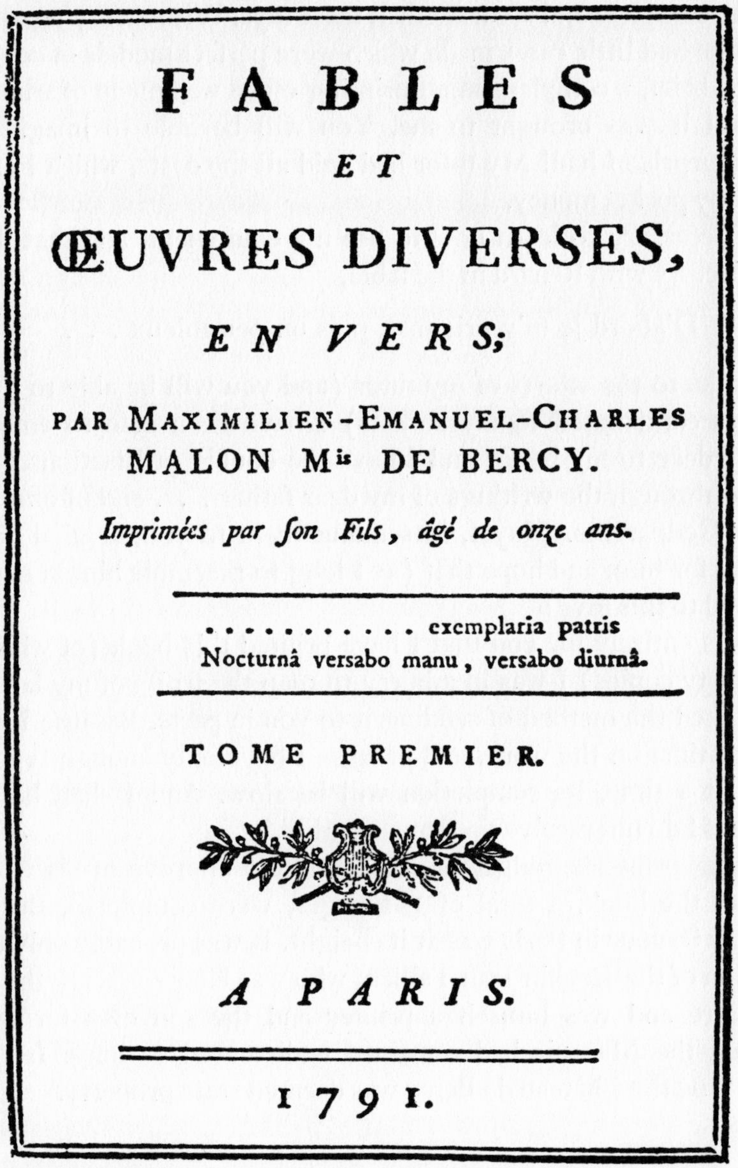

FABLES
ET
ŒUVRES DIVERSES,
EN VERS;
PAR MAXIMILIEN-EMANUEL-CHARLES
MALON Mis DE BERCY.
Imprimées par ſon Fils, âgé de onze ans.

. . . . exemplaria patris
Nocturnâ versabo manu, versabo diurnâ.

TOME PREMIER.

A PARIS.

1791.

Fig. 6. Title-page of a book set up and printed by the eleven-year-old Marquis de Bercy

English printing sets as New Years gifts. With these they could print a few lines. This gave them very great pleasure, which they were not slow in letting me share. After I had played with them, my enthusiasm showed my tutor how much I would like to have a printing press of my own. Always anxious to satisfy my wishes when they are reasonable, he sought a way of enabling me to print more complete and accurate than these toys. Without saying anything to me about it he had little cases made which were perfect models of compositors' cases—to be brief, a complete small printing office was made of which I knew nothing until it was brought to me. You will be able to imagine what a marvellous surprise I had! My tutor had paid all the costs, which I am paying back out of my pocket money.

'It was necessary to learn how to use my equipment, and that demanded much practice. As with Renard in the fable,

D'abord je m'y pris mal, puis un peu mieux . . .

At last, thanks to the efforts of my tutor (and you will be able to guess how much he has contributed to my success) I have been able to embark on a project very dear to my heart, and I have the double satisfaction of knowing through and through the writings of my dear father . . . and of offering them to you, my Godparents. May I, in sending them to you, remind you of the love you had for him, and hope that (as I long to resemble him in every way) I may succeed to this love?

'As it was entirely for you that I have printed this book (of which I have produced thirty copies) I was in a hurry to reap the fruits of my labours, and so have adopted the method of sending it to you in parts. Because I can spend only my free time on the work, and because I have only enough type to print four pages at a time, its completion will be slow. And I shall be afraid of losing heart if I do not receive your approbation.'

The young printer's godparents evidently did approve of his work, since four parts of the book, a total of 144 pages, were completed. But in 1791 revolutionary fervour in Paris was at its height. It was probably only thanks to the protection of the Jacobin Jean Tallien, who was later to secure the downfall of Robespierre and was himself a printer and the son of a former family steward, that the Marquis had remained undisturbed so long. It could not last, and in 1792 the Château de Bercy was decreed state property.

5

The aristocratic plaything

The *Gentleman's magazine* had not been the only periodical to report on Samuel Palmer's demonstration of printing at St. James's Palace in 1731. A fuller report appeared in *The craftsman*, which concluded with the observation that 'it must be the greatest Mortification to *Those*, whose guilt makes them enemies to this useful Invention, to see it encouraged by their Majesties, in such a Manner, and even to behold some of the Royal Family initiating Themselves in the noble Arts of *Writing* and *Printing.*—We could wish that our *Nobility* and *Gentry* would follow this Royal Example, and set up a *Printing-Press* in their Houses; which, we apprehend, would be a much more polite, as well as a more instructive Amusement for Themselves and their Heirs, than the modern fashionable Diversions of *Billiard-Tables* and *Fox-hunting.*' A cutting of this passage was to be pasted at the beginning of the Journal of the most famous of eighteenth-century private presses, that of Horace Walpole at his Gothick villa Strawberry Hill.

The Strawberry Hill Press which was set up in one of the outbuildings of Walpole's house in 1757 was in the words of Wilmarth S. Lewis 'for his own pleasure and convenience; he would bring out only books and trifles by his friends and himself and unpublished manuscripts of antiquarian interest. He would control their distribution. He let Dodsley, the leading London publisher, sell some; others he sold for charity—the poor of Twickenham, a learned and indigent tailor, his friend Bentley—but most he gave away. His political pieces continued to appear anonymously in London. Strawberry was not to be defiled by them.'

The first stage was the appointment of a printer and the installation of equipment. In his first printer, William Robinson, who started work on 25 June 1757, Walpole had chosen moderately well; during the two years that he worked for Walpole he printed competently and extensively if not exceptionally well. But Robinson left in a huff in March 1759: '. . . my printer, who was a foolish Irishman, and who took himself for a genius, and who grew angry when I thought him extremely the former and not the least of the latter, has left me', Walpole wrote to Lord Zouch. His next few appointments to the position were most unsuccessful, and the record in Walpole's *Journal of the Printing Office* reads very amusingly:

'1759 March 5th Robinson the Printer went away
             29th My new printer, Benjamin Williams, came
   May   25th He went away
   June   19th James Lister, a new Printer, came; staid but a week.'

Eventually, after a number of printers had departed rapidly, leaving debts or pregnant girls behind them, Walpole appointed Thomas Kirgate as his printer in 1765. Kirgate was no more skilled at his craft than his predecessors, but he fitted in to the Strawberry Hill household well enough to become Walpole's secretary, librarian and curator of prints, remaining in his employ until Walpole's death in 1797. Yet he too was a not altogether desirable servant, abusing Walpole's confidence in his secretarial capacity, and as printer issuing several forgeries of Strawberry Hill books.

Wilmarth S. Lewis has claimed that the Press 'has to its credit the first editions of more books of lasting interest than any other private press in England before or since'. Certainly the publishing programme started splendidly, with an edition of two of Gray's *Odes*. 'On Monday next the Officina Arbuteana opens in form,' wrote Walpole to Chute on 12 July 1757. 'The Stationers' Company, that is Mr Dodsley, Mr Tonson, &c. are summoned to meet here on Sunday night. And with what do you think we open? *Cedite, Romani Impressores*—with nothing under *Graii Carmina*. I found him in town last week: he had brought his two Odes to be printed. I snatched them out of Dodsley's hands, and they are to be the first-fruits of my press . . .'

The books printed at the Strawberry Hill Press during the thirty-two years of its life included a good number from Walpole's own pen, including his *Catalogue of the royal and noble authors of England* (1758), *Anecdotes of painting in England* (1762–3), *Hieroglyphic tales* (1785) and *The Mysterious mother* (1768), the least bad of tragedies in a period of bad tragedy—but not, surprisingly, his *Castle of Otranto*. The Press also produced guides to the contents of Strawberry Hill, tickets of admission to view the house and similar pieces, but it was in no sense a vanity press. Much important material by other authors was also produced: an edition of Lucan, of the autobiography of Lord

O D E S

BY

Mr. G R A Y.

ΦΩΝΑΝΤΑ ΣΥΝΕΤΟΙΣΙ‒‒‒‒‒‒‒
PINDAR, Olymp. II.

PRINTED AT STRAWBERRY-HILL,
For R. and J. DODSLEY in Pall-Mall.
MDCCLVII.

Fig. 7. Gray's *Odes*, the first book to be printed at the Strawberry Hill Press

Herbert of Cherbury, of Hamilton's *Memoirs of the Count de Grammont,* and several others of lasting importance.

Walpole's press had another much less serious side which fitted better with his claim that 'present amusement is all my object'; a side much more characteristic of the aristocrat's plaything. On 17th May 1763, for example, Walpole recorded in his *Journal* that 'Mesdames de Boufflers and Dusson, two French Ladies who came to England this year, breakfasted at Strawberry Hill, and were carried to see the Printinghouse; where desiring to see something printed, the following lines which had been set ready, were taken off.

> *The Press speaks.*
> *For Madame de Boufflers.*
> *The gracefull Fair, who loves to know,*
> *Nor dreads the North's inclement Snow;*
> *Who bids her polish'd accent wear*
> *The British diction's harsher air;*
> *Shall read her praise in ev'ry clime,*
> *Where types can speak or Poets rhyme . . . '*

Strawberry Hill produced a good many of these trifles which were typical of the eighteenth-century private press, in France as much as in England. There is a story of Louis XV visiting a press, and finding a pair of spectacles lying on a sheet of paper. On examining the sheet through them, he found that it contained 'a panegyric of his person as majestic as it was delicate. "Ah," exclaimed the King, "these lenses are too strong. They make everything appear larger than life".' But though such pieces today fetch very high prices, it was not through these that Strawberry Hill achieved the fame it had in its own time. And of its fame there is no doubt: as early as 1759 broadsheets were being hawked in the London streets with the imprint of Strawberry Hill on them to make them sell, and in 1792 Walpole wrote that 'some years ago Count Potocki brought me a message from the present King of Poland . . . desiring my *Anecdotes of painting.* It distressed me as they were out of print . . . I was reduced to buy a second-hand set . . . and, though the original set sold for less than thirty shillings, I was forced to pay thirteen guineas from their scarcity.'

During the nineteenth century Walpole himself was extraordinarily misunderstood and undervalued—'a gentleman-usher at heart,' said Macaulay —and Strawberry Hill books were also attacked, although they never lost their value to book collectors. In 1854, for example, Bolton Corney commented in *Notes and queries* on Walpole's edition of the *Memoirs of the Count de Grammont*: 'In reprinting the dedication to Madame du Deffand, I had to insert *eight* accents to make decent French of it! The *avis* is a mere medley of fragments: I could not ask a compositor to set it up!' And so on, and so on. All this would not have worried Walpole; writing to his friend Mason in May 1773 he had confided that 'I have not the patience necessary for correcting the press. Gray was ever reproaching me with it, and in one of the letters I have just turned over, he says: "Pray send me the proof-sheets to correct, for you know you are not capable of it." It is very true; and I hope future edition-mongers will say of those of Strawberry Hill, they have all the beautiful negligence of a gentleman.'

From the point of view of book design, modern authorities have not been flattering. Stanley Morison conceded that the Press encouraged interest in typography, but insisted that much finer work was done by commercial printers of the day. Updike was more forthright: 'Among its rather indifferent printing the . . . Lucan is worthy of moderate praise' was the best that he could find to say. Yet the books have a certain modest elegance of their own, and are without doubt a pleasure to handle and read.

The Strawberry Hill Press was almost the only private press of any importance in England in the eighteenth century. In France, *The craftsman*'s recommendation to the nobility and gentry would have been entirely super-fluous, as in the seventeenth and eighteenth centuries there were many such aristocratic playthings. These presses were particularly common at Versailles, where the mother of Louis XVI had a little press in the 1750s which the Duc de Bourgogne continued to run in the following decade. In her apartments 'au nord' Madame de Pompadour also had a small press from which an edition of Corneille's *Rodogune*, with an etching by her hand, was issued in 1770. Nearly all of these were serious presses, and their work had a high moral tone about it: the Duc de Bourgogne's edition of a prayer-book for the use of the royal family is typical. In complete contrast was another earlier royal press: in 1730 the Duchesse de Bourbon-Condé, aided and abetted by the unsavoury abbé Grécourt, had a little press ('L'Imprimerie du Vourst') installed in the Palais de Bourbon, from which she issued an odd little volume called *Maranzakiniana*. This was a collection of queer sayings and *sottises* (a perfect parody of the typical *ana* of the period, in fact) of a certain Maranzac, who had formerly been an equerry in the service of Louis XIV's son, and after the latter's death had been taken into the Duchesse's household as a sort of court buffoon. A chapter in Nodier's *Mélanges* is devoted to this piece of nonsense.

The nobility as well as the royal family had their presses. The Marquis de Lussay in the 1730s, the Duc d'Aiguillon at the same period, the Duc de Choiseuil and *Président* Saron in the 1770s, all had presses from which were printed (occasionally with their own hands) volumes of memoirs, family histories, and similar pieces. Among the more interesting of these were the presses of Capronnier de Gauffecourt, a friend of Voltaire and of Madame d'Epinay (who had a press of her own at Geneva) who in 1763 published the first manual on bookbinding; and that of Leorier de Lisle, who in the 1780s printed two books on papers he had made from nettles, couch-grass, moss, marshmallow and other unusual materials.

It was into such a situation that Benjamin Franklin entered when he was appointed the first American Minister to the French court in 1776. It was natural indeed that a man who thought of himself first and last as a printer should install a press in his residence at Passy. The conventional picture is of the old man (he was then in his seventies) using his press as a relaxation from the cares of public service, to teach his grandson Benjamin Franklin Bache how to print, and producing the series of 'bagatelles' which charmed the French salons of the time. Yet there was a much more serious side to Franklin's work at the Passy Press. As well as the bagatelles, which were propaganda of the subtlest sort for the American cause, Franklin produced a range of official documents—blank passports, orders against American bank balances in France, promissory notes and bonds, regulations about the capture of prizes at sea and similar pieces. All these demonstrate how much Franklin had to work on his own initiative as the American Minister Plenipotentiary: the Passy Press was virtually a government printing office as well as the hobby of an aged man. How much more than this Franklin's press was still remains to be discovered. The bagatelles and official pieces already mentioned were all small pieces, and the first dated document from the Passy Press was a dinner invitation in July 1779. Yet in 1777 and 1778 large purchases of type were made; in 1780 Franklin had at least three presses, and in the same year he bought typefounding equipment extensively. Four employees, a foreman and three assistants, were engaged full time in typefounding at this time, and even allowing for the fact that some of this type was produced for American printers cut off from their normal English sources of supply, the Passy Press was obviously operating on a much larger scale than can be explained by the pieces known to have been produced.

The French revolution naturally put a stop to much of the amateur printing of the aristocracy. But such presses did not necessarily disappear straight away, as we have seen from the Marquis de Bercy's little press; in at least one case the revolution was the principal cause of such a press being set up.

The events of the revolution in France, which compelled so many of the aristocracy to become *emigrés*, persuaded the Duc de Luynes that it would be wise to retire to the country, and he and his wife and family spent the troubled years of the 1790s living quietly and discreetly at the Château de Dampierre. His wife, Guyonne de Montmorency-Laval, had at court been a lady-in-waiting to Marie-Antoinette; a post for which she seems to have been singularly ill-suited—she was something of a blue-stocking and in addition was a strong masculine character who always dressed in an extraordinarily unfashionable manner, and at times in men's clothes—and which she disliked heartily. Country life must have wearied her, and when in company with Madame Récamier she visited the printing house of Ballanche, she was unable to restrain her enthusiasm. Hoisting up her skirts, she set herself before a case of type and quickly and accurately set up a passage, to the amazement and admiration (so we are told) of all the workmen. She had found the ideal hobby.

A press and equipment were quickly installed at Dampierre, and in 1797 the first book from the press was issued: *Robinson Crusoe*, with an interlinear French translation by the Duchesse. From then until 1810 a steady stream of books came from the press—translations of Gray's *Elegy*, of the life of Dean Swift, anthologies of verse 'for the use of friends living in the country', and many others. The Duchesse appears to have done most of the typesetting and presswork, as well as editing the texts herself. But she was not interested in binding, and the books were sewn into paper covers by an Irish lady, Mme Felz, who lived at the Château. In 1810, however, an imperial decree by Napoleon forbade all such private presses, and the Duchesse was compelled to abandon her hobby. Instead of printing she devoted herself to writing, and more than forty volumes of her manuscripts survive at Dampierre.

Another private press which disappeared as a result of Napoleon's decree was that owned by the Baron de Villenfagne, an historian who while he was Burgomaster of Liège in the 1790s had a press erected in his house from which he published his *Histoire de Spa* among other works. But this press fades into insignificance beside another Belgian private press of about the same period: that of the Mareschal Prince de Ligne. In his magnificent Château de Bel Oeil the Prince set up a small press about 1780, on which it amused him to print small editions of books (mainly from his own hand) for presentation to his friends. So enthusiastic was the Prince, in fact, that some authorities have suggested that he had a second press in his house in Brussels. Among the

Fig. 8. Title-page of the most celebrated of the Prince de Ligne's 'Imprimerie de Bel Oeil' publications, 1781

books he printed by far the best known is his *Coup d'oeil de Bel Oeil* of which fifty copies were produced in 1781, but some of his other works, such as his *Mélanges de litterature* published with the imprint 'à Philisopolis' in 1783, are of equal interest. It seems that much of the printing was done by the Prince himself, with assistance from his son and perhaps from his chaplain; it has been surmised that he also bound the books, so far do surviving copies fall below professional standards!

In 1794 the events of the revolution compelled the Prince to leave his country, his home, his fortune and his press, and he retired to Vienna where he set up house in the suburbs, living in straitened circumstances. Here he once more set up his press, and between 1795 and 1811 a collected edition of his works, *Mélanges militaires, littéraires et sentimentaires*, was issued.

The most richly endowed of all eighteenth-century private presses was that which Frederick the Great of Prussia maintained 'au donjon du chateau' in Berlin. Even before he succeeded to the throne, Frederick had been contemplating the operation of a press at Rheinsberg, in order to print an edition of Voltaire's *Henriade*. His original idea was not to produce the work at his own press, but to have it produced by the English engraver John Pine. He had been greatly impressed by Pine's *Horace* published between 1733 and 1737, and dreamed of a *Henriade* engraved by Pine with decorations by the Prussian artist Knobelsdorff. But Pine was busy with other work, and demanded seven years in which to produce the book. Neither Voltaire nor Frederick was willing to wait so long, and so they turned to the idea of a carefully-printed edition to be produced under Frederick's personal supervision. In October 1739 Frederick wrote to Voltaire to say that a printing-office was to be installed in the tower he was having built to house his library at Rheinsberg. Soon afterwards Algarotti was asked to find out the cost of purchasing printing equipment in England; Frederick wrote a Preface and the artist's preliminary sketches for the designs were well advanced. 'No matter what the cost, we shall create a masterpiece, worthy of its text' Frederick wrote. But the *Henriade* was never to appear: on the death of his father Frederick had to leave Rheinsberg for Berlin, and for some years afterwards cares of state prevented him from contemplating his own personal press.

Eventually, however, Frederick found the leisure to return to his dreams of having books for private circulation printed under his personal direction. As a result of researches by Hans Dreysen and Paul Seidel in the Hohenzollern archives at the beginning of this century it has become clear that in 1748 the official royal printer Christian Friedrich Henning was instructed to equip a

ŒUVRES

DU

PHILOSOPHE

DE

SANS-SOUCI.

Au Donjon du Chateau.

Avec Privilége d'Apollon.

M. DCC. L.

Fig. 9. Title-page of the first book to be printed at Frederick the Great's press in Berlin, 1750

printing office in the King's residence. The engraver George Friedrich Schmidt, who in 1743 had been tempted to return from a brilliant career in Paris to become court engraver, was placed in charge of the press's operations.

The first book to be printed by the new press was, appropriately enough, an edition of Frederick's own literary pieces: *Œuvres du philosophe de Sans Souci*, published 'au donjon du chateau, avec privilége d'Apollon, MDCCL'. The first part of the first volume, a mock-epic poem about the French ambassador Valory entitled *Palladion*, had in fact been printed in 1749, but the King could not bring himself to pass proofs without changing and expanding his text. As he wrote to Algarotti, 'Vous faites bien plus sagement que moi, avec vos ouvrages; vous les limez et après vous imprimez; pour moi j'imprime, je me repens et puis je corrige.'

Despite the secrecy with which *Palladion* had been printed, knowledge of its existence leaked out, and Frederick was considerably embarrassed by a request which Valory transmitted from the French court requesting a copy—so embarrassed, in fact, that even his friend Voltaire was told that if he wished to see a copy he could do so only in Berlin. This was not an outright refusal, for Voltaire was already planning to come. When he arrived in July 1750 he found the press's second book, Frederick's *Mémoires pour servir à l'histoire de la maison de Brandebourg*, already well advanced. But after Voltaire had read through the sheets, covering them with his characteristic ironic comments, printing was interrupted so that the book could be rewritten. The corrected edition was completed the following year, and copies were distributed to Valory and others. Meanwhile, the scandal of *Palladion* was still alive, and in order to put an end to it the King decided to suppress the offending edition of his *Œuvres* and to reprint in a single volume, suppressing some pieces and adding others such as his essay on the art of war. A copy of the new edition, completed in 1751, was sent to Valory: 'Je ne saurais vous envoyer ce que votre politesse vous engage de me demander avec tant d'instance', wrote Frederick. 'Je n'ai fait tirer que très peu d'exemplaires de la dernier édition et les anciennes sont si imparfaites et si incomplètes que je me propose d'en faire brûler tous les exemplaires.' As far as he was concerned, the affair was now closed.

These early books were not different in essence from the work produced by other aristocratic presses, though undertaken on a grander scale. But Frederick's press had another more serious side to it, just as Franklin at Passy was more than a printer of bagatelles. In 1752 a small octavo manual *Principes généraux de la guerre appliqué à la tactique et à la discipline des troupes prussiennes* was

FRÉDERIC-GUILLAUME, LE GRAND ELECTEUR.

RÉDÉRIC-GUILLAUME nâquit à Berlin, le 6. de Février 1620. Il reçut le nom de GRAND, & il l'étoit effectivement. Le Ciel l'avoit formé exprès, pour rétablir, par son activité, l'ordre, dans

N 3

il semble qu'il eut le nom de grand au berceau, comme louis 14 celuy de Desdans il me semble qu'on

pourroit attendre pour luy donner ce nom, le temps ou il le merita ainsi dans l'histoire de louis 14 je dirois qu'il receu le nom de grand en 1650.

Si on veut donner le nom de grand a federic guillaume des les premieres lignes ne pourroit on pas dire

fed Guill, surnommé le grand et qui merita ce titra

ou

a qui les vertus ont merité le nom de grand

ou

digne du nom de grand que ses peuples et ses voisins luy ont donné

ou —

Fig. 10. Part of the proof-sheet of Frederick the Great's *Mémoires pour servir à l'histoire de la maison de Brandebourg*, with annotations by Voltaire, 1750

printed under conditions of the strictest secrecy and circulated to some (though it seems not all) of the generals commanding his forces. Their silence on the book was ordered, and to confuse the issue in the event of a leak an octavo edition of another military work, selections from the commentaries of the Chevalier de Folard on Polybius 'pour l'usage d'un officier', was prepared for circulation to his commanders.

Only one more book was to be printed 'au donjon du chateau', the King's *Réflexions sur les talens militaires . . . de Charles XII*. Frederick was unable to supervise the printing personally, since he was away in the battlefield, but this did not prevent him from finding fault with the edition sent him in November 1759 by the Marquis d'Argens to whom he had entrusted the production. 'Les Huns et les Visigoths s'ils avaient eu des imprimeurs, n'auraient pas plus mal fait,' he commented acidly. A corrected edition was hastily prepared, and accepted without comment by the King in January 1760. By now the seven years' war was well under way, and Frederick had no more time for such pleasures. Even after the end of the war, the King had no heart for printing, and his press was never revived.

Occasionally such presses were to be found in the unlikeliest places. Robinson, in his *Last days of Bishop Heber*, recorded that the Rajah of Tanjore in south India had a good library and philosophical instruments, and adds 'that of which he is most justly proud, as the rarest curiosity of an Indian court, is an English printing press worked by native Christians, on which they struck off a sentence in Mahratta in the Bishop's presence, in honour of his visit.'

6

Private printing and the bibliomania

———◆———

The early years of the nineteenth century in England, the period of the Napoleonic wars, were also a period in which book-collecting was to boom. An aristocratic interest in early printed books, assiduously fanned by Dr. Dibdin in his *Bibliomania* (1809, enlarged edition 1811), reached its height at the celebrated sale of the library of the Duke of Roxburghe, which spread over some six days in May and June 1812, and at which the Marquis of Blandford paid the previously unheard-of price of £2,260 for the famous Valdorfer *Boccaccio*.

It was in celebration of this sale that the Roxburghe Club was founded: Dibdin and some seventeen like-minded friends agreed to meet for a celebration dinner annually, at which toasts were to be drunk to 'the immortal memory of John Duke of Roxburghe, Christopher Valdarfer, Gutemberg, Fust and Schoeffer . . . and to the cause of bibliomania all over the world.' In this it probably did not differ from many similar convivial meetings arranged to celebrate prize fights, race meetings and the like. Had this been all there was to the Roxburghe Club it would probably have survived only a few years, but at the first anniversary dinner on 17 June 1814 it was proposed and agreed, as James Markland recorded in the *Gentleman's magazine*, that 'upon each successive anniversary, one of the members is to produce a reprint of a scarce and curious tract, or to print some original manuscript, and the number of copies will be confined to that of [the members of]the Club.' With the first of these books, Bolland's reprint of the Earl of Surrey's translation of Virgil (1814), the Roxburghe Club became the first of the many publishing societies which were so prominent a feature of nineteenth-century England.

The idea of reprinting early works was by no means new in 1813; it was at least a century old. The Gothick spirit which Horace Walpole understood so well, and the reprints of early ballads in Percy's *Reliques* and in the work of

Ritson and Sir Walter Scott, must all have stimulated the interest of the original Roxburghe members and of other contemporary book collectors.

Few of the Roxburghe Club's publications were printed at private presses (though they were usually well-printed and were for a restricted audience in the private press tradition); in any case a further account of its work has been rendered superfluous by Nicolas Barker's *The publications of the Roxburghe Club, 1814–1962* (Cambridge, for the Roxburghe Club, 1964). But its work was closely akin to that of a number of private presses which flourished in the early years of the nineteenth century: presses owned by wealthy book collectors who used them for reprinting scarce works or manuscripts never before printed. These were not the elegant playthings of the previous century; they had a serious scholarly purpose.

The earliest of these presses was in fact where one would least have expected to find it, in remotest Wales. Colonel Thomas Johnes, a Cardiganshire squire, set up a press in his home Hafod House near Aberystwyth in 1803. For some years before this Johnes had been engaged in translating Froissart's *Chronicles*, of which there had been no translation since that made by Lord Berners in 1523–5. The problems of supervising its printing in London without neglecting his Cardiganshire interests had troubled him sorely. Eventually—perhaps inspired by the example of Lewis Morris, who in 1731 had attempted to print specimens of Welsh poetry in the locality—he decided the best solution was to have his own printing-house in Wales. Two printing presses and enough type for five folio pages were purchased; and early in 1803 a printer was brought down from London. But despite good working conditions and wages he (or as Johnes believed, his wife) could not settle in the quiet Welsh countryside. An appeal for help to a Scottish friend produced a more satisfactory employee, however, and the printer his friend suggested, James Henderson, was to continue as Johnes's printer until the Hafod Press closed in 1810. It seems to have been an ideal partnership; Henderson's pride in his craft made the production of the books slower than Johnes would have wished, but the Colonel had the good sense to bow to his printer's feelings, with the result that the publications of the Hafod Press compare well with commercial printing of the time.

The first volume of the Froissart appeared by Christmas 1803, the fourth in 1805. Despite some reservations by reviewers, the book sold well. Even at the ten guineas charged for each set sold, Johnes lost money on his venture, but he had been seized with the urge to continue with translations. Froissart was followed by an edition of the *Chronicle* of Joinville in 1807, of the travels of

Bertrandon de la Brocquiere in the same year, the *Chronicles* of Monstrelet in 1808–9, and a final volume of Froissart in 1810. In the intervals of producing these very substantial volumes Henderson was engaged on printing reports for the Cardiganshire Agricultural Society, a *Cardiganshire Landlord's advice to his tenants* and other works of the same sort. On occasion his work was interrupted by Johnes's visitors who, in the good old manner of the preceding century, would be invited to try their own hand at the press.

In 1810 Johnes decided to call a halt to his printing activities. A disastrous fire at Hafod in 1807 had destroyed much of his library, and the death of a favourite daughter three years later seems to have overwhelmed him, and the press was closed.

A few years later, in 1813, Sir Egerton Brydges started a press at Lee Priory near Canterbury which was far more typical of these nineteenth-century scholarly presses than Hafod had been. One of the original members of the Roxburghe Club, Brydges had for some years before its establishment been issuing antiquarian reprints which were printed for him by the firm of Thomas Bensley in London.

Brydges was a strange figure with his Gothick-romantic melancholy, his fondness for picturesque solitude and his interest in the books and literature of the past. But however much in period he was in these tastes he was profoundly out of sympathy with his times in his passionate anti-democratic prejudices— only made worse by his failure in his claim to the ancient Barony of Chandos, and by his almost feudal extravagance which caused him considerable financial embarrassment—and he became a soured and despairing man. It was almost a matter of course that when he set up his press it should prove a source of vexation and worry to him.

To start with, all went well: in 1813 Brydges enticed two of Bensley's workmen, John Johnson (the author of *Typographia*) and John Warwick, with a novel proposal. If they provided presses, type, paper and labour he would find them premises, supply them with copy and undertake the editorial work; the profits of the venture would be shared. There was an experimental edition of the poems of the Duchess of Newcastle produced for private circulation in 1813, and in the next book (the first placed on sale) Brydges's own *Sylvan wanderer*, the policy of the Press was defined as 'furnishing the literary collectors with reprints of some of the most curious tracts of former days, in which there shall be an attempt to add beauty of typography and wood-engraving, to the interest of the matter selected from the rarities of the Black Letter Stores.'

Modern writers have tended to damn the Lee Priory books with faint praise, and certainly the quality of their production was overshadowed by the commercial printing of Bulmer and later of William Pickering. Yet the books have an agreeable elegance, and at the time of their publication they were highly admired and advance-subscribed with a speed characteristic of periods of book-market inflation. All was apparently going sweetly, reprints of Raleigh, of Nicolas Breton, of Wither and others appearing rapidly. But in May 1816 there was a serious quarrel between Brydges and Johnson which eventually led to Chancery proceedings. The Press carried on under Warwick alone, but it is clear that Johnson had been responsible for whatever typographical excellence the earlier books possessed, and the later publications are far inferior. Brydges himself left England to live on the Continent in 1818, but the Press continued to work at Lee Priory until 1822, some forty-five books and pamphlets being produced in all.

Contemporary with the Lee Priory Press was that set up at Auchinleck by Sir Alexander Boswell, the son of Johnson's biographer, in 1815. Like Brydges's press, it was concerned in reprinting early literature (although in this case Scottish literature) and it shared with it the distinction of printing one of the early Roxburghe books. In Dibdin's *Bibliographical Decameron* (1817), Sir Alexander's own account of the establishment of the press is given. Having resolved to reprint the text of the disputation between John Knox and Fr. Quentin Kennedy of which he possessed the only surviving copy, 'I was constrained to purchase two small founts of black letter, and to have punches cut for eighteen or twenty double letters and contractions. I was thus enlisted and articled into the service, and being infected with the *type* fever, the fits have periodically returned. In the year 1815, having viewed a portable press invented by Mr John Ruthven, an ingenious printer in Edinburgh, I purchased one, and commenced compositor. At this period, my brother having it in contemplation to present [a volume of the poems of] Barnfield to the Roxburghe Club, and not aware of the poverty and insignificance of my establishment, expressed a wish that his tract should issue from the Auchinleck Press. I determined to gratify him, and the portable press being too small for general purposes, I exchanged it for one of Mr Ruthven's full-sized ones; and having increased my stock to *eight* small founts, roman and italic, with the necessary appurtenances, I placed the whole in a cottage, built originally for another purpose . . . not a quarter of a mile from my house.' In the three years of its life from 1815 to 1818 the Auchinleck Press produced some fifteen or sixteen booklets, mostly in editions limited to forty copies. Though John Hill Burton

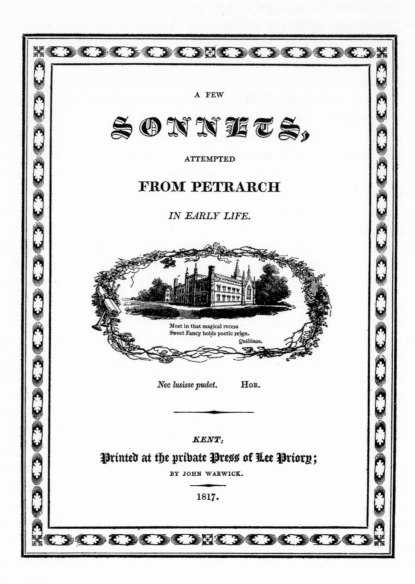

Fig. 11. Archdeacon Wrangham's translations from Petrarch:
a typical Lee Priory Press title-page

exaggerated in claiming in *The book hunter* that Boswell 'alone and single-handed, set the example of printing the kind of books which it was afterwards the merit of the book clubs to promulgate' the work of the Auchinleck Press is unjustly neglected today.

Undoubtedly the private press which should have been pre-eminent among these bibliographical and antiquarian undertakings was that which belonged to Sir Thomas Phillipps, the world's greatest book collector. 'I wish to have one copy of every book in the world,' he said, and his immense collection of manuscripts and printed books is not yet completely dispersed. Phillipps started collecting books seriously while still an undergraduate at Oxford in 1812. By 1822, the year in which he started his own press, his obsessive book-buying had got him into such financial straits that a period of retrenchment on the Continent had become necessary. His reasons for starting his press were unexceptionable: 'The public is probably aware that I do not print for profit,' he wrote in one of his prefaces. 'My object is to preserve information which is lying in [manuscripts possessed by] public libraries; and to put in the power of those who desire that information to have it in their own house, without the trouble and expense of having copies made . . .' And in another he wrote 'Twenty-five copies only are printed, my object being merely to prevent unique records from being utterly destroyed by a single accident.' But there were also less creditable private reasons as well as these public statements of his aims in setting up his private press: for several years before 1822 Phillipps had employed commercial printers to print the texts of manuscripts in his collection and had found that they were expensive—and worse still, they expected to be paid promptly, a thing at which he was particularly bad. Soon after Phillipps had left England in 1822, an Evesham printer named John Agg to whom he owed money nearly sent the bailiffs into Phillipps' house Middle Hill, Broadway; only prompt action by his father-in-law prevented the distraint. Phillipps may well have considered that a private press, operated by a printer in his own service, would be cheaper as well as more convenient.

Cheaper and more convenient it was to prove—for Phillipps; less so for his unfortunate printers. The story of the first, a young man from Bungay in Suffolk named Adolphus Brightley, was to be only too typical. Brightley had been engaged by Phillipps before the latter went abroad, and had been promised quarters in Broadway Tower. When he arrived in August 1822 he found the conditions considerably less than ideal. 'My dear Sir,' wrote Phillipps' agent to his absent master, 'Your printer is come to the Tower & I am very sorry for him indeed he seems so much Distress'd & disappointed in the Place; it is he

Heir followis ane tractat of a part
of ye **Yngliss Cronikle,** *shaw-*
and of yar kings part of
yar ewill & cursit
governance.

FOrſamekle as we haue ſene and vn-
dirſtading zour falſs and ſenzeit writ
that ze call ane cronikle, in ye quhilk
yaj mak zow to ſchaw ye defaltſ of
our Scotts nacioun, and yat certane of our
kings ſuld haf maid homage vnto zour kings
of Yngland, the quhilk is weray falſs in ye
ſelf, as baith our comikles and zours bers ex-
preſs witneſs, to ye quhilk ze ſall be anſwerit
as efferſ.

Item, In ye firſt we vndirſtand how ze ar
cumyn of Brut⁹, yat is ye maſt faltyf pepill of
all ye warld, yat was ye treſonable tratoꝛs of
Troye, of quhais wikit falſs deidſ all ye warld
reidſ, and will do vnto ye end ȝof. And we ar
cumyn and diſcendit of ye maſt noble peple yat
ebir was i all ye warld, baith of our manhed
and treuth, that is, of ye noble Grekȝ yat we
ar cumyn of on ye mānis ſyd. And attour to

Yat our kings maid homage vnto ȝ kings of Yngland is weray falſs.

Ye Scotts ar diſcendit of ye nobit Grekſ. Ye Yngliſs of ȝ treſonable tratoꝛs of Trope ȝ ye debill.

A ij — mak

Fig. 12. A page from Sir Alexander Boswell's edition of *Ye Yngliss Cronikle*,
printed at his Auchinleck Press, 1818

says impossible for him to think of Living there neither do I think it fit for him or any one else, in the state it is now in, the Windows are so bad Broken that the wet when it rains floods every Room, & runs through the floors & Ceilings so that the Plaistering is coming down in many places, & as there is but one Lodging room it wou'd never do for him & his Sister, therefore he cannot think of having her come down. Another Objection to the Place as being unfit for the Business, is that there is no Water, which he shall be often wanting; I really am very sorry for the Young Man he seems so much Distress'd & says that he had but little Money & he has laid it all out in types & one thing or another that he knew he shou'd want for the Business, that will never be of any use to him or any other Printer only for this work of yours. Therefore hope you will give me an Order to assist him with a little Money to Pay him for what he has laid out & the Expense of his coming Down . . .'

Through the agent's good offices, Brightley's living and working conditions in the tower were gradually improved, and for a year or two he seems to have enjoyed his position. '. . . I am still in the Tower,' he wrote in the spring of 1823, 'now Summer is approaching I find it the most delightful situation imagination can conceive . . .' and he set himself conscientiously to learning Latin and Anglo-Saxon in order to perform his work the better. Though when Phillipps had gone abroad he had left a good deal of copy for his printer, it was frequently illegible and always ill-arranged, and Brightley was often at a loss to know how to proceed. Worse, Phillipps was either unable or unwilling to pay his employees regularly, and by the end of 1825 the arrears due to his wretched printer were over two hundred pounds. Eventually Brightley decided to cut his losses, and gave notice to leave. After vainly advertising for a successor able to compose types in 'Saxon, Greek, Latin, French, German, Persian, Arabic and Domesday characters' Phillipps engaged a London printer, F. T. G. Crees, who remained only six months. He was replaced by a local boy, Edwyn Offer, who had been an assistant to Brightley. He lasted until 1829: 'I am not aware,' he wrote to Phillipps, 'whether you imagine that the refusal of any pecuniary remuneration for nearly six years of faithful service will stimulate me to any fresh exertions—*I should think not* . . .'

For some years the press lay idle, and much of Phillipps' printing was done away from Middle Hill, but there were at least seven other printers who worked at the press at different times before Phillipps' death in 1872. The only one of them to last for long was James Rogers who with his sons worked for him from 1854 to 1872.

In such circumstances it is scarcely to be wondered at that the productions of the Middle Hill Press were of a sort which, as A. N. L. Munby has observed, 'it would be charitable to describe as mediocre'. The most important work of the press was the catalogue of Phillipps' manuscripts produced over the period 1824 to 1871—abominably printed on paper of different colours and sizes, with uncorrected as well as corrected sheets used in different copies. In several of his publications the list of errata was fantastically long, as Phillipps was always prone to rush into print and was a very careless editor. He printed his books in very small editions, which he then distributed in an utterly unsystematic manner. The end result has been that many of the works which Phillipps had put into print for the first time are today almost as inaccessible to the scholar as if the Middle Hill Press had never existed.

Few private presses were quite so idiosyncratic, nor were their owners often such abominable employers as Phillipps. In *The working man's way in the world*, that remarkable autobiographical account of the printing trade which Charles Manby Smith wrote in *Tait's Edinburgh magazine* in 1851–2 (reprinted by the Printing Historical Society, 1967), the author records how in the summer of 1830 he was taken into the service of a Rev. Dr. D——e who had retired to Freshford in Somerset, and wanted to have his own sermons printed. For the next two years Smith lived as a member of the family, spending his days in printing, and his evenings in fishing for trout with his patron, or in winter in teaching him the violin or playing chess with his wife.

Rather less idyllic, but more interesting as a late press inspired by the bibliomania is that which the antiquary E. V. Utterson set up at Beldornie House, near Ryde in the Isle of Wight, in 1840. Utterson was an early member of the Roxburghe Club, presenting books to it in 1820 and again in 1836, and had edited two volumes of *Early popular poetry* for general publication in 1817. His decision to set up his own press came late in life, and its productions seem to have been exclusively type-facsimiles of books in his own collection, with the original woodcuts and ornaments carefully copied from the originals. Between 1840 and 1843 he reprinted such pieces as Samuel Rowlands' *Looke to it: for Ile stabbe ye* (1604), Patrick Hannay's *Songs and sonnets* (1622) and— echoing the Auchinleck Press—Barnfield's *Cynthia*. All were well printed on good paper, in editions limited to twelve or fifteen copies for presentation to fellow book collectors. The press seems to have been a summer amusement, as in November 1841 Utterson told Philip Bliss (the Oxford book collector) that he had discharged his printer for the winter, but hoped 'to set tympan and fresket at work again in the Spring'.

In what was perhaps the last of these scholarly private presses to be

———ooo———

Ex Bibliotheca Mac Carthy.

1 Livy. [*Gallice.*] 4 vols. *folio. vel. sæc. xv.* [*With many illuminations.*]
2 Do. Do. 3 vols. *folio. vel. sæc. xiv.* [*With many illuminations.*]
3 Thucydides. [*Latine.*] *folio. vel.*
4 Sallust. [*Scriptura Italica.*] *vel.*
5 Suetonius. *vel. sæc. xii.*
6 Virgil. [*Beautifully illuminated.*]
7 Lactantius. [*Italian.*] *vel. sæc. xv.*
8 Liber Precum.

Debure.

9 Ordonnances Religieuses. *vel. sæc. xiv.*
10 Apicius. *vel. sæc. x.*
11 Hippocrates. *vel. sæc. x.*
12 Cristine de Pise Mutation de Fortune.
13 Extraits de Seneque. *vel.*
14 Plato sur l'Immortalité. *vel.*
15 Berosus. *vel. sæc. xiv.*

Royez.

16 Croniques de Jean de St Tre.
17 Ordre de St Michel. *vel. sæc. xvi.*
18 Galfrid Monumetensis. *vel. sæc. xiii.*
19 Cartularium de Fontevraud. *vel. sæc. xiii.*
20 Do. Saumur. *vel. sæc. xi.*
21 Do. Laon. *vel. sæc. xiii.*
22 Do. Sauve Majeur. *vel. sæc. xiii.*
23 Do. S. Severini de Bourdeaux. *vel. sæc. xiii.*
24 Do. Metz. *vel. sæc. xiii.*
25 Do. Laudun or Laon. *vel. sæc. xiii.*
26 Do. S André de Bourdeaux. *vel. sæc. xiii.*
27 Do. Belver. *vel. sæc xiii.*
28 Cronique de St Denis. *vel. sæc. xiv.*
29 Revenues de l'Archeveché de Bourdeaux. *vel.*
30 Romant de la Rose. *vel. sæc. xiv.* (1375.)
31 Cronique de France. *vel. sæc. xiv.*
32 Calendarium Benefactorum Sti Petri Salmuri. *vel. sæc. xiii.*
33 Tresor des Histoires. *vel. sæc. xiii.*
34 Tresorerie de la Marine. *vel. sæc. xv.*
35 Revenues de diverses Abbayes &c. *folio.*
36 Cossa's Livre des Temps. *Vel.*
37 Croniques de Gennes. *Vel.*
38 Loi Salique et Miroir Histoire de France. *Vil.*
39 Chemin de Paradis. *Vel.*
40 Entrevues des Roys.
41 Custumale Andegavense. *vel. sæc. xv.*
42 Terrier du Captal de Buch. *vel. sæc. xiv.*
43 Computus Monetæ receptæ in Andegavia. *vel. sæc. xiii.*
44 Rentale Domini de Gastines. *vel. sæc. xiii.*
45 Statuta Collegii de Marche.
46 Repertorium Cartarum de Champagne.
47 Juvenal et Persius.
48 Vitæ Amici et Caroli Magni. *Vel.*
49 Confessio Soliloqua. *Vel.*
50 Registrum i recedentium Legis Ecclesiasticæ. *Vel.*
51 Fiefs de la Ville de Craon.
52 Traités des Roys de France avec les Papes.
53 Histoire de Du Guesclin, *vel.*

Royez or Paris.

54 Æsopi Fabulæ. *vel.*
55 Nobiliaire de Normandy.
56 Mich. de Vouges Collection de Prieres. *vel.*
57 Lectionarium Ecclesiæ S. Germani. *vel. sæc. xvii.*
58 Galfridus Monumetensis
59 Alexander de Villa Dei Doctinale. *vel. sæc. xv.*
60 Hippocratis Opera. *vel. sæc. xiv.*
61 Hori de Sapience. *sæc. xv.*
62 Legende Doree. *vel.*
63 Psaulmes en Plein Chant. *Vel.*

64 Leonard Aretino de Bello Gothico. *Vel.*
65 La Spina Rosa.
66 Pelerinage de la Vie Humaine. *Vel.*
67 Christine de Pise Debat sur le Roman de la Rose. *Vel. sæc xv.*
68 Bernard de Humilitate. *Vel.*
69 Generalités de France.
70 Interpretatio Nominum Hebraicorum. *Vel.*
71 De Oculo Morali. *Vel.*
72 Raymundi Lullii Opera. *Vel. sæc. xiv.*
73 Vita Christi. *Vel.*
74 Marci Evangelium. *Vel.*
75 Petri de Alliaco ———. *Vel.*
76 Comment. in Apocalyps. *Vel.*
77 P. Gregorii Dialogi. *Vel.*
78 Villare Gallicum.
79 Pupilla Oculi Johannis de Burgh. *sæc. xv.*
80 S. Anselmi Opus quoddam. *Vel.*
81 Ligues de la Suisse. *Vol. 2. vel. sæc. xvi.*
82 Do. Universelle.
83 Jean Cara Vita sur les Constitutions des Chevaliers de Malta. 2 *vols. folio. ch.*
84 Sti Thomæ Aquinatis Opera. *vel.* 4to.

Brodie and Dowding, Salisbury. ☞ **Ex Insulâ Jersey.**

85 Histoire des Arabes. *folio. ch.*
86 Do. de Malthe. *folio. ch.*
87 Brantome's Memoires des Hommes Illustres. *Vol.1. folio. ch.*
88 Job cum Glossis. *vel. sæc. xiii.*
89 Turrecremata de Potestate Ecclesiæ. *folio. ch.*
90 Principes de Marine. *folio. ch.*
91 Remarques sur l'Isle de Malthe. *folio. ch.*
92 Principia Cartesiana. *folio. ch.*
93 Bonifacii VI. Decretalium. *vel. sæc. xiv. folio.*

Thorpe.

94 Catalogue of American Books. 5 *vols.* 8vo. *ch.*
95 Stevens' Collectanea de Monasteriis, &c. 3 *vols. folio. ch.*
96 Review of Parliaments. *ch.*
97 Rules of the House of Commons. *ch.*
98 Journal of Do. Do. in 1640. *ch.*
99 Judicature in Parliament. *ch.*
100 Cotton's Remonstrance of the House of Commons to James 1. *ch.*
101 Pedigrees of Berkshire Families.
102 Account of the Peshall Family. *folio. ch.*
103 Do. of the Argyle Do. *ch.*
104 Do. of the Navy. *ch.*
105 History of Edward IV. *ch.*
106 Parliamentum Pacificum. *ch.*
107 Exactions on the State. *ch.*
108 General Assembly of ———.
109 Of the Irish Plantations. *ch.*
110 Valor Beneficiorum. *folio. ch.*
111 St George's Grants of Arms. 18mo. *ch. sæc. xvii.*
112 Cases of Habeas Corpus. *folio. ch.*
113 Curia Wardorum. *folio. ch.* [*Olim Comitis Grey de Stamford.*]
113 Snelling's View of Silver Coinage. *folio. ch.*
114 Burlington and Gainsbro' Pedigrees.
115 Maffei de Republica Venetæ.
116 Flower's Derby Visitation. *folio.*
117 Norfolk Do. 12mo.
118 York (query ?) Do.
119 Leicester Do. [*Query from Nichols?*]
120 Cambridge Do. 1620.
121 Benolt's Devon Visitation. [*Query ?*]
122 Sir Peter Thomson's History of Poole.
123 Alphabet of Arms. [*Query ?*]
124 Arms of Knights of the Bath.
125 Do Do. of the Round Table.
126 Pedigree of Sydenham. [*Query.*] *vel.* Roll.
127 Do. of Bullen. Do. Do.
128 Do. of Gifford of Wilts. Do. Do.
129 Do. of Botiler of Sudely. Do. Do.
130 Do. of Bagge. *Paper roll.*

Fig. 13. A page from Sir Thomas Phillipps' *Catalogue of manuscripts*, second edition (1828) printed at the Middle Hill Press by Edwyn Offer

established, that of Prince Louis-Lucien Bonaparte, we find a reversion from the antiquarian bibliophile presses of the Lee Priory or Beldornie pattern to the more purely learned presses of an earlier era. Most authorities have regarded the philological publications of the Prince as privately published, but produced by commercial printers, and it was not until Albert Ehrman's research into his publishing activities that the existence of the Prince's private

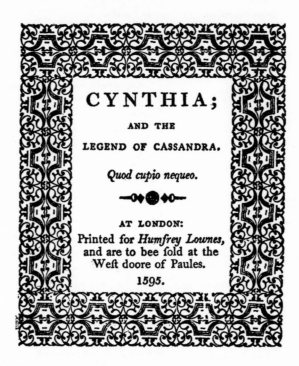

Fig. 14. Title-page of one of E. V. Utterson's type facsimiles, printed at his Beldornie Press in the Isle of Wight, 1841

press was authenticated. Prince Louis-Lucien, nephew of the Emperor, had been born in England, where his father the Prince of Canino was a prisoner of state, in 1813; and his long life was spent mainly in England or in Italy. In his day he was well-known as a philologist, and especially as an authority on the Basque language and on dialects. It was in order to print his own contributions in these fields that he set up a press in his home in Norfolk Terrace, Bayswater, in the mid-1850s. '. . . J'ai une petite imprimerie chez moi,' he wrote to a friend in 1856, 'uniquement pour les Evangiles de St-Matthieu en Basque et pour d'autres raretés bibliographiques.' In 1857 he produced ten works from his press, and in the following year five more. They varied in length from single sheets to books of more than one hundred and fifty pages, all in limited editions of no more than two hundred and fifty copies. The earliest books from the press bear no indication of the printer's name, but most carry the name of W. H. Billing and a few that of E. Billing. But after 1858 the Prince seems to have abandoned his private press, and for the rest of his publishing career his work was printed by commercial firms in the usual way. Whether the Prince was dissatisfied with the quality of the books (which have no special typographical merit) is uncertain, though he confided to a Basque friend that his printer was not skilful enough for him to consider printing on vellum. Most of the Prince's publications consisted of parallel versions in different languages and dialects of Biblical texts, intended for comparative linguistic study. The translators of these texts into the various dialects were not always prompt in submitting their copy. One of the tardier contributors was reminded that the printer 'was paid by the day, and was often idle for lack of copy'. This seems to indicate the real reason for Prince Louis-Lucien's abandonment of his own press.

7

The author as publisher

Of the many different private presses described in earlier chapters, few indeed were as a matter of course operated by the owner of the press personally. These owners had presses, which were operated by printers whom they had employed for reasons which seemed to them sufficient; but there is little doubt that—at any rate after the craft of printing had become thoroughly established—had they chosen to have their work printed in the usual way employing commercial firms, they could have done so easily enough.

Sometimes authors have avoided commercial publication because they felt that to print their work privately would be more rewarding. In this class is Charles Viner, who had prepared a *General abridgement of Law and Equity* on which he is said to have started work soon after he had been admitted to the Middle Temple in 1700. When the work was eventually completed in 1738 it was offered to a commercial publisher, but Viner regarded his offer of £500 for the work as 'very trifling' and decided to publish the book himself. He had presses and other equipment installed in his house at Aldershot, had paper manufactured with a special watermark, and between 1742 and 1753 his printers produced a twenty-three volume edition of the *Abridgement* which was sold at £26 the set. Although it has been aptly described as 'a vast and labyrinthine encyclopaedia . . . ill arranged and worse digested' the work was by no means unsuccessful, though whether Viner gained sufficient recompense for the inconvenience this method of publication must have caused him, to say nothing of the very considerable financial outlay it must have involved, is uncertain. In financial terms his self-confidence certainly paid off handsomely; it was in part from the profits of his *Abridgement* that the Vinerian Professorship of Common Law at Oxford was endowed after his death in 1756.

Viner had received an offer from a commercial publisher. But for the author who is unable to persuade any publisher to accept his work on normal terms, and too poor to have his book produced at his expense by vanity publishers or to commission a printer to produce it, a private press often seems the only way of giving his work the authority and power of print.

Probably the most famous example of this usually misdirected endeavour was in the printing activities of William Davy at Lustleigh in Devon at the end of the eighteenth century. Born to poor parents near Tavistock in 1744, and educated at Exeter Grammar School and later at Balliol College, Oxford, Davy took holy orders and at his examination 'Received great encomiums for his Biblical knowledge'. For a few years he was a curate at Moretonhampstead and later at Drewsteignton, where his sermons were 'of so disagreeable a nature that the most respectable part of his parish could not, without painful feelings, attend his ministry'. Or so they complained to his Bishop. Summoned to Exeter to explain, Davy took with him some twelve volumes of a 'System of divinity' on which he had started work while still at Oxford, and the explanation became clear: the sermons complained of had been on the 'Vices of the Age'; a previous series on the 'Virtues of the Age' had been received with approval by his parishioners. The Bishop inspected his sermons carefully, and praised his zeal; adding that when a living became vacant Davy would not be forgotten.

Filled with enthusiasm, Davy determined to publish his system of divinity, incomplete as it was. An impressive list of subscribers was collected, and in 1785–6 six duodecimo volumes were printed for the author by the proprietors of the *Exeter flying post*.

Davy's sanguine hopes were soon shattered; a good many of the subscribers failed to pay for their copies, the public received his book with complete indifference, and he was left with a debt of £100 to his printer—a very serious matter, for the annual stipend of the perpetual curacy of Lustleigh (to which he had been appointed in 1786) was only £40. But he was determined not to abandon his work, being convinced of its practical usefulness in making his parishioners 'willingly attend the Church, when they found they had some *Equivalent* for their money'. By 1795 Davy had as he thought perfected his work, which had grown to such proportions that the proprietor of the *Flying post* estimated that it would cost two thousand pounds to have it printed. Even if Davy had been able to find patrons it would have been very difficult to raise such a sum, and the Archbishop and Bishops whom he attempted to interest in his project were emphatic in their refusal.

With most men the projected book would have been abandoned, however regretfully. But Davy was a man of pronounced mechanical ability: at the age of eight he had watched carpenters building a watermill, and had carved himself a scale model which worked better than its original; and it seems probable that what little he had seen in his printer's shop convinced him that he could easily overcome his problem by printing a specimen volume of his work himself. Armed with this, he probably reasoned, he could no doubt attract enough support to continue with his original plan of having the whole work printed commercially.

Accordingly 'he resolved *to do what he could*. He borrowed money to purchase a fount of castaway types of a printer in Exeter'. The proprietor of the *Flying post* received him tolerantly, and sold him a case of battered type, but could not resist saying 'I expect that in less than a month you will come and entreat me to take all again from you.' Yet before the month was up, Davy built himself a press, which his son many years later described as being 'of a very substantial and convenient form, and on a principle very different from those in general use' and had taught himself enough of composition and presswork to produce a specimen which he showed his supplier in triumph. The latter remarked with evident surprise 'Well Sir, if you have done this, you will do anything.'

How substantial the 'anything' was to prove would have astonished him even more. Within five months Davy had succeeded in printing forty copies of a volume of some three hundred and twenty-eight pages—an altogether remarkable achievement when one remembers that he had at this time only sufficient type to set and work off a page at a time. Once more with high hopes he sent twenty-six copies away to the two universities, to the Archbishop of Canterbury, to the Royal Society, to a number of literary reviews and to individuals he thought might be willing to help his work. Once more he was disappointed. Most of the recipients ignored the book; the reviews were at best patronizing. The Secretary of the Royal Society got as far as sending a letter of thanks, but failed to have the letter franked so that Davy was obliged to pay the postage himself—no mean consideration for so poor a man in the days before the penny post.

Even this disappointment did not deter him; he was a very dogged man. He still had fourteen copies of the first volume by him, and he determined to finish the work as he had started it, at his own press. He managed to reduce the extent of his own labours by training a housemaid, Mary Hole, to act as compositor, while he cut the paper, read the proofs, printed the sheets and bound the completed volumes. A welcome increase of his stipend (to £60 per annum!) made the expense of the undertaking a little less burdensome, but it was only Davy's indomitable spirit which enabled him to produce three volumes in 1796—and it is perhaps scarcely coincidence that there were no entries in the Parish Register that year—another two volumes in 1797, and so on until the twenty-sixth and final volume was finished in 1807.

A system of divinity was not a handsome example of printing. The press-work was very poor, some lines being starved of ink and others blurred with an excess of it; the work abounded in additions and afterthoughts which were printed on slips and pasted in; while Davy's lack of Greek and Hebrew types, and the consequent additions in manuscript, do not help the effect. But Davy's long years of work were not without reward: Isaac D'Israeli gave the book a favourable notice in the *Quarterly review*, and the Bishops of Durham and of Gloucester wrote to express their appreciation. But not all the recipients of copies were so polite: the Bishop of Exeter (presumably in reply to an enquiry from Davy on whether he had received his set) observed 'that he could not be supposed to be able to notice every trifle that appeared in print.' This was more than Davy could take: 'if his Lordship considered 26 volumes octavo, the labour of fifty years in collecting, compiling, and printing, a *trifle*,' he retorted, 'he certainly could not allow himself to expect from his Lordship either approbation or encouragement.'

One might have expected that after all these labours, so ill rewarded, Davy would have had more than enough of printing for a lifetime; and that as he was now in easier financial circumstances he would have turned to commercial printers for anything further he wished to publish. And for ten or fifteen years his press seems to have lain idle. But in 1823, at the age of eighty, he once more set to work with a volume of selections from his *System*, and without any assistance whatsoever produced another octavo volume of 480 pages. This time the worth of his work was recognized by the new Bishop of Exeter, and in December 1825 he was presented with the living of Winkleigh. He was not to enjoy it long, dying there the following June. In his will he remembered Mary Hole, 'my old and faithful servant'. Though his life may have been one of misguided application, there can be little doubt that in the labours of printing which he had shared with her for so long he had probably been happier than most men are in their work.

Although it would be difficult to find other instances of such devotion as Davy's it is by no means hard to find other examples of authors turning printer. Cotton in his *Typographical gazetteer* mentions one such at Carrick-on-Suir in County Tipperary: '. . . Mr Patrick Lynch . . . was born . . . in 1757. He was educated at Ennis by Donough au Charrain . . . His master knew no

English, and young Lynch learned the classics through the medium of the Irish language. After acquiring in this way an excellent knowledge of Greek, Hebrew and Latin he was compelled, by family misfortunes, to turn farmer, and for five years held a plough. From this employment he was happily relieved . . . and settled at Carrick-on-Suir. Here he commenced author. He had written a Chronoscope, but had no means of publishing it. In concert with a barber in the town he procured some types, and by means of a bellows press, he actually set and printed his first work with his own hands and established the first printing-press ever seen in that place . . .'

The private press seems to have had considerable fascination for the clergy in the past, to judge from the numbers who possessed them in the eighteenth and nineteenth centuries. Often it was probably because more than other educated men they had sufficient leisure, and insufficient funds for commercial printing. Sometimes the books that they printed on their presses were in the field of local history, like the Rev. Francis Blomefield's *History of Norfolk* of which the first volume was printed on his own press at Fersfield in 1739 (the presswork so unsatisfactory that the second volume was printed commercially) or like *The history of Lacock Abbey* which was compiled and printed at Lacock by the Chaplain to the Countess of Shrewsbury in 1806— another unsatisfactory example of bookmaking. More usually they were concerned with religious or church matters, like that operated at Wisbech by the Rev. Henry Burrough in the 1770s, or that at Whitburn, near Linlithgow, by the Rev. Archibald Bruce in the 1800s, or the Rev. Frederick Nolan's press at Prittlewell in Essex in the 1820s. Sometimes these presses were run with true missionary zeal: between 1852 and 1875 the Rev. George Hay Forbes, the Episcopal Minister at Burntisland, operated a press which produced a monthly magazine, *The Gospel messenger*, and his own liturgical writings; after his death the Pitsligo Press (as it was called) was continued for some years by a trust set up by his will.

Quite often, however, these clerical presses were also used for more frivolous work, as for example that of the Rev. John Fletcher at Madeley, Shropshire, who as well as printing the usual series of sermons in 1792 produced Dr. Beddowes's *Alexander's expedition down the Hydaspes*—a book which has been described as '. . . in every way a curiosity, having been printed by a woman and illustrated with woodcuts by a Parish Clerk'. The poem itself is very strange, having apparently been written with the twofold object of demonstrating the possibility of imitating Erasmus Darwin's *Botanic garden* and of denouncing English expansionism in India.

The clergy did not of course have a monopoly of printing their own books. At least one volume of poems by Lewis Way was printed by the author at Stansted in 1822; in the middle of the nineteenth century Albany Wallace, a wealthy eccentric who lived at Worthing, had a press on which he printed a number of books which he had written or translated. Wallace had originally had his press in London, where he produced *The reigns of the Stuarts dramatised* in six parts between 1835 and 1843. He moved to Worthing some time before 1850 when he printed his *Elfrida*, following this with translations of Voltaire and Racine in 1854 and 1861. One of his Prefaces is amusing:

'A certain picture was said by a connoisseur to be "very well painted for a *gentleman!*" a species of negative praise which gave but little satisfaction to the artist.—Should the *Amateur-Printer*, however, meet with as much, he will be very well contented.—All he can say himself for his work is, "that it is legible"; and his type being of a pretty tolerable rotundity, he does not think it will need an additional pair of spectacles to be made out.'

Something of the carefree attitude of those who regarded themselves as amateur authors as well as amateur printers, and had few illusions about the importance of their work, can be obtained from this Preface. A very engaging picture of another earlier press is given by Martin in his *Catalogue of books privately printed* (1834) in which he quotes a letter from a correspondent:

'I was acquainted for many years with Charles Dickinson Esq. of Somerset-shire, . . . He, during a portion of his life, devoted himself to auto-printing; he kept presses and types in his apartments, and composed in a leaden style— I mean to say, that the patriotic, ultra-liberal principles which he professed he embodied in excellent poetry, and as Apollo gave him the verse, he printed, but wrote not his poem. Mr Dickinson read his poems to me, portions indeed, for they formed some volumes quarto, of perhaps eight hundred pages each, in large type and with some margins to receive corrections . . .'

Presses of the kind described are not, of course, things of the past. Kempton Bunton, who removed Goya's portrait of the Duke of Wellington from the National Gallery in London some years ago, was reported by the *Daily Mail* to have written a novel called *Micky Lowbrow* in the late 1930s. Finding that no publisher would accept it, he became convinced that the reason for the refusal was that the book was in longhand, and that it would have to be printed before they would look at it. 'So he decided to build his own press. With tremendous patience he made a press of wood and lumps of old iron collected from scrapheaps and it worked.' The publisher who eventually accepted the novel received one of the several copies which were printed, but the paper shortages in the Second World War compelled him to abandon his plans for publishing the book. If any copies of Bunton's book survive, they will be real curiosities of literature.

It should not be thought that all such author-as-printer enterprises are unsuccessful; there are also many instances of books of acknowledged importance having been produced in this way. To quote one example only, in the late 1920s a Trinidadian lawyer named Charles Reis wrote a *History of the constitution of Trinidad*. There were at that time no commercial publishers in the island who might have been willing to publish it, and Mr Reis's enquiries at the offices of the *Port of Spain Gazette*, at Yuille's Printerie and other commercial firms showed him that it would cost him far too much to be able to consider having it printed at his own expense. So while on leave in London he bought himself a small treadle press, a small fount of Cheltenham type, and on his return home printed the book himself, completing it in 1929. After finishing the book—still the standard text in its field—he used his press for some years to produce ephemera for the Portuguese Club in Port of Spain, but it was essentially a one-book press.

Trinidadian history, and the difficulties of getting the source materials for its study into print, were to be responsible for the establishment of another private press some years later. When the Historical Society of Trinidad and Tobago was founded in the early 1940s one of its principal objects was the publication of documentary sources, but the difficulties caused by the war together with the rising cost of printing threatened to put an end to its work until Professor K. S. Wise, who was retiring from the Imperial College of Tropical Agriculture to live in England, bought a hand-press and occupied his retirement by selecting, translating, editing and printing some hundreds of pieces for publication by the Society. As with Mr. Reis, Dr. Wise made no money from his work, in fact he must have subsidized the Society to a considerable extent, but he had the satisfaction of collecting and making available the materials from which Eric Williams and others have subsequently drawn for their historical studies, and sets of his documents form an important part of all collections of West Indiana.

The presses so far described in this chapter all existed for the single purpose of getting material dear to the owner into print. In this they are not so far from the private presses of the bibliomania, except that they were for the most part printing material of less intrinsic importance, the owner was himself the printer and not an employer of printers, and the quality of production was a matter of relatively minor importance to the owners—though few of them were worse than the Middle Hill Press. As long as the books were got into print it was enough. But there were and are presses operated by authors who deliberately choose this method of production for aesthetic reasons: in some cases an author has felt that only if he can personally design and decorate the vehicle for his texts can the full artistic aim of his work be realized.

The outstanding example of such work—so outstanding that it is almost an impertinence to discuss it briefly in the present context; so far above most private press work that it is seldom recognized as such—is to be found in the 'illuminated' poetic and prophetic books which were printed by William Blake. Blake's earliest published verse, *Poetical sketches*, was printed (at the expense of his friends) in the conventional way in 1783. Blake was not himself satisfied with this method of production, and when about 1788 he began to collect together some of the poems which had originally been included in the manuscript of his burlesque novel *An island in the moon* he was unsure at first how they could best be presented. By this time Blake was fully aware that he was a *complete* artist—he knew that poetry and design are different forms of the same thing, and that he possessed the originality and craftsmanship which both demand. He was not contented therefore to have his poems only in written or printed form: he wished to clothe them so that they were more than poems; they would be poem-pictures forming an artistic whole.

The methods used by Blake for his 'illuminated printing' have been the subject of considerable speculation over the past century. Blake himself believed that this method of producing his poetry was communicated to him in a dream by his dead brother Robert, but it was not until the experiments made by S. W. Hayter and Ruthven Todd in the 1940s that anyone had a clear understanding of his methods. That Blake's books were produced by a method of relief etching had been clear enough, but the means by which he had written his poems in reverse on the surface of the plate before etching had never been explained satisfactorily. Todd and Hayter's investigations revealed that Blake probably got his ideas from a suggestion on methods of transferring writing from paper to the surface of a copper plate in Alexander Browne's *Ars pictoria* (1675). Blake improved on Browne's method, and it seems that he wrote the text of his poems, and drew the outlines of the decorations on paper in a mixture of bituminous and resinous varnish. When the paper was pressed into contact with a heated copper plate, the varnish was transferred to the surface of the plate, and very little retouching was necessary. The plate was then etched in the usual way, leaving the text and decorations, which had been protected by the varnish resist, in relief. To ink and print these plates as for normal intaglio copper engravings would not have been possible, and Todd's experiments suggest that a plain unengraved plate would have been painted over with a special ink compounded from egg-yolk and water colour, this pressed into contact with the etched plate which would take the ink on the raised areas and which could then be printed in the usual way. After printing Blake added further decoration in watercolour with pen or brush to each print, varying them on each copy made.

The series of Blake's now famous illuminated books was started with his *Songs of innocence*, dated 1789. His method of illustration was elaborated in the course of time through *The book of Thel, The marriage of Heaven and Hell* and other works; and the contrast in style between the decoration of the *Songs of innocence* and the *Songs of experience* with which it was issued from 1794 onwards is most marked.

Blake's technique was too slow for him to be able to produce many copies of his books, and it was not until many years after his death, and largely because of the enthusiasm of such men as Richard Monckton Milnes and Alexander Gilchrist (whose *Life* of Blake was first published in 1863) that his poems were extensively reprinted. When they were reprinted, they normally appeared as ordinary letterpress printed pages; it is only in the last few years that the work of the William Blake Trust and the Trianon Press has made it possible for many readers to see Blake's poetry in the form in which Blake wished it to be seen.

Among the enormous number of writers and artists who have been inspired by Blake's work a few have worked in the tradition of Blake's private printing. On Iona in the 1880s J. W. Cormick and W. Muir produced small lithographic editions of Gaelic poetry (*The blessing of the ship*, 1887, and *The death of Fraoch*, 1888, are the only two known to me, though they may have produced more) in the design of which the style of the prophetic books was followed closely. And in this century there have been two other presses which are equally in Blake's tradition, unlike most other modern private presses whose owners normally owe their inspiration (however indirectly) to William Morris and the Arts and Crafts Movement.

The first of the two to be established was that of Ralph Chubb, himself a mystic and very conscious of following Blake. In a prospectus called *My path* which he issued in 1932 he said that 'Blake, faced with an almost identical problem solved it in almost the same way. I accept his tradition, and am grateful, and own my obligation; still, I am no copier nor follower. Rather I take up the thread where he left it and develop the plan . . .' This was, to say the least of it, a bold claim, but one which had the support of at least one critic, P. G. Konody. Chubb, he wrote, 'is not an imitator of Blake, but his mind dwells in the same spirit regions, and he is technically better equipped to give pictorial form to his visions.'

Ralph Chubb (1892–1960) was educated at St. Alban's Grammar School (memories of which recur constantly in his later books) and at Selwyn College Cambridge. After serving in the First World War, he studied at the Slade School of Art, and afterwards had pictures hung at the Royal Academy and elsewhere, with one-man shows at Chenil's in 1922 and 1924 and at Goupil's in

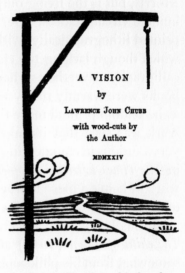

Fig. 15. The first booklet to be printed on the press made for Ralph Chubb by his brother, who also wrote and printed the text to demonstrate the methods of letterpress printing

1929. He seemed in fact to be destined for a fairly conventional artistic career. However, from early childhood he had been obsessed with a desire to make books, and painting alone was not proving an adequate creative outlet. In 1924, he turned to printing. The cost of a press proving too high, his brother (a distinguished geologist) built him a primitive press out of a carpenters' screw and some odd pieces of timber. The first production of the press was in fact *A vision*, a macabre poem written and printed by his brother in an edition of twenty-seven copies so that they could learn the craft of printing. With this crude press Chubb set to work. For the next few years he produced a number of volumes of his own verse, such as *The sacrifice of youth* (1924) and *The cloud and the voice* (1927) often illustrating them with his own woodcuts. But he became increasingly dissatisfied with letterpress printing: the mystical element in his work was growing greater and he found the impersonal effect of type as constricting as Blake had done a century and a half earlier. And so he started to experiment, finally buying a lithographic press so that he could 'combine poetical idea, script, and designs, in free and harmonious rhythm—all unified together—so as to be mutually dependent and significant.' At the same time, he decided to renounce painting and engraving entirely except in the production of his books, so that it was with complete justice that he wrote 'My object is ideal, my work is not a pastime even to the extent that it was with William Morris, but is the living output of one who labours for humane ends content in humble circumstances.' During the 1930s Chubb was to produce four books printed lithographically, with the text written out in a highly formalized script which though lacking the clarity and elegance of Edward Johnston's school of calligraphy nevertheless harmonized excellently with the illustrations. The books were warmly received by a small circle—it was necessarily a small one, as he seldom printed more than thirty or forty copies, though the nature of his work was such that its appeal would always be restricted—and critics were very cautious in commenting on books so far out of the ordinary, but a reviewer in *The Times Literary Supplement* observed that 'no one could suspect Chubb's work of being a mere literary imitation [of Blake]; it is obviously an instance of the parallel working of a similar mind.'

In his last book completed in the 1930s, *The secret country* (1939), and in *The child of dawn* (1948) and *Flames of Sunrise* (1953) Chubb moved away somewhat from his philosophical and mystical preoccupations, and the volumes include a number of stories of occult adventures and Gothick tales which would not have disgraced 'Monk' Lewis. At the same time he reached the peak of his powers as an illustrator, but he was by this time a sick man, and his last books (*Treasure trove*, 1957, and *The golden city*, published posthumously in 1961) show some falling off. But a collection of his books shows an impressive body of work, and though his mysticism at times is too strong for the average reader, Chubb deserves to be far better known than his method of publication made possible.

Though Chubb devised no new methods of printing his books, as Blake had done, another contemporary printer, Morris Cox, has been far more of an innovator. In some respects Cox's reasons for starting his press were those of William Davy rather than those of Blake; the magazines in which his stories and poems had been published had become defunct, and the publishers of his first book, *Whirligig* (1954), were not convinced that the style of his work would

Plate 2. A group of Gog Magog Press bindings

She parts the curtains,
the Unknown who has ever known me.
Cockled of darkness, uncurled of light,
pricked from the spleen, a sweat of breath,
waking in me to think in me:
thinner than a giggle, piddling as peas,
head without body, hands without arms:
she parts the curtains and peers at me.

Plate 3. Opening from *The Curtain* (Gog Magog Press, 1960)

Plate 4. Opening from *Mummer's fool* (Gog Magog Press, 1965)

Plate 5. Morris Cox at the Gog Magog Press

interest more than a very limited circle of readers, and were not prepared to lose money on future books. So Cox was presented with a classic problem: to abandon writing altogether, to attempt to adapt his style to one which might have more sales-appeal, to go to a firm of vanity publishers—or to take up printing himself. In this there was nothing except the very high quality of his poetry to distinguish him from a host of other writers; the difference was that he was an artist who since the 1920s had been experimenting with autographic illustration processes, and had achieved a considerable measure of success in print-making. So in 1956, already in his fifties, he bought his first fount of type, modified a press which he had made for printing linocuts, and set to work. His first book, *Yule gammon*, was completed early in 1957 but of the twenty copies printed only a few had been sold before Cox decided that the standard of production was too low and scrapped the remainder. A fresh start was made with *The slumbering virgin*, a blank-verse interpretation of the old tale of the sleeping princess, which was published under the imprint of 'The GogMagog Press'.

The aims which he should pursue with his press were now clear to Cox: to publish original texts supported in full by his own illustrations. His own philosophy suggested that however much it reduced the volume of work produced, *all* the tasks involved in the production should be undertaken by the author-artist—nor has increased success made him budge from this decision; though today his books are distributed by Bertram Rota he still produces them entirely by his own unaided efforts. But however clear the aims of the Press, Cox still had not arrived at what he considered a satisfactory production, nor found a paper which had the qualities for which he was looking. Of two books printed in 1959, one was never issued, the other, *Nine poems from nature*, nearly suffered the same fate. But with his next book, *The curtain*, Cox was very much better pleased, and it remains one of the most completely satisfying of all GogMagog books. In it he employed for the first time some of his highly individual techniques of printing; techniques which sometimes call for a combination of direct with offset printing, of hand-inking in several colours on blocks which have been built up from cardboard, lace, wire netting, dried leaves and other objects into a surface from which it would be impossible to print by any conventional method. Often Cox's blocks are very simple, as the time spent on producing his prints is very largely devoted to the presswork; some of the more complex prints having to be cleaned and inked in three or four different colours for each impression so that no more than half a dozen impressions can be made in an hour. The resulting prints often have a very distinct and satisfying tactile quality—they are more than two-dimensional in a way which no other book illustrations (and only the French *beaux livres* with their *estampilles*) have attempted. Occasionally some of Cox's techniques, such as printing direct from brocade, have been adopted with varying success by other private printers but most of his methods defy imitation.

Fig. 16. A prospectus drawn and written on to the stone by Ralph Chubb, and printed on his lithographic press, 1939. Characteristic of his later work

Though GogMagog was set up originally as a means of publishing his own work, Cox has occasionally produced books which have been written by others, such as *Chimneypots* (1961) and *A mediaeval dream book* (1963) though such have in general been less successful than those books in which the whole conception was Cox's own. He has occasionally, as in his landscape panoramas of the four seasons (1965–6), moved away from written text almost completely; in these volumes an initial text of twelve or fifteen lines—virtually a programme note—is followed by as many pages of illustration.

To the typographical purist—and there are plenty in the private press world—Cox's philosophy is a considerable irritation. 'No serious work should be attempted that cannot be done as well or better by the average commercial printer' he has said. On the choice of type he is undoubtedly heretical: 'There is no ideal type. Perhaps type faces should be one's own, with a character of one's own. However, better an ugly face married to the mood of the work than one which sits pretentiously in a vacuum'; and at times his choice of face—Matura, Bodoni Wide and others—contradicts all that these amateur printers hold sacred. And yet they have to admit that Cox's books have a sense of unity and purpose which is all too often absent from the production of fine books. GogMagog has been aptly described as 'the most poetic and creative private press in England' and it represents the author as printer in a manner which few could hope to emulate.

8

Clandestine presses I: Moral

'With twenty-six soldiers of lead I shall conquer the world' is an old boast of the printer. It was not long after the introduction of printing into western Europe that rulers began to realize the power that producers of the printed word could wield—power that could be harnessed (as in case of the Emperor Maximilian, with his ambitious programme of over a hundred books which were to broadcast the glories of the house of Habsburg) but which could be disastrous in the hands of the opposition. A solution to the problem was sought in censorship; not a new idea, for in the late Middle Ages the ecclesiastical authorities, particularly in the universities, had always attempted to control the written word and naturally extended their censorship to the printed book. It was not until 1501, however, that the Pope (Alexander VI) attempted to impose preventive censorship on non-theological books—previously the Church had been interested only in the suppression of heresy—and this position was to harden under the attacks of the Protestant Reformation and of the increasing power of the secular rulers until the first *Index librorum prohibitorum* was promulgated by Pope Paul IV in 1559. Meanwhile temporal rulers were also claiming the right of censorship as their own prerogative: the first secular censorship office had been set up by the electorate of Mainz and the imperial city of Frankfurt as early as 1486.

The result of such action was not to silence those presses publishing material unwelcome to the secular or ecclesiastical authorities, but to drive it underground, and clandestine presses have flourished whenever and wherever there has been political, religious or moral oppression.

Not all such presses have been operated by amateurs, of course, however private they may have been. Some of them have covered up their traces so successfully that the true identity of the printers, or the very existence of the press remains in doubt. The commonest subterfuge in evading the attentions

92

of the censor was the use of false imprints on the books printed, and these were used extensively by reputable publishers. In London, J. Charlesworth had enough courage to publish the revolutionary tracts of Giordano Bruno, but compounded it with prudence by making the books appear as if printed in Venice and Paris. On occasion the lack of censorship was a trouble to printers: the laxity of the Dutch censorship in the seventeenth century made any book on a controversial subject which declared its Dutch origin more than usually suspect to foreign censors; and so for example when the Elzevirs in Amsterdam published Pascal's *Provinciales* in 1657 they used the imprint 'Cologne, chez Pierre de Vallée'.

The path of the bibliographer is made very treacherous by these false imprints, and many writers have been deceived by them. For generations it had been believed that Ulrich von Hutten, the political publicist of German humanism, maintained a press in his castle of Stekelberg, a place from which he could with impunity publish his attacks on the Duke of Wurtemberg. Cotton, Peignot, Brunet and other authorities all support the story, and only modern bibliographical examination of type and ornaments has shown that the books with this imprint were produced by a commercial printer elsewhere, and that the imprint *In arce Stekelberk* was used only to mislead the censor.

In England the religious and political controversies of the sixteenth and seventeenth centuries provided an excellent field for such presses to flourish. One of the most famous of these was that of the Jesuit martyr Edmund Campion. In the course of his work in rallying the spirits of the persecuted English catholics, early in 1581 he wrote his famous *Decem rationes*—'Ten reasons for the confidence with which Edmund Campion offered to dispute with his adversaries on behalf of the Faith'. The difficulties of producing the book were very great: it was essential that the textual references with which the work was copiously endowed should be given accurately, as any slip would have been pounced upon eagerly by his opponents and quoted as evidence of dishonesty. It was originally intended that the book should be printed in secret by Stephen Brinkley, who had installed a surreptitious press at Greenstreet House in East Ham some time in 1580, and had printed several works for Campion's fellow-missionary Robert Persons in 1580 and 1581. Campion therefore came up to London to supervise its production. But the search which was being made for him was closing in; Walsingham's government spies were very efficient, and when one of the servants of Ronald Jenks, a stationer who had supplied many of the materials, turned informer, it was obviously unsafe to continue where they were. The press was quickly moved to Stonor-on-Thames, where Dame Cecilia Stonor had put her house at the missionaries' disposal. It was an ideal spot; easily accessible by river from London and Oxford, and yet well-hidden from prying eyes in dense beech woods. Here under Brinkley's supervision four workmen printed the *Decem rationes*, and the completed copies were sent to a Fr. Hartley at Oxford, who in time for Commencement on 27 June 1581 placed copies on the benches in St. Mary's church.

Viewed as an example of book production, Campion's tract shows relatively few signs of the haste and difficulties of its production. The presswork is good, the composition correct. Yet there are signs which show that it was produced with very limited typographical resources. There was a shortage of some sorts —Æ had at times to be represented by *Æ* or by E; the question mark is from a blackletter fount; the Greek quotations had to be represented in italic type. In its day, however, the design of the book was of no interest; the romantic manner of its appearance in St. Mary's and Campion's polished and urbane style caused a great effect in the University. Lord Burghley regarded its publication as a matter of gravity, and enlisted the aid of the Bishop of London and of the Regius Professors of Divinity at the two universities to produce replies to the book. The hunt for Campion was intensified, and in July he was taken. Offered his life if he would abjure his faith, offered the prospect of high advancement if he would enter the Protestant ministry, he refused. On 1 December 1581 he was hung, drawn and quartered at Tyburn.

After the seizure of the Stonor press it seems that Richard Rowland (or Verstegan, as he was later known), a printer in Smithfield, intended to carry on with Catholic printing. But soon after his first clandestine book (*A true report of the death and martyrdome of M. Campion*) had been printed his press also was seized. Rowland evaded capture and managed to flee the country, to continue printing recusant books in Paris and later in Antwerp.

Though these presses were troublesome enough to the authorities (as were to be the later secret presses of Robert Southwell and others) it was not only on the Catholic side that clandestine presses were at work. In the 1580s the danger to the English Church from the rising tide of puritanism was very great, and Archbishop Whitgift found it necessary to adopt the most stringent methods to keep the puritans in check. In 1586 he obtained a decree from the Star Chamber which forbade the publication of any book unless authorized by himself or the Bishop of London, limited the number of printing presses and revived an old law imposing the severest penalties for the publication of slanderous or seditious works. One result was the rise of what has become known in literary history as the Marprelate controversy.

Among those who suffered most severely from Whitgift's policy was the printer Robert Waldegrave. He had already had several terms of imprisonment for printing unauthorized tracts, when in April 1588 he printed John Udall's *The state of the Church of Englande*, an attack on the Church far more dangerous and outspoken than earlier works which had been savagely prosecuted. At Whitgift's order his house was raided by officers of the Stationers' Company on 16 April, and a press, types and copies of Udall's tract were seized and confiscated. Waldegrave himself managed to escape, but his occupation was gone and he had a wife and children to support. With nothing further to lose, he conveyed some type he had rescued to the London home of a certain Mistress Crane, while he himself seems to have moved to Kingston-on-Thames, where a new edition of Udall's book was printed with equipment belonging to John Penry, 'the father of Welsh non-conformity' who had previously suffered under Whitgift and been associated with Waldegrave. Probably by June Waldegrave had moved to Mistress Crane's country house in the near-by village of East Molesey, where the type had been conveyed from London. He was soon at work on another pamphlet by Udall, and by October was engaged on the first of the Marprelate tracts, commonly called *An epistle*.

An epistle burst on the world with startling effect: the work of 'Martin Marprelate' was devastating in the success with which it covered the Bishops with ridicule while at the same time leading the reader on into the traps of puritan doctrine. The stir the tract caused was so great that by 14 November Burghley was writing urgently to Whitgift telling him to spare no pains in arresting those responsible. But this was not to be too easy; as early as June Whitgift's pursuivants had searched for Waldegrave at Kingston, and by November he had moved to the greater safety of Northamptonshire, setting up his press once more in the house of Sir Richard Knightley, a friend of Penry. Here the second Marprelate tract (*The epitome*) was printed before December. Early in January 1589 the Press had moved again to Coventry, where more tracts (*The minerall conclusions* and *Hay any work for Cooper*) were also produced. But Waldegrave was tiring of his work; quite apart from the very considerable personal danger involved he seems (like a good many puritans) to have disliked Martin's methods. He is next to be heard of in La Rochelle where he retired for safety, and where he seems to have printed some other pamphlets by Penry and by Job Throckmorton, another of the Marprelate writers. They took some time to find another printer to replace him, but early in the summer of 1589 John Hodgkins, 'a salt-petre man', was engaged. He printed two further pamphlets, *Theses Martinianae* and *The just censure and reproof of Martin junior* on the press belonging to Penry, which had been moved to a new home in the house of a Mistress Wigston in a village some miles south of Coventry. But Hodgkins disliked the press and moved to Manchester, where there was another press, to work on *More work for the Cooper*. He and his assistants were caught while engaged on this work in late August, and carried off to London for examination under torture.

This was not to be the end of Martin Marprelate, however. Penry's old press in Mistress Wigston's house was still undiscovered, and it was quickly moved to Throckmorton's house at Hasely, and used to print the last Marprelate tract, *The protestation*, in September 1589. The first half-sheet of the book is very obviously amateur work—perhaps that of Penry and Throckmorton—but the rest shows all the marks of a skilled printer, so that it has been conjectured that it was completed by Waldegrave, who had returned to England. Soon after the book had been finished Penry and Waldegrave left for Scotland. They were only just in time: in October an informer gave away the secret of the press and all those concerned were arrested and imprisoned. A few years later Penry returned from Scotland, and was seized on a trumped-up charge of treason, paying with his life for the part he had played in the affair. Waldegrave more prudently stayed in Scotland (where he became King's Printer) until King James succeeded to the English throne.

As well as the recusant printing carried on openly abroad at Douay and elsewhere, there seems to have been at least one long-lived Catholic press at Birchley Hall in Lancashire, operated by members of the Anderton family from about 1608 until 1642. But with the later increase of religious and political tolerance in Britain, there was naturally a decline in the number of clandestine presses of this sort. One of the last in England was a Jacobite press which printed *A collection of loyal songs* with the imprint Ragland Castle in 1750. But in Ireland such presses flourished very much later, particularly in the troubled years after 1916, when clandestine work was ably directed by Michael Collins. Much of this printing was undertaken in secret by commercial printers who were sympathetic to the cause of Irish independence—the bonds and promotional literature produced for the 'National loan' for example, which were printed at Dollard's Printing House right by Dublin Castle. But Collins did not consider it sufficient to rely only on the services of sympathisers, and special printing equipment was also obtained and secreted in Aungier Street, where Dick McKee was engaged in setting up and printing *An tOglách*, the news-sheet of the Republican Army, in the intervals he could find from his work as a member of the Dublin Brigade.

On the continent such presses have been equally numerous. At one extreme there have been the relatively public presses set up by those powerful enough to defy government censorship. Jan Potocki (the author of *The Saragossa manuscript*, and one of the founders of Slavic archaeology) quarrelled with the government of Poland over the freedom of the press and in 1789 set up a free printing press in his castle from which numerous books were issued. These Wolny Drukarnia publications were scarcely seditious—*A chronological atlas of European Russia, An essay on universal history, A description of the new machine for coining money* are typical titles—and though the authorities may have been annoyed at the flouting of their authority, the work of the press can not have caused them much worry. At the other extreme there was at about the same time as Count Potocki's press a surreptitious undertaking operating in Brabant. The Austrian police there were seriously concerned by the appearance of the revolutionary writings of the Abbé François Xavier de Feller, and spared no efforts in their search for the Abbé and his press. To escape from their pursuit he is said to have set up a press at the bottom of a coal-mine near Liège, from which his seditious sheets were produced and distributed throughout the whole of the Austrian Netherlands with impunity.

Presses of this kind were to be found frequently in the nineteenth century and later. In Russia there were very many underground presses before 1917; in occupied Belgium during the First World War the Abbé de Feller provided the example for many ventures of the same kind. And in occupied Europe during the Second World War clandestine printing was by no means the least important aspect of the various resistance movements.

In Vichy France the difficulties of organizing clandestine presses were very considerable. France was split into the occupied and unoccupied zones; the French divided into the supporters of Vichy who were prepared to collaborate with the Germans and their opponents who were by no means prepared to do so—a situation which like the religious dissensions of the sixteenth century made it very difficult to recognize who could be trusted and who not. The vast majority of publishing houses, and many individual writers, gave in to *force majeure*. Many were willing to collaborate. Many of the editors and printers of the first resistance presses and newspapers—of *Pantagruel*, of *La pensée libre*—were caught and shot. But out of the failure of *La pensée libre* came a development which was to lead to the establishment of the most successful of all presses of the resistance: Les Éditions de Minuit.

Jean Bruller, an engraver and illustrator and journalist, had at the invitation of Pierre de Lescure written a story called *Le silence de la mer* which was to have appeared in the next issue of *La pensée libre* under the pseudonym of Vercors. Suddenly he was left, an author without a publisher. But before the war Bruller had been his own publisher for various books—why should he not now publish his story in the same way?

In his autobiography *The battle of silence* (1967) Vercors records that he was influenced to a very slight degree by a story which he had heard about some rebels against Napoleon III who at a dinner party were startled by their host putting a bust of the hated emperor in the place of honour in the centre of the table—but that at the end of the meal the host struck the bust in the face with a hammer, and out tumbled dozens of copies of Victor Hugo's incendiary poem *Les Châtiments* . . . But it was no mere adolescent romanticism which spurred Vercors in his venture. If he could set up the organization needed for his book, it could serve to produce other books. The propaganda which the resistance movements would produce would not be enough, he reasoned; there was also a need for a clandestine press which by producing books of a high intellectual content would demonstrate that French literary life still survived in defiance of Nazi domination, and would provide a rallying point for intellectual resistance.

Jean Bruller found a jobbing printer, Georges Oudeville, who was willing to run the risks that would be involved in the undertaking from a tiny printing office right by the Pitié hospital which had been taken over by the Germans as a military hospital. Oudeville had just enough type to set and print an eight-page forme, which had to be distributed before he could set the type for the next eight pages. For three months, with German troops constantly passing and repassing his open door Oudeville printed *Le silence de la mer* in whatever time he could take from his legitimate work of producing wedding and funeral announcements. Then the printed sections were taken in small batches to the flat of a friend, Yvonne Paraf, who organized a team of helpers to sew the sections and to glue them into covers.

Le silence de la mer eventually appeared in a small edition of three hundred and fifty copies in February 1942. The secret of the authorship was well kept; of the team of workers only Pierre Lescure knew who Vercors was, and his true identity was not revealed until the liberation. But Vercors became very well known; copies of the book found their way into the unoccupied zone of France, were taken to England and reprinted extensively—in London, in New York, Dakar, Quebec, Beirut. At the orders of General de Gaulle it was reprinted by the Free French in London, and tens of thousands of miniature copies on india paper were dropped over France by the RAF. An English version by Cyril Connolly sold fifteen thousand copies; one of these was taken to Tunis where the novelist Pierre Moinot retranslated it into French in order to circulate it further.

With loans of three and later five thousand francs from a close friend Bruller was able to continue with his publishing. By the time of the liberation in 1944 he and his assistants had managed the remarkable feat of publishing twenty-five books, nearly one a month. Far from depending on help from resistance funds, they sold the books so successfully that they realized a total profit of three hundred thousand francs, a sum which was later distributed through the Comité National des Écrivains to the families of those printers who had died for their country in the resistance.

Although the printers had many anxious moments, neither the Vichy authorities nor the Gestapo succeeded in stopping the production of the Éditions de Minuit. In fact near the end they despaired of doing so, and instead conceived the idea of producing spurious editions of its books themselves, which because of the veiled propaganda which they would contain would bring the real books into discredit. But though the idea was excellent, its successful execution eluded the Germans. Eighty thousand copies of the first of these false editions were printed and delivered to Hachette, the official distribution agency. So that they should appear clandestine, the *justification du tirage* carried an obviously false censorship permit, No. 00002. Immediately Hachette seized on this: if they distributed the books, they would be liable to prosecution for illegal distribution, so they demanded a written order to protect themselves. But if the Germans were to issue the written order, the books would be clandestine no longer, and the cat would be out of the bag. It was too difficult a problem for the Teutonic mind: at the liberation the eighty thousand copies were still in Hachette's basement!

In the Netherlands the production of books and newspapers from the resistance presses reached astonishing proportions. In a country in which access to printing presses was strictly guarded, in which the sale of printing ink and paper was rigidly controlled, it has been estimated that the eighty or more clandestine printing groups managed to produce well over a million copies of their news-sheets. There were in addition a good number of pamphlets printed as well, and the number of serious and thoughtful articles on post-war development and similar topics shows very clearly the total intellectual rejection by the Dutch of the German occupier.

Most of the publications of these presses are naturally enough typographically undistinguished. The circumstances under which they were printed

rendered this inevitable, but it was also sound policy—undistinguished printing is much harder to trace than that having a recognizable 'house style'. But
one of the most interesting features of these Dutch presses is the number of
them which set out deliberately to produce their clandestine editions in the
finest typographical style possible; producing exquisite little editions of
classical works or of Dutch poets who had officially been silenced for their
refusal to join the German-sponsored 'Kultuurkamer'. In this endeavour they
were doing much the same as the Éditions de Minuit which had tried to provide a vehicle for those writers who refused to work for the Vichy press;
naturally enough in typographical terms the Dutch succeeded far better.

Among the first of these clandestine fine presses was that of A. A. Balkema,
the Amsterdam bookseller and publisher. His 'Five Pound Press'—so called
because five pounds of paper was the maximum which could be obtained without special permits—and his other imprints A A B and 'The Black Sheep'
produced about fifty small books. The typographer Jan van Krimpen was a
partner in the venture, and the books—which include poetry by Blake, Pushkin,
Emily Brontë, Heraclitus and others—were beautifully produced.

One of the largest of these organizations was De Bezige Bij (The Busy
Bee) which produced *rijmprents*—illustrated broadsides of poetry which were
sold extensively by tobacconists, grocers and others. So successful was this
undertaking that it was able to contribute a sum in the region of £80,000 to
resistance funds. And there were many others: A. A. M. Stols issued some
books under his own imprint, but antedating them to before the war; there
were books produced under the imprints of the Bayard-Pers, In agris occupatis,
Le lapin et le chat, and others. There were many disasters (over a hundred
writers and printers died for their work for the resistance) but they had no
effect on the determination of the other printers or their distributors. It is said
that babies in prams were one of the most frequent and successful vehicles for
the distribution of the clandestine publications.

One of the printers who perished for his work was the artist-printer
Hendrik Nicolaas Werkman. Between the wars, Werkman had been very
closely connected with the art group De Ploeg in Groningen, a group much
influenced by German expressionism. Although some of his early work, such
as his *Het boek van Trijntje Soldaats* (1928), had been widely praised, his
amazing *druksels*, pamphlets and prints produced by a mixture of various printing techniques, were too exclusive in their appeal, and were regarded by many
as belonging to the lunatic fringe of printing. At the beginning of the war his
artistic experiments ceased for a while, but in November 1940 some friends

persuaded him to print M. Nijhoff's poem *Het jaar 1572* as a gift to be sent to friends at the New Year. This was to be the first of forty similar publications of De Blawe Schuit (The Blue Barge) which were intended to stiffen readers' spiritual resistance to the occupation. These and other prints continued to be produced through until the summer of 1944, when the general state of tension resulting from the battle of Arnhem compelled him to stop. In March 1945 he was arrested by the Nazis on suspicion of illicit printing, and on April 10— three days before Groningen was liberated by the Allies—was shot out of hand.

Werkman's influence on later Dutch graphic work has been very considerable. During the war he had become closely associated with W. Sandberg, whose own *experimenta typographica* had been worked out while he was in hiding, and soon after Sandberg became Director of the Stedelijk Museum in Amsterdam he devoted an exhibition to Werkman's graphics. Like Dr. van Royen (whose Kunera-Pers is described in a later chapter) Werkman was not killed by the occupier because he committed acts of sabotage; he was put out of the way because he was a nuisance, and was later sacrificed by the executioners.

It might be thought that in contemporary England clandestine presses of this sort have disappeared completely, but this is not so. Soon after Rhodesia's declaration of independence, it was reported in the press that the police were trying to find the printers of some anti-government, pro-Rhodesian pieces 'to assist them in their enquiries' and in connection with other political protest the police would seem to have been used in an attempt to suppress printing. In 1968 there were two cases of indictments for forgery—poor quality prints of dollar bills with the slogan 'Is this worth the slaughter in Vietnam?' printed over them (a slogan which a U.S. Treasury official concerned with protection against counterfeiting commented was 'not usually found on genuine U.S. banknotes'). Such prosecutions on legal technicalities are as alarming as they are futile. In Beatrice Warde's splendid phrases, 'any private press has fearsome claws sheathed in its velvet pads. What keeps them sheathed is not *force majeure* but free will . . . Every private press is in some sense a Press of the Resistance. In its ancestry is the blood of martyrs who crept by night to secret cellars with forbidden texts; its heroes of our own century are the men who risked their lives to purloin handfuls of precious type from Nazi-guarded composing rooms. And if you see anything in this modern world that makes you cry "No, I resist", you need not try to capture the nearest radio station. Goliath has a more insidious enemy. He can keep a sharp eye on the millionfold instruments of communication and yet never see what doom is awaiting him from the perfidious Albion.'

9

Clandestine presses II: Immoral

I t is not only to avoid religious or political oppression that presses may prefer to operate in secret. An author may have excellent reasons for wishing a purely private circulation for books which he does not want attributed to him, or which he does not want to be regarded as in the main current of his work: there are contemporary examples of private presses operated under a pseudonym because the owner feels that his identity as a printer should not be confused with his identity in his real profession. To avoid public censure was perhaps the reason for the privacy with which Thomas Ilive, a printer and typefounder, printed a famous literary forgery, *The book of Jasher*, in 1751. Ilive was a man of very odd beliefs, in 1773 having published the text of an oration he had delivered a few years earlier, in which he attempted to prove the plurality of worlds, that this earth is hell, that men's souls are apostate angels, and similar fancies. *The book of Jasher* was a pretended translation from the Hebrew, supposedly made by 'Alcuin of Britain'.

'The account given of the translation,' wrote Edward Rowe Mores in his *Dissertation upon English typographical founders* (1778), 'is full of glaring absurdities: but of the publication this we can say from the information of the Only-One who is capable of informing us, because the business was a secret between the Two: *Mr Ilive* in the night-time had constantly an *Hebr.* bible before him (*sed qu. de hoc*) and cases in his closet. he produced the copy for *Jasher*, and it was composed in private, and the forms worked off in the night-time in a private press-room by these Two after the men of the Printing-house had left their work.—*Mr Ilive* was an expeditious compositor though he worked in a night-gown and swept his case *to pye* with the sleeves . . .'

The normal reason for most printers wishing to avoid public censure is much more straightforward than this: it is the printing of pornography. One of the most interesting of these—most of them are very dull indeed—was the press maintained by the Duc d'Aiguillon on his estate at Verets in Touraine. On this press a small edition (perhaps of twelve copies) of erotic Italian and French poetry was printed in 1735. Edited by Paradis de Moncrif and the Abbé Grécourt (who was connected also with the Imprimerie du Vourst and its tasteless *Maranzakiniana*) the volume bore the title of *Recueil de pièces choisies, rassemblées par les soins du Cosmopolite*, and was published with the punning imprint of 'À Anconne, chez Uriel Bandant, à l'enseigne de la liberté'.

According to Gustave Werdet, writing in the prudish 1860s, this was the most licentious book ever printed. It was certainly run close by another book which came from the same press in 1742; a bawdy song book, *Les Muses en belle humeur*, issued from 'Ville Franche' and probably also edited by Moncrif and Grécourt. Gerhson Legman, whose *The horn book* (1964) is packed with curious learning, has suggested that the 'Cosmopolite' for whom the books were printed was not the pseudonym of a single person, but instead of an orgiastic group of noblemen and women who met under the Duc d'Aiguillon's protection to engage in what was then called devil worship. Legman quotes a magnificent story from a suppressed page in the Pixerécourt catalogue; of how the young Duchesse d'Aiguillon was put to setting type for the *Recueil des pièces choisies*, and asked her husband if there should be two Rs [=heures] in *foutre*. 'Indeed there should,' replied the Duke gravely, 'but one normally gives it only one.'

In England the most famous of all clandestine presses of this kind was that of John Wilkes. Following the publication in April 1763 of the famous 'number 45' of the *North Briton*, which stirred a sluggish government into the ill-considered action of issuing a general warrant against the unnamed authors, printers and publishers—an action which was to lead to the recognition of the illegality of such warrants—Wilkes was unable to find any commercial printer willing to take the risk of working for him. Wilkes therefore had two presses installed in his house in Great George Street in Westminster, and engaged two journeymen printers to work them. Originally his idea seems to have been to publish an account of his own persecution, but the idea was not received well by his friends. The two printers were therefore set to printing a number of relevant items, such as Lord Temple's *A letter to Lords Halifax and Egremont*, which dealt with the seizure of Wilkes's papers by government agents. An edition of the forty-five numbers of the *North Briton* was also put in hand. But in a foolish moment in May 1763 Wilkes instructed his printer Michael Curry to set to work on an indecent parody of Pope, the *Essay on woman*. Some years earlier Wilkes had become a member of the notorious Hell Fire Club, that

society whose members—Sir Francis Dashwood, Lord Sandwich, Bubb Dod-
ington and others—engaged in extravagant ceremonies and orgiastic rites
similar to those practised by the Duc d'Aiguillon's group at Verets. The *Essay
on woman* was probably written by Thomas Potter, the libertine son of a former
Archbishop of Canterbury, and it had circulated in manuscript among the
members of the Hell Fire Club. Despite a good opening it is (like most similar
pieces) remarkably tedious; but in the printed version the facetious and
scandalous notes (wickedly ascribed to Dr. Warburton, the editor of Pope, but
probably written by Wilkes himself) give the *Essay* considerably more sparkle.

Wilkes cannot have considered how dangerous the *Essay* could prove to
him when he ordered the edition of twelve copies to be printed for presentation
to his intimates. It was not long before he found out. The government spies
who were sniffing around his press got wind of the *Essay* and by insinuating
themselves into the confidence of one of the workmen they managed to obtain
a copy of it while Wilkes was abroad. The government made the best use they
could of the *Essay* to support their general case against the *North Briton*. In
the House of Lords the attack was led by Lord Sandwich, Wilkes's erstwhile
companion in Hell Fire meetings.

Sandwich had good reason for disliking Wilkes. At a meeting of the Hell
Fire Club at Medmenham, Wilkes had secretly introduced a baboon into the
company. The frightened beast leaped on to Sandwich's back and clung there
while Sandwich fell on his knees crying 'Spare me, gracious Devil. I am as yet
but half a sinner. I have never been half as wicked as I have pretended.' His
humiliation when he realized that he was not in Satan's clutches was acute. At
another well-known encounter with Wilkes he also came off badly: when he
observed that Wilkes would die of a pox or on the gallows he was shattered
by the retort that it depended whether Wilkes embraced his Lordship's
mistress or his principles. Sandwich's attack was therefore a ferocious one,
and he was strongly supported by Warburton, who was Bishop of Gloucester,
and solemnly protested against the attribution of the notes in the *Essay* to him.
The result was a resolution of the House of Lords condemning the publication
as 'a most scandalous, obscene and impious libel'.

For once the public was less susceptible than Parliament to this mass
hypocrisy. During a current performance of the *Beggar's opera*, at MacHeath's
line 'That Jemmy Twitcher should peach I own surprises me' the whole
theatre collapsed in laughter; Lord Sandwich remained 'Jemmy Twitcher' to
the end of his life. Nevertheless, because of the *Essay* Wilkes had become a
political liability, and was thrown over by the ailing Pitt.

Wilkes's press was by no means the only private press set up for a more serious purpose which dabbled in the production of erotica. In 1783 a volume bearing the imprint of *Londres* was published under the title of *Amusemens, gayetés et frivolités poetiques, pour un bon Picard*. This very rare book was written by a certain Pierre-Antoine de la Place, and contains a selection of songs, stories and epigrams of a decidedly free nature. La Place recorded in one copy that the book was printed by the Prince de Ligne and his son, using a manuscript pilfered from the author as 'copy', and that a few copies of the small edition were stolen by a valet who took them to Paris, and where at the author's request they were seized and destroyed.

Many amateurs of all periods have indulged themselves by printing little pieces of this nature. Mark Twain's *1601*, variorum editions of *Eskimo Nell* and the like are common enough—and harmless. The traditional hand-press is no tool for the hard-core pornographer, who prefers more speedy methods of producing the wares he has to peddle. In contemporary society commercial publishers can issue erotic books with little fear of prosecution, *Last exit to Brooklyn* notwithstanding. But during those periods in which the fear of censorship lies heavily upon the literary world, private presses have often succeeded in publishing questionable material when other more commercial undertakings would almost certainly have been prosecuted. There has always, at any rate in this century, been a market for expensively got-up and lusciously illustrated editions of the more lubricious classics. Some of the private and quasi-private presses of the 1920s and 1930s jumped in to supply this market, confident in the fact that prosecution was unlikely: the authorities in England seem to have worked on the assumption that the expensive book would not corrupt its purchasers, whereas cheaper editions would . . . This taste for printing and reprinting the more erotic classics *ad nauseam* has almost disappeared among today's private presses—and what need for it in a permissive society?—but in its day it certainly made the idea of 'private presses' or 'fine editions' suspect to many.

Some of the private presses were not above a little baiting of the censors. The Nonesuch was by no means one of the publishers of erotica, but they pretended to feel in danger in their 1929 catalogue:

'In these days of literary censorship exercised by Sir Archibald Bodkin (of Savidge case fame), Sir William Joynson-Hicks and a Detective-Inspector of Scotland Yard, no publisher can be positive in his announcement that he will issue such and such a book. Chaucer? Fie, his language is coarse. Plato? The less said about Socrates and his young friends, *if* you please, the better.

Shakespeare? He will perhaps pass unchallenged, for Lamb's Tales doubtless exhausted the censors' interest in this prurient author. Farquhar, Don Quixote even—these too may corrupt the corrupt, which is the current legal test of obscenity. With a propitiatory bow to Sir Archibald and to the potent and anonymous Detective-Inspector (the unlamented Home Secretary gets no more than a distant nod) we therefore give to this list of announcements the precautionary title, "Bodkin Permitting".'

One private printer who suffered considerably under the obscenity laws in the 1930s was Count Potocki of Montalk. Geoffrey Wladislas Vaile Potocki is one of the most extraordinary and original figures of the literary world; in interest far surpassing Baron Corvo, with whom he bears several points of resemblance, although unlike Corvo he has not become a cult figure. Born in New Zealand of Polish descent, in 1928 he came to London to seek his fortune in the world of letters, like Jack Lindsay and others before him. Whereas Lindsay was to move to the far left in his rejection of bourgeois life, Potocki was and remains a man of the extreme right wing. He claimed to be a poet by divine right and Wladislaw V King of Poland by heredity—a claim which though fantastic is not altogether lacking in foundation. Potocki is in fact a man born out of his time; if one came across him in Casanova's *Memoirs* he would fit in perfectly.

Early in 1932 Potocki and a friend, Douglas Glass, accosted a policeman on duty outside the Old Bailey. They wished to have some poems containing the four-letter words then taboo, set up in type so that they could print them on a hand-press for distribution to friends; could the constable direct them to a printer. The policeman was obviously a man with a sense of humour: the near-by firm to which he sent them turned out to be the publishers of the *Methodist recorder*. Eventually Potocki and Glass found a firm of Linotype setters who expressed themselves willing to set the poems for Potocki if he could not get the work done more cheaply elsewhere, and the manuscript was left in the manager's hands. Next thing, Potocki and Glass found themselves in Brixton charged with publishing obscene verse—the 'publication' had been by showing the manuscript to the printer. In the Magistrate's Court, Potocki elected for trial by jury; Glass, who did not, was discharged. When the case came up before Sir Ernest Wild at the Old Bailey, Potocki received a sentence of six months imprisonment. This 'criminally brutal sentence' as W. B. Yeats described it, produced a host of supporters for Potocki—Aldous Huxley, Leonard Woolf, H. G. Wells, Walter de la Mare, T. S. Eliot and others—but his appeal was in vain.

After his release from gaol, Potocki published *Prison poems* from 'The Montalk Press for the Divine Right of Kings', but then moved to Provence and later to Warsaw, returning to England in 1935. The following year, with financial assistance from Aldous Huxley, he purchased a small press and set up the ultra-monarchist anti-democratic *Right review*. On this press as well as seventeen numbers of the *Review* Potocki printed a number of small books and other pieces—*Snobbery with violence*, *Whited sepulchres*, *Social climbers in Bloomsbury* and *The unconstitutional crisis* (published on the day of Edward VIII's abdication, and for which the Count found himself once more briefly in gaol). These books, like all his subsequent publications, are vilely printed. He described *Whited sepulchres* as 'badly printed, well written' which perfectly summarizes his attitude to his press. Like the good pamphleteer he is, the physical presentation of his work is of no importance to him.

During the Second World War, Potocki's printing activities were for a time brought to a halt. He had intended to print the poems of Maurras, but 'We were prevented,' he wrote, 'not merely by the Fall of France . . . and by the ghoulists having control of all French matters here, but also by the circumstances that the British Authorities [*i.e.* MI5] with the sneaking brutality that characterises them, caused Our press printing plant and all Our paper supplies to be stolen . . . and saw to it that We were unable to obtain any real redress.' By the time that Potocki had the money to buy a new press 'We were in the thick of the fight about 18B and the like, and then about Katyn and all the other atrocities against Poland, as a result of which We were involved in further illegal persecution and were gaoled by unlawful means, exiled in a forced labour camp in the British Soviet "punishment republic" of Northumberland, and were cut off from access to Our printing press . . .'

After the war, Potocki resumed printing, at first in Islington and later in Bookham. In 1956 he set up his press (now named the Mélissa Press) at Draguignan in the south of France. In 1962 or 1963 he moved back to England again, installing a press in his home near Dorchester. A few more characteristic pieces were produced—*One more folly*, some observations on the Hinton St. Mary mosaic, against the sale of which an injunction was swiftly sought; his views on apartheid in *Two blacks don't make a white*; *Thomas Hardy from behind*, and other pieces to divert his friends and enrage his enemies. These were available for sale, but the Count's terms of sale are rather different from those usual in the book trade: his *YTT YZZ czyli*, 'the first surrealist poem to be issued by this anti surrealist press', was offered post free 'to Japanese 3d, to Hungarians, Balts, Germans, 18Bs, and sexy women 6d, otherwise 1s 6d.'

A few years ago Potocki left Dorset to take up residence once more in Draguignan. A good poet, a splendid pamphleteer, a magnificent enemy, he is still continuing to print small volumes of verse and attacks on those who annoy him. To a small band of collectors of Potockiana his work is a constant delight.

Fig. 17. Count Potocki at his press in Dorset. Drawing by Rigby Graham

There remains one variety of clandestine press still undescribed: the printers who work in secret because they are engaged in forgery. Not all fraudulent printing is undertaken in secret: the forgeries of T. J. Wise, perhaps the most famous of modern times, were openly and innocently printed for Wise by the firm of Richard Clay & Sons. But it is obviously more usual for such fraudulent activities to be undertaken in secret using private equipment.

Presses of this nature are by no means new. Paper currency was in use in Britain's American colonies from 1690 onwards, and whether printed by letterpress or from engraved copper plates was widely and successfully counterfeited. It was in an attempt to render such imitation more difficult that many of the more interesting developments in the printer's craft have taken place, in such instances as Benjamin Franklin's nature printing—in which he appears to have successfully used a method of making metal castings from leaves, which he could use as a printing surface which was almost impossible to copy—or in Congreve's compound plate printing. But such counterfeiting is too remote from normal private press activity to warrant detailed discussion here. Legitimate private presses have often suffered from their association with the illegitimate in the mind of authority: Sir Francis Meynell has recorded how a Scotland Yard Detective in pursuit of the printer of some subversive pamphlets arrived at the Nonesuch Press, an obviously suspect concern . . . But it is the manufacturers of presses who really suffer: at one time the office staff of the Kelsey Company (which specializes in making small presses for the amateur market in the United States) lost a great deal of time in attending court hearings at which they had to give evidence against customers who had interpreted their 'Print—make money' advertising too literally.

In eastern Europe, it is naturally assumed that any private press must be clandestine. In an article about his Keepsake Press, Roy Lewis has described how while he was on a visit to one of the Russian satellites he mentioned casually that he owned a private press. There was instant attention: whatever subversive revolutionary things did he produce? Equally instant disillusion; small books of poetry printed *for pleasure*—that is the effete bourgeois for you!

10

Printing for pleasure:
the growth of a middle-class hobby

ntil the late eighteenth century private presses seldom existed as a hobby for the owners' personal operation. The well-to-do could install a printing office complete with workmen, but their printing equipment would differ hardly at all from that which one would have found in commercial printing houses of the time. The cumbersome old wooden press, which had undergone very little change since the fifteenth century, did not readily lend itself to miniaturization, and although several half-scale models exist there is no evidence that they were regularly made. The full-size press called for more effort in operation than one would expect an amateur to be willing to give, unless (as in Edward Rowe Mores's case) he had a special interest in the craft.

There were, no doubt, a few who might experiment in printing without using a press; one of these, a Mr. Passmore Stevens, has gained a certain immortality in a footnote in Mores's *Dissertation*:

'*Mr Stevens* was a gentleman of a typographical turn, but no great adept. he purchased some letter at *The Hague*, and when he came home he printed for his recreation, he used wooden chases nailed upon planks: no composing stick: no head-sticks, foot-sticks, side-sticks, gutter-sticks, quoins, or other furniture, but nails only with which he pegged his matter together: his balls were a bunch of waste paper: his tympans and frisket a dirty handerkchief: his press for small work the ball of his thumb; for larger a rolling-pin and old rags. he was an antient bachelor of odd humour and of *Dutch* taste, in his garb and gesture antique indeed, and the furniture of his house was of the reign of *Qu. Eliz,* the work in which he delighted was below the degree of *Drops* or *Patters* or *Chaunts* or *Runs.* he devised and printed *title-pages* of strange and ludicrous books *speedily to be published* which were never to be published, nor indeed had any existence; and these title pages he dabbed up in the cool of the evening at the corners of the public streets to stir up the expectation of those who stopped there.—this was *his* amusement, and harmless enough.—he printed likewise the epitaphs of his friends richly bedizened with

"The sun, the moon, and all the stars."

the greatest of his performances was the epitaph of *Dr Holmes* late Pres. of *S. John's coll. Oxon.* which he conceived himself in honour bound to print (and we have it in *black* letter and *red* ink) for some favour shewn by the coll. in the renewal of a lease. it makes a *whole*-half-sheet, and for work of this bulk wooden chases may suffice.—*Sutter*'s portables are little more.—*Mr S.* was an honest inoffensive and a good natured gent.. . .'

'*Sutter*'s portables' may have been a version of the bellows press which was used by the commercial printer for small cards and labels of which only limited numbers were required. The name of the press came naturally enough from its appearance : two thick rectangular boards hinged at one end, with two handles at the other which would be grasped to give the necessary pressure. Several refinements of the bellows press were being introduced in the last part of the eighteenth century, such as the 'Leaver printing press' patented by Isaac Moore and William Pine in 1770, or the press invented by Philippe-Denis Pierres in the late 1780s. Various 'pocket printing offices' were sold by German typefounders who were fairly obviously aiming at an amateur market. And customers for these presses probably existed in fairly large numbers. In 1776 Boswell and Johnson visited the museum of Richard Green, an apothecary of Lichfield, which Boswell described as 'a wonderful collection . . . He had all the articles accurately arranged, with their names upon labels, printed at his own little press', which was probably of the bellows variety. Occasionally the bellows press could be used for work much more extensive than it was really suited for; in Paris Jean Castaing printed three volumes of his own *Théâtre* on such a press—volumes which Peignot regarded as altogether without merit, ridiculous text abominably printed—though he admitted Castaing's good sense in limiting his edition to thirty copies so that no more than that number could be bored by his work!

In Mr. Albert Ehrman's collection is a price-list issued by the Breitkopf Typefoundry of Leipzig in 1787 which advertised a little English printing office suitable for marking washing at 5 thalers, and on a larger scale a press suitable for the studies of *grosse Herren* which comprised a large chest containing cases of type, stands, a press and founts of type both roman and black letter, which would suffice for four octavo pages each, priced at fifty to eighty thalers.

The 'petites imprimeries anglaises' which the friends of the Marquis de Bercy were given as New Year gifts in 1790 were almost certainly of the kind marketed by Breitkopf. Such small amateur printing offices were to be found in many parts of Europe: to quote only one further example, in 1786 the poet Alfieri wrote to a friend enclosing a sonnet which he explained he had printed on a little portable press which was just large enough to handle the fourteen lines.

Some amateurs were not content with the presses which were on the market. William Davy's press at Lustleigh which he built 'on a principle very different from those in general use' must have answered well enough, as it served for the production of the whole of his *System of divinity*—but Davy was a skilful carpenter and mechanic, to whom the devising of a suitable press would have given added pleasure. Yet he was by no means the only amateur to build a press of his own design: Peter Buchan, the author-printer of Peterhead, in 1819 'constructed a new press on an original plan, to work with the feet instead of with the hands, and which printed equally well from stone, copper and wood, and would have been as suitable for printing on cloth.' Buchan used this press—about the design of which nothing further is known—to print his *Annals of Peterhead* and other books which he issued from his Auchmedden Press.

On a very much slighter scale than this was a printing press which was operated by a fifteen-year-old boy named Howard Dudley at Midhurst in Sussex in the middle 1830s. Dudley's press was a very small one, on which he could print no more than a page at a time (and his pages were no more than $4\frac{1}{2}$ by $3\frac{1}{2}$ inches), but it was of his own design, and substantial enough for him to be able to print his 140-page *Juvenile researches, or a description of some of the principal towns in the west of Sussex and the borders of Hants* which he wrote, printed and illustrated with his own wood-engravings in 1835. Despite the crudity of the work the small edition was much sought after, and a second edition of fifty copies was printed in the same year. In 1836, having removed to London where he adopted the trade of wood-engraver, he issued a much larger book, *The history and antiquities of Horsham*. This was illustrated with wood-engravings and lithographs, and it seems probable that it was printed on a more amenable press than his home-made effort. It was the last book from Dudley's private press: although some years later he issued a prospectus for a book of the history of Midhurst, it was never published.

In Ireland, in Ladiston, Co. Westmeath, there was an unusual instance of an amateur printer abandoning a purchased press for one which he built

JUVENILE

RESEARCHES,

OR A

DESCRIPTION OF SOME OF THE PRINCIPAL
Towns in the Western part of Sussex,
and the borders of Hants.

INTERSPERSED WITH VARIOUS PIECES OF
POETRY, BY A SISTER:
and illustrated by numerous wood engravings
executed by the Author.

The whole being composed and printed,
BY A BOY OF 14.
D. H.

"I pencill'd things I saw,
And profited by things I heard."

EASEBOURNE.

1835.

Fig. 18. Title-opening printed by the young Howard Dudley on a press of his own design

himself. John Lyons, a member of the vanished race of Anglo-Irish gentry and 'a gentleman of varied attainments, and a most ingenious mechanic', in 1820 bought a small press in Edinburgh. It may have been one of Ruthven's presses, of the same sort as that used by Sir Alexander Boswell, but Lyons did not find it satisfactory. After a few years he replaced it by a much larger machine which he constructed on a plan of his own, and with this he printed the results of his own antiquarian and horticultural research for the next thirty years. His *Remarks on the management of orchidaceous plants* (1843) was of considerable importance in its time as the first manual on orchid growing, and he received the gold medal of the Horticultural Society of Dublin for the second edition which was printed commercially in 1845. Among the many other works from his press was *A book of surveys and distributions of the estates forfeited in the County of Westmeath in the rebellion of 1641*, which had the unusual feature of possessing two prefaces printed in parallel text—one written from the Catholic and the other from the Protestant point of view!

These men were all unusual amateurs in that they were enthusiastically determined to print, and would take very considerable pains to overcome the difficulties which lay in their way. For the average man looking for a recreation, the lack of a satisfactory simple and portable press was enough to prevent him from taking up printing at all.

All this was to change in the nineteenth century. The development of the iron press at the beginning of the century in England—the Stanhope, the Albion, the Ruthven—meant that much more consistently reliable presses of varying sizes became readily available. In America there was the Columbian press, while the work of Adam Ramage succeeded in producing wooden hand-presses which were relatively portable and which were widely used in printing houses on the moving frontier.

At the same time the rapid increase in population in England, and the growing prosperity of the middle classes, meant that in thousands of surburban villas springing up all over the country there were many who had sufficient time, money and education to find printing a profitable and amusing pastime if it were presented to them in the right way. But if printing were to enter the parlours of these villas it would have to be shown as useful, elegant and fool-proof. By the 1840s engineering firms were attempting in their advertising to show that it was all of these.

As early as 1834 Messrs Holtzapffel & Co, 'Engineer, lathe and tool manufacturers' of Long Acre were advertising printing presses 'on the Stanhope and other principles, in small sizes' and over the following decade they appear to have built up a good business selling presses and printing equipment to amateurs.

In the St. Bride Printing Library is a copy of the third edition of a manual published in 1846 entitled *Printing apparatus for the use of amateurs, containing full and practical instructions for the use of Cowper's Parlour Printing Press, also . . . various other apparatus for the amateur typographer*. Edward Cowper (a partner with Applegath in building cylinder presses for *The Times*) had devised this press, the manual declared, 'for the amusement and education of youth, by enabling them to print any little subject they had previously written.' The design was derived from the old bellows press, but with the impression obtained from a lever incorporating a knuckle-joint at the other end of the platen from the hinges. As a method of applying pressure it has disadvantages, but for simplicity of operation can scarcely be bettered (the Adana flatbed presses used by many amateur printers today works on the same principle) and there is little doubt that the mahogany Parlour Press was used in many Victorian homes. Holtzapffel & Co. did not offer the press alone; theirs was a complete printing outfit, and the pamphlet also describes and illustrates a four-drawer cabinet which contained specially designed type cases and furniture, roller, composing stick and other tools 'modified to suit the con- venience of the amateur'. The handbook included a fourteen-page specimen of types (at prices ranging upwards from 3d per dozen sorts) and finally a price-list of the apparatus described: £5 6s for the plain press with deal cases, or £7 2s for a press 'japanned and finished in the best manner' and with cases of mahogany. Larger presses were also available.

That the Parlour Press undoubtedly met a need for a cheap press can be seen from the replies to an enquiry in *Notes and queries* in December 1862: a writer signing himself Γ asked what sort of press he should use for printing a duodecimo half-sheet. There were two replies, both recommending Holt-zapffel's equipment, which the second correspondent said he had used successfully on an octavo half-sheet. Should Γ really wish to print a larger sheet, he continued, he thought that he would need a regular Albion press costing fifteen to twenty pounds—a fairly considerable increase.

Though the manufacturers made much of the virtues of Cowper's press 'for the amusement and education of youth' they were by no means slow to point out its advantages for other less high-minded purposes. 'Companies, institutions and individuals, have found it convenient for circular letters, invoices, and papers subservient to the despatch and methodical arrangement of business; naturalists and travellers, for short memoirs of scientific researches, or labels of specimens.' Schoolmasters and clergymen are among the others whom they suggest could find 'some new application of this useful little apparatus'. By implication, the purchaser of one of these presses could save himself money which otherwise might have to be paid out to commercial printers.

Later nineteenth-century manufacturers of small presses in England were to strike a similar note in their advertising. D. G. Berri's *The art of printing* (3rd edition 1871) speaks of the advantages to owners of his 'People's Printing Press' in very explicit terms: 'Men in business could print more rapidly than can be done by any other press or hand machine now in use, *and at a tithe of a printer's charges*, their circulars, cards, handbills, invoices . . . Many persons also, not in business, frequently wish to have printed notes, . . catalogues of their libraries [etc] . . . but are deterred by the price charged by printers for doing what would be to themselves a very instructive and agreeable employment.' But it remained for American enterprise to develop and publicize the idea of amateur printing as a means of making money in one's spare time.

In the United States, though portable presses of the Ramage type, or the iron Washington, Columbian and Ruthven presses were commonplace in commercial printing shops, there was nothing designed specifically for the

A RYGHTE

Goodlie Lyttle Booke

OF

Frisket Fancies

SET FORTH FOR

BIBLIOMANIACS !

BY

Edwin Roffe.

PRIVATELY PRINTED.

ROCHESTER PRESS.

TWELVE COPIES.

LONDON:

Set up, and Im L *printed, in Leisure-time, by*

EDWIN ROFFE:

At his Birth-place, 48, Ossulston Street,
SOMERS' TOWN. MDCCCLXI.

Fig. 19. A typical example of a book printed by Edwin Roffe, a prolific Victorian amateur

use of amateurs for over fifteen years after the debut of the Parlour Press in England. But in 1857 Samuel W. Lowe of Boston exhibited a press which was an attempt at providing for amateur needs, at the fair of the American Institute held at the New York Crystal Palace. Lowe's press, which he had patented the previous year, had a heavy conical roller which moved in an arc backwards and forwards, pressing the tympan down on to the type. It was not a very satisfactory press in use (though at his Between-Hours Press in New York Ben Grauer has used a surviving example with considerable success). Two other small presses which were developed in the early 1860s and used extensively in the field throughout the campaigns of the Civil War—Adam's Cottage Press and its close relation the Army Press—were very much simpler and more efficient. They were essentially a modification of the traditional copper plate or etching press, with the pressure applied by means of a cylinder across the tympan.

By 1869 another sort of press designed for amateur use was in production; a machine which like the Parlour Press was to have a long line of descendants, right down to the present day. This was an adaptation of the commercial printers' treadle platen presses, of which the first models had appeared in 1851. In these presses the chase was held not on a flat bed, but vertically—a frequent cause of disaster to the amateur printer who has not locked his type up tightly enough—in a bed to which the platen was hinged: in principle a bellows press stood on end. The first platen press to be made for amateurs was the Novelty, made by B. O. Woods & Company of Boston; with modifications this press continued to be manufactured until 1883 when the firm was taken over by its great rival, the Kelsey Company of Meriden, Connecticut.

The career of William A. Kelsey, the founder of the firm, was in many respects an epitome of the American dream. While still in his teens he had run a stamp business, worked for the Parker Gun Company and by the age of twenty become editor of their magazine (which was to become *Forest and stream*)—not only this, but he had tried out all the amateur presses on the market and come to the conclusions that he could make one which would be better and cheaper. In his spare time from working for the Parker Company he tried to design a press which could sell at a price which he thought the average boy would pay. On 19 December 1872 he advertised his first press in *The youth's companion*:

'$5 Printing Press! A *perfect* Press at the *right price*. **Business Men** save expense and increase business by doing their own printing and advertising. **For BOYS** delightful, *money-making* amusement . . .'

Unfortunately for Kelsey his press (which like the Novelty Press was a hand-platen) had not been sufficiently tested, and would not work. He was left with a host of orders, and no means of filling them. After much burning of midnight oil he devised a new press, the Excelsior, which *would* work, and which he patented in the spring of 1873. He was abashed not at all by his previous blunder: 'Great changes have been made from the original plan of our Press,' he boldly advertised, 'till we have reached what we firmly believe perfection.' His confidence in the new press was not misplaced; it was a thoroughly satisfactory machine. By dint of advertising in all the leading American journals of the day, such as *Harper's weekly*, and in practically everything else available—from Southern revivalist magazines to Barnum & Bailey's Circus programme—a large mail-order business was built up. At the Philadelphia Centennial Exhibition of 1876 an improved version of the press with automatic inking received a medal: the Kelsey Company was firmly established.

The Excelsior was not the only press made for the amateur market in the United States. Though the Kelsey Company did most of its business through mail order, in its early days a number of publishing firms were used as sales agents. One of these, realizing the market potential, decided to go into business themselves, and produced the Model Press, another excellent hand-press which continued to be manufactured until well into this century. Many Model presses survive and are still used by amateurs.

Other rivals to the Kelsey Company were also dangerous. Curtis & Mitchell made the Caxton Press and the very good Columbian Press until the 1890s; in Boston Golding's Pearl and Official Presses—two more sound machines which are still often used by pastime printers—were made until the 1920s when Golding (who had attempted to move into a larger scale of business building presses for commercial use) were absorbed by the mammoth American Type Founders Company, for whom the amateur market was of little interest.

Most other attempts to siphon off potential Kelsey customers failed. The firm of J. Cook & Company—in whose Meriden workshops the first Kelsey presses were made until Kelsey built his own factory—made the Victor and Enterprise Presses. They were good machines, but Cook could not rival Kelsey's masterly advertising and ferocious price-cutting. In 1883 the Kelsey *Catalog* contained this obituary notice:

DEAD. Competitors of this establishment do not seem to prosper. We have bought out B. O. Woods & Co., Novelty Presses, started in Boston in 1864. J. Cook & Co., after spending $20,000 in attempting to compete with our excellent presses, have sold out to us at a great sacrifice. Our machines are too good to allow much chance for competition. We shall meet all rivals with cut prices!

Another rival to be absorbed by Kelsey was Joseph Watson, who as the manufacturer of Lowe and Adam's Cottage presses had been in the business much longer than Kelsey. He manufactured a range of hand-platens which gave the Excelsior more competition that these earlier lines could, but in 1896 his firm finally succumbed.

In England too, the 1870s saw the introduction of new presses for the amateur market, many of them derived from American machines. Berri's 'People's Printing Press' was based upon the conventional copper plate press, and seems to have been inspired by the American Army Press, though unlike that it had a bed moving by means of a gear wheel under a fixed cylinder instead of a fixed bed and moving cylinder as in the Army Press. Berri claimed that as the pressure of cylinder could be adjusted on his press it could be used

Fig. 20. Berri's 'People's Printing Press', 1871, designed for the amateur market

for printing letterpress, lithographically, or from copper plates. It seems doubtful whether in fact the construction of his press was rigid enough for copper plate printing: it is noticeable that although several satisfied customers vouched for its efficiency in lithographic and letterpress work in the testimonials printed at the end of his handbook on *The art of printing*, there is no reference to its use for intaglio work.

The great advantage of Berri's press was that its use of a cylinder meant that a large surface could be printed without the need for a massive platen. It

119

was relatively cheap (the smallest size, to print an area of $5\frac{5}{8}$ by $4\frac{3}{8}$ inches, cost two guineas; the largest, 22 by $15\frac{1}{2}$ inches, was eight guineas) and it was simple to operate. Berri, though pointing out the advantage of his press for business use, was also confident of its value to amateurs. 'It may be suggested that this machine might be made the means of great and pleasing amusement among residents in the country, in issuing gazettes for circulation among their

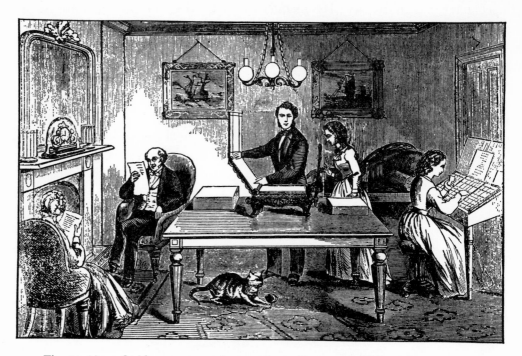

Fig. 21. 'A profitable amusement for many'; wood-engraving from Jabez Francis's
Printing at home, 1870

friends,' he suggested. In a fine expansionist vein he continued that 'for those pioneers who daily leave our shores to establish a home midst the pathless forests and the rolling prairies, and to perpetuate our industry with our language on the continents of Asia and Africa, and the distant islands of Polynesia' it would also be useful. There was nothing of the brash Yankee commercialism of Kelsey's 'Print—make money' about this.

One of Berri's closest competitors for the growing amateur market was Jabez Francis of Rochford, Essex. Francis's press was a cast-iron variation on the theme of the wooden Parlour Press, and rather cheaper than Berri's presses (twenty-five shillings for the smallest, printing an area six by four inches, to three guineas for a larger, $9\frac{1}{2}$-inch model). His pamphlet *Printing at home* was aimed almost entirely at the amateur. 'Printing may be made to afford a profitable amusement for many,' he wrote. 'Either parent may write an essay, poem, or a note to friends at a distance, a young lady daughter may "compose" it . . . the proofs may be read by all and corrected, it is then "made ready", and one rolls the "forme" or type, while another prints at the press.' To reinforce the appeal of a hobby for all the family he included a wood-engraving of such printing in the parlour.

Francis was wise to concentrate his attentions upon the purely amateur market. Both his and Berri's presses were designed for hand-inking, and must have been very slow in operation. Competition from the newer and faster self-inking platens must have hurt their sales to those wishing to make money by their printing. For the pure amateur, the older presses were simpler to use, and in a veiled attack upon the newer platens Francis claimed that his presses could not go wrong and would last a lifetime.

Of the American presses introduced into England, the Model Press, developed by Kelsey's rival, was the most successful. Originally manufactured and sold in England by C. Squintani & Company of Liverpool Street, it was taken over in the late 1880s by the Model Printing Press Company of Ludgate Circus, and finally by the Excelsior Printers Supply Company of Farringdon Street (a firm which had originally been organized for the distribution of Kelsey's Excelsior presses in England) who continued to manufacture the press until World War Two. The Excelsior Printers Supply Company still deals in second-hand Model presses as part of its general trade in printers' sundries.

The Model Press was (as in America) advertised in a much more aggressive way than its earlier rivals had been. Much less emphasis was placed on its value for the amusement and education of youth, and much more on its advantages in business practice: the use of cheap office labour to print labels, letterheads, invoices and the like cheaper than a commercial printer. Squintani advertised complete printing outfits at prices ranging from five to one hundred guineas.

There were native English presses able to compete with the Model and Excelsior. As well as the larger Albions (which continued to be made into the 1930s) there were many firms of printers' engineers who developed their own lines of small platen presses. One such was the Simplissimus Press, a lighter and cheaper variation of the platen principle manufactured by the Birmingham

121

Machinists Company and advertised by them in their *Eclectic handbook of printing* of about 1875. It was highly regarded by professionals (who used it for small jobbing work) as well as amateurs. And there were other presses aimed more exclusively at the hobby printer. One was manufactured by C. Morton of City Road. In his *The art of printing simplified for amateurs* (1875) he made large claims: 'An uncontracted experience of the requirements of an Amateur Printer has enabled me to thoroughly comprehend the difficulties he has to contend with', he wrote. 'As a Typefounder and Press Manufacturer, I, in a business way, continually make the acquaintance of "distressed" Amateur Printers, to whom I have had, as it were, to be a physician.' His own press was distantly related to the Albion in design, but was suspiciously cheap: the physician seems in fact to have been something of a quack.

By no means all printing firms had welcomed the expanding amateur market with enthusiasm. The printers themselves were scarcely surprisingly unhappy at the growth in the numbers of what they derisively called back-bedroom printers, who worked at cut rates; some suppliers were also distinctly uncooperative. In July 1879 the Caslon Foundry, finding that they had been included in a list of suppliers printed in a handbook for amateurs announced in their *Circular* that 'We cannot undertake to supply founts of type smaller in quantity or assortment than are required by regular professional printers . . . We are not among those who are alarmed at the increase in amateur printing in this country, though we will not encourage it. In the majority of cases amateur dabblers in a handicraft about which they know nothing, discover sooner or later that they have spent all their money to no purpose, and return to the professional printer with a higher and more professional appreciation of his service . . .' It is to the credit of the Caslons' sense of ethics, if not their business acumen, that they did not resort to selling small founts of type to amateurs at prices far higher than those charged the trade, as many suppliers did.

What sort of work was produced by the amateur purchasers of all these different presses, and who were the purchasers? Among those who played with printing at one time or another were such men as Thomas Edison, Rudyard Kipling, Lord Northcliffe and—unlikely picture—the son of Mrs. Hodgson Burnett, 'Little Lord Fauntleroy' himself, who printed a little magazine and two small books in 1891–2. At one extreme of the craze there was the appeal of Yankee entrepreneurism at its most highly developed, as we have seen. At the other extreme there was the quintessence of Victorian high-mindedness: at the 1862 Exhibition Mrs. Daniel Jones exhibited a miniature Albion Press, together with a prayer for peace printed in forty-six languages which she had produced on it. In the words of *Cassell's illustrated exhibitor*, her entry was 'an appeal to ladies to turn their attention to a private study to produce gems of thought, in elegancies of well-assorted type, and clever arrangement, so as to relieve the fingers from the ornamental intricate worsted work and crochet labyrinthal pattern, and to exert the same perseverance in leisure hours to the

Fig. 22. Mrs. Daniel Jones and her miniature Albion at the 1862 Exhibition. She 'undertook to instruct ladies in the mysteries of printing'

cultivation of private circulation of new ideas, which would soon grow into a pleasure in the doing and a necessity for fireside entertainment.'

'In speaking of the merits of this undertaking,' continued the *Exhibitor*, 'we see a useful, neat, powerful printing press, suited to the library . . . and the boudoir of the lady, whose ingenuity and reflective habits would be greatly assisted could she, in her leisure hours, be enabled to print many beautiful passing thoughts, which would otherwise float away, and have no means of being retained in the private manner which her judgment and sympathies would suggest.' Ladies were given to understand that Mrs. Jones was willing to give instructions to any who wished to try the black art for themselves. What response she received is not known; although there were presses operated by ladies in mid- and late-Victorian England, it was unusual for them to print entirely without masculine assistance. Despite the enthusiasm of the writer in the *Exhibitor*, it is improbable that many ladies, having once touched and smelled printers' ink would admit a press to their boudoir.

An interesting example of a press operated on the distaff side was that owned by Jane Bickersteth at Roehampton from 1848 to 1851. Presumably the child (she was about twelve years of age at the time) had a Parlour Press, and on it she laboriously printed a number of magazines, *The elf*, *The fairy*, and *The mite*, each consisting of only a single page, 'price one farthing'. Her assistant in producing these was Anthony Panizzi, and though it would be easy for those who dislike him to find the explanation for his assuming this unfamiliar role in the fact that Jane's father, Lord Langdale, was one of the Trustees of the British Museum, and therefore a very useful man for Panizzi to cultivate (he certainly proved useful when Panizzi's appointment to the Principal Librarianship of the British Museum was being mooted in 1856) there seems no doubt that there was genuine kindliness and affection in his assistance to the young printer.

Panizzi was by no means the only man of eminence to play with printing in this manner, nor was it anything new at the time. Davies Gilbert, who was President of the Royal Society from 1828 to 1831, set up a small press in his house at Eastbourne in 1825 for the amusement of his family circle. Type and probably the other equipment was obtained from B. Nichols of Parliament Street. Most of the work of the Press seems to have been done by Gilbert's eldest daughter Catherine, and for fourteen years (until his death in 1839 called a halt to the hobby) a large number of single sheets of poems and ephemera were printed. No serious or extensive work was undertaken; it was purely printing for pleasure.

An interesting press of the 1840s was that owned by Gaetano Polidori at Park Village East, Regents Park. Polidori had formerly been the head of a London firm of printers and publishers, and when in his mid seventies he once more felt an urge for his old craft he set up a press in his own home. It cannot have been a small affair, and without doubt Polidori had the assistance of workmen in its operation, for in 1840 he issued a three-volume edition of Milton's works in Italian, translated by himself. Two years later he followed this with some of his own dramas, and then, in 1843, with the first of two books which were of real importance. Polidori's daughter was the mother of Dante Gabriel and Christina Rossetti, and their grandfather printed a small edition of *Sir Hugh the heron* which Dante Gabriel had written at the age of thirteen. Four years later, in 1847, he printed a duodecimo volume of *Verses* by Christina, with a note recording that the poems had been written while she was still of tender age, and that it was only with difficulty that he had persuaded her to allow him to print them. The last book from this press was an unfinished Italian poem by an ancestor, *Il Losario* by Francesco Polidori, and this is also of considerable interest as it included a conclusion composed by Dante Gabriel Rossetti.

Another early Victorian private press which is remarkably little known (considering the high standards of workmanship its work displayed) was the Duncairn Press, near Belfast. It was operated from 1850 onwards by Edmund MacRory, a Bencher of the Middle Temple, who used to while away the long vacations which he spent in his father's Irish home by printing. The press was set up in a very workmanlike manner: a small foolscap folio Albion Press was first purchased, to be joined by a larger Columbian in 1852. Type was obtained from Robert Bensley and from H. W. Caslon, ornaments from Paris typefounders, and wood-engravings were commissioned from Robert Branston and from H. Swain in London. Although the press lay idle for more than ten months in every year, during the ten years or so that the equipment was in use a respectable number of very substantial books were produced. The largest was a 247-page octavo edition of *The private diary of Elizabeth Viscountess Mordaunt AD 1656–68*, of which one hundred copies were completed in 1856. Other works included a catalogue of pictures in Duncairn House, *Notes on the Temple Organ* (later reissued commercially), and the usual offering of poetry written by the friends of the printer.

By far the most important of all these Victorian printers for pleasure was the Reverend C. H. O. Daniel (1836–1919). He started on his printing activites in a commonplace way: while a child at Frome in Somerset, where his father

THE

DIARIE OF THE

VISCOUNTESS MORDAUNT.

A. D. 1656.

LORD God Almyty, Father, Soun, and Holy Goste, I the unworthyest of all cretuers Liveing, doe here cume with my harte, and mouthe, full of all thanks Geuing and prays, accept them from me Lorde, for thou haste inabelede me to render them unto thee, for the grete and unspekabel mercy which I have this day receued from thee, of that sperittuall Ioy

(1 *rec.*)

B which

Fig. 23. Page from a book printed by Edmund MacRory at his Duncairn Press, 1856

was Vicar, he and his brother George were given some type to play with in 1845. With this they laboriously printed a number of small pieces, inking them with their thumbs and impressing the type by hand in the manner of Mores's Mr. Passmore Stevens. One of the earliest surviving pieces of their printing, produced in the summer or autumn of 1846, recorded a great advance in their resources: the Vicar, well pleased with his sons' interest in the craft, had given them a small press (almost certainly one of Holtzapffel's Parlour Presses). Charles printed a letter of thanks to his father, promising good conduct and pathetically asking 'qlease do not mind my very bad printing, for when any one looks on any part of it, it is really immensely, terribly, and dreadfully horrible' —which was no exaggeration. Then Charles went away to boarding school for a year, and when he returned home in 1848 he did not resume his pastime. But in the spring of 1850 he turned again to his hobby, and when in July of that year he was given a miniature Albion he continued still more enthusiastically, producing texts for his father's sermons, invitation cards, small pamphlets of verse and the like. From 1853 to 1854 he was again away at boarding school, so the press at Frome languished, and it might have gone the way of most childhood hobbies had not Charles's two youngest brothers taken it over and continued to print until the 1860s. Charles Daniel himself had gone on from school to Worcester College, Oxford, in 1854, and after graduating taught in London for a few years before returning to Oxford to take up a fellowship at his old college in 1863.

Were this the whole history of the Daniel Press, it would be no more interesting or remarkable than that of dozens of other parlour printers in mid-Victorian England. Where it was to differ was in its revival and triumphant growth, so that as well as being an example of printing for pleasure the Daniel Press can with equal justice be regarded as one of the presses concerned with printing as a fine art, which flourished at the end of Victoria's reign.

In 1874 Dr. Daniel, after a visit home, took back the miniature Albion and the store of type with him to Oxford and set to work on printing some *Notes from a catalogue of pamphlets* in Worcester College Library, printing some twenty-five copies which he circulated to friends towards the end of the year. It was not in itself a pretty piece of printing: in the long period since he had last used the press the printer had evidently lost much of his cunning. He was himself well aware of its shortcomings, for a continuation of the same work, though an improvement in layout and arrangement, was abandoned before completion and most copies were destroyed. Then came the turning point in the career of the Daniel Press, with the revival of the Fell types—the types

CHRISTMAS :

A Vigil.

BY

C. J. C., ESQUIRE.

IMPRINTED AT THE PRIVATE PRESS
OF H. DANIEL.
1851.

Fig. 24. An early Daniel Press title-page

with which Dr. John Fell had lavishly endowed the Oxford University Press nearly two centuries earlier, but which had fallen almost entirely into disuse during the eighteenth century, and by the 1870s were virtually forgotten.

The tradition of Daniel's revival of these types is a romantic one. According to the *Memoir* by Sir Herbert Warren in *The Daniel Press, Memorials of C. H. O. Daniel with a Bibliography of the Press 1845–1919* (Oxford, 1921) Dr. Daniel 'had recourse to the Clarendon Press for type, and as he turned over their old stocks his artistic eye lit on a broken and imperfect fount, a dusty, disused legacy left by "the unreasonably hated" Dean Fell, and called after his name. He divined the possibilities, and spurred by its charm . . . went on to new elaborations . . .' In fact, the credit for Daniel's adoption of this type must rest equally with Professor Bartholomew Price, who had for many years been Secretary to the Delegates of the Press. Stanley Morison in his splendid study of *John Fell, the University Press and the 'Fell' types* (Oxford, 1967) suggested that during Price's discussions with Daniel of the latter's printing problems it must have become apparent to Daniel that to use Victorian black letter or roman type for reprinting seventeenth-century material using the old spelling was a typographical crime. Obviously the best way to avoid the crime would be for the University Press to supply Daniel with a fount of the Fell types. Whether the suggestion came from Price or Daniel is unimportant; what is interesting is that early in 1876 Dr. Daniel purchased some of the Fell type, to which he was to remain faithful as long as he printed, and that it was as an indirect result of Daniel's use of the types that the University Press itself came to revive them in its own splendid typographical renaissance at the beginning of this century.

The first use at the Daniel Press of its new types was in *A new sermon of the newest fashion*, printed from manuscript and originally written about 1643 (1877). This was followed by Erasmus's *Colloquia* (1880) of which Walter Pater wrote that 'it is, I suppose, the most exquisite specimen of printing that I have ever seen'; from him remarkable praise, and indicating how much improvement there had been in the work of the press since Daniel had resumed his hobby six years earlier. But the most celebrated of all his books was still to come. Some time in 1880 Thomas Humphry Ward suggested to Daniel that the first birthday of Daniel's infant daughter Rachel should be celebrated with special poems written by his friends and printed at the press, after the mode of the famous *Guirlande de Julie*. Enough of Daniel's friends responded for *The garland of Rachel* to be a considerable literary success when it appeared in October 1881, with contributions from Austin Dobson, Andrew Lang, Edmund Gosse, James Addington Symonds, Lewis Carroll, Robert Bridges and a host of others. Nor was it impressive only from a textual point of view; the design and execution of the book, set in the Fell types and miniated by Mrs. Daniel, was of a very high order, so that the book was as successful a cradle-crowning of the Daniel Press as it was of Rachel. Each of the seventeen contributors was presented with a copy of the book containing a special title-page naming it as by him 'and divers kindly hands'. Only thirty-six copies in all were printed;

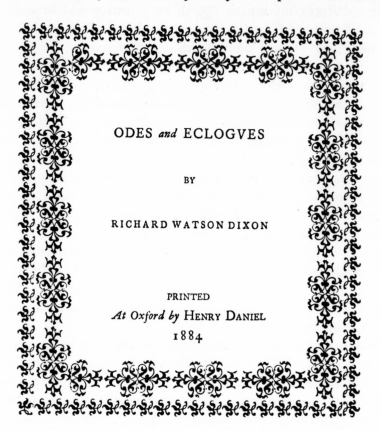

ODES *and* ECLOGVES

BY

RICHARD WATSON DIXON

PRINTED
At Oxford by HENRY DANIEL
1884

Fig. 25. A Daniel Press title set in the Fell types and ornaments

these have always commanded a high price on the antiquarian market, and the book had the distinction (if that is the right word) of being pirated in a sort of type facsimile by Thomas Bird Mosher at Portland, Maine, in 1902.

The very favourable reception that *The garland* received inspired Daniel to continue with his hobby, and in the winter of 1881–2 he purchased his first press which was more than a toy for amateur use: an Albion Press which had been made by J. & J. Barrett in 1835. His first experiment on this, *Hymni ecclesiae*, proving satisfactory, he set to work on an Elizabethan translation of Theocritus, *Sixe Idillia*, which was published in 1883; the first book he had offered for sale. From then on until 1903 the Albion was seldom idle, another

130

fifty-two substantial books of considerable literary interest being produced in the time that Daniel could spare from his work as Bursar of his College and his many appointments in the University and City. Not that he was without assistance; just as the press at Frome had been operated jointly with his brothers, so at Oxford Mrs. Daniel and his two daughters Rachel and Ruth once they were old enough assisted with the composition and presswork, in some instances producing whole books by themselves.

In 1903 Dr. Daniel was elected Provost of Worcester College, and he decided that the Press should be discontinued. Despite the pleas and protests of his many friends, he would not move from this decision. He relented only once, in 1906, when his daughters printed a form of prayers used in the College for the Gaudy. One more book was to be printed on the Press: the *Memorials* and bibliography of its work, which were printed in the Bodleian Library to which the press was presented on Dr. Daniel's death in 1919.

The significance of the Daniel Press came from two things: the excellence of the texts selected for printing—they included more than a few first printings of the work of Robert Bridges—allied to the charm of the production. Daniel Press books were quite unlike other private press books produced at the turn of the century. There is nothing of the pseudo-gothic or would-be renaissance spirit about Daniel Press books. Though unmistakably of their time, Daniel's deep interest in seventeenth-century literature allied to his use of the Fell types and ornaments made him produce a series of books which hark back to the printing of the period in a very refreshing manner.

Though the nineteenth century saw the development of presses which were designed specially for amateur use, there remained—as there still remains—a small number of individuals who found part of their pleasure in building their own presses. One such was at work between 1871 and 1892 in the Old Vicarage, Grantchester; an address more commonly associated with Rupert Brooke. Its owner, Samuel Page Widnall, was decidedly an original: a retired farmer, who built a pseudo-medieval folly, 'Burgherst Tower', at the bottom of his garden and occupied his leisure time with stone and wood-carving, with photography, with making architectural models, and with inventions of one sort or another. That such a man, seized of the idea of printing, should construct his own press was scarcely surprising. Whatever the form of his press, it worked well enough for him to be able to print four pages at a time upon it, and with it he printed some seven books between 1871 and 1892. The first book, *The millar's daughter, a legend of the Granta*, was illustrated with lithographs which were his first attempt in the medium. With the exception of the third book from his press, a very substantial volume of records of *The Smith-Carrington family* which he printed to oblige his brother-in-law in 1884 (and the only one of his books which is at all common), all his publications were written as well as illustrated and printed by himself. They are interesting examples of substantial amateur work, but in layout, ornament and type little different from the work of any small jobbing printer of the time—in Professor Bruce Dickinson's words, 'it would be idle to claim for him distinction as a printer.'

By the time that Widnall's last book had appeared, the boom in amateur printing was past. A writer in the *British and colonial printer* for 1902 recalled 'the period between 1875 and 1885, when amateur printing was at its zenith and numbered its votaries by thousands', and discussed some of the presses which had been produced. 'What brought about the decadence of amateur printing as a hobby? is a question that has often been asked, but never satisfactorily answered. Certainly it is, that after 1886 the number of amateurs became fewer, and continued to dwindle until now their ranks are very much thinned, and instead of being—as at one time they threatened to be—a menace to the professional, they are now only to be found in rare and isolated instances' he wrote. His own opinion was that the reason for the decline of interest in printing for pleasure was that the development of the dry plate had made photography so much more straightforward that many amateurs abandoned their presses for the quicker rewards of the camera. In this belief the writer in the *British and colonial printer* had probably hit upon the truth. But he was less happy in his conclusion that 'amateur printing is no longer what it was, and we are not likely ever again to have a recrudescence of the hobby'.

11

Printing as one of the fine arts:
William Morris and the Kelmscott Press

On 15 November 1888 Emery Walker gave a lecture on printing at the first exhibition of the Arts and Crafts Exhibition Society. Walker had been a close friend of William Morris since 1884, and in the preparation of his lecture and of the lantern-slides with which it was to be illustrated, he and Morris had long discussions on what constituted good printing, on the virtues possessed by various incunabula and the like. Morris had been interested in book production long before this; as early as 1866 he had been planning a lavishly illustrated edition of *The earthly paradise* which never came to fruition (although some of Burne-Jones's designs for it were used very much later in the Gregynog Press edition of *Eros and Psyche*), and in the 1880s was engaged on the production of *The house of the Wolfings* which was being printed for him by the Chiswick Press. But Morris's interest in book design had previously been slight; Walker's talks with him, and the examination of the details of fifteenth-century printing, transformed it into a strong enthusiasm. 'Let's make a new fount of type' he proposed to Walker as they walked home to Hammersmith after the meeting. It was from this stimulus that Morris's 'endeavour . . . to re-attain a long-lost standard of craftsmanship of book printing' was to grow, and it is from this date that one may trace the development of those private presses which have been concerned with the printing of books as an art form.

At first it was by no means clear in Morris's mind that he wanted a press of his own. With help from Walker he embarked on designing a fount of type, but while that was still in progress he was continuing experiments with C. T. Jacobi of the Chiswick Press, producing *The roots of the mountains* in 1889. This showed an improvement in layout over his earlier experiment, and Morris declared it 'the best-looking book issued since the seventeenth century'. 'I am so pleased with my book,' he wrote soon after it was published, '. . . that I am any day to be seen huggling it up, and am become a spectacle to Gods and men because of it'—and for a time it seemed possible that his interest in book production would continue to be satisfied by the employment of the Chiswick Press for his work, in the same sort of way that in 1899 Robert Bridges was to commission the Oxford University Press to print *The Yattendon hymnal*. But, as Morris was to write to F. S. Ellis in November 1889 about *The roots of the mountains*, 'the difficulty of getting [the printing] really well done shows us the old story again. It seems it is no easy matter to get good hand-press men, so little work is done by the hand-press: that accounts for some defects in the book, caused by want of care in distributing the ink. I really am thinking of turning printer myself in a small way . . .'

A last experiment at the Chiswick Press, *The story of Gunnlaug Worm-tongue*, though completed, was never published. In December 1889 Morris finally decided to set up his own press as a solution to these problems, and invited Emery Walker to go into partnership with him. 'Mind you, I shall want my own way!' he is reputed to have said. Walker refused the offer, 'having some sense of proportion' (as he said later) but nevertheless he remained an *eminence grise*. In Sir Sydney Cockerell's words, 'no important step was taken without his advice and approval'.

What were Morris's aims in setting up the Kelmscott Press? He had been struck, while he was selecting examples of the best commercial printing of the time for the Arts and Crafts Exhibition, by the fact that not one of his own many books was of such a standard as to merit inclusion, and undoubtedly he was equally struck by the inferiority of contemporary books to the incunabula which he and Walker had been examining. He would not have been Morris had this not been enough to make him determine to try his own hand at achieving the standards of the fifteenth century, nor would he have been true to himself had he not made an intensive study of all the various technical aspects of printing. As W. R. Lethaby wrote, these studies by Morris were 'not of the superficial look of things, but of their very elements and essence. When . . . first producing textiles, Morris was a practical dyer; when it was tapestry, he wove the first pieces with his own hand; when he did illumination, he had to find a special vellum in Rome and have a special gold beaten; when he did printing, he had to explore papermaking, inkmaking, type cutting, and other dozen branches of the trade. His ornaments and the treatment of Burne-Jones's illustrations were based on his personal practice as a woodcutter. Morris was no mere "designer" of type and ornaments for books, but probably the most competent book-maker ever known. Indeed, it is a mistake to get into the habit of thinking of him as a "designer"; he was a work-master . . .' This is to overstate Morris's importance, but Lethaby's description of his methods clearly indicates that Morris did not ignorantly attempt to clear typography of the mess of centuries; before the Kelmscott Press started work he made a thorough investigation into the various materials and processes which go into a book, individually and in relation to one another. Then, and only then, he 'began printing books with the hope of producing some which would have a definite claim to beauty, while at the same time they should be easy to read and should not dazzle the eye, or trouble the intellect of the reader by eccentricity of form in the letters'—the opening statement in his *Note . . . on his aims in founding the Kelmscott Press*.

The production of the new type (of which fuller details are given in Chapter 23) was under way. The selection of the right sort of paper was another problem: after some searching Morris decided that a Bolognese paper of about 1473 (a 'neat, subtle and courtlike' paper as Fuller described such papers in the seventeenth century) was the best. He had some little difficulty in getting paper of this quality made—'We can do nothing with Whatman but take what he has on the shelves'—until he went with Emery Walker to visit Batchelor's mill at Little Chart, Ashford, in the autumn of 1890. While there he tried his own hand at papermaking (doing very creditably, according to J. W. Mackail) but finding Joseph Batchelor as enthusiastic as himself he was content to let the latter experiment in producing the right paper. By February 1891 Batchelor had produced one which was satisfactory, and he continued to make all the paper ever used for Kelmscott Press books.

As well as paper, vellum was thought to be necessary for 'superior' editions. A small stock of that which he had obtained years before from Rome for illumination remained unused, but when Morris tried to purchase a further supply he found that the whole supply had been bespoken by the Vatican. In desperation he contemplated a direct appeal to the Pope (on the grounds that *The golden legend*, which he intended to print, was a book in which the Pope should be interested!) when a friend suggested that Henry Band, who made binding vellums at Brentford, might, like Batchelor be willing to try to produce the right kind of surface. It was a happy suggestion: though Band's experiments took too long for vellum copies of *The golden legend* to be printed, by 1892 satisfactory skins were being produced in England. Ink was to present another problem, 'as one might have known, seeing that those damned chemists have a freer hand with it!' Morris commented bitterly. Though after many trials he found an English ink which with a little modification would have been satisfactory, its manufacturers adopted a take-it-or-leave-it attitude. Eventually he found an ink said to be made from the old-fashioned pure ingredients by Jaenecke of Hanover. With this, unwilling to turn ink-maker himself, Morris was content.

For a press, he found the Albion perfectly satisfactory. As his printing activities grew, he added two further Albions and a proofing press. For printing with the sort of ink and paper that he intended to use these were far better than powered presses; for the short runs which he was to print they were far more economical. That Morris was content with nineteenth-century cast-iron presses, and inking with rollers, is a sufficient proof that his was not merely an antiquarian hobby. It would have been perfectly simple for him to have had common presses built of wood, and to have distributed the ink using the age-old method of ink-balls; had he merely wished to print in the fifteenth-century manner this is what he would have done. But this would have been less satisfactory technically, and Morris unhesitatingly turned to nineteenth-century equipment and methods when they could do the work better. Nevertheless, as a medievalist in spirit he was not altogether without regrets. 'Pleased as I am with my printing,' he was to write in May 1891, 'when I saw my two men at work on the press yesterday with their sticky printers' ink, I couldn't help lamenting the simplicity of the scribe and his desk, and his black ink and blue and red ink, and I felt almost ashamed of my press after all.'

By January 1891, with type and paper nearly ready, premises were taken at 16 Upper Mall, Hammersmith, and a compositor and pressman appointed— W. H. Bowden, who was later to be joined by his daughter and his son. The Kelmscott Press was born. Bowden later told a splendid story of its christening: 'When the type came in from the founders, he [Morris] was very anxious to help lay it in the cases; but not having served his time to the business, more often than not put the type into the wrong box. It was very amusing to hear him saying to himself "There, bother it; wrong box again!" But he was perfectly good humoured, and presently ran off and came back, bustling up the path . . . without a hat, and with a bottle of wine under each arm, with which to drink the health of the Kelmscott Press.'

But was the Kelmscott Press a *private* press at all? Morris's 'little typographical adventure' (as he had described it to Bowden when offering him a post), which in the seven years of its existence was to have a turnover of over £50,000, was obviously on a very different scale from even so important and successful a press as that of Dr. Daniel. Many have regarded Kelmscott as too commercial to warrant the name of private press, yet undoubtedly in its infancy it *was* private in the strictest definition of the term. Morris set it up for his own interest, to see what could be done in the way of producing a good book at his own expense, and his original intention was to print only twenty copies of its first publication (*The story of the glittering plain*) for distribution to personal friends. Only when news of the forthcoming book had leaked out to the press, and Morris was being badgered to make copies available for purchase did he decide (with some misgivings) to print extra copies for sale. He was no remote aesthete but a practical man, and if the public was prepared to give financial support to his experiments in printing what he wanted in the manner he wanted he was happy to let them do so. That the Kelmscott Press was successful enough to cover the very heavy production costs of its books was no slur on its amateur status.

The golden legend had been intended as the first book from the Press, but the first sizes of paper supplied by Batchelor were wrong for the work, so *The story of the glittering plain* was printed instead. Work on *The golden legend* started as soon as it was completed, but because of its length five other books had been issued before it was completed in November 1892. By that time the style of the Kelmscott books had become clear: volumes carefully designed, with wide and well-proportioned margins, magnificently decorated with borders designed by Morris and illustrations by Burne-Jones engraved on wood (usually by W. H. Hooper, one of the old master engravers), splendidly printed on the best materials available.

Up to and including *The golden legend* all the books were printed in Morris's 'Golden' type, based upon Jenson's roman letter of 1470. But already Morris's appetite had been whetted, and in June 1891 he had started on the designs for a black letter which was cut and cast at the end of the year; in the same month, realizing that the single press and the existing premises were inadequate, he moved the Press to a new home next to Sussex House (in which Emery Walker's process-engraving business was already situated) and added a second press so that the output of work could be increased.

The first book to be printed in the larger size of the black letter (the 'Troy' type) was Caxton's translation of *The recuyell of the historyes of Troye*, the first book printed in English and long one of Morris's favourites, which was published through Bernard Quaritch in November 1892. Quaritch had also published *The golden legend* (earlier books had been handled by Morris's old publishers Reeves and Turner) but so many enquiries were received at the Kelmscott Press that a book list had to be prepared, and from July 1892

Halliday Sparling was named as Secretary of the Press—a position to which Sydney Cockerell was to succeed in 1894, becoming Morris's right-hand man, after Sparling's marriage with Morris's daughter May had broken up. A few more books were published through these firms, but from *The history of Godefrey of Boloyne* (1893) onwards it became normal practice for the Press to publish directly. This is a course much more usual with private presses, and it had the advantage of saving bookkeeping, giving Morris information on sales —placing him in a position to guard against overprinting—and enabling him to give preference to purchasers of individual copies over booksellers laying in stock against an anticipated rise in price. A few more books were commissioned by publishers or booksellers, and in the case of one, Tennyson's *Maud* published by Macmillan in 1893, there was an apparent case of overprinting. Three hundred copies were sold at once, but the other two hundred hanging fire, Macmillans announced that they would be sold as a remainder. And sold they were, by noon on the day following the announcement!

Undoubtedly the most important of the Kelmscott publications was the *Chaucer*, hailed by the editor of the *Nineteenth century* as 'the greatest triumph of English typography'. Work on this started in the summer of 1892 (though Morris had been talking of it a year earlier) but it was not until June 1896 that the book was ready to be issued. By the time that it appeared, Morris—whose health had been visibly failing since 1894—was a very sick man. He knew that he was dying, and in August 1896 asked Sydney Cockerell whether he and Walker would be prepared to carry on the Press after his death. Cockerell was in favour of it ceasing, lest it should fizzle out by degrees. After Morris's death on 3 October 1896 he continued to run the Press with Walker and F. S. Ellis for another eighteen months in order to complete work which was already in hand. Much of the work was abandoned as being in too early a stage of preparation to be carried through (including a splendid *Froissart*), but in the seven years of its life the Press published fifty-two books in sixty-six volumes —no small achievement for the 'little typographical adventure' of an elderly man.

Nobody can judge of the printing of the Kelmscott Press without handling the books themselves; no reproduction, however good, can convey the colour of the ink, the feel of the paper and the impression of the types on the page (which is why Morris refused to allow Edward F. Strange to reproduce Kelmscott work in his *Alphabets* published in 1895). The books were books such as the late Victorian public had never seen before. There were many critics. Walter Crane was probably the first to comment unfavourably that

Fig. 26. Specimen leaf of the Kelmscott *Froissart*. At William Morris's death the planning of the book was not far advanced, and its production was abandoned

Morris's first type was more gothic-looking than its model, a criticism with which even the most ardent supporter of Morris would today agree, but Morris himself was unrepentant: 'this is a fact, and a cheerful one to me,' he wrote. Others objected to the presswork of the books, his *imprinting* of the type into the dampened paper instead of giving the kiss impression of a machine-press. 'Witness has been born against Morris,' wrote Frank Colebrook in the *Printing times*, 'in regard to what is called the embossing of the back of the page, an evidence that the other side of the page we are reading is also printed upon. The effect is displeasing to most eyes, and it detracts from the vividness of the letter which is being read, to the degree to which it detracts from the whiteness of the intervening space between the words. I don't think this con-comitant of the hand-press, with its enormous vertical pressure, is really gratifying to Morris, however indulgently he may look upon it for its reminis-cences of old-world books. It is simply the lesser of two evils. If a perfect, dense, deep black is not to be obtained without the drawbacks of the embossing of the back of the page, well, on the balancing of advantages, he chooses to have the more legible letter. He, indeed, procures so deep a black it can afford the sacrifice of a little white in the contrasting spacing . . .' Despite Colebrook's comment, Morris certainly did look too indulgently on this fault. Bodoni had dried his printed sheets under pressure between heated copper sheets in order to remove the indentations left by the type, and so painstaking a craftsman as Morris would certainly have resorted to a similar method (just as the more fastidious of today's private printers borrow their wives' irons for the pur-pose!) had he felt the indentation to be a blemish. Very probably he regarded it as an essential part and evidence of hand work, and as such not to be concealed.

At times there were protests that too many of the books he printed were written by himself; a foolish argument to advance against a *private* press. For the politically-minded attacks—that he was 'preaching socialism and going away to prepare books which none but the rich could buy'—there was little to be said. Many of his prices were certainly high (the vellum *Chaucer* was 120 guineas) but others were low: his own lecture on *Gothic architecture*, printed at the Arts and Crafts Exhibition in 1893, cost half a crown. In Frank Cole-brook's words again, 'he sets up his press, not really to make money, whether out of the rich or the poor, but to produce a book as beautiful as he can make it. When he has paid a high price for his paper . . . When he has used black ink at about 10s. a pound, when he has designed his three types and had them cut; when he has paid fair wages to his workmen . . . he is not able to sell the product of all this for a less sum.' But Morris's quest for perfection was beyond the comprehension of some: in his *The Kelmscott Press and William Morris, master-craftsman* (1924) Halliday Sparling tells how he once took 'the head of a large commercial printing works, with some pretensions to artistic leanings, over the Press. The visitor watched the careful setting and justifying of the compositors, watched the pressmen examining each sheet as it was pulled and commented "That's all very well for Mr Morris, but there isn't a man here that would be worth a penny an hour to me after he'd been here a week!"'

The commercial printer might grumble that it was 'all very well for Mr Morris', but the books sold very well indeed. One writer who made good use of the fashion for Kelmscott books was Thorstein Veblen, who saw it as an example of his theory of conspicuous consumption:

'Here we have a somewhat cruder type, printed on hand-laid, deckle-edged paper, with excessive margins and uncut leaves, with bindings of a painstaking crudeness and elaborate ineptitude. The Kelmscott Press reduced the matter to an absurdity—as seen from the point of view of brute serviceability alone—by issuing books for modern use, edited with obsolete spelling, printed in black-letter, and bound in limp vellum fitted with thongs. As a further characteristic feature which fixes the economic place of artistic book-making, there is the fact that these more elegant books are, at their best, printed in limited editions. A limited edition is in effect a guarantee—somewhat crude, it is true—that this book is scarce and that it therefore is costly and lends pecuniary distinction to its consumer . . .'

Though most other contemporary criticisms of the Kelmscott Press were unimportant, being based very largely on misunderstanding, time has not dealt kindly with the work of the Press. There was the inevitable reaction against what had been so highly admired and imitated. In a fighting speech delivered at the William Morris Centenary Dinner of the Double Crown Club (a speech later included in his *The printing of books*, 1938) Holbrook Jackson commented that the books were 'typographical curiosities from birth, and so far removed from the common way of readers that they have become models of what a book should not be . . . His typefaces became picturesque, his margins inclined to pomposity, and his paper was pretentious. The Kelmscott books are over-dressed. They ask you to look at them rather than to read them. You can't get away from their overwhelming typography . . .' In fact, Jackson concluded, they are 'museum pieces, typographical monuments—beautiful and ineffectual angels beating in the void their luminous wings in vain'. Undoubtedly Jackson was laying it on rather thickly for his audience, but this is more than just a witty after-dinner speech. And Daniel Berkeley Updike's statement that 'William Morris was a great printer because he was a great man who printed greatly' was carefully ambiguous. As works of art the publications of the Kelmscott Press are magnificent; as revolutionary manifestos in the cause of better printing they were of very real importance. But they were not *books*.

12

After Kelmscott: the fine press in Britain

Villiam Morris's typographical adventure was by no means the only essay in printing as an art in late Victorian England. But it was the first, and its influence for good or bad on the work of its successors was considerable. Not all private presses which were set up a few years after Kelmscott were under Morris's influence, needless to say: in the books which Sir George Sitwell had printed under his supervision at Scarborough in the 1890s, or in the long series of genealogical publications produced at the private press of Frederick Arthur Crisp there is no evidence of an awareness of Kelmscott work. These were in fact survivors of earlier amateur work, in the tradition of the Middle Hill Press or Prince Louis-Lucien Bonaparte.

In point of time one of the earliest followers of Kelmscott was the Ashendene Press, which was started by C. H. St. John Hornby in 1894, and which survived until 1935. Hornby was a member of the Board of W. H. Smith & Son, and named his press from the family estate in Hertfordshire, where it was set up originally in a little summer house. In its original form the Press was not unlike some of the earlier Victorian amateur affairs, at first being operated by Hornby and his sisters without outside help. But there was an important difference from most of the parlour printers: Hornby was a warm admirer of Morris's work at Kelmscott, and while a student at Oxford he had become acquainted with the work of the Daniel Press. At first the Daniel influence was the stronger: after printing three books in Caslon type Hornby managed to obtain the loan of various founts of Fell types from Oxford University Press, and used these to print a further ten books. In 1900 he moved his Press to Shelley House in Chelsea, which remained its home until it closed.

Though Dr. Daniel's work strongly influenced the outward appearance of these early books, it was an influence which did not last. 'How well I remember that afternoon in March 1895 when I came to Kelmscott House,' Hornby wrote to Sir Sydney Cockerell in 1940. 'It was shortly after I started the Ashendene Press, and I was brimful of enthusiasm for Morris and all his works. I remember my talk with him in his book-lined room, and going with you to see the sheets of the *Chaucer* on the Press . . . all as if it were yesterday . . .' Probably much more important than the example of Kelmscott (which was an inspiration rather than a direct influence) was the friendship which Hornby struck up with Cockerell and through him with Emery Walker. 'From these two,' he wrote in the Foreword to the *Ashendene Press bibliography* in 1935, '. . . I received inspiration and encouragement in my venture, and unstinted help and advice. The friendship then formed has lasted unbroken for more than thirty years, and has been a source of much happiness in my life. Cockerell was an unsparing and outspoken but withal kindly critic, and Walker a mine from which to draw a wealth of counsel ever at the free disposal of any struggling beginner. I owe them a debt which can never be repaid . . .'

The earliest substantial effect that Walker and Cockerell had on Hornby's books was that of persuading him to have his own proprietary typeface cut. In 1900 his 'Subiaco' type, originally projected by Morris for Kelmscott use, was cut, and for the next quarter century the Ashendene Press used it exclusively. Based upon the type which Sweynheym and Pannartz, the first printers in Italy, had used at Subiaco, the design had a sturdy elegance which suited Hornby's typographical style admirably. From the first book in which it was used, *Lo Inferno di Dante* (1902), the style of the Ashendene Press was to develop and be refined, but never to change considerably. It was a more restrained style than that of Kelmscott, with very much more of renaissance subtlety replacing gothic exuberance. Nor was there any self-conscious proclamation of intent or object: Hornby was content to produce books as well as could be done (admittedly in circumstances of complete economic freedom) and let them stand as a statement of his aims. He was not above being chaffed about his hobby (for hobby it was, 'a wonderful relaxation . . . from all the cares of life and business worries'). 'If you want to satisfy yourself that I really *do* do my own printing,' he wrote to Cockerell in 1902, 'look in here tomorrow about teatime and stay to dinner . . . Bring Walker with you, so that I may convince both the unbelievers of my *bona fides.*' There were to be many such little dinners over the next thirty years, as the friendship became closer.

The Ashendene Press was to publish many books in the Subiaco type. A good many were enriched with woodcut initials designed by Eric Gill, by Graily Hewitt and Louise Powell—all early pupils of Edward Johnston in the calligraphic revival of the beginning of the century. Cockerell was instrumental in introducing Hornby to their work. In some cases the initials were not printed, but instead spaces were left for the scribe to add them by hand afterwards. In one case, *The song of songs* (1902), the initials were illuminated exquisitely by Florence Kingsford, who was to become Cockerell's wife a few years later.

In 1925 Hornby added a second proprietary typeface to his repertoire, a recutting of a face first used by Holle at Ulm for the first edition of Ptolemy's *Cosmographia* in 1482. As a design it lacked the virtues of the Subiaco face, but was used with great success in a number of books, notably in a fine *Don Quixote* published in 1927. Long before this the Press had grown beyond its original humble form, and Hornby employed a craftsman printer to help with the work. Although Hornby still did much of the composition himself, the presswork was normally left for his assistants to carry out, just as Morris had done. The high quality of the work of many of the private presses of the late Victorian and Edwardian period is due in no small measure to these under-praised men. Finally, in 1935, Hornby decided that he should call a halt to his Press, and concluded his work with a splendid *Bibliography*, copiously illus-trated with specimen pages from the books he had produced. 'Perfect . . . as an example of printing and as a compilation' was how Cockerell (who was not given to fulsome praise) described it. Hornby's own pressman had died before it was produced, and the presswork was carried out by H. Gage-Cole, who at that time was working at the Stourton Press for B. Fairfax Hall. He was a hand-press craftsman of the old school, having worked at Kelmscott and later at the Doves Press.

St. John Hornby's influence on commercial printing was considerable. But this influence came largely through his professional work, not his hobby; through his employment of such men as Eric Gill, Joseph Thorp and Bernard Newdigate on work for W. H. Smith & Son. The Ashendene Press itself was of only minor importance in this respect, though in the forty-odd years of its life it had established and maintained a standard of production quite as high as that of Kelmscott, and it fully deserves its place as one of the trinity of great English private presses.

The third member of this trinity was the Doves Press which was established by Thomas James Cobden-Sanderson and Emery Walker in 1900. Cobden-Sanderson was a strange figure. The son of a senior civil servant, in his youth he was apprenticed to a shipbuilder, abandoned that to read for holy orders at Cambridge, but left without a degree after a breakdown, and for eight years went through a period of mental anguish 'about it and about'. In 1871 he was called to the Bar, but after some time spent in codifying the London & North-western Railway's various acts his health once more collapsed. While re-cuperating in Italy, he met Annie Cobden, the daughter of the great Free Trader, who later became his wife. At a suggestion from William Morris's wife, and with encouragement from his wife, he found an answer to his search for 'something which should give me means to live upon simply and in independence, and at the same time something beautiful, and, as far as human things may be, permanent' in bookbinding. Though his wife and the Morrises encouraged him, most other members of his circle were appalled. 'I heard of your book binding, but I own with regret,' wrote Lady Russell in 1884. 'With an education such as yours I should like better to hear that you were employing your mind on something which others of less cultivated interests could not do. I can, however, well understand the interest of being brought into contact with a class of human beings of whom we know little except by the articles they produce.'

Others were to hear of Cobden-Sanderson's bookbinding with less regret. After learning his craft under de Coverley, he rapidly acquired a high reputa-tion for the beauty of his bindings, and today is generally regarded as one of the leading figures in the revival of fine binding at the end of the nineteenth century.

From the establishment of the Arts and Crafts Exhibition Society (the phrase 'Arts and Crafts' was of his invention) Cobden-Sanderson was closely associated with William Morris, and followed the fortunes of the Kelmscott Press closely—so closely, in fact, that in 1894 he set up the Doves Bindery close to Morris's Press in Hammersmith with the initial aim of 'Beginning a tradition in association with the Kelmscott Press . . . The idea of a workshop; a young, active, imaginative printing press to feed the Bindery; a house to let immediately opposite to that printing press; the first link in the formation of a Tradition, and an apprentice ready to hand!' As it turned out, the Doves Bindery was never to work in collaboration with Kelmscott; but in any case Cobden-Sanderson found that bookbinding alone was not enough to satisfy his search for 'man's ultimate and infinite ideal'.

Towards the end of 1898 he wrote in his *Journals* 'I must, before I die, create the type for today of "the Book Beautiful" and actualise it—paper, ink, writing, ornament and binding. I will learn to write, to print and to decorate.' A catalytic role was now played by Sydney Cockerell, when he remarked that it was strange that nobody had yet revived Jenson's roman in its pure form— *here* was Cobden-Sanderson's model for his ideal type! By 1900 his resolutions were being carried out: with his son and daughter he enrolled for Edward Johnston's classes in lettering at the Central School of Arts and Crafts. Despite his aside, while watching a demonstration by Johnston that 'It is like watching some strange bird' he and Johnston soon became firm friends, and were discussing plans for a scriptorium to be associated with the Doves Bindery and with Cobden-Sanderson's new press. His decision to print was also no longer passive: work on the typeface was already progressing. In his *Journals* for 29 April 1900 he recorded that 'I have in hand now 1) *Organisation of printing press*. We are now in treaty for No. 1 in the Terrace, and propose to install our printing press there . . . We have taken No. 1 Hammersmith Terrace, and it is now whitewashed throughout, and is sweetly clean . . . And we have engaged a compositor, J. H. Mason . . . He began work last Monday week on *Agricola* at the Bindery, in the attic over my room. This has at last set us in motion; we have ordered "oddments" of all "sorts", and an additional fount to keep him going, and finally a press and paper . . . Proofs have been taken at the Bindery presses and have been sent to Mackail for revision . . .'

What Cobden-Sanderson did not record in his *Journals*—unless the references were removed through filial piety when his son published them in 1926—is that the Doves Press was not a solitary adventure on his part, but had been started in partnership with Emery Walker. They were a peculiarly ill-assorted pair; Cobden-Sanderson the enthusiastic, idealistic and obstinate visionary, and Walker the sober prosaic partner whose technical knowledge was sorely necessary to make the enterprise a success. But a success it was, from the publication of the *Agricola* in January 1901 onwards. As Ruari MacLean has remarked, the pages of the Doves Press books were the most devastating criticism ever made of Morris's work at the Kelmscott Press. Completely without ornament or illustration, they depended for their beauty almost entirely upon the clarity of the type, the excellence of the layout, and the perfection of the presswork—they were in fact the ruthlessly simple application of Cobden-Sanderson's dictum that 'the whole duty of typography . . . is to communicate, without loss by the way, the thought or image intended to be communicated by the author.' It was this restraint, and not Morris's lavish romanticism, which was to point the way for printing in the first half of the twentieth century (a way in danger of being forgotten). Beatrice Warde's statement that 'Printing should be invisible' is another way of saying the same thing that the Doves books were trying to express. Though it seems obvious enough today, it was by no means plain in the aftermath of Kelmscott, as those who remember the sub-Morrisian extravagances of the endpapers and title-pages of the early volumes in the Everyman's Library will readily appreciate. The simplicity of the Doves pages was of course deceptive. Johnston's masterly calligraphic initials, like the unforgettable opening to Genesis, in the *Bible* (1903–5), were a perfect example of how to marry calligraphy and typography, and Mason's setting was full of those almost invisible refinements that only another printer can recognize.

With most of the other 'fine art' presses one can trace a development in style: in the Doves books there was little change from first to last because Cobden-Sanderson's 'ideal book' was realized almost from the start.

After some twenty volumes had been produced at the Press, in 1909 the partnership between Walker and Cobden-Sanderson broke up, and at much the same time Mason left. The reason for the rupture was not hard to find: Cobden-Sanderson was a man who found collaboration with others very difficult, and seems to have regarded it almost as an attack on his own identity. Though he had set up the Doves Bindery with the avowed aim of working in conjunction with Kelmscott, when it came to the point Cobden-Sanderson felt that 'we had in the first place to establish ourselves—to be independent. I therefore fought shy of Morris and his ideas. I had first to develop my own', with the result that the Doves Bindery never worked on Kelmscott books. Although Walker was by no means as dominating a personality as Morris, he believed strongly that the Doves type should be made available for general, commercial use. Cobden-Sanderson, on the other hand 'regarded it as a consecrated instrument, and shrank away from what he regarded as desecration', as Mason put it. No reconciliation of views was possible, so Walker withdrew from the Press, and Cobden-Sanderson continued to direct it alone. In 1911 he made 'the last will and testament of the Doves Press':

'To the Bed of the River Thames, the river on whose banks I have printed all my printed books, I bequeath The Doves Press Fount of Type—the punches, the matrices and the type in use at the time of my death, and may the river in its tides and flow pass over them to and from the great sea for ever and for ever, or until its tides and flow for ever cease; then may they share the fate of all the world, and pass from change to change for ever upon the Tides of Time, untouched of other use and all else.' In various places in his *Journals* he recorded his growing resolve to close the Press, and in 1916 he finally did so with a last *Catalogue raisonné*, having previously thrown the punches and matrices and ultimately the types themselves into the Thames at Hammersmith Bridge. 'I stood upon the bridge, and I walked to and fro and bethought me of the time when I had crossed and recrossed it in winter time, in the darkness, and as the buses brought protection threw the type from the bridge into the river. Then I lifted my thoughts to the wonder of the scene before me, full of an awful beauty, God's universe and man's—joint creators. How wonderful! And my Type, the Doves type was part of it.'

Cobden-Sanderson's bequest of the type to the Thames was no doubt a splendid gesture, sincerely meant. But its splendour was tarnished by the fact that he was throwing away another man's property. When the partnership between Walker and himself had finally collapsed, Cobden-Sanderson had refused to allow Walker any of the Doves type unless hedged around with so many limitations as to make it useless to him. With his patience worn out (for disagreement had built up over several years) Walker commenced a legal action against his partner. To Sydney Cockerell—who had for some time been trying to repair the breach between his two friends—Cobden-Sanderson wrote 'to implore you, as you at the outset implored me, to make an end of these disgraceful "proceedings". And this I ask not for my own sake but for E. W.'s own. His "proceedings" at the utmost can only result in "damages" or in imprisonment: and think of that! for nothing on earth will now induce me to part with the Type. I have "devoted" it to the press and I have full power to do so. I have the will, and I have in my actual possession the punches and the matrices without which it is impossible to have a Fount of Type . . . I am, what he does not appear to realise, a Visionary and a Fanatic, and against a Visionary and a Fanatic he will beat himself in vain.'

Cockerell found a formula that seemed satisfactory—that Cobden-Sanderson (by far the older man) should have the sole use of the type for his life, and that if Walker survived him it should then pass into his possession. Walker agreed to this, but with misgivings: '. . . If I tell you I agree to the suggestion . . . he may by some means circumvent me. I can't trust him after what he has done' he confided to Cockerell. And how right he was! After Cobden-Sanderson's destruction of the types, Walker did not attempt to obtain legal redress—which would have been poor compensation indeed for his loss. 'Of unswerving rectitude of thought and deed' (as Cockerell described him in *The Times* obituary) he must have realized that Cobden-Sanderson was hardly answerable for his actions, and forebore to press the old man. The last words must be Cobden-Sanderson's own, written to Cockerell in 1917: 'If you, and the other old friends who lament my action and the shipwreck of my reputation, cannot enter into my feelings [in committing the types to the Thames] I may indeed weep, but I cannot help it. All things I was prepared to sacrifice for that one action and the dedication of the type, as I had dedicated all that I had done by its means, to the symbolism of life, as I had dreamed it among the stars, my witnesses . . .'

Cobden-Sanderson's gesture in destroying his Doves type in this way was perhaps disgraceful, certainly dramatic. But it was not original. Years before, in 1903, Charles Ricketts had similarly destroyed his typefaces by throwing them in the Thames, but in his case the action was less distressing. The types were his own property, and the designs were so bad that it was better that the Thames than typography should be polluted by them. Ricketts had started work in book design, much as Morris had, with a number of preliminary publications (such as *Daphnis and Chloe* in 1893) before he set up a press of his own in 1896.

Purists have objected that the Vale Press (as it was called) was not private with even more vigour than they have about Kelmscott. The original intention had been that Ricketts should set up his press in the Vale, Chelsea, but planning regulations forbade him starting what was technically a shop in a residential quarter. He therefore arranged for a press and workmen at the Ballantyne Press (a commercial firm of printers) to be reserved to work exclusively on Vale Press books under his personal supervision. Part of the purists' objection no doubt stemmed from the fact that the Vale Press books were advertised and sold with considerable efficiency. John Lane acted as publisher, Ricketts's partner W. L. Hacon supplied the financial backing, leaving Ricketts himself free to concentrate upon the design of the books. He was no mere follower of Kelmscott; though he admired Morris's work he was not uncritical of it, and for his own books he had thought out his own aesthetic which he applied with fastidious care.

The Vale Press books—of which there were to be forty-six different titles, including a Shakespeare in thirty-nine volumes—were far truer to the spirit of fifteenth-century Italian printing than Kelmscott work (not that this would have worried Morris) and were designed throughout by Ricketts. From the design of the watermarks on the paper (which was hand-made by Arnolds), through the types, decorations, wood-engravings, and the bindings, all was the work of Ricketts. In the patterned papers used on the boards of some of the ordinary editions, and in the full-leather bindings which he designed, the work is particularly good.

If one must look for 'lessons' taught by the private presses of the 1890s, there can be little doubt that the lesson of the Vale Press was that of the control of the whole production of the book in a consistent design, which has had the greatest influence on modern book production. Unfortunately in Ricketts's case the theory conflicted with the practice: whereas in Kelmscott books one gets the impression that type and decoration have grown naturally together and could keep on growing (like some monstrous hot-house plant) in the Vale Press work there is the feeling of deliberate construction according to a rigid formula, with the result that many of the books have a self-conscious good taste which has become ostentatious. 'The aim of the revival of printing,' Ricketts said, was 'to give a permanent and beautiful form to that portion of our literature which is secure of permanence . . . I mean permanent in the sense that the work reflects that conscious aim towards beauty and order which are ever interesting elements in themselves.' By trying to make every part of his books exquisite Ricketts too often made them merely precious.

By the beginning of the twentieth century Ricketts had decided that the time was approaching for him to close his press, as he believed that it had already carried out nearly all the work he had set out to produce. A disastrous fire at the Ballantyne Press in which most of his blocks and material were destroyed made up his mind for him, and in 1903 he cast the punches and matrices of his types into the Thames, retaining only enough type to print a *Bibliography of books printed by Hacon and Ricketts* (1904). The type was then melted down.

For some years the Vale Press was very closely associated with the Eragny Press, which was run by the artist Lucien Pissarro. Ricketts and his life-long companion Charles Shannon had befriended the young Lucien soon after he came to London from France, and had encouraged him to contribute to their publication *The dial*. In 1894 Pissarro had purchased a hand-press and laboriously printed *The queen of fishes*, the text of which was reproduced by process-engraving from hand-lettering, with coloured wood-engravings. As neither Pissarro nor his wife knew anything of printing the work gave endless trouble, but the results were sufficiently good for John Lane to agree to market the book, for Pissarro to decide to continue with printing, and for Ricketts to offer Pissarro the use of his Vale type for subsequent publications. The next fifteen books printed at the Eragny Press between 1896 and 1903 were accordingly all in Ricketts's type, and published through the Vale Press. But they were by no means imitations of the Vale manner; Eragny books had a charm and freshness quite unlike anything to be found in the work of any other private press, and in the printing of coloured wood-engravings in particular the Press excelled.

After 1903, when the Vale Press types were no longer available, Pissarro continued to print, using his own fount of type for a further sixteen books. The greater part of the work of producing these was done by himself and his wife Esther (who engraved his blocks), but when funds permitted a local printer, Thomas Taylor, was employed to assist with the presswork. *When funds permitted*: the Eragny Press was no money-spinner, nor was Pissarro sufficiently businesslike to price his books highly enough to compensate for the time and work which he lavished upon each book in an attempt to make it as perfect as possible. Although Pissarro's books were highly praised, and he had the distinction of being commissioned by the Societé des Cent Bibliophiles and by the Societé du Livre Contemporain to produce books for them (and magnificent books they were!), the First World War and the consequent loss of continental subscribers hit him too hard for the Press to be able to continue. Although he did not dispose of the press until after the war, *Whym Chow*, privately printed in 1914 for two friends of Ricketts, was to be the last book from the Eragny Press. Posterity was the poorer.

After Kelmscott had closed, several of the workmen employed there moved to the Essex House Press, started by C. R. Ashbee in 1898 as one of the several crafts practised by the Guild of Handicrafts, originally at Essex House in Mile End Road, London, and from 1902 onwards at Chipping Camden. It was different from the other private affairs of the time in that it was deliberately conceived as a part of a larger whole: it 'was but one of a group of workshops . . . working with such machinery as could be controlled in the interests of the corporate life, working with a common purpose in which the life was the first consideration,' wrote Ashbee. '. . . In a mechanical age that had destroyed the crafts, the unit was not the individual designer, as Morris and some of the older men had at first supposed, but the small workshop group.' The Essex House Press was then an Arts and Crafts press *par excellence*; alas, it was also a supreme example of 'articraftiness' of the worst sort. Though some of its publications were textually of real importance, like its surveys of historic buildings in London, others were completely unnecessary. Indeed, a projected lectern *Bible* had to be abandoned for lack of support. The books were printed (some of the early volumes very badly, which is strange considering the standards to which the workmen had become accustomed at the Kelmscott Press) in vile types on unsuitable paper . . .

Little that is good can be said about the Essex House Press, which finally closed in 1910, save that it was an honestly meant if misguided enterprise, and that it was by no means the worst of the presses in its misunderstanding of what Morris's 'little typographical adventure' had been about. If one compares an Essex House book with, for example, one of those printed by H. G. Webb at his Caradoc Press between 1899 and 1909, the former will seem a superb example of design and execution. But the real standard of comparison should not be with such misbegotten efforts, but with the work of Doves, or Eragny, or Ashendene. Compared with these, the books printed by the Essex House craftsmen are indeed vain things fondly invented.

13

Morris in America

———

Long before the hectic English typographical experimentation of the 1890s there had been private presses in America. In the Community at Ephrata in the middle of the eighteenth century there had been a late example of the sort of religious press which flourished in Europe in the fifteenth and sixteenth centuries. But in so young a country there was no rich leisured class among whom the plaything presses of the sort so common in Europe could flourish. Even on the eastern seaboard there seems to have been little amateur printing until the second half of the nineteenth century, when the efforts of Kelsey and other manufacturers fostered the growth of amateur journalism and parlour printing.

Of the presses which grew up then, that established at Hamden, Connecticut, by W. J. Linton the wood-engraver, was the most professional, producing some charming books illustrated with Linton's wood-engravings in the 1870s —and this was virtually an English press in exile, with all its roots in the English tradition. Of the many other American amateur efforts of the 1870s and 1880s, such as that of W. J. Brodie, little needs to be said; they amused their owners, but there was no pretence of making fine books or of improving commercial standards.

It was not long after the establishment of the Kelmscott Press that news of Morris's work and ideals was being filtered throughout the United States. In the pages of the *Inland printer*, the Midwestern trade journal, the concepts of 'the book beautiful' were being transmitted; in the work of Elbert Hubbard of East Aurora in New York State they were being interpreted in a curious way. Hubbard (1856–1915) is a figure who for many years has been derided—in England he was never regarded seriously, and May Morris who dismissed him as 'that obnoxious imitator of my dear father' was only airing the general opinion. Having made a modest fortune in Chicago, in 1892 he retired from business and following a visit to Morris in England he became an ardent champion and exponent of what he conceived Morris's aims to be in the crafts generally. On his return home he set up the Roycroft Shop, a body not unlike the Essex House community, which grew into a vast pseudo-medieval combination of inn, printing-shop, smithy, furniture factory and other crafts, which at its height employed some five hundred men. Hubbard was a born salesman, and his journal, *The Philistine*, which was written almost entirely by himself, had a circulation of nearly a quarter of a million. The Roycroft books, which included a series of Hubbard's *Little journeys* to the homes of the great, and his amazingly successful *A message to Garcia* were not really private press work. But they were 'articrafty' in the most vulgar and meretricious sense—poorly printed on rough, heavy paper, using ugly types with the nastiest of art nouveau decoration, and bound in the cheap soft suede known appropriately in the trade as 'limp ooze'. They were horrid indeed—Holbrook Jackson commented that the Kelmscott Press 'found its nemesis in Elbert Hubbard's Roycroft books'—but they, and the other Roycroft crafts, did awaken thousands of Americans to ideals of craftsmanship and help to produce the idea that there could be something better than mass-produced factory goods.

A more important centre for fine printing was Chicago, where a small group of young men interested in private presses gathered towards the end of the century. Some were commercial artists, or students at the Art Institute of Chicago, others newspapermen or writers. McClurg's Bookstore, where the new books of the English private presses were to be seen, was a centre for their devotions. Perhaps the earliest on the scene, and certainly the most important of all, was Frederic W. Goudy (1865–1947) who had moved to Chicago in 1890 to become a book-keeper. From childhood he had been interested in illustration and design, and though without any formal training he gradually moved into commercial art. With financial backing from a friend he started the Camelot Press, a small commercial printing shop for which he designed his first typeface and printed a number of books for Stone and Kimball. But the Press was not a success, and Goudy had to retire to the security of book-keeping again. He kept up his type designing, producing a number of advertising types, until encouraged by his wife he turned to full-time commercial art.

Among those who were influenced most strongly by Elbert Hubbard had been a young man in Snohomish, Washington: Will Ransom. Even as a child he had been fascinated by the idea of producing books, an idea which influenced his decision to take a job with the local newspaper when he left high school. With financial assistance of a friend in the autumn of 1901 he produced his first book, 'after the dainty style set by the Roycrofts', using the newspaper's equipment but rubricating and binding the volumes at home. Another book followed in 1902. Encouraged by the mild success that they had, Ransom decided to go east to Chicago, where he had been told prospects were good for a young man interested in fine printing, and where he could enrol at the Art Institute. In Chicago he soon became a friend of the Goudys.

In 1903 Goudy decided to start his own private press and invited Ransom to join him in the undertaking. Undoubtedly spurred by the English work which he had seen, and probably also by the private printing which a number of his Chicago friends were beginning to produce, Goudy found the reason for setting up his press in a wish to make his 'Village' type known to the printing world. This face had originally been designed as an advertising type for the exclusive use of the Kuppenheimer clothing firm, but the clients had balked at the cost of having the type cut and cast. Ransom managed to persuade a friend to advance the $250 needed, the new type was ordered from Robert Wiebking and by the end of July 1903 the Village Press had been set up in the Goudys' home in the Chicago suburb of Park Ridge and had issued its first piece. Appropriately this was a quotation from Cobden-Sanderson's *The Ideal book*. By September of the same year the Press's first book was completed: a reprint of the essay on printing which William Morris and Emery Walker had contributed to *Arts and crafts essays*. In the appearance just as much as in its content this book showed the Kelmscott influence very strongly, as did much more of the Village Press work for a considerable time afterwards. But from 1904 onwards the Press was run by the Goudys (Bertha Goudy was always a very active partner in its work) alone. Ransom withdrew when they decided to move from Chicago to Hingham, Massachusetts. He issued one more book, *A vision* and *The dream of Petrarca* in one volume under the Handcraft Shop imprint, but he found that interest in private printing was waning rapidly, and for some years had to abandon his dreams of book-building; like Goudy he found employment as a book-keeper. In 1921 Ransom again set up a private press, publishing some ten volumes of contemporary verse; again the public response was insufficiently encouraging for him to be able to continue beyond 1923. But he kept up his interest in private printing, and his *Private presses and their books* (1929) and *Selective check lists of press books* (1945–50) remain standard reference works in the field. To the many amateur printers in the 1930s and later who turned to him for advice he was extraordinarily generous and encouraging: in his very different way he was perhaps as significant a figure as Emery Walker had been in the English private press movement.

The Goudys' Village Press had only a short stay at Hingham, issuing a few more books (including William Morris's *The hollow land*, which had been designed by Ransom, in 1905) before moving to New York in 1906. Goudy eked out a living as a freelance designer while continuing to run the Press, until a studio fire in 1908 destroyed his press, types, books—in fact almost all his possessions. The Village Press was restarted in 1911, producing a few more books, but by now Goudy had built up a connection with the Lanston Monotype Corporation, a connection which was to last into the 1940s. There was no need for him to use the Village Press as a means of publicizing his types any more. His interest in private printing continued—in 1924, following a move to Marlborough-on-Hudson, New York, he purchased one of the Albions used to print the Kelmscott *Chaucer*—but by now the Press was far more a hobby than anything else, and not much more work of real substance was printed.

Goudy's influence on American printing was considerable though not entirely beneficial. It stemmed almost entirely from his very large number of type designs. With one or two exceptions these have never been admired extensively in the Old World, and most of them have dated very badly.

Among Goudy's circle in Chicago had been Frank Holme, the newspaper artist, with whom Goudy worked at Holme's School of Illustration—a short-lived affair, but one which turned out some very competent lettering artists, including Oswald Cooper and W. A. Dwiggins. In 1895 Holme printed seventy-four copies of a little book called *Just for fun* which included a selection of verses such as *Casey at the bat*. The imprint used, The Bandarlog Press, came from the *Jungle book* nicknames given to Holme and his wife by friends who accused them of 'always pecking at new things'. It was a light-hearted effort, typical of much work produced by printers for pleasure, and little more might have come from the Press had not Holme been compelled by tuberculosis to give up his newspaper work. While he was in a sanatorium in Asheville, North Carolina, he produced a second book, *Swanson, able seaman*, of which 174 copies were printed for presentation to friends. In a vain search for health Holme decided in 1902 to go to Arizona, and in order to help him the Bandarlog Press was incorporated, many of his friends (including Mark Twain, Booth Tarkington and George Ade) taking up shares in the company at $25 each. The control of the Press remained entirely in Holme's hands, and before he died at the age of thirty-six in 1904 he managed to produce another seven books. Some of these had a serious artistic intent, like *Her Navajo lover* (1903) but others were very light-hearted. There were three burlesques by George Ade of the dime novels then popular, published in a series called the 'Strenuous

Lad's Library' which Holme illustrated in an appropriate style. The titles give some idea of these splendid stories: *Rollo Johnson the boy inventor, or the demon bicycle and its daring rider; Handsome Cyril, or the messenger boy with the warm feet;* and *Clarence Allen, the hypnotic boy journalist.* They were by no means well printed, but were deliberately produced as 'a bum job' to be in keeping with their models. Though Holme was certainly in sympathy with the aims of the Arts and Crafts Movement, he had a sense of proportion and an ability to laugh at his own beliefs which was very unusual among private printers at that time. By a good many others beside Cobden-Sanderson, private printing was regarded with an almost religious devotion. After reading through some of the pompous Credos they solemnly issued, Holme's *All about the Bandarlog Press* comes as a very refreshing change:

'In every article relating to printing that you pick up nowadays you are bound to run across the words "dignity" and "simplicity" and "legitimate use of materials".

'Now "dignity" being a sort of extraneous husk or shell rather than an inherent quality, it is sometimes liable to stand in the way of one's having a good time. It is all right for those who like it and who have the patience to keep it up—because it's largely a matter of opinion anyhow, so the Bandarlog Press will have to pass it up as a steady thing and let the other Presses corner it if they choose . . .

'But when it comes to "legitimate use of materials", that's the Bandarlog Press's long suit.

'That's where it shines.

'In the revolt against machinery it accompanies the pendulum to the limit of its swing.'

Precisely what Holme meant by this can be seen in some of his colophons: 'This rare and limited edition was done into type and the refined and elegant illustrations were done into wood cuts on best grade North Carolina yaller poplar timber with an IXL jackknife (two blades), and the whole business was done into its present shape in the month of December. AD 1901, by F. Holme, who at that time had nothing else to do . . .'

Two other Chicago presses of the time are also of interest. The Blue Sky Press was started as a purely private venture by Thomas Wood Stevens and Alfred Langworthy in 1899, and produced competent if not particularly distinguished volumes of contemporary writing at a time when most private printers were turning out dreary new editions of *Sonnets from the Portuguese.* The other was Ralph Fletcher Seymour's Alderbrink Press Seymour's introduction to fine printing had been something like that of Will Ransom; as a schoolboy in Cincinnati he had been inspired by seeing reproductions of old blockbooks in the Museum Library, and tried his hand at hand-lettered pages in the same manner. Soon after he had come to Chicago, where he obtained

THE STRENUOUS LADS LIBRARY.

ROLLO JOHNSON

THE BOY INVENTOR

:OR:

The Demon Bicycle and Its Daring Rider

BY GEORGE ADE

Author of "Eddie Parks, the Newsboy Detective," Etc.

Copyright 1903 by George Ade. All rights Reserved.

Fig. 27. The Bandarlog Press's 'Strenuous Lad's Library'; a skilful pastiche of the dime novel

employment as a commercial artist with the Manz Engraving Company, he decided to have line-blocks made of one of these, Keats's *Ode to melancholy*. An edition of six copies of this was printed on one of his employer's proofing presses in 1897. Pleased with the effect he produced another hand-lettered

book, *Three merry old tales*, by the same method. A copy of this fell by chance into the hands of the Rev. F. W. Gunsaulus, a well-known Chicago book-collector, who encouraged Seymour to continue and by persuading many of his friends to subscribe to his next book enabled Seymour to set up in business for himself. Seymour built up a commercial art practice alongside his press, on which he progressed from hand-lettering through the use of Caslon type to his own fount, the Alderbrink type. In the design of this he had considerable help from Goudy, and in 1902 he had his first book printed in it by a friend, Morris's *The art of the people*. It was produced on handmade paper using imported German ink, and was a very successful exercise in the Kelmscott manner, and one indicating the future of the Alderbrink Press. But with that future we are not concerned, for the Press soon moved over into a purely commercial sphere. Though Seymour continued to produce books in a workmanlike manner for many more years, the elements of complete personal selection and control—the real criteria of a *private* press—had gone.

Chicago was by no means the only American city in which private presses were set up as a result of Morris's influence. At the opposite extreme from Elbert Hubbard's commercialized Roycroft work was the Cranbrook Press which the manager of the *Detroit evening news*, George Booth, ran from 1900 until 1902. Booth was familiar with the work of the Kelmscott Press and had travelled to East Aurora to examine the work of the Roycrofters at first hand. He had enough taste to decide which was the better model for his own press, and the design of his books was to be closer to Kelmscott than those of any other private printer. Not only in design, in fact, but also in execution; Booth worked hard to emulate the craftsmanship of Morris. His reasons for setting up his press were irreproachable: having seen thousands of rare books in the Lennox Library in New York he had concluded that to print more was 'excusable only if the printer chose such works as his best judgement told him were worthy of preservation'. Though he tempered this by adding '. . . I conceive it also to be the sphere of good books to entertain, if devised only to amuse, providing the influence is good' the Cranbrook Press books maintained a high seriousness of intent. None were devised only to amuse; they were such books as *The dictes and sayings of the philosophers*, *The Revelation of St John the divine*, and *Utopia*.

In starting his own press Booth did it in style. A room in the top floor of his office building was altered to resemble a medieval workshop and filled with furniture in the same style; a hand-press was purchased and a printer engaged 'who had learned his trade before the days of Linotypes'. Paper was specially made, and type pirated from the Kelmscott designs by American founders was purchased. Much of the work of the Press was performed by his workmen, but under Booth's close and careful supervision. Like Morris before him he designed many of the elaborate strapwork borders used in the books.

Almost as closely imitative of Kelmscott in its earliest years was the Elston Press at New Rochelle, New York, at which Clarke Conwell printed some twenty books between 1900 and 1904. Conwell outgrew his Kelmscott phase and turned to the use of Caslon type, producing some excellently printed volumes. They were, however, the usual dreary predictable classics—*Sonnets from the Portuguese*, *Aucassin and Nicolette*, *Cupid and Psyche*—with which so many of these eager amateurs thought to make the art of the book more appetizing to a satiated world. The Kirgate Press which Lewis Buddy operated at Canton, Pennsylvania, during the first five years of this century seems all the more interesting therefore for being cast in a different mould. Named after Horace Walpole's printer, the Press was concerned very largely with reprinting various Walpole pieces. Its most ambitious production was a type facsimile of Emerson's quarterly journal *The dial*, which was reprinted with painstaking care in the same type and style as the original. Another press of interest was the Marion Press, originally set up 'as a relief from ordinary suburban amusements' by Frank Hopkins in 1896. Hopkins was manager of the Fine Books Department of the De Vinne Press, and produced some excellently printed (if rather too conventionally designed) books. In 1898 he changed his Press into a full-time commercial undertaking.

Though the influence of the English private presses in the Arts and Crafts Movement was very considerable, it was not through private press work that it flowered most luxuriantly. It was through the designers and printers in the commercial field—through such men as D. B. Updike, Bruce Rogers, Carl Rollins and T. M. Cleland—that Morris's ideas spread most effectively across the Atlantic. And these were men with the ability and the understanding to abandon mere facile imitations of the Kelmscott style very early. One or two of them toyed with private presses; Cleland at the turn of the century ran the Cornhill Press whose books, as he said, 'were printed in black letter types and were very hard to read, and I had a notion at that time that being so made them especially romantic and beautiful.' Such notions were pretty general at the time; their replacement in good commercial work by such firms as the Merrymount Press or the Riverside Press is unfortunately outside the scope of this volume.

14

Fine printing on the continent

The influence of William Morris and of the other English private presses was as considerable on the continent as it was in England and America. But one country in which his ideas on book design had no influence whatsoever, either at the time or since, was France; hence the separate tradition of the *beau livre*, so different from our 'fine books'.

A few years before Emery Walker's 1888 lecture, Octave Uzanne had written in a splendidly chauvinistic vein that 'the art of producing beautiful books is the only one that foreigners have been unable to imitate. Essentially it is a purely French art . . . Printing, illustration, sewing, binding, make us the absolute superior of all others in Europe and America, and this is true not only of our artists' talents, but of the perfect taste of our principal publishers.' In such soil it would have been unlikely for Morris's notions to catch root.

There had in 1883 been a splendid suggestion of what a French private press could be. In Huysmans' *À rebours* we read how Des Esseintes

'had in the past had certain books set up just for himself and printed on hand-presses by workmen specially hired for the job. Sometimes he would commission Perrin of Lyons, whose thin clear types were well suited for antiquarian reprints of old texts; sometimes he would send to England or to America for new founts to print modern works; sometimes he would apply to a Lille printing house which for centuries had possessed a complete fount of black letter; sometimes again he would employ the old Enschedé foundry at Haarlem, which had preserved the punches of the civilité types.

'For the paper of his books he had done the same. Deciding that he was bored with the usual expensive papers—silver from China, pearly gold from Japan, white from Whatman's, grey-brown from Holland, buff from

Turkey and the Seychel Mills—and disgusted by machine-made papers, he had ordered special papers to be made by hand for him at the old paper-mills at Vire, where they still used pestles once employed on crushing hempseed. In order to introduce a little variety into his collections, he had on several occasions imported flock papers, linen woves and the like from London; while to show his contempt for other book collectors he had a Lübeck merchant supply him with an improved greaseproof paper of a bluish tint, crackly and brittle to the touch, in which instead of straw fibres there were flecks of gold like those in Dantziger Goldwasser.

'In this way he had made some books which were unique, and for which he always chose unusual formats; having them bound by Lortic, by Trautz-Bauzonnet, by Chambolle, or by Cape's successors; irreproachable bindings of old silk, of embossed oxhide, of Cape morocco—all full-bindings, tooled and inlaid, with endpapers of watered silk; enriched in ecclesiastical fashion with metal clasps and corners, sometimes even decorated by Gruel-Engelmann in oxidized silver and gleaming enamel.

'Thus he had commissioned Baudelaire's works to be printed in the admirable episcopal type of the old firm of Le Clere, using a large format similar to that of a missal, on very light Japanese paper; a porous paper as soft as elder-pith, its milky whiteness tinged faintly with pink. This edition, limited to the single copy and printed in a rich velvety black, had been bound in a wonderful flesh-coloured pigskin—one in a thousand—dotted all over where the bristles had been, and tooled in black with marvellously apt designs by a great artist.'

This is what a French private press should have been; had it existed in fact Uzanne would perhaps have had more justification for his ridiculous boast about the quality of French book production. But Huysmans' dreams were not to be fulfilled; in the smug self-satisfaction of the Third Republic there was little likelihood of any attempts at improvement taking place. Though in the eighteenth century there had been many amateur printers in France, the Victorian middle-class hobby of printing in the parlour does not seem to have spread across the channel.

Outside France Morris has been universally recognized as *the* pioneer in typographic reform and revival. In the establishment of private presses, his influence was to show itself first in Belgium, where it coincided with the renaissance of Flemish literature that was a feature of the 1890s. As far as French language printing in Belgium was concerned, he had no influence, but as early as 1889—before Morris started work at the Kelmscott Press—the artist Henry van der Velde had made his work in arts and crafts the theme of lectures he gave at Antwerp. It was natural that van der Velde should follow the work of the Kelmscott Press closely, and in fact his wife Maria visited the Press while in England to find out more about it for him. When his friend Auguste Vermeylen, who was planning to publish a literary magazine called *Van Nu en Straks*, asked him to take charge of its layout and design in 1892 he investigated the possibilities of having a special typeface cut for the magazine, but unfortunately had to reject the idea. For his own shortlived little private press, La Joyeuse, he used Caslon type in the *Six chansons* (1895) written by his partner in the venture, Max Elskamp. But van der Velde's most important contribution to the fine press movement before 1914 was to be in Germany, where he had moved before the turn of the century. Another amateur Flemish press which operated in the 1890s indirectly under the Kelmscott influence was that of Julius de Praetere. At Laethem St. Martin he printed a number of exquisite little volumes of poetry by H. Teirlinck and others, illustrated with his own woodcuts. But for de Praetere as for van der Velde Belgium did not prove a satisfactory environment in which to work, and he moved to Zürich where he became the first director of the Kunstgewerbeschule.

In Germany, where Morris's influence was to be far strongest, it did not sweep triumphantly into a vacuum. Though in 1887 Ludwig Meper, Director of the Leipzig Akademie der Graphischen Künste, had said that 'printing, even in the edition de luxe, is *not* an art', there had been a restlessness, a dissatisfaction with the traditional development in the arts in Germany just as much as elsewhere. One result had been the growth of *Jugendstil*. It was not with the old dreary tradition of bad design (or more often than not no design at all) that Morris's teaching had to compete, but rather with the freedom, the anarchy of art nouveau's tangled ribbons and tendrils which were overpowering the German book. It is often very difficult today to separate the historicism of the private presses from art nouveau influences (to separate the two streams in Charles Ricketts' work, for instance) and it is usually pointless to do so. In Henry van der Velde's work in Germany Morris's teaching was transmuted into art nouveau forms—though van der Velde would have denied that his work was art nouveau at all, as he had rejected the plant patterns used by Otto Eckmann in his book design and instead used more abstract patterns. In van der Velde's work for the Insel Verlag, in *Ecce homo* and *Also sprach Zarathustra* —not of course private press work, but in the direct tradition—there was an application of the Morris principles allied to a completely modern system of decoration. But by this time the reaction against the nightmare foliage of Eckmann and his school had set in; as early as 1901 a working group of young graphic artists, the Steglitzer Werkstatt, had called for a stand against exaggerated decorative trends in book design.

The influences spreading from England were not restricted to the work of William Morris: of even more importance in the spread of the private press movement in Germany were the books of the Doves Press and the calligraphic teaching of Edward Johnston, which had been taken back to Germany by his pupil Anna Simons who was to translate his seminal *Writing and illuminating and lettering* a few years later in 1910.

An important figure in this work was Count Harry Kessler (1868–1937). As early as 1900 he had encouraged the designing of a new type by the Belgian artist George Lemmen (the face used later in van der Velde's books for the Insel Verlag) and following a visit to England in 1904, during which he met Edward Johnston, Eric Gill and others, he invited Emery Walker to design a series of German classics, the *Grossherzog Wilhelm Ernst* series, for the Insel Verlag. This series, with its calligraphic title-pages designed by Johnston and Gill, was to have a marked effect on German book design—not least by its use of roman type in place of black letter.

August Kippenberg, who at that time was jointly responsible with Kessler for the work of the Insel Verlag, had a large degree of responsibility for the establishment of one of the first truly private German presses of this period: the Ernst-Ludwig-Presse at Darmstadt, which was started under the patronage of the Grand Duke of Hesse (for whom it was named) in 1907. This press was under the artistic direction of the brothers Friedrich Wilhelm and Christian Heinrich Kleukens. Friedrich Wilhelm, who had been a member of the Steglitzer Werkstatt from 1901 to 1903, remained at the Ernst-Ludwig-Presse only until 1914; but his brother continued to direct its work until 1937—from 1918 onwards with an expanded programme, only occasionally producing work for the Grand-ducal house. The style of the press was relatively severe; all illustration was eschewed, the only decoration being in title-pages and initials, and in the types used. To a considerable degree the press was a vehicle for experiment with the typefaces designed by the Kleukens brothers; a practice followed by several other German private presses, most of which went far beyond the one or two proprietary faces used by the English arts and crafts printers. The result was that many of their volumes look mannered and intentional. In Daniel Berkeley Updike's words, 'they produce a certain sensation, but not that of pleasure; they astonish rather than charm.'

ἔχεις γεγωνεῖν τῆς πολυφθόρου πλάνης,
λέγ᾽· εἰ δὲ πάντ᾽ εἴρηκας, ἡμῖν αὖ χάριν
δὸς ἥντιν᾽ αἰτούμεσθα, μέμνησαι δέ που.

ΠΡΟΜΗΘΕΥΣ

τὸ πᾶν πορείας ἥδε τέρμ᾽ ἀκήκοεν.
ὅπως δ᾽ ἂν εἰδῇ μὴ μάτην κλύουσά μου,
ἃ πρὶν μολεῖν δεῦρ᾽ ἐκμεμόχθηκεν φράσω,
τεκμήριον τοῦτ᾽ αὐτὸ δοὺς μύθων ἐμῶν.

οὗτός σ᾽ ὁδώσει τὴν τρίγωνον ἐς χθόνα
Νειλῶτιν, οὗ δὴ τὴν μακρὰν ἀποικίαν
Ἰοῖ πέπρωται σοί τε καὶ τέκνοις κτίσαι.
τῶν δ᾽ εἴ τί σοι ψελλόν τε καὶ δυσεύρετον,
ἐπανδίπλαζε καὶ σαφῶς ἐκμάνθανε·
σχολὴ δὲ πλείων ἢ θέλω πάρεστί μοι.

ΧΟΡΟΣ

εἰ μέν τι τῇδε λοιπὸν ἢ παρειμένον

Fig. 28. Aeschylus' *Prometheus*, printed by the Bremer Presse, 1926. Set in the Press's own Greek type, with woodcuts by Ludwig von Hofmann

Very closely modelled on the work of the Doves Press was the Janus-Presse, founded in Leipzig by Walter Tiemann and C. E. Poeschel in 1907. Poeschel was a printer (and for some years Kippenberg's partner in the Insel Verlag), Tiemann a typographic designer and lecturer at the Akademie der Graphischen Künste in Leipzig. The Press was a sort of busman's holiday at which the two of them carried out the operations of presswork and composition themselves as a change from directing the operations of others. Tiemann designed the Press's special typeface (a forerunner of his well-known 'Mediaeval' type) and cut the titles and initials in wood. Strictly a spare-time occupation, in the sixteen years of its life the Press published only five books, two in 1907 and 1910, and three more after the end of the war; but what they lacked in number they made up in quality—they were superbly produced, and the texts selected were of real worth.

There were more than a few other private presses in Germany in the years before the First World War. The Officina Serpentis, founded by E. W. Tieffenbach in 1911, though based closely upon the English private presses in its working methods adopted a much more decorative manner in its work than was usual. Less influenced by non-German sources than almost any other press was the Rupprecht-Presse. Founded in Munich in 1913 by the typographer F. H. Ehmcke, and named for the popular crown-prince of Bavaria (who acted as godfather at its christening) in the twenty years of its life the Press produced some fifty-seven books, mostly German literature. All were printed in Ehmcke's own typefaces; roman, fraktur, schwabacher, and they convey the German tradition in typography with splendid effect. Even more steeped in the Teutonic past were the 'Rudolfinische Drucke', occasional pieces of printing issued by Rudolf Gerstung and Rudolf Koch. Koch was the German equivalent of William Morris and Edward Johnston rolled into one; a craftsman of very great talent he was responsible above all others for the splendid flowering of black letter in the first third of this century, a flowering that was at its best in the blockbooks *Elia* and *Jesaia* which were produced at his private press. This work is far too Germanic for most English tastes; though lip service is paid to Koch's achievements I have found few others who share my own enthusiasm—though Morris would have relished it.

Much more closely in the traditions of the typographic work of Emery Walker and Cobden-Sanderson (and therefore more admired in the English-speaking world) was the Bremer Presse. Founded in 1911 by a group of whom Willy Wiegand was the chief, the Press was very much in the grand tradition; a few good special typefaces being cut and used with magnificent effect in

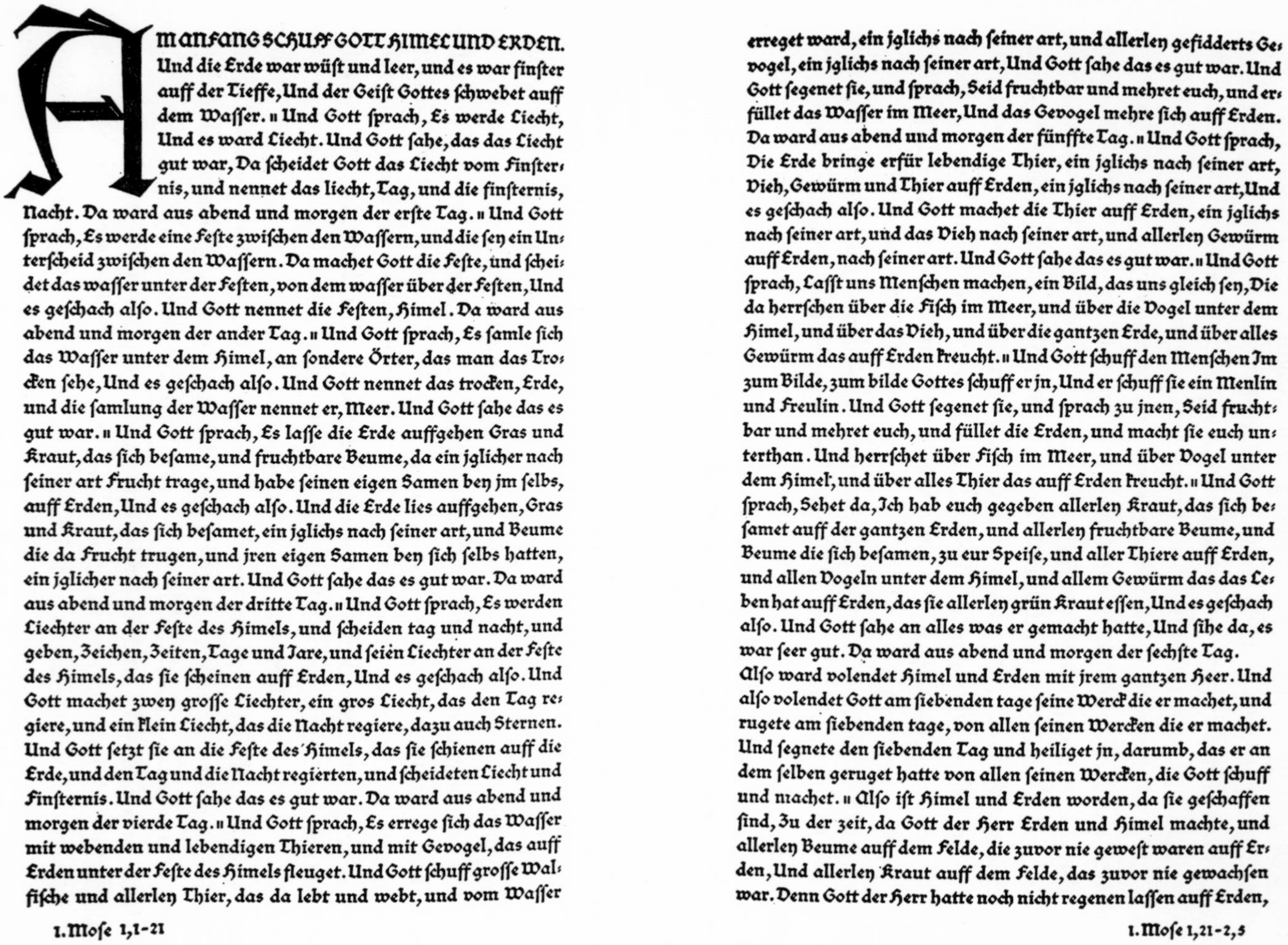

AM ANFANG SCHUFF GOTT HIMEL UND ERDEN. Und die Erde war wüst und leer, und es war finster auff der Tieffe, Und der Geist Gottes schwebet auff dem Wasser. ¶ Und Gott sprach, Es werde Liecht, Und es ward Liecht. Und Gott sahe, das das Liecht gut war, Da scheidet Gott das Liecht vom finsternis, und nennet das liecht, Tag, und die finsternis, Nacht. Da ward aus abend und morgen der erste Tag. ¶ Und Gott sprach, Es werde eine Feste zwischen den Wassern, und die sey ein Unterscheid zwischen den Wassern. Da machet Gott die Feste, und scheidet das wasser unter der Festen, von dem wasser über der Festen, Und es geschach also. Und Gott nennet die Festen, Himel. Da ward aus abend und morgen der ander Tag. ¶ Und Gott sprach, Es samle sich das Wasser unter dem Himel, an sondere Örter, das man das trocken sehe, Und es geschach also. Und Gott nennet das trocken, Erde, und die samlung der Wasser nennet er, Meer. Und Gott sahe das es gut war. ¶ Und Gott sprach, Es lasse die Erde auffgehen Gras und kraut, das sich besame, und fruchtbare Beume, da ein iglicher nach seiner art frucht trage, und habe seinen eigen Samen bey jm selbs, auff Erden, Und es geschach also. Und die Erde lies auffgehen, Gras und kraut, das sich besamet, ein iglichs nach seiner art, und Beume die da frucht trugen, und jren eigen Samen bey sich selbs hatten, ein iglicher nach seiner art. Und Gott sahe das es gut war. Da ward aus abend und morgen der dritte Tag. ¶ Und Gott sprach, Es werden Liechter an der Feste des Himels, und scheiden tag und nacht, und geben, Zeichen, Zeiten, Tage und Jare, und seien Liechter an der Feste des Himels, das sie scheinen auff Erden, Und es geschach also. Und Gott machet zwen grosse Liechter, ein gros Liecht, das den Tag regiere, und ein klein Liecht, das die Nacht regiere, dazu auch Sternen. Und Gott setzt sie an die Feste des Himels, das sie schienen auff die Erde, und den Tag und die Nacht regierten, und scheideten Liecht und Finsternis. Und Gott sahe das es gut war. Da ward aus abend und morgen der vierde Tag. ¶ Und Gott sprach, Es errege das Wasser mit webenden und lebendigen Thieren, und mit Gevogel, das auff Erden unter der Feste des Himels fleuget. Und Gott schuff grosse Walfische und allerley Thier, das da lebt und webt, und vom Wasser

1.Mose 1,1-21

erreget ward, ein iglichs nach seiner art, und allerley gefidderts Gevogel, ein iglichs nach seiner art, Und Gott sahe das es gut war. Und Gott segenet sie, und sprach, Seid fruchtbar und mehret euch, und erfüllet das Wasser im Meer, Und das Gevogel mehre sich auff Erden. Da ward aus abend und morgen der fünffte Tag. ¶ Und Gott sprach, Die Erde bringe erfür lebendige Thier, ein iglichs nach seiner art, Vieh, Gewürm und Thier auff Erden, ein iglichs nach seiner art, Und es geschach also. Und Gott machet die Thier auff Erden, ein iglichs nach seiner art, und das Vieh nach seiner art, und allerley Gewürm auff Erden, nach seiner art. Und Gott sahe das es gut war. ¶ Und Gott sprach, Lasst uns Menschen machen, ein Bild, das uns gleich sey, Die da herrschen über die Fisch im Meer, und über die Vogel unter dem Himel, und über das Vieh, und über die gantzen Erde, und über alles Gewürm das auff Erden kreucht. ¶ Und Gott schuff den Menschen Jm zum Bilde, zum bilde Gottes schuff er jn, Und er schuff sie ein Menlin und Frewlin. Und Gott segenet sie, und sprach zu jnen, Seid fruchtbar und mehret euch, und füllet die Erden, und macht sie euch unterthan. Und herrschet über Fisch im Meer, und über Vogel unter dem Himel, und über alles Thier das auff Erden kreucht. ¶ Und Gott sprach, Sehet da, Ich hab euch gegeben allerley Kraut, das sich besamet auff der gantzen Erden, und allerley fruchtbare Beume, und Beume die sich besamen, zu eur Speise, und aller Thiere auff Erden, und allem Vogeln unter dem Himel, und allem Gewürm das das Leben hat auff Erden, das sie allerley grün Kraut essen, Und es geschach also. Und Gott sahe an alles was er gemacht hatte, Und sihe da, es war seer gut. Da ward aus abend und morgen der sechste Tag. ¶ Also ward volendet Himel und Erden mit jrem gantzen Heer. Und also volendet Gott am siebenden tage seine Werck die er machet, und rugete am siebenden tage, von allen seinen Wercken die er machet. Und segnete den siebenden Tag und heiliget jn, darumb, das er an dem selben geruget hatte von allen seinen Wercken, die Gott schuff und machet. ¶ Also ist Himel und Erden worden, da sie geschaffen sind, Zu der zeit, da Gott der Herr Erden und Himel machte, und allerley Beume auff dem Felde, die zuvor nie gewest waren auff Erden, Und allerley Kraut auff dem Felde, das zuvor nie gewachsen war. Denn Gott der Herr hatte noch nicht regenen lassen auff Erden,

1.Mose 1,21-2,5

Fig. 29. The Luther *Bible*, printed by the Bremer Presse, 1926–8, set in the Press's own blackletter types

large-format editions of Homer, Dante, Tacitus, the Luther *Bible* and similar books. Apart from splendid initials drawn by Johnston's pupil Anna Simons the books were entirely without ornament, and only one—*Vesalius*, printed for an American medical society—was illustrated. In 1922 the Press expanded and produced a number of educational books such as Hofmannthal's *Deutsches Lesebuch* which were printed on powered presses, an example of the extension of private press ideals into the commercial field. For some years the hand-press tradition and good commercial printing were carried on side by side. After the Nazis came to power economic and political difficulties killed the Bremer Presse, but in its long life its influence on German printing was probably greater and longer lasting than that of any of the other fine presses.

As the 'Rudolfinische Drucke' were the most purely Germanic privately printed books, so when Count Kessler at length set up his own private press at Weimar in 1913, it was to be the most international in spirit. Kessler himself was equally at home in Paris or London as in Berlin or Weimar. Educated in England, he was to become an international diplomatist, but he devoted a good deal of his very considerable wealth to intelligent patronage of ballet, music, and the fine arts. As has already been said, he had obtained the services of Emery Walker, Johnston and Gill for the Insel Verlag in 1904; when he decided to set up the Cranach Presse in 1910 or 1911 he naturally turned to Walker for advice and assistance. Edward Johnston was engaged to advise on type designs, and when in 1913 the type was at last ready J. H. Mason (the former Doves Press compositor) went to Weimar for a few months to supervise the installation of the hand presses and assist in engaging compositors and pressmen. Finding that it was far from easy to get workmen skilled in hand press work in Germany, Mason arranged for H. Gage-Cole, also from the Doves, to go to Weimar. Work was proceeding apace; Kessler had persuaded Aristide Maillol to try his hand at woodcuts for a projected edition of Virgil's *Eclogues*, and Gordon Craig to prepare woodcuts for *Hamlet*. Caspard Maillol (nephew of Aristide) was making special paper for the exclusive use of the Press. By the summer of 1914 the *Eclogues* were well advanced, despite the fact that there were to be three different editions (with translations in English, German and French respectively, as parallel texts to the Latin) and despite the delays caused by Kessler's many other engagements—collaborating with Richard Strauss on *Der Rosenkavalier* at Munich, or helping with the production of Diaghileff's ballets at Covent Garden. The war stopped all these preparations.

Although one or two very minor pieces seem to have been produced during the war years, and there were a few more publications of a private nature during

Idee der Transcendental-Philosophie.

ERFAHRUNG ist ohne Zweifel das erste Product, welches unser Verstand hervorbringt indem er den rohen Stoff sinnlicher Empfindungen bearbeitet. Sie ist eben dadurch die erste Belehrung und im Fortgange so unerschöpflich an neuem Unterricht, daß das zusammengekettete Leben aller künftigen Zeugungen an neuer Kenntniß, die auf diesem Boden gesammelt werden können, niemals Mangel haben wird. Gleichwohl ist sie bei weitem nicht das einzige, darin sich unser Verstand einschränken läßt. Sie sagt uns zwar, was da sei, aber nicht, daß es notwendiger Weise, so und nicht anders, sein müsse. Eben darum gibt sie uns auch keine wahre Allgemeinheit, und die Vernunft, welche nach dieser Art von Erkenntnissen so begierig ist, wird durch sie mehr gereizt, als befriedigt. Solche allgemeine Erkenntnisse nun, die zugleich den Charakter der inneren Notwendigkeit haben, müssen, von der Erfahrung unabhängig, vor sich selbst klar und gewiß sein; man nennt sie daher Erkenntnisse a priori: da im Gegenteil das, was lediglich von der Erfahrung erborgt ist, wie man sich ausdrückt, nur a posteriori, oder empirisch erkannt wird. ¶ Nun zeigt es sich, welches überaus merkwürdig ist, daß selbst unter unsere Erfahrungen sich Erkenntnisse mengen, die ihren Ursprung a priori haben müssen und die vielleicht nur dazu dienen, um unsern Vorstellungen der Sinne Zusammenhang zu verschaffen. Denn, wenn man aus den ersteren auch alles wegschafft,

Von dem Unterschiede der reinen und empirischen Erkenntniß.

DASS alle unsere Erkenntniß mit der Erfahrung anfange, daran ist gar kein Zweifel; denn wodurch sollte das Erkenntnißvermögen sonst zur Ausübung erweckt werden, geschähe es nicht durch Gegenstände, die unsere Sinne rühren und theils von selbst Vorstellungen bewirken, theils unsere Verstandesthätigkeit in Bewegung bringen, diese zu vergleichen, sie zu verknüpfen oder zu trennen, und so den rohen Stoff sinnlicher Eindrücke zu einer Erkenntniß der Gegenstände zu verarbeiten, die Erfahrung heißt? Der Zeit nach geht also keine Erkenntniß in uns vor der Erfahrung vorher, und mit dieser fängt alle an. ¶ Wenn aber gleich alle unsere Erkenntniß mit der Erfahrung anhebt, so entspringt sie darum doch nicht eben alle aus der Erfahrung. Denn es könnte wol seyn, daß selbst unsere Erfahrungserkenntniß ein Zusammengesetztes aus ihm sey, was wir durch Eindrücke empfangen, und dem, was unser eigenes Erkenntnißvermögen (durch sinnliche Eindrücke bloß veranlaßt,) aus sich selbst hergiebt, welchen Zusatz wir von jenem Grundstoffe nicht eher unterscheiden, als bis lange Übung uns darauf aufmerksam und zur Absonderung desselben geschickt gemacht hat. ¶ Es ist also wenigstens eine der näheren Untersuchung noch benöthigte und nicht auf den ersten Anschein sogleich abzufertigende Frage: ob es ein dergleichen von der Erfahrung und selbst von allen Eindrücken der Sinne unabhängiges Erkenntniß gebe. Man nennt

Fig. 30. A specimen sheet from the Officina Serpentis, 1928

the early twenties—such as the volume *In memoriam Walter Rathenau* in 1922 —Kessler's preoccupation with international diplomacy in the aftermath of the war prevented him from resuming work on his half-completed projects until the mid-twenties. But in 1926 the German edition of the *Eclogues* appeared, to be followed by the English version the following year.

In view of the part played by Emery Walker in advising Kessler and in suggesting the design of the roman type, the similarity of these to the best work of the Doves Press was not surprising. The *Hamlet*, when it eventually appeared in 1930, was however completely individual in style; Shakespeare's text was set in a large black letter face designed by Johnston, with the text of the sources (Saxo-Grammaticus and Belleforest) printed in a smaller size around the text, with the most marvellously conceived and perfectly printed woodcuts as illustration. Gage-Cole's skill in printing these showed the ability of the pressman at its best: of all private press work in the Kelmscott tradition, the Cranach *Hamlet* is the greatest.

A few more books from the Press were to appear; a very attractive *Canticum canticorum* with wood-engravings by Eric Gill, and Rilke's *Duineser Elegien*, both published in 1931. At least six other titles were being planned in the early thirties, but when Hitler came to power they had to be abandoned; as the friend and biographer of Rathenau, whose politics and race were equally detested by the Nazis, Kessler had to abandon his home and his possessions at a moments notice, and the Press produced nothing more.

Because of the international nature of its work, the Cranach Presse has received a disproportionate amount of notice in the past. With the exception of the *Eclogues*, the *Hamlet* and the *Canticum canticorum* its work was not altogether satisfactory. For the fruits of over twenty years' work three satisfactory books may seem a poor showing—but this is to judge the press in terms which are not really valid: this was a press in the grand tradition, and time was of no more importance than cost.

In the Netherlands the influence of William Morris and of Cobden-Sanderson was slower to penetrate than it had been in neighbouring Belgium, although from the early 1890s the work of Kelmscott had been studied with interest. It was an interest mixed with caution; there was a feeling that the Belgians in such publications as *Van Nu en Straks* had been taking things too easily—that their principles of design were illogical and impure, and lacked the earnestness of English work—and neither the Belgians nor the English were by any means eagerly copied. The revival of fine printing in Holland came through the book trade; through the influence of such men as Jan Kalf,

J. W. Enschedé and S. H. de Roos (whose first commission was to design a translation of some of Morris's essays under the title of *Kunst en Maatschappij* in 1903) rather than through indigenous private press work.

The first true private press in the Netherlands was De Zilverdistel, operated by Dr. J. F. van Royen (1878-1942). After studying law at Leyden van Royen had entered the Dutch postal service. During the early years of this century he became a member of the circle of the three poets Jan Greshoff, Jacques Bloem and P. N. van Eyck and the architect K. P. C. de Bazel, all of whom were strongly interested in typographic design. Van Royen's own practically applied interest in the subject, and in the improvement of standards was shown in 1912 when (though still in a relatively subordinate position in the postal service, the P.T.T.) he was instrumental in having de Bazel commissioned to design a new series of postage stamps. In the same year he was to publish a vehement attack on the low standards of official printing in the first issue of a book-collectors' magazine called *De Witte Meier*. (The improvement of government printing in the Netherlands was to be largely his doing; over the next thirty years, during which he was to rise to the influential position of Secretary-General of the Post Office, he influenced standards as thoroughly as later Francis Meynell was to effect improvements at His Majesty's Stationery Office.)

In 1910 Greshoff and the other two poets had started De Zilverdistel, a bibliophile series of books of a sort to become very much commoner in the 1920s, in which the design of the books was undertaken by the partners, but the printers (Enschedé at Haarlem or van der Wiel of Arnhem) were responsible for interpretation and execution of the designs. The programme of the press was well within the Kelmscott-Doves tradition; they aimed at 'pure, non-ornamental book typography' and although their editions were both expensive and limited in size, this was intended to be only a temporary factor: 'a luxury of beauty, not of rarity, is what we need.' They were well aware of the dangers which afflicted presses, as well as of their ideals: 'There is one aim, inwardly and outwardly a perfect harmony. There is one risk; snobbery, dilletantism, affectation combining to produce preciousness.' On their models (if this was not already clear) they were quite frank: 'They would be less German and more English, and among these less the books of the Kelmscott or Vale Presses than the work of the Doves Press.'

After the production of three of these semi-private press books between 1910 and 1912, Greshoff and Bloem withdrew from the undertaking, leaving van Eyck to carry on alone. Van Royen joined him in 1913, but following a trip to England in 1914 during which he visited Cobden-Sanderson, St. John Hornby and Pissarro, he determined to return to the purer private press tradition by doing his own printing. Van Eyck was not altogether willing, and a few more books were printed commercially; but in 1915 van Eyck left Holland to become a newspaper correspondent in Italy, and had to become virtually a sleeping partner and leave van Royen to produce the books as he thought best. As it was to turn out, De Zilverdistel was to become more like St. John Hornby's Ashendene Press than its former model Doves, and it is perhaps the only example of a semi-commercial press becoming truly private. Two special type designs were commissioned; one to be used for contemporary work, which was designed by S. H. de Roos; and one for the printing of older texts which was the work of Lucien Pissarro. Pissarro was also instrumental in the purchase of an Albion press, which was soon installed in van Royen's home in The Hague.

The first book to be printed on the hand press and in de Roos's new Zilvertype was a joint statement by van Royen and van Eyck of their aims, *Over Boekkunst en De Zilverdistel* (1916). For this de Roos also designed the initials. Van Royen printed the next two books in the same type, Jan Hendrik Leopold's *Cheops* (1916) and Shelley's *Prometheus unbound* (1918); the first use of Pissarro's Disteltype was in a late medieval Dutch text, *Een boecxken gemaket van Suster Bertken* printed in 1918. There was to be one more book from De Zilverdistel in the following year, but after that for some years there was a pause in van Royen's printing; the collaboration with van Eyck did not work as happily as it might, and van Royen wanted to be completely his own master.

In 1923 he resumed his hobby under the new name of the Kunera Pers, starting with an edition of Leopold's *Oosterch*, for which he designed and cut the title and initials himself, as he was to do for all the other books from his press. There were to be very few of them, for van Royen's philosophy did not allow him to employ others for the composition or presswork as most of these other private presses did; except for the binding all the work in the production of his books was done by himself, and his official duties at the Post Office left him little time. There was a *Villon* in 1926 (with splendid red and blue initials, the printing of which was very highly praised by St. John Hornby), Arthur van Schenel's *Maneschijn* in 1927, Péguy's *La tapisserie de Notre Dame* in 1929, and then no more—until the early 1940s, under the German occupation, when he printed a few small pieces (such as the ninety-third psalm) for circulation to friends, and a book, P. C. Boutens's *In den keerking*, which he completed on

1 March 1942. Four days later van Royen was arrested by the Germans; he died in the concentration camp at Amersfoort three months later. To prevent confiscation of his press and equipment they were hidden away by friends and colleagues. After remaining in storage for some twenty years, in 1964 van Royen's workshop was carefully reconstructed in the former coach-house of the Rijksmuseum Meermanno-Westreenianum (that most attractive of all book museums) in The Hague.

The work of De Zilverdistel and of the Kunera Pers, though exquisite of its kind and very highly praised abroad, has never met with unanimous approval in its native land. Jan van Krimpen, a High-Church typographer if ever there was one, and whose criticism was as frankly expressed as it was without malice, described its work as 'bibelot' books, and van Royen as a printer of 'modern incunabula'. S. H. de Roos was less condemning: the books, he believed, were among the finest made either in the Netherlands or abroad. But de Roos shared some of van Royen's romanticism, and between 1926 and 1935 he ran the second Dutch press in the Kelmscott-Doves tradition, the Heuvelpers. He designed a special type (the Meidoorn type) for the press in 1928, and printed several books such as Spinoza's *Tractatus politicus* and Fromentin's *Les maitres d'autrefois* which were very closely in the old tradition. All the setting and printing was done by himself. But the economic crisis of the early thirties which killed so many private presses in England and the United States compelled de Roos to give up, and in 1935 he disposed of the type to J. F. Duwaer en Zonen of Amsterdam. He was in fact to use it once more after his retirement from the Typefoundry Amsterdam in 1941; in Jacques Perk's *Eene helle- und hemelvaart*, published as one of the clandestine editions of A. A. Balkema's Five Pound Press in 1943.

'As books they had sometimes many, sometimes few merits,' wrote G. W. Ovink of the work of van Royen and de Roos. 'As models in a period when one has to produce with machine paper and machine composition on cylinder presses with automatic feeding, they were valueless . . . Only as examples of striving after beauty without compromise could they inspire those who . . . hoped to raise the standards of the commercial book.' As examples their work was indeed far less valuable than the work of those who followed the original Zilverdistel pattern of commissioning good commercial printers: Jan van Krimpen with his Palladium Editions, or A. A. M. Stols's 'Trajectum ad Mosam' series, for instance. But these are beyond our scope.

Of all the private presses which were set up on the continent between the wars the greatest, as well as the longest lived, has undoubtedly been the

legimus: mortuo enim Salomone, qui filiam Regis Ægypti
sibi matrimonio junxerat, filius ejus Rehabeam bellum cum
Susaco Ægyptiorum Rege infelicissimè gessit, à quo omni-
nò subactus est. Matrimonium præterea Ludovici 14. Regis
Galliarum cum filiâ Philippi quarti novi belli semen fuit, &
præter hæc plurima exempla in historiis leguntur.
¶ XXV. Imperii facies una, eademque servari, & consequenter Rex unus, & ejusdem sexûs, & imperium indivisibile esse
debet. Quòd autem dixerim, ut filius Regis natu major patri
jure succedat, vel (si nulli sint liberi) qui Regi sanguine pro-
ximus est, patet tam ex Artic. 13. præced. Cap. quàm quia
Regis electio, quæ à multitudine fit, æterna, si fieri potest
esse debet; aliàs necessariò fiet, ut summa imperii potestas
sæpe ad multitudinem transeat, quæ mutatio summa est,
& consequenter periculosissima. Qui autem statuunt, Re-
gem ex eo, quòd imperii Dominus est, idque jure absoluto
tenet, posse, cui vellet, idem tradere, & successorem, quem
velit, eligere, atque adeò Regis filium imperii hæredem jure
esse, falluntur sanè. Nam Regis voluntas tam diu vim juris
habet, quamdiu Civitatis gladium tenet; imperii namque jus
solâ potentiâ definitur. Rex igitur regno cedere quidem potest, sed non imperium alteri tradere, nisi connivente multitudine, vel parte ejus validiore. Quod ut clariùs intelligatur,
venit notandum, quòd liberi non jure naturali, sed civili
parentum hæredes sunt: nam solâ Civitatis potentiâ fit, ut
unusquisque quorundam bonorum sit dominus; quare eâ-
dem potentiâ, sive jure, quo fit, ut voluntas alicujus, quâ de
suis bonis statuit, rata sit, eodem fit, ut eadem voluntas etiam
post ipsius mortem rata maneat, quamdiu Civitas perma-
net, & hâc ratione unusquisque in statu civili idem jus, quod

57

Fig. 31. S. H. de Roos' Meidoorn type, which he designed for his Heuvelpers

Officina Bodoni. Named for Giambattista Bodoni, the great eighteenth-century Parma printer, it was founded in Rome in 1922 by Hans Mardersteig (born 1892), and issued its first book from Montagnola in the Ticino in the following year. Mardersteig was devoted to the hand press, believing it to be the only instrument which could encourage the strictest attention to detail and give the greatest subtlety of impression. In this belief he was echoing William Morris, but he was not influenced by romantic quasi-medieval ideals: there was nothing of the spirit of handicraft which prevailed at the Essex House Press, nor of the obsessive search for the perfect book which drove Cobden-Sanderson. In Stanley Morison's words Mardersteig 'acted on the belief that to confer fine typographic form upon a fine piece of literature is a justifiable use of time and labour, material and skill; secondly that no quality of impression, however fine, can excuse inattention to textual precision.'

Mardersteig had obtained from the Italian government the exclusive right to cast type from some of Bodoni's matrices preserved in the Biblioteca Palatina, and most of the books printed at the Officina Bodoni for the first few years were in these faces. The quality of the setting was excellent, and the press-work was superb. Handmade papers from Italy, France, Germany and Holland were used; for many of the books a very few copies were also pulled on vellum supplied by Band of Brentford (so thoroughly had William Morris done this work, that this was considered superior to Roman vellum). Such skill was shown in the printing of these vellum copies that Friedrich Ewald, in a critical survey of the work of the Officina Bodoni published in the final number of *The Fleuron* (1930), proclaimed that he 'did not believe that the perfection of printing upon vellum has ever been carried to a higher degree'.

Such enthusiasm from the leaders of the typographic world for the work of a private press was by no means common by the late 1920s, yet Mardersteig had early established among them a reputation that he had never lost. In part this was a result of the splendid design of his books: though most of the early volumes were in Bodoni's sixteen-point roman, there were signs that the Officina would not stick to one typographic style, as had most private presses from Kelmscott on. In Goethe's *Das Römische Carneval* (1924), for example, Mardersteig employed a larger ornamented italic of Bodoni's which had been cut at almost the same time that Goethe had written the text. This was skating perilously close to 'period typography', as Mardersteig has done on several occasions, though his skill is such that the design never degenerates into pastiche.

Typographically the work of the Officina Bodoni was fully up to Bodoni's own standards. But a good deal of Bodoni's work had been textually abominable (like the calligraphic masterpieces of the fifteenth century), and it was as much for the excellence of his texts as the perfection of his printing that Mardersteig gained such high esteem. This was not luck: in a brief account of the work of the Officina Bodoni which he published in 1929 Mardersteig stated that 'All texts before being set up are thoroughly examined. The best critical edition is chosen, and if it does not agree with the latest research, a new revised text is established by comparison with the original manuscript or the first edition.' In this Mardersteig's approach was closer to that of the early scholar printers like Aldus Manutius or Robert Estienne than to the dilettantes of the Arts and Crafts Movement; the result has been that Officina Bodoni books have a value far above their success as examples of fine printing: they are (like the books of the Nonesuch Press) designed *to be read*.

In 1927 the first phase of Mardersteig's work came to an end with a move from Switzerland to Verona. During the previous five years he had published ten books under his own imprint, the *Editiones Officinae Bodoni*, and printed a further eleven commissioned by other publishers. To the purist, the Officina Bodoni should from the start be regarded not as a private press but as a commercial undertaking, but a less appropriate description for Mardersteig's undertaking would be difficult to find. These books ranged very considerably in language—seven were in English, five each in German and Italian, the others in French and Latin—and in text; from Lord Chesterfield to Seneca, Politian to Alfred de Musset, Shelley to Frederick the Great. Of those printed for outside publication two were for the booksellers and publishers Elkin Mathews and Marrot, and two for Frederic Warde in Paris, including a facsimile of the writing books of Ludovico degli Arrighi which was edited by Stanley Morison (who later edited several other classical manuals of calligraphy which were printed at the Officina Bodoni for the Pegasus Press, Paris). The two books for Warde were printed in the two versions of Arrighi's italic, Arrighi and Vicenza; most of the others were in Bodoni types.

The reason for the move to Verona was simple: Mardersteig had won a limited competition for the design and execution of the Italian national edition of the *Opera omnia* of Gabriel d'Annunzio, and the Italian government stipulated that it must be printed in Italy. It was a very considerable undertaking: forty-nine quarto volumes, many of five hundred pages or more, and presenting many problems in the layout of the verse. All were to be set by hand in the Bodoni types, and printed in an edition of 300 copies on vellum and Imperial Japanese vellum on the hand press. There was in addition a 'trade edition' (if that is an adequate term to describe these volumes which were superbly printed

GABRIELE D'ANNUNZIO

ATTO I

E voi data m'avete la mia sorte,
madre; la sposa voi l'avete scelta
pel vostro figlio nella vostra casa.
Madre, voi me l'avete accompagnata
perché dorma con me sopra il guanciale,
perché mangi con me nella scodella.
Io pascevo la mandra alla montagna,
alla montagna debbo ritornare.

La madre gli toccherà la fronte con la palma,
come per cacciarne un'ombra funesta.

CANDIA

Àlzati, figlio. Come strano parli!
La tua parola cangia di colore,
come quando l'ulivo è sotto il vento.

Il figlio s'alzerà, smarrito.

ALIGI

E il mio padre dov'è, che non lo veggo?

CANDIA

A mietitura con la compagnia,
a far mannelle, in grazia del Signore.

ALIGI

Io ho mietuto all'ombra del suo corpo
prima ch'io fossi cresimato in fronte,

12

LA FIGLIA DI IORIO

SCENA II

quando il mio capo al fianco gli giungeva.
La prima volta mi tagliai la vena
qui dov'è il segno. Con le foglie trite
fu ristagnato il sangue che colava.
«Figlio Aligi» mi disse «figlio Aligi,
lascia la falce e prenditi la mazza;
fatti pastore e va sulla montagna.»
E fu guardato il suo comandamento.

CANDIA

Figlio, qual è la pena che t'accora?
Il segno incubo forse ti fu sopra?
La tua parola è come quando annotta
e sul ciglio del fosso uno si siede
e non segue la via perché conosce
che arrivare non può dov'è il suo cuore,
quando annotta e l'avemaria non s'ode.

ALIGI

Alla montagna debbo ritornare.
Madre, dov'è la mazza del pastore,
che giorno e notte sa le vie dell'erba?
Io l'abbia, quando viene il parentado,
che la veda com'io la lavorai.

La madre andrà a prendere la mazza pog-
giata in un canto, presso il focolare.

13

Fig. 32. The Officina Bodoni's edition of d'Annunzio, set in Bodoni types

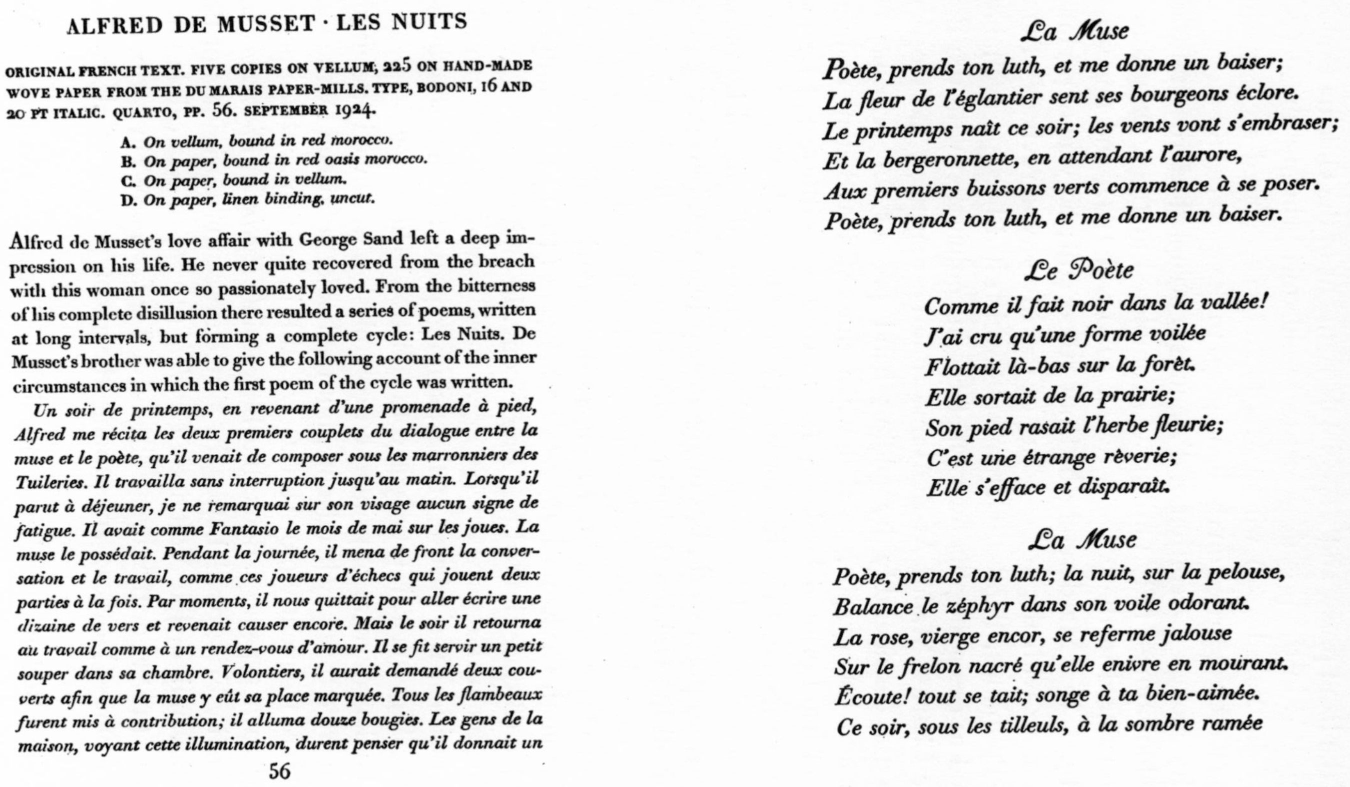

ALFRED DE MUSSET · LES NUITS

ORIGINAL FRENCH TEXT. FIVE COPIES ON VELLUM, 225 ON HAND-MADE WOVE PAPER FROM THE DU MARAIS PAPER-MILLS. TYPE, BODONI, 16 AND 20 PT ITALIC. QUARTO, PP. 56. SEPTEMBER 1924.

A. *On vellum, bound in red morocco.*
B. *On paper, bound in red oasis morocco.*
C. *On paper, bound in vellum.*
D. *On paper, linen binding, uncut.*

Alfred de Musset's love affair with George Sand left a deep impression on his life. He never quite recovered from the breach with this woman once so passionately loved. From the bitterness of his complete disillusion there resulted a series of poems, written at long intervals, but forming a complete cycle: Les Nuits. De Musset's brother was able to give the following account of the inner circumstances in which the first poem of the cycle was written.

Un soir de printemps, en revenant d'une promenade à pied, Alfred me récita les deux premiers couplets du dialogue entre la muse et le poète, qu'il venait de composer sous les marronniers des Tuileries. Il travailla sans interruption jusqu'au matin. Lorsqu'il parut à déjeuner, je ne remarquai sur son visage aucun signe de fatigue. Il avait comme Fantasio le mois de mai sur les joues. La muse le possédait. Pendant la journée, il mena de front la conversation et le travail, comme ces joueurs d'échecs qui jouent deux parties à la fois. Par moments, il nous quittait pour aller écrire une dizaine de vers et revenait causer encore. Mais le soir il retourna au travail comme à un rendez-vous d'amour. Il se fit servir un petit souper dans sa chambre. Volontiers, il aurait demandé deux couverts comme la muse y eût sa place marquée. Tous les flambeaux furent mis à contribution; il alluma douze bougies. Les gens de la maison, voyant cette illumination, durent penser qu'il donnait un

La Muse

Poète, prends ton luth, et me donne un baiser;
La fleur de l'églantier sent ses bourgeons éclore.
Le printemps naît ce soir; les vents vont s'embraser;
Et la bergeronnette, en attendant l'aurore,
Aux premiers buissons verts commence à se poser.
Poète, prends ton luth, et me donne un baiser.

Le Poète

Comme il fait noir dans la vallée!
J'ai cru qu'une forme voilée
Flottait là-bas sur la forêt.
Elle sortait de la prairie;
Son pied rasait l'herbe fleurie;
C'est une étrange rêverie;
Elle s'efface et disparaît.

La Muse

Poète, prends ton luth; la nuit, sur la pelouse,
Balance le zéphyr dans son voile odorant.
La rose, vierge encor, se referme jalouse
Sur le frelon nacré qu'elle enivre en mourant.
Écoute! tout se tait; songe à ta bien-aimée.
Ce soir, sous les tilleuls, à la sombre ramée

Fig. 33. Mardersteig's *The Officina Bodoni*, 1929, showing a leaf from his edition of Alfred de Musset's *Les nuits*, 1924.

on hand-made Fabriano paper) of 2,500 copies. This was clearly beyond the capacity of the hand press, and a special department of the Officina Bodoni was therefore opened in the premises of the Mondadori printing house (echoing the work of the Vale Press) where Mardersteig supervised their machining, applying the lessons learned on the hand press to the powered press.

Naturally enough the edition of d'Annunzio occupied Mardersteig and the Officina Bodoni almost fully until it was completed in 1936. Only four other books were printed in the years between 1930 and 1932, and none between 1933 and 1935. But Mardersteig had not stood still; he was experimenting very much more with the use of some of the Monotype revivals of classical typefaces—Poliphilus, Bembo, Garamond—which had become available, and was engaged in designing his own typefaces in conjunction with the Parisian punchcutter Charles Malin. At the same time he expanded the scope of his printing house considerably by adding hand presses for printing copper engravings and lithographs, so that when the Officina Bodoni resumed its production of hand-printed books in 1936 many were illustrated by modern artists of the calibre of Fritz Kredel and Franz Masereel. As before many of these were commissioned by clients, and so could be dismissed by purists as not really private press work, but many were private editions never placed on sale, and for all the Officina Bodoni remained true to its ideals and standards. Some of these commissions took the concept of the limited edition to the logical conclusions of Des Esseintes in *À rebours*: Berto Barbarini's *San Zen che ride* (1938) or Kenneth Grahame's *The reluctant dragon* (1941) for example, were both printed in editions limited to a single copy. In undertaking this work and countenancing its mad logic Mardersteig was seriously at fault: the manufacture of artificial rarities, the misuse of the printing press in what should be the sphere of the calligrapher, is utterly in contradiction to his other aims.

All the books which were printed on commission were well executed, and most of them are extremely handsome, but the books published by the Officina Bodoni itself are frequently more attractive still, in particular those printed in Mardersteig's own typefaces. Books like Boccaccio's *Il Ninfale Fiesolano* (1940), with woodcuts by Fritz Kredel after the sixteenth-century originals of Bartolommeo di Giovanni, or like Voltaire's *Candide* (1944) or Marcel de Guerin's *Poèmes en prose* (1954) or the three editions of *The four gospels* in Latin, English and Italian (1962-3)—these are among the most perfect of all twentieth-century books.

The Officina Bodoni weathered the difficult years of the Second World War successfully, and still continues to print today. Faithful to the hand press

Fig. 34. Wood-engraving by Otto Rohse from *Kikeriki*; Maximilian-Gesellschaft, 1954

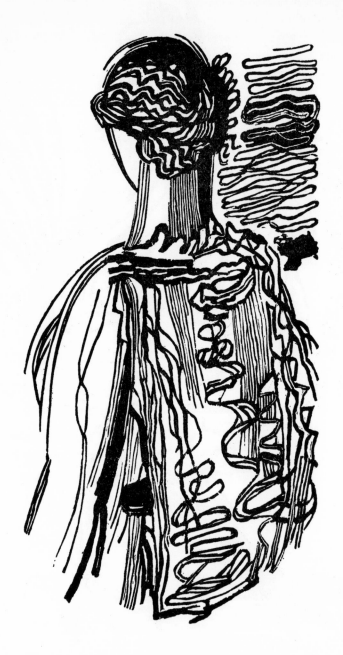

Fig. 35. Wood-engraving by Hans Orlowski from *Orpheus und Eurydice*, printed by the Drei König Presse, a modern German press in the English tradition, 1961

which has served him (and which he has served) so well, Mardersteig restricts its output to what can be set and printed by hand. But profiting from his earlier experience with the production of the trade edition of the works of d'Annunzio, and in order to make finely printed books available to a larger number of readers at a lower price, in 1948 he founded the Stamperia Valdonega,

Fig. *36*. Wood-engraving by Imre Reiner from *Die Frösche*, printed by the Trajanus-Presse, perhaps the finest contemporary German private press, *1962*

which produced books which have been machine-set and printed on powered presses. Working in very close collaboration with the Officina Bodoni, its bread-and-butter has been the publication of the excellent series of Ricciardi classics, which (as might be expected) are also distinguished by the excellence of their texts. A fine example of the excellent work of the Stamperia Valdonega (which is now directed by Mardersteig's son Martino) can be seen in the catalogue *Officina Bodoni Verona,* produced for the exhibition held in the British Museum in 1954; or in the similar catalogue published a decade later for the exhibitions held in the Royal Libraries in The Hague and in Brussels.

15

England between the wars I: the great presses

By 1920 a world war was over, and so was a period of experiment and development in printing techniques, especially in machine composition and process engraving. And by 1920 there was a new generation of typographers who had grown up since Morris's 'little typographical adventure' and who were considerably less under the glamour of the private press movement than had been the case ten or fifteen years earlier. Those interested in book design in Britain had nearly all come around to the views expressed by the Dutch writers Kalf and Simons, who in the 1890s had objected that the slow and archaic Kelmscott methods would never guide them to good work in the everyday production of printed matter. Such views were by no means unknown in England before 1914, of course; the lamentably short-lived journal *The imprint* had been intended primarily to interpret the private press gospel in practical terms for commercial printers. The cutting of the Imprint type, a reformed and regularized version of Caslon design by J. H. Mason and Gerard Meynell which was made generally available for Monotype composition, was a first step to this end. But it took the world war to break down the Kelmscott tradition completely.

Most of the major presses of the private press movement had come to a halt before 1914, and when the war came Eragny was killed, work at Ashendene was suspended and only the Doves Press continued for a while. Other newer promising presses were killed by the outbreak of hostilities; the most promising of which was 'Flying Fame', the publishing title chosen in 1912 by Claud Lovat Fraser, Holbrook Jackson and Ralph Hodgson for a charming and lively series of broadsheet and chapbooks which rapidly won a high reputation.

There were of course to be a few ventures in the private press field between 1914 and 1918, but the times were not propitious for such experiments. One which is of interest is the Mall Press, operated by Emery Walker and Bruce

Rogers, who in 1916 came to London from America to work at it. Only one book was produced; an English translation of Albrecht Dürer's *Of the just shaping of letters*, of which 315 copies on paper and three on vellum were printed for the Grolier Club in 1917. Set in Centaur, the version of Jenson's roman type which Rogers had designed and Robert Wiebking cut two years earlier, the book was to prove rather a labour for Rogers. He professed 'a lack of enthusiasm for the printer's craft *as* a craft, a distaste for printer's ink'; but the Mall Press's one workman having been conscripted into the army Rogers had to make ready and print the book himself. Being a thoroughgoing Yankee he succeeded splendidly, but one such experience was enough for him, and when (at the instigation of Sydney Cockerell, then director of the Fitzwilliam Museum) the Syndics of Cambridge University Press invited him to become the Press's typographical adviser Rogers quickly agreed. A second book was to result from his collaboration with Emery Walker many years afterwards, T. E. Lawrence's translation of the *Odyssey* published in 1932.

The first fruit of what was to be a very much richer harvest than this had come from Francis Meynell in 1915. Cousin of Gerard Meynell of *The imprint* and the Westminster Press, son of Alice and Wilfred Meynell, magazine proprietor, editor, writer, printer and publisher, Francis Meynell had grown up in a literary atmosphere in which the practicalities of printing also figured largely. He started his career at Burns & Oates (where his father was managing director) in 1913, where he was soon joined by Stanley Morison who had earlier abandoned work as a bank clerk to work for Gerard Meynell at *The imprint*. In 1914 Francis had (as a personal venture, distinct from his workaday life) purchased a hand press, which he kept in his dining room. Like Daniel and St. John Hornby before him he negotiated with the Delegates of Oxford University Press for some of the Fell types, which were sold to him with the proviso that the type could be recalled if they felt he was misusing it. In 1915 he issued a prospectus; years later he said he regarded it 'with mixed feelings of shame and admiration at my audacity; for if ever there was a gold-brick prospectus this was one.' This was how it read:

'The Romney Street Press at 67 Romney Street, Westminster, has been set up for the better and unaffected production of Books, & Pamphlets, & single sheets of poetry. The type of the Press (used for this Prospectus) is the finest of the series imported from Holland in about 1660 by Bishop Fell for the Oxford University Press, by whose courtesy it is now used. The editions of the Romney Street Press will be limited to a maximum of fifty copies. The preliminary costs of equipment amount to £40, & Francis Meynell, the Director of the Press, invites subscriptions to cover this amount.

'Subscribers will have first call upon the publications of the Press at cost price up to the amount of their subscriptions.

'The first publications will be seven poems by Alice Meynell, written since the issue of the Collected Poems. There will follow Mary Cary, [sic] the meditations, occasional poems and spiritual diary of the wife of a Cromwellian captain, now first published, from her Ms. Note-book; & Love in Dian's Lap, by Francis Thompson. But the process of production will be but slow. Suggestions for other books, particularly of seventeenth century reference, will be welcome.'

Although three books were announced, in the end only two were produced —*Ten poems* by Alice Meynell in December 1915 (for which Edward Johnston wrote in the initials in each poem) and Mary Carey's *Meditations*, which were printed on Japanese vellum and issued in 1918 (an earlier impression of this, which was printed on hand-made paper in 1917, proved unsatisfactory and was never issued). Despite the persuasiveness of the prospectus, there were no general subscriptions to the Press, and the fifty copies of the two books published were sold only with great difficulty. So, disheartened with this reception and finding the single-handed production of the books irksome, Meynell discontinued his private printing; concentrating his attention on the development of the Pelican Press, an offshoot of the Victoria House Publishing Company, which with the help of George Lansbury he had started in 1916.

Morris's influence still made itself felt at times. The chance sight of the Kelmscott *Chaucer* in Sotheran's window in 1919 persuaded the recently demobilized Oliver Simon to abandon his vague plans for entering the cotton trade or taking up forestry; 'it was plain to me that I *must* become a printer,' he said. By 1922, as a traveller for the Curwen Press, he had become a member of a small informal group of those interested in advancing the cause of good printing. With Bernard Newdigate, Holbrook Jackson, Morison and Meynell he was responsible for forming the Fleuron Society which he had suggested should produce one book every year as a demonstration to collectors and others that books set by machine could be quite as successful aesthetically as the books of the private presses before the war. The Society lasted for two stormy meetings, then collapsed; Newdigate's firm belief in the superiority of the hand press prevented any progress. But good came from the Society nevertheless;

Simon and Morison went on together to publish *The fleuron*, the greatest of all English typographical journals, and Meynell decided to go ahead with publishing books on his own. Soon after the war had ended he had tried without success to persuade publishers to allow the Pelican Press to print fine editions for them; with the collapse of the Fleuron Society he persuaded David Garnett (at that time a partner in the bookselling firm of Birrell and Garnett) and Vera Mendel to join him in making books 'for those among collectors who also use books for reading'. The Nonesuch Press was born.

The propriety of their use of the word 'Press' was called in question by Arnold Bennett and others (for those who attempt to define the term 'private press' Nonesuch remains a stumbling block). It was not a Press in the arts and crafts tradition of Kelmscott or Doves, with all the work being done by hand under the direct personal supervision of the owner. It was not even to make special use of the resources of a single commercial printer, as Ricketts had used the Ballantyne Press for the Vale books, or Robert Bridges had employed Oxford University Press for the *Yattendon hymnal*. Instead, as Meynell wrote in *The Nonesuch century* (1936), its stock in trade was 'the theory that mechanical means could be made to serve fine ends; that the machine in printing was a controllable tool. Therefore we set out to be mobilisers of other people's resources; to be designers, specifiers, rather than manufacturers; architects of books rather than builders.' Accordingly books were printed for Nonesuch by good commercial printers—by the Kynoch Press, by T. & A. Constable, by the two university presses, by Joh. Enschedé en Zonen and others—in order to exploit the various skills and the wide range of excellent typographical material which was becoming available and which no single printing house could possess no matter its size. In this, Nonesuch was doing no more than any commercial publisher might; where it differed from the commercial publishers of the time (apart from doing it far better than they) was in its possession of a small printing plant of its own, on which experimental pages for the Press's books were printed as a part of the process of designing them before the production was finally handed over to a commercial firm. Whole books were composed on the premises in Janson types (of which Nonesuch was then the only English possessor) and on occasion the Press printed them as well—in the delightful volume of Thomas Beedome's *Select poems* (1928) for example.

In such work as this, Nonesuch was adhering strictly to the tradition of Doves or Ashendene, and in the books commissioned from commercial firms the perfectionism of the private press spirit was certainly predominant—for

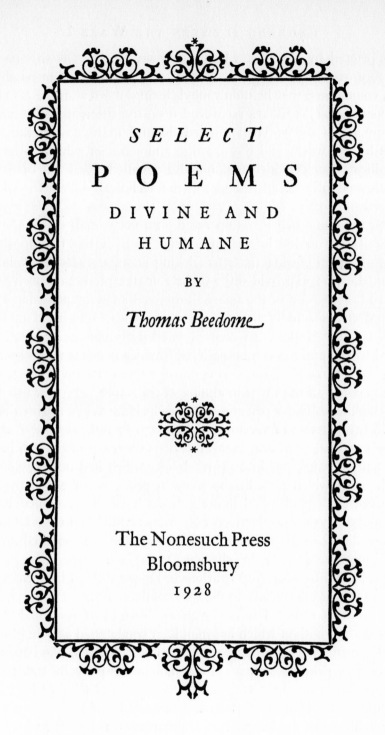

Fig. 37. A Nonesuch title-page, from one of the few books set and printed by the Press itself

one book printed by R. & R. Clark thirty-seven different title-pages were set up before Meynell was satisfied. William Maxwell, the manager of R. & R. Clark, commented that he didn't mind 'losing' money on the text of Nonesuch books because he always recovered it on the title-page! But none of the printers employed by Meynell minded 'losing' in this way; the challenge presented by the work, and the prestige and sense of achievement obtained from producing books which undoubtedly equalled the work of the prewar private presses fully compensated for the technical difficulties which they encountered.

At first the Nonesuch Press operated on a very small scale; Garnett was working full-time in his bookshop and Meynell at the Pelican Press; the routine work, from editing texts to sticking stamps on letters, was done by Vera Mendel, who had provided the Press's small capital. Nonesuch could very easily have become one of the many short-lived amateur publishing ventures which appeared and rapidly disappeared in the 1920s. That it did not do so was due in part to the skill with which Meynell designed the books; in part to sheer hard work (enlivened by occasional 'invoice bees' at which friends were enlisted to write invoices, statements and the like between drinks), but most of all to the policy of the Press in aiming at collectors 'who also use books for reading'. Unlike so many private and quasi-private presses with their seemingly endless repetition of versions of *The song of songs*, *The Rubaiyat*, *Sonnets from the Portuguese*, et cetera, Nonesuch books were books which had a very good reason for being put into print—books which had not previously been published, or of which no editions were in print, or of which the existing editions were inadequate. And though an extraordinary amount of care was lavished on the physical production of Nonesuch editions, no less attention was paid to the editing of the texts. In such books as the collected editions of the works of Congreve (1923), Wycherley (1924) and of the other Restoration dramatists; in Geoffrey Keynes's editions of Donne and of Blake, the Press was to perform a very useful service to the cause of literature.

There were of course failures, such as *The book of Ruth* and Apuleius's *Cupid and Psyche* (both of which Meynell later condemned as being 'toy' books in the bad private press tradition). There were frivolities, like Amanda Ros's *Irene Iddesleigh*, printed with a suitable solemn gravity in 1926; or James Laver's splendid mock eighteenth-century verses in *A stitch in time* and other slim volumes. The Nonesuch Press never took itself too seriously (as the splendid ebullience of the long series of prospectuses shows) and it is evident that the producers of the books had as much pleasure in their work as the readers were later to receive. One instance of this was given by Sir Francis Meynell at an address he delivered at the opening of The Times Bookshop's exhibition of private press books in 1961: a memory of the Rev. Montague Summers, who had edited several of the seventeenth-century dramatists for the Press, arriving with his typescript of Rochester's poems. 'I have discovered some hitherto unknown couplets, which are, regrettably, very indecent,' he announced cheerfully. 'Fortunately in the original text the most opprobrious words are replaced by dashes, but' (very cheerfully) 'I regret infinitely to report that these words almost always come at the end of lines and therefore' (with a joyous chuckle) 'the rhymes unfortunately indicate the missing word!'

Although the Nonesuch Press started in such a humble way, the excellence of its work soon became known, and instead of having to boost sales the partners found themselves in the pleasant position of having to ration orders. In 1925 they moved from their cellar under Birrell and Garnett's shop to new premises in Great James Street, and incorporated the firm legally. Thanks to the quality of their work they were able to continue operations with very little difficulty right through the years of the Depression, when other presses which seemed equally secure died.

It is almost impossible to give any idea of the richness and variety of the Nonesuch books by word or by illustrations. Almost all were different, for it was Meynell's deliberate policy to avoid anything like a house style. 'I did not want people to be able to say at the first sight of our books "Oh yes, that must be a Nonesuch book." I wanted them to say "That's not a bad-looking book" and then to find it was ours.' As a substitute for handling and reading the books themselves *The Nonesuch century*, an account of the first twelve years and hundred books of the Press, is well worth examining. But it remains no more than a substitute.

After Nonesuch, the most important of the private presses which grew up between the wars was the Golden Cockerel Press. In its earliest form (it changed hands and character several times) the Press did not show much promise of adding anything to the art of making books, for its owner, Harold Midgely Taylor, had founded it in 1920 with the object of publishing new books of literary merit by young authors on a co-operative basis (an up-dating of the Essex House ideal, in fact). He equipped a large wooden hut in his garden at Waltham St. Lawrence, Berkshire, with a Wharfedale press (powered by a Ruston-Hornby engine in an outhouse), with a bookbinding stitching machine and with other equipment; and succeeded in persuading Martin Armstrong, A. E. Coppard and a few other young writers that to produce their books as a team (setting, printing and binding their books themselves) would be rewarding. In his autobiography *It's me, oh Lord*, Coppard later recalled how Taylor bicycled twenty-five miles across the Berkshire Downs to his cottage at Headington to ask him to join in the venture, and allow his *Adam and Eve and Pinch Me* to become the Press's first book. It was eventually published on All Fools' Day in 1921. Coppard helped with the production, 'doing some of the printing, folding, pasting, binding and labelling. In the end my eyes were so bedazed by the titlepage that they were blind to the inadequacies of the rest; the type was poor, the paper bad, the leaves fell out, the cover collapsed . . .'

The standards of production soon improved, but (as might have been expected) it was not long before Taylor's assistants began to lose their enthusiasm for the work, and one by one they dropped away, leaving Taylor and his wife to carry on alone. They were determined to carry on, though they had to change their policy to concentrate on producing 'fine editions of books of established worth' (ominous phrase!). A pressman and compositors were engaged, the bookbinding equipment was sold, and a Victoria platen purchased. On this they started to print their editions of the classics in the good old-fashioned way using handmade paper damped before printing. Several of the books produced in this manner during 1923, such as Sir Thomas Browne's *Hydrotaphia*, were pleasant though unexciting books. But at the beginning of 1924 Taylor's health broke down, and he was compelled to dispose of his Press. It was bought by Robert Gibbings, a founder-member of the Society of Wood-Engravers, whose work at that time was still little known. In his hands it was to be transformed into the principal vehicle for the renaissance of wood-engraved book-illustration which took place in the years between the wars.

From the first book produced by Gibbings (an edition of Brantôme's *Lives of gallant ladies*, which had been planned by Taylor) to the last printed at the Cockerel under his direction, only a handful were not to be illustrated with wood-engravings or woodcuts. Many were the work of his own hand, but he also commissioned many of the other wood-engravers of the day to illustrate books for him—such men as Eric Gill, John Nash, David Jones and John Farleigh. At first Caslon type was normally used, and in several of the earlier books from the Press the colour of the type and of the engravings did not harmonise altogether satisfactorily. But Gibbings possessed considerable typographical skill as well as consummate ability as an engraver, and the books produced by the Golden Cockerel Press were in general remarkably good examples of how well type and wood-engraving can be blended together.

For a considerable period Gibbing's policy at the Golden Cockerel paid off handsomely in financial as well as aesthetic terms. An extra platen press (as well as a Columbian, which was used extensively for proofing the engravings) was installed, and in the late twenties two extra pressmen were employed to work on the books. But the Depression hit the Golden Cockerel hard, much harder than it had hit Nonesuch, and although in artistic terms the work the Press did in the early thirties was even better than before—the Cockerel *Four gospels*, printed in 1931, with engravings by Eric Gill and set in a new proprietary typeface which Gill had designed is arguably the finest of all private press books printed between the wars—it did not pay its way. The Press was no rich man's plaything; Gibbings had to make his living from its work. In 1933 he felt compelled to call an end to his book making, and the Press was taken over by Christopher Sandford, Francis Newbery and Owen Rutter. Under their regime the Cockerel took on a new lease of life.

Sandford was not new to fine press work when he took over Golden Cockerel. While still an undergraduate at Cambridge he had come under what he described as the 'fascinating influence' of William Morris, and after some years abroad he joined the Chiswick Press of which he subsequently became a director. In 1930 he started the Boar's Head Press at Manaton in Devon, from which until 1936 he issued a number of books, mainly by contemporary authors and many of them with wood-engravings by his wife Lettice. For the first few of these he set the type himself, but all were printed at the Chiswick Press under his supervision—a reversion to Charles Ricketts's method with the Vale Press books. In 1932, together with Francis Newbery, he succeeded in persuading the Chiswick Press to back a larger publishing enterprise, the Golden Hours Press, which was intended to produce an edition of the works of Christopher Marlowe in nine volumes. The Press died after only three volumes of Marlowe and one other book had appeared. They were very well produced, Eric Ravilious's illustrations for *The Jew of Malta* and Blair Hughes-Stanton's for *Faustus* being particularly good, but they did not sell. (Indeed, even though the unsold copies were remaindered and sold off in a cheaper binding it took a very long time for the stocks to be cleared, and the volumes can still be bought much more cheaply than much inferior private press work of the time.) Whether Newbery and Sandford would have found a way of continuing the Golden Hours Press after 1933 had they not purchased the Golden Cockerel is a matter for conjecture; with an ailing Cockerel to care for it was an obvious impossibility.

Sandford's partners left the active direction of their Press in his hands, and his solution to the economic problems of its survival was the obvious one for a man with his background. The maintenance of their own equipment and skilled labour was abandoned, and an arrangement was made with the Chiswick Press so that they were able to use its plant and men when needed: in other words to the purist the Cockerel became like Nonesuch no more than an imprint. It was a drastic remedy, but it worked, and for the remainder of the 1930s the Golden Cockerel Press continued to produce books finely illustrated with wood-engravings. For some of these the proprietary Golden Cockerel

Fig. 38. Wood-engraving by Eric Gill for the Golden Cockerel *Four Gospels*, 1931

type was used, but not by any means for all; the Press made use of several of the many good faces available for Monotype composition—an indication of Nonesuch influence. To improve the justification of the lines, Monotype-set matter was normally 'put through the stick' by hand afterwards (a practice still followed by several private presses) but the machine had conquered. As Sandford freely admitted it could produce work equal or superior to setting by hand, at considerably less cost.

The third of the triumvirate of private presses to be set up in the early 1920s was not English, but Welsh. In 1919 the great country house of

Gregynog, near Newtown in Montgomeryshire, had been purchased by two wealthy sisters, the Misses Gwendoline and Margaret Davies. Deeply interested in the fine arts, they formed a magnificent collection of paintings, and had dreams of making Gregynog a centre for the encouragement of many crafts: pottery, weaving, furniture design and fine printing. Such a project would need a competent controller; advised by Hugh Blaker the ladies appointed a young artist, R. A. Maynard. He was sent to London to learn as much as possible in a short stay about the various crafts, and in particular printing which he studied under J. H. Mason at the Central School of Arts and Crafts. In July 1922 Maynard took up residence on the Gregynog estate; though the crafts project as a whole came to nothing (it was planned on too grandiose a scale to be easily or quickly practicable) by the end of the year the founders had decided their policy in printing, and Maynard had installed the basic equipment of the Press.

The aims of the Gregynog Press were very much in the great tradition:

1. To introduce and encourage fine printing in Wales.
2. To print certain literature, in both English and Welsh, which relates to Wales and the Welsh, and which has been hitherto unavailable except in rare volumes.
3. To print editions of English classics.
4. To give great attention to decoration and to carry out at the Press itself the whole of the design of woodcut decoration, illustrations and initials.
5. To bind all work at the Press bindery.

It was obviously impossible for Maynard to attempt to carry out this programme single-handed. Through Dr. Thomas Jones, Deputy Secretary to the Cabinet and a good friend to the Misses Davies, and who took a great interest in the work of the Press throughout its life, J. H. Mason was asked for his advice. The most suitable assistant he could suggest was his own son, John Mason, who at that time was bookbinding overseer in a firm at Eton. He joined Maynard in the summer of 1923.

At first Maynard and Mason were concerned principally in printing programmes for the concerts for which Gregynog was to become so well-known to music lovers, but when a Victoria platen had been installed (to supplement the Albion which had been purchased initially) they were able to start on their first book. This had been suggested and was to be edited by Sir Walford Davies, *Poems by George Herbert*. This was followed, at Dr. Thomas

Jones's suggestion, by *Poems by Henry Vaughan* edited by Ernest Rhys (1924). The third book was to be a volume of Welsh poems by John Ceriog Hughes, *Caneuon Ceiriog*, and to make the composition easier for the non-Welsh-speaking printers a young man from Anglesey was appointed to the staff of the Press to learn the trade.

It was a pleasant though somewhat monotonous life for the 'immigrant' staff of the Press, with Mason taking charge of the setting and the binding while Maynard planned the books and engraved the blocks for them. But the increasing tempo of the work made it desirable to have another increase in staff, and half-way through the production of *Caneuon Ceiriog* they were joined by an old friend of Maynard's, Horace Bray. With Maynard he was to be responsible for illustrating most of the books produced before 1930.

The first three books from the Press were printed in Kennerley type, but it was felt that a change was desirable, and that some of the newer typefaces which Monotype was (under Morison's guiding hand) making available would be better. The difficulty was that the Gregynog printers were using hard-surfaced hand- and mould-made papers supplied by Grosvenor Chater from their mills at Holywell in Flintshire, and this called for a harder type-metal than was usual in Monotype casting. After discussions in London Maynard purchased a Monotype caster, with the intention of using a harder metal than usual and putting up with the consequent frequent jamming of the mould. Gregynog never purchased a Monotype keyboard; the caster was used only to supply type for subsequent hand-setting. More staff were engaged: Idris Jones as pressman and from the beginning of 1926 George Fisher as a binder. Originally Fisher was to stay for a year only, but as events turned out he was to take charge of the bindery and stay working at Gregynog until 1945, years after the Press itself had closed.

For the rest of the 1920s the Maynard-Bray partnership flourished, and produced some remarkably attractive books. Among these were *The life of St David* and *The autobiography of Edward, Lord Herbert of Cherbury*. But the first period of Gregynog's work was coming to an end: Mason had left to join the Shakespeare Head Press at Stratford-upon-Avon in the autumn of 1926, and in 1930 Maynard and Bray also left, setting up their own Raven Press at Harrow Weald. This press was intended to carry on where Bray and Maynard had left off at Gregynog, but it was set up at the wrong time to have any chance of success. Though its work was good, like the Golden Hours Press the enterprise had to close after four books had been printed.

Meanwhile back in Montgomeryshire William McCance and Blair

Hughes-Stanton had arrived in 1931 to take charge of Gregynog as controller and designer respectively. It was a useful appointment, for they brought with them their wives Agnes Miller Parker and Gertrude Hermes who were both thoroughly accomplished wood-engravers in their own right.

This second period in the history of the Press was remarkable for the very fine wood-engravings used to illustrate the books. At first the fine lines and the delicacy of tone in Hughes-Stanton's engravings gave the printers considerable trouble; and in such books as *Comus* (1931) the presswork was not completely satisfactory. But in another immigrant Londoner, Herbert Hodgson, the Press acquired a pressman who rose magnificently to the challenge of Hughes-Stanton's work. Hodgson was capable of bringing out the subtlest tones, the finest lines—his make-ready was a real essay in devoted skill—and in such books as *The Revelation of St John the divine* (1932) and *The lamentations of Jeremiah* the skill of both engraver and printer could be seen at its best. But the book which received most attention at the time, and is still perhaps to be regarded as the most successful of all Gregynog books, was *The fables of Esope* (1931) for which Agnes Miller Parker cut many engravings which are delightful studies of wild life.

In 1933 Hughes-Stanton and McCance left the Gregynog Press, and for a short while it had no controller. Fisher in the bindery and the other staff carried on with work already in hand; with the enthusiastic aid of Mrs. Dora Herbert-Jones—the Secretary of the Press, whose knowledge of Welsh was absolutely vital to the various Controllers—they were to manage successfully for the remaining six years of the Press's active life, for the two last Controllers were to work only in a part-time capacity.

In 1934 an Oregonian, Loyd Haberly, a Rhodes Scholar who had settled at Long Crendon in Buckinghamshire to build and set up his Seven Acres Press, was invited to become Controller for a year. (According to Haberly, the Misses Davies were misled by his name and had expected a Welshman!) As it turned out, he was to stay for two years, supervising the production of such books as Xenophon's *Cyropaedia* in Philemon Holland's translation (1936). The principal book to be produced during his regime was an edition of Robert Bridges's *Eros and Psyche*. For this some early pencil drawings by Burne-Jones were prepared for engraving by Professor Catterson-Smith (who many years earlier had worked with Burne-Jones on the illustrations for the Kelmscott *Chaucer*) and then engraved by Haberly and John Beedham. A special proprietary typeface, based on an early model, was designed by Graily Hewitt and Haberly, and Hewitt also designed special initials for the edition.

The book was undeniably handsome, but equally undeniably it was a throw-back: had it appeared forty years earlier it would have been praised highly, but in 1935 even such kindly disposed critics as St. John Hornby could find little to say in its favour. The proprietary type was not used again by Gregynog; a music type which Haberly had also designed regrettably met with the same fate.

In the late summer of 1936 James Wardrop of the Victoria and Albert Museum took over from Haberly, and supervised the production of a further six books. Of these de Joinville's *History of St Louis* was the most successful as it was also the most ambitious, employing the talents of Alfred Fairbank, John Beedham, Reynolds Stone and Berthold Wolpe on the decorations and the maps.

The outbreak of war in 1939 was to signal the end of the Gregynog Press. The books that were already in hand were completed, but by the time the Press closed in 1940 most of the workmen had already been called up. Only the bindery continued; George Fisher had a backlog of fine binding that was to occupy him until 1945, and the equipment was also used to bind up paperbacks to be sent to the forces.

There was some question of reopening the Press after the end of the war, but the difficulties were too great, and the equipment lay almost idle. After the death of Miss Gwendoline Davies in 1951, her sister presented much of the type and equipment to the National Library of Wales at Aberystwyth, though for a few years more the Press at Gregynog continued to print the orders of service and the programmes for the music festivals which were so prominent a feature of its cultural activities.

In the eighteen years of its life the Gregynog Press printed forty-two different books, which more than bear comparison with the work of any other private press. In the design and execution of bindings it was far superior to any, the Doves Press included. Though it was in the arts and crafts tradition, Gregynog was in its conception far closer to some of the aristocratic presses of the eighteenth century. It has been said that there have been only two *real* private presses in the twentieth century: Cranach and Gregynog. Though this is to overstate it, the munificence with which Count Kessler and the Misses Davies endowed the pursuit of the perfect book is altogether without modern parallel. The money 'lost' on the Gregynog Press ran into many thousands of pounds every year: that in these more egalitarian days we shall see another press of this sort in Britain is beyond belief.

16

England between the wars II: backwaters and tributaries

———

Although the First World War was to force a halt in the work of all the major presses engaged in the production of 'fine books', there were a good many private printers of a rather different sort who successfully survived or started in the difficult years between 1914 and 1920.

The earliest of these, and one of the most important, was a press which had been set up in 1902 by Elizabeth and Lily Yeats, the sisters of the poet William Butler Yeats. Started at Dundrum in County Dublin, it was initially part of a larger enterprise which was intended to stimulate Irish industry and to give training and employment to Irish girls by the production of such things as rugs and embroidery. The press was named the Dun Emer Press after the Lady Emer, famous in early Irish history for her embroidery.

The printing and publishing side of the enterprise was under the direction of Miss Elizabeth Yeats, who had studied the craft at the Women's Printing Society in London and had—like so many others—received advice from Emery Walker. Equipped with an Albion Press and Caslon type, and using paper specially made at the near-by Saggert Mills, the Press set to work with a programme of producing new works by modern Irish writers, and of new editions or translations of classical Irish works. This programme was obviously made an easier one to follow through the association of W. B. Yeats with the Press, and a very distinguished list of books by such writers as Lady Gregory, Synge, and Gogarty was to be produced. The printing was sound and workmanlike, but with no pretentions of being 'fine printing'; the merit of the books lay in their content and not the packaging.

In 1908 the Press was moved, and the name changed to the Cuala Press, under which style it continued to produce good work right through the troubled years of the war and the 1920s, and indeed until the late 1940s. As well as its long series of books, the Press produced series of broad-sheets, calendars, greeting-cards and similar small pieces. Jobbing work was not disdained, and a number of publications were printed for private distribution. Some of the most interesting of these were produced for Mrs Dora Herbert-Jones, who persuaded Miss Yeats to print for her some small broad-sheets of Welsh songs in the early 1920s. They were a valiant attempt to promote interest among the Welsh in their own poetry, attractively presented. But they did not arouse much interest among the audience at whom they were aimed, and the difficulties of production were considerable. After a final broad-sheet of a poem opening 'Cymru fach i mi' in which Mrs. Herbert-Jones found to her horror that the Cuala printers had left enough room for a coach-and-four to drive through the space between the initial C and the rest of the word, she abandoned the experiment in disgust.

Another press of at least equal importance in literary terms was to be started in a very different way in 1917—Leonard and Virginia Woolf's Hogarth Press. This was originally intended purely as a hobby: Leonard Woolf was anxious to find a manual occupation which would interest his wife, in an attempt to reduce her intense and exhausting absorption in her writing, which had on previous occasions caused her collapse. During 1916 they had decided that they would learn to print, but attempts to enroll in classes at St. Bride's met with a rebuff—the trade had no welcome for amateurs. It seemed that some other means of relaxation would have to be found; then in March 1917 they found themselves by chance passing the Excelsior Printing Supply Company's shop—that haven for the earlier spare-time printers. They went in and explained their predicament. But there was no need for training or apprenticeships, the shopman said; with the aid of his sixteen-page pamphlet they would soon find themselves to be competent printers . . .

Half an hour later when they left the shop they had purchased a small hand-platen, type and other equipment—in all this, the episode was typical of thousands of the same sort since the introduction of Cowper's Parlour Printing Press three-quarters of a century earlier; where it differed from these was in the growth of the hobby into a distinguished publishing house.

When the press and the other materials were supplied to their home, Hogarth House at Richmond, they installed it in their dining room and started to experiment. The man at the suppliers had been quite right; with the aid of his booklet they were soon able to set the type and print a page, and after a month's practice they felt sufficiently competent to start work on a pamphlet. They decided to produce a paper-covered booklet containing one story by each of them, which they would sell on subscription; if it were a success they could proceed further with the printing and publishing of short works which would be of no interest to the commercial publisher.

Considering the printers' lack of experience, the production of *Two stories*, the first publication of the 'Hogarth Press', was very fair. Some features betrayed their inexperience (the backing-up in particular was poor) but they had gone to a good deal of trouble to make the pamphlet attractive, binding it in a gay Japanese paper—a practice which at that time was very uncommon. This use of unusual and attractive cover papers was to become a feature of the Hogarth Press, for later they imported some brilliant patterned papers from Prague, from Roger Fry's daughter in Paris and from other sources; to some degrees they may have been responsible for starting the fashion there was in the 1920s for such cover papers. They tried to produce their books well, but they were not in the least interested in producing fine books as such; their concern was with the text above all.

The reception given to *Two stories* was excellent; it was published in July 1917 and by the end of the month almost all the edition had been sold. Encouraged by this, the Woolfs went ahead with something more ambitious, Katherine Mansfield's *Prelude*. This was a substantial undertaking; a sixty-eight-page book—too substantial for them to print a page at a time on their hand press, so Leonard Woolf machined it on a larger press belonging to a near-by jobbing printer with whom they had become friendly.

The story of the Hogarth Press from its very modest beginnings to a full-scale publishing house has been told by Leonard Woolf in two volumes of his autobiography, *Beginning again* (1964) and *Downhill all the way* (1967). The success of the first books printed at the Press between 1917 and 1920 was so great that they were unable to cope with the orders which they received for them. (When one considers that they were by the Woolfs, Katherine Mansfield and T. S. Eliot, and that the editions were of less than three hundred copies, it does not today seem so surprising.) They were compelled to fall back on the services of commercial printers to reprint the books, and gradually a steadily increasing number of Hogarth Press books were produced through normal trade channels, although for many years a number of the Press's books continued to be printed on the premises at Hogarth House or later from the Woolfs' new home at 52 Tavistock Square, where the printing press was installed in an old scullery. Here, until well into the 1930s, some of the Hogarth Press books were printed, although the majority of the books appearing on its lists, such as Freud's *Collected works*, or the novels of V. Sackville West, were printed by commercial firms.

Among the many amateurs of fine printing who had considered setting up a private press was T. E. Lawrence. As early as 1906 he and a fellow-undergraduate at Jesus College Oxford, Vyvyan Richards, had discovered a mutual enthusiasm for the work of Kelmscott and its followers. For many years they planned the private press that they would establish together: in the middle of the First World War, for example, Lawrence wrote from Cairo 'Shall we begin by printing Apuleius' *The golden ass*, my present stand-by?' After the war, their press came near to being set up at Pole Hill in Epping Forest; but as Richards was later to write, 'there was much planning about it, but it never came off'. In the end Richards started a press of his own in St. John's Wood, though only one book (of no special typographical merit), Caxton's *Prologues and epilogues* (1927), was to appear from it.

Though so little came directly from Lawrence or Richards, their influence was by no means absent from one of the most interesting and important of the literary private presses; that of Laura Riding and Robert Graves. Both these writers knew of the Woolfs' work at the Hogarth Press: Graves's *The feather bed* had been printed by them in 1923; Laura Riding's *The close chaplet* and *Voltaire* in 1924 and 1927. Graves had known Lawrence at Oxford, and through him had met Richards. Yet the idea of setting up a press of their own did not occur to the two poets until Richards made a friendly visit to their home in St. Peter's Square, Hammersmith. At the time Richards's conversation was full of his own press, and in Laura Riding's words 'His talk about the possibility of doing one's own printing fired thoughts in us of publishing possibilities outside the regular-publisher channels . . . Poems are difficult commodities to market; publishers tend to accept them in the sense of doing a favour. The idea of a press, and publishing one's own poems, seemed to spell freedom; it intrigued us, then excited us . . .'

The press was quickly to develop from an idea into reality. An old Albion press was procured—according to some accounts Richards's own press was transferred from St. John's Wood to Hammersmith, though Laura Riding's recollection is of purchasing a press from a printer's supplier to whom Richards directed them. Richards helped the two collaborators in learning how to handle it. A few lessons were sufficient; Laura Riding and Graves were not interested in producing 'fine books' any more than the Woolfs had been. Laura Riding soon found a name for their undertaking; the idea of ownership, 'of possession of ground of life for making the Good come into words' was in her imagination. Roget yielded 'Seizin'. It seemed right, and they sought no other.

The first book from the Seizin Press ('Seizin One') was a slim demy octavo, Laura Riding's *Love as love, death as death* (1928). Published in 1928, it was laboriously printed on Batchelor hand-made paper from type which had been Monotype-set and put through the stick by hand. Plainly bound in a pleasant linen-canvas, its only decoration was a design on the title-page by Len Lye. He had recently made what is sometimes described as the first abstract film, *Tusalava*, and was to become very closely associated with the Press, designing the very gay bindings which were a feature of the later Seizin books. For 'Seizin Two', Gertrude Stein's *An acquaintance with description* and 'Seizin Three', Graves's *Poems* (both published in 1929), the same methods of production were employed.

Printing at Hammersmith ceased in 1929. For personal reasons (touched on briefly in Graves's *Goodbye to all that*) the two poets wished to leave England and find a new home from which to continue their work, and the printing equipment was put into storage. After spending a while in France with Gertrude Stein (near whom they almost decided to settle) they moved briefly to Germany and from there to Majorca. Finding a village which they liked, they settled in Deyá, and had the press and the other printing equipment shipped out to them from England.

A good deal more printing was to be produced from the Press's new home despite the difficulties of obtaining type and paper. Four more books and a number of slighter pieces were to be printed by hand: Len Lye's *No trouble* (1930), Laura Riding's *Though gently* (1930) and *Laura and Francisca* (1931) and Graves's *To whom else?* (1931). Something of the difficulties that the printers encountered in their work can be seen in these volumes—change in size, change in paper used, italic type that does not always match the roman with which it was used—but the work was by no means bad for two amateurs less interested in the medium than in the message.

In *Laura and Francisca* there is a passage on the work of the Seizin Press:

> How's that? How's anything you know or don't?
> You can't believe . . . on ordinary paper . . .
> Printed by myself, and Robert . . .
> He's human, by every imperfection
> He's made a dogged art of . . .
> Yes, I ink, he pulls, we patch a greyness
> Or clean the thickened letters out . . .

As time went on, Laura Riding's part in the physical production of the hand-printed volumes grew smaller as she concentrated more on the editorial side of the Press's work. The hand press was proving inadequate as a vehicle for the public expression of the Seizin programme, and she negotiated an agreement with Constable (the London publishers) whereby they published books sponsored by Graves and herself. Several books of importance were published under the imprint 'Seizin Press—Constable', including the critical volumes *Epilogue* (1935–7), Laura Riding's *A Trojan ending*, Honor Wyatt's *The heathen* and Graves's *Antigua penny puce*. With the outbreak of the Spanish civil war their use of the hand press in Majorca was brought to an abrupt and forced halt. It was not to be revived; when Laura Riding and Graves parted company in 1939, the life of the Press was over. The printing equipment and the premises were by arrangement put into Graves's exclusive ownership, but the Seizin identity had been extinguished. On his return to Majorca in 1946, Graves sold the printing press, though he applied the Seizin imprint on at least one pamphlet, Jay MacPherson's *Nine poems*, which he had printed commercially in Palma in 1955.

Hogarth and Seizin followed a not uncommon pattern in changing from being purely private presses into commercial (albeit highly individual) publishing concerns. In the Netherlands De Zilverdistel had followed the opposite pattern as van Royen's influence became stronger. But it remained for an Australian press to go full circle, starting with books printed privately on a hand press, then commissioning work from outside commercial printers, and finally reverting to printing its own books once. This was the Fanfrolico Press.

The Press was conceived about 1922 by John T. Kirtley, Jack Lindsay and Percy Stephensen: Kirtley had installed a small hand platen press in his flat in a Sydney suburb on which the three of them were soon printing little items of curiosa, such as *Panurge's codpiece*—it was from this interest in Rabelais that the name of the Press was later derived as a whimsical variant of the 'Fanfrelucke' of *Gargantua and Pantagruel*. They soon progressed to more serious work, the first real book from Kirtley's hand press being Jack Lindsay's *Fauns and ladies*, illustrated with woodcuts by his father Norman Lindsay, Australia's most famous and influential artist. A second book by Jack Lindsay entitled *The passionate neatherd* was printed, but never published because of the faults in its production, and very few copies survive. A third volume was rather more successful and was put on sale: Kenneth Slessor's *Thief of the moon*. There was to be one more substantial production on the hand press in Sydney; Jack Lindsay's translation of the *Lysistrata* of Aristophanes, which was published under the Fanfrolico imprint in 1925. But this was the last; Stephensen had already left to take up a Rhodes Scholarship at Oxford some time earlier, and in 1926 Kirtley and Lindsay also left Sydney for London, a natural centre of gravity for young men with literary ambitions, and where interest in private printing was also very much greater.

The Fanfrolico Press was re-established in Bloomsbury Square, and in December 1926 another edition of the *Lysistrata* was printed. But not by the Press itself, for the printing equipment had been left behind in Sydney, and for a while Fanfrolico followed the Nonesuch pattern in commissioning the work from commercial firms like the Chiswick and Curwen Presses.

Soon after the establishment of the Press in London Kirtley withdrew from the undertaking and returned to Australia. The Press remained under the literary control of Jack Lindsay, while P. R. Stephensen rejoined him and acted as its business manager. An impressive list of books was produced by Fanfrolico, many of them being edited by Lindsay. Some were new editions of the books already printed in Australia, but many others were translations of the classics—Petronius, Propertius, Aristophanes, Theocritus and others. There were in addition a number of editions of English literature which were well worth producing: selections from the works of Robert Eyres Landor (a title later taken over by Eric Partridge's 'Scholartis Press', which was one of the most interesting semi-private publishing imprints of the time), the works of Tourneur and of Beddoes—and there were a few literary oddities, like the reprint of Sir John Harington's *Metamorphosis of Ajax*, or *Loving mad Tom*, a splendid anthology of Bedlamite verses of the sixteenth and seventeenth centuries. In Fanfrolico's deliberate adopting of the mode of the sixteenth-century scholar-printers who themselves edited the texts they published, or in the choice of texts for printing or their typographical presentation, the influence of the Nonesuch Press was very considerable. This can be seen clearly enough from the statement of aims in *Fanfrolicana* (1928) that an attempt was made 'adequately to express the individuality of each book' and that 'in fine book production the question is not merely *how* to print finely, but *what* to print finely'. One difference from Nonesuch was in regard to book illustration, which at Fanfrolico was regarded as 'almost the *sine qua non* of a book with character'; the other real difference was the degree of success with which these high ideals were pursued. There are a few aesthetic failures among Nonesuch books; there are many more among those of the Fanfrolico Press—like the almost unreadable *Antichrist* of Nietzsche, which was set throughout in sixteen-point capitals, or Byron's *Manfred* with its illustrations printed in purple—

and those books which were successful were less completely so. It was probably partly because he was aware of these faults that in 1929 Jack Lindsay turned to printing the Fanfrolico books himself.

Stephensen withdrew from the Press, to set up the Mandrake Press (another of the short-lived quasi-private presses with a few interesting books to its name) and Lindsay, assisted by his brother Philip—who had recently arrived from Australia, and had yet to make his name as a historical novelist—and by Brian Penton, installed a treadle platen in a Hampstead cellar. Here they painfully printed a few more books themselves. They were very much simpler and less ambitious than the commercially printed Fanfrolico books; very much closer to the Kelmscott tradition. Among this last group of its books my own favourite is *A patchwork quilt*, translations of Ausonius by Lindsay, illustrated with vignettes by Edward Bawden; almost as effective was an edition of William Morris's *Guenevere* illustrated with eight of Rossetti's drawings. But despite the success of these volumes the Press was doomed; in 1928 it had started publication of *The London Aphrodite*, a deliberately outrageous and iconoclastic 'little magazine'. Like most little magazines it was a complete financial failure. Only six numbers were planned, and all were published, but they ruined the Press. Although in point of sales Fanfrolico had been second only to Nonesuch, its financial state had never been other than precarious. In 1930 the stock of unsold books was disposed of to Simpkin Marshall for remaindering; an inglorious end for 'fine books', but at least the Press's creditors were paid in full. In its brief life Fanfrolico had published some very interesting books, and the 1920s would have been poorer without its attempts to storm the battlements of the English literary establishment with a new critique.

To those whose interest was in the craft of printing, the Depression was to be less of a stumbling block. The most private and at the same time the most commercial (and certainly the most individual) of these was Hilary Pepler at the St. Dominic's Press. Originally a Quaker, Pepler had in the early years of the century been engaged in social work, running Hampshire House, a working men's club in Hammersmith, for the London County Council. While there he had become close friends with two of his neighbours in Hammersmith Terrace, Eric Gill and Edward Johnston. Emery Walker and Cobden-Sanderson were also near by, and it was almost inevitable that he should become interested in printing. His own emotional involvement in the Arts and Crafts Movement could not have been greater, and after Gill and Johnston had both moved to Ditchling in Sussex he felt that he 'wanted to escape from the town and earn my living in the country . . . Moreover, in my ignorance, I thought any fool could print. And there were books I wanted to print—books about crafts which machinery threatened with extinction. I felt that the Press, which had destroyed the kind of civilisation I loved, should be used to restore it, or at least help in preserving such records of it as came my way'. So in 1916, as a convert to Catholicism, he also moved to Ditchling to set up his press.

The St. Dominic's Press was not a private press in the sense that, say, the Doves had been. Pepler did not establish the Press in order to produce the Book Beautiful. He did not think very much of the more fanciful claims of the private presses: in his fascinating essay on *The hand press* (originally printed by him for the Society of Typographic Arts, Chicago, in 1934, and reprinted by the Ditchling Press in 1952) he quoted from a claim made by the Bremer Presse that the real aim of the book 'should be to act as mediator between the artistic creation of genius and the mind of the reader . . . the printed page should reflect the sound and rhythm of the language and the character and form of the work itself . . .' God help us, he commented; 'it would be an impertinent and grotesque performance because the function of the printer is no more (and no less) than that of the pump which conveys water from the well to the bucket.' He was a *craftsman*, with the craftsman's wholesome contempt for the more absurd fancies of those who would like to be thought artists. As such, he did not consider commercial commissions for books or for jobbing printing beneath him: his first printing, in fact, was a beer bottle label for a Ditchling publican. His press was, then, not a private press at all in the 'art' sense; its privacy consisted in the honest production by hand of books which the printer thought deserved to be printed; books which he printed as well as he was able.

There is, no doubt, a rather alarming air about all this. In rejecting the aesthetic ideals of the presses which he thought pretentious, there was a danger that Pepler's work would be at the other extreme of the Arts and Crafts Movement: a bibliographical equivalent of the terrible hairy tweeds and heavy uncomfortable furniture which an obsession with craft so often produced. In practice his achievement was nothing like that. Perhaps as a result of his close association with Johnston and with Gill (both of whom left their mark on the St. Dominic's Press), Pepler's work from the start had a simple grace which was particularly attractive. Among its earliest publications the Press issued a little periodical called *The game*. It was produced by Johnston, Pepler and Gill, because they had decided 'to print our views about things in general which we regarded, as all men regard games, as of supreme importance'. For the Christmas number in 1916 Johnston wrote out in each copy a full page *Gloria in altissimis Deo*. The price? Half a crown.

Throughout the 1920s Pepler produced a long series of books, posters, rhyme sheets, penny tracts, calendars and the like, which are at once the delight and despair of collectors. Their bibliography is, to say the least of it, confused. One instance will suffice: for the first poster printed by the Press Pepler used a block of a basket of flowers for decoration. This was worked with four inkers— one for the black and one each for the three colours, with the blocks being lifted and the ink dabbed on the flowers between each impression. In this way they were able to achieve four-colour printing with a single impression, but to make the work more interesting, more of a game, they did not stick to the same colours for the same flowers, nor to replacing the flowers always in the same position, but instead made many changes during the course of the printing. The result of such experiments has been that for a good many of the St. Dominic's productions, each copy has an individuality rare indeed among printed books.

The venture was completely successful; by 1934, when so many private presses were dead or dying, it had six men working full-time with as much work to do as they cared to undertake. But in 1937, when the Press attained its majority, there was a change of pace with the installation of a Linotype machine. At about the same time Pepler's own involvement with the day-to-day work of the Press became less, as after G. K. Chesterton's death Pepler had become manager of *G.K.'s weekly* and Secretary of the Distributist League, and was later to become editor of *The weekly review*. The St. Dominic's Press was no longer private in any sense of the word, and in 1940 when it came under new management it was renamed the Ditchling Press; a commercial firm but one producing good work in a way in which Pepler would have approved.

Another press which combined the elements of commercial printing and of privacy, the Walpole Press of Norwich, remains remarkably little known. Mr. Martin Kinder set up his press in 1913, inspired by a visit which he had paid to the Cuala Press while on a tour to Dublin with Nugent Monck, founder of the Norwich Players, who was then producing a play at the Abbey Theatre. Encouraged by Monck he bought an Albion press and some Caslon type, and having taught himself to print he set to work on producing material for Monck's productions with the Norwich Players—playbills, tickets, programmes and the like. One book was also produced, an edition of Monck's *The Interlude of Holly and Ivy*, which had been performed in 1911. After the interruption of the First World War, his printing activity was resumed with the production of similar theatrical ephemera; with the acquisition of a treadle press and an increasing repertoire of types he branched out into jobbing work of good quality, producing concert programmes, wedding services, Christmas cards and similar work for friends and acquaintances in the Norwich area. He was, in fact, considering giving up his work in insurance and devoting himself to a career as a jobbing printer (rather in the way that later Will Carter was to do so successfully) but because of ill health he never took the plunge, and remained always a spare-time printer.

Songs from the Dramatiſts

Thomas Dekker

Norwich
Printed and Publiſhed by Martin Kinder
at the Walpole Preſs, 36 Elm Hill
1931

Fig. 39. A Walpole Press title-page

Some of his personal ephemera produced between the wars has a very real charm; like, for example, the invitations (individually addressed in type) to a fancy-dress party:

> Will you help us celebrate
> This (for us) auspicious date
> By coming here on Satur*dy*
> The 27th of July
> Punctually at half past eight,
> Disguised as beggar, sans-culotte,
> Ragamuffin, tramp, or what
> You like? . . .

But the real interest of the Press lies in the books which it produced. These included an edition of Sir Thomas Browne *On dreams,* and two volumes of 'Songs from the dramatists'; *Thomas Nashe* in 1929 and *Thomas Dekker* in 1931. There were to have been two more volumes in the series, containing the songs of Lyly and of Peele, but the inhibiting effects of the Depression (again!) on the sales of the volumes already published prevented their appearance. Had Kinder's work become well known outside the Norwich area there is no doubt that they would have sold readily, for at three shillings and sixpence each they were remarkably good value. This was no amateur printer battening on the collectors' market to sell his books at high prices; had Kinder done so he would probably have sold his work far more readily, but as it was stocks of the books remained unsold until well into the 1960s.

There were a few more pamphlets published by the Walpole Press between the wars; in 1945 an edition of *The book of Tobit* with gravure reproductions of paintings by old masters, and right up until his death in 1967 Kinder continued with his jobbing printing. He was not a great printer, but he was a good one; his books were not 'fine books', but they are honest workmanlike editions of worthwhile texts, pleasant to handle and to read. It is surprising that collectors of private press work have paid so little attention to his work, for the Walpole Press was a link between the great presses of the Edwardian era and the amateurs of today.

Of the many other private presses which grew up in the hectic atmosphere of the 1920s, few survived the years of the Depression if the sale of the books that they printed was a matter of real importance to their owners. Many of those which died were of little importance, and their demise scarcely a matter for regret. One notable exception was the Beaumont Press, which the bookseller Cyril W. Beaumont had set up in the basement of his Charing Cross Road bookshop in 1917. Inspired by the example of Morris, Pissarro *et al.*, Beaumont's object in learning to print was originally to present the work of

A Ballad
Upon a Wedding

I TELL thee, Dick, where I have been,
  Where I the rarest things have seen;
    O, things without compare!
Such sights again cannot be found
In any place on English ground,
    Be it at wake or fair.

At Charing Cross, hard by the way,
Where we (thou know'st) do sell our hay,
    There is a house with stairs;
And there did I see coming down
Such folk as are not in our town,
    Forty at least, in pairs.

Fig. 40. *A ballad upon a wedding*, printed by the Walpole Press, 1932

contemporary writers in a distinguished form, though later he improved on this general aim by endeavouring to make the physical presentation of each book reflect its literary content. With this object he enlisted the assistance of artists and designers such as Ethelbert White and Paul Nash and throughout

211

the 1920s he produced a charming series of previously unpublished books by such writers as Walter de la Mare, Edmund Blunden and D. H. Lawrence—volumes with a distinct style, a sort of sophisticated naïveté which is very refreshing beside the pompous pretentiousness of some other books of the period. Twenty-six books in all were published, the last in 1931, before economic conditions forced Beaumont to close his press.

Others who tried in the same sort of way to further the production of well-printed editions of modern authors were less successful. John Rodker started the Ovid Press in Hampstead in 1919 intending 'to bring before the public work that was then considered advanced', and produced a few volumes of poetry by Ezra Pound and T. S. Eliot, and a number of volumes of drawings by Wyndham Lewis and Gaudier-Brzeska. But the public response was very cool, and at the end of 1920 Rodker abandoned his private press to continue his missionary activities through more conventional publishing channels.

Another short-lived press which has close affinities with the Seizin Press was that which was operated from La Chapelle-Réanville, Eure, in Normandy, by Nancy Cunard. She had bought a little peasant house there named 'Le Puits Carré' in the spring of 1928, and wanted to try printing for herself. Various friends tried to put her off—Virginia Woolf, who had hand-set her long poem *Parallax* for the Hogarth Press in 1925 pointed out what a messy business it could be, while John Rodker, with memories of his lack of success at the Ovid Press, was most discouraging. But she was not deterred, and when William Bird (whose 'Three Mountains Press' in Paris had been one of the ornaments of expatriate America) offered to sell her his equipment at a bargain price she accepted without hesitation. Bird came down from Paris to supervise the installation of the old Mathieu press, and was instrumental in obtaining for her the assistance of a first-rate printer, Maurice Levy.

The success of the Hours Press (as she named her venture) was never in doubt except at the very beginning, when Nancy Cunard had only vague ideas of producing contemporary poetry—for George Moore offered to send her something 'to start off your press with a good bang', and very soon other friends like Norman Douglas, Arthur Symons and Richard Aldington offered her work of theirs to print. Of the first eight books printed at the Hours Press, six were to be by these authors. (The first, Norman Douglas's *Report on the pumice-stone industry of the Lipari Islands* which he had written as a report for the Foreign Office in 1895, was produced as a present for the author. It must have been an abominably difficult book on which to learn typesetting and printing.) In Moore's *Peronnik the fool*, the first book offered for sale, the work was much better. Caslon type on Rives paper was used, as in most of the later books, though its binding was relatively plain—in later Hours Press books much use was to be made of bindings decorated with photo-montages by Len Lye, Man Ray and others.

One book of remarkable interest was produced in Normandy in 1929, Aragon's *La chasse au Snark*, a *tour de force* of translation (Aragon regarded Lewis Carroll as well within the realm of surrealism), and the only Hours Press book not in English. But in the winter of 1929–30, after many a sixteen-hour day at the press, Nancy Cunard decided to move back to Paris. George Sadoul found her a little shop on the Left Bank, the equipment was brought from Normandy, another press purchased, and the Hours Press resumed work. There was to be much more contemporary poetry produced—by Roy Campbell, by Laura Riding, by Robert Graves and others, including *Whoroscope*, Samuel Beckett's first separately published work. But the management of the Press took up far too much of Nancy Cunard's time—and she wanted to be printing herself, not to employ others to do the work for her. One or two books were farmed out to commercial printers: Ezra Pound's *A draft of XXX cantos* to Bernouard of Paris, and John Rodker's *Collected poems* to the Curwen Press in England. Two works were to be produced at the Hours Press by a temporary manager working without supervision—indeed one of them, Havelock Ellis's *The revaluation of obscenity*, was printed without Miss Cunard's knowledge. There was no pleasure in this for the owner, so at the height of its literary success in 1931 the Press was closed. One of its presses was sold to Guy Lévis-Mano, the other taken back to Réanville. This, and the African sculpture and other possessions which Nancy Cunard had there, was to be destroyed by German and French looters during the war: the remaining stock of books was trodden into the mud and destroyed. In its three years the Hours Press was typographically insignificant (despite its exciting bindings) but in literary terms it was one of the most important of all the private presses.

With so many private and quasi-private presses on the fringe of the literary world, one might have expected them to figure occasionally in contemporary novels. But the fictional private presses of the period between the wars are no more typical of their time than Des Esseintes' had been in *À rebours*—and they are a good deal less interesting. Henry Wimbush's *History of Crome*, written over a period of a quarter of a century, and then occupying four years in the printing, was clearly a delightful book, as the exerpts from the life of Sir Ferdinando Lapith in Huxley's *Crome yellow* show. But one suspects that the printing was only pedestrian; it was a press in the tradition of Sir George

Sitwell rather than that of St. John Hornby. Jasper Shoon's press was a much more ambitious affair, and the idea of having a press in a gothick cellar equipped with clanking chains and gesticulating skeletons would have amused other amateur printers as well as the author of *The castle of Otranto*. But they would have been doubtful about the use of a powered press, and would have wanted to know more about the work of the Shoon Abbey Press beside its complimentary verses before giving their approval—alas, the plot of Michael Innes's *Stop press* does not give it.

Among the private presses which safely survived the Depression, there were some which were more in the tradition of the Victorian parlour printers or of the Daniel Press, than that of Kelmscott and the Arts and Crafts Movement. The earliest of these to be established was the hand press of E. H. Blakeney, who started printing for his own diversion at Ely in 1908. Some ten booklets, mostly of poetry, were printed in small editions before 1918, when the printer (who for some years was Secretary of the Amateur Printers' Association) moved to Winchester to become a master at the College. For a while he ceased printing, but in 1925 he resumed his hobby, and continued to produce respectable and collectable little books from his Press until the early 1950s. Most of these were intended purely for private circulation to friends, though a few copies were occasionally sold for a shilling or two.

The High House Press which was run as a hobby by another schoolmaster, John Masters of Shaftesbury, was a very much more ambitious affair than Blakeney's had been. It was set up, like most of such presses, purely for the pleasure that the owner found in printing texts which interested him. All the work of composition, presswork, and binding was carried out by Masters and his wife, and the many books which they produced show very clearly the mastery they had gained in the craft. They were handsomely produced books, all of considerable literary interest; some reprints of classical works, but other editions of contemporary verse. It was a long-lived press; after his retirement to Westbury-on-Trym Masters continued with his printing until his death in 1943. Other purely amateur presses producing work of a high standard in the 1920s were seldom so long lived; at the Priory Press in Tynemouth Robert King printed a number of books of north-country interest, such as his *Old Tyneside street cries* (1924); at Wembley Hill Richard Stanton-Lambert and his wife produced a few books of some merit, of which their edition of Walafrid Strabo's *Hortulus* (1924) was perhaps the most attractive.

At a much lower standard of technical accomplishment, Giles Dixey's press at Oxford is interesting. From 1919 to 1945 he was a master at the Dragon

School, and started printing at the School with an Adana flatbed press about 1922, producing school programmes, Christmas cards and such pieces as a part of the work of a handicrafts hut under his charge. When he handed over his responsibilities for handicrafts to another master he took his press home and used it for printing verses, producing a little volume every two or three years.

WINTER FACETS

December the second
    The Robin sings
    this dullest day.
    What pleasure wrings
    from him a lay?

Third
    Weak joy to me
    this Monthly Rose
    that tenderly
    and faintly blows.

Fig. 41. From *One hundred facets of winter and spring*, printed by the High House Press, 1931

After his retirement in 1945 his rate of production increased, and little pamphlets still appear occasionally from his press. They are not great printing, nor do they contain great poetry, but they are interesting examples of the work of the most genuine of all private printers; those whose owners would say with Walpole that 'present amusement is all my object', and leave theorizing about the book beautiful strictly alone.

17

Between the wars in the U.S.A.

he period of the First World War was far less of a great divide in the new world than it was in the old. Several presses started work in those years—Dard Hunter's Mountain House Press (which is described more fully in a later chapter) being the most important—while Village and others continued work.

Of the older private presses, the Palmetto Press had the earliest origins, its owner William Lewis Washburn having played with a toy press and published a miniature newspaper while a small boy in Connecticut in the 1870s. The hobby languished, but in 1900 when Washburn had become associated with a newspaper in South Carolina the 'typus fever' again attacked him, and during a long and peripatetic career the Palmetto imprint was to be used on many small and attractive books.

A far more solid programme of work was undertaken by the Rev. Charles C. Bubb at his press which he set up in his Rectory at Fremont, Ohio, in 1908. Most of its work (originally issued under the imprint of the Grace Church Press, but from 1909 onwards as from the Clerk's Press) was connected with the Church, such as his excellent *Eight greater antiphons for Advent*, which he printed complete with the music, black notes on red staves in the good old manner. Most of it was in the form of small pamphlets, produced in small editions. A small hand press operated in spare moments does not readily lend itself to the production of lengthy books, and few amateurs would attempt anything more than booklets, but at least one publication of the Clerk's Press— Thomas Stanley's 1655 translation of *The clouds* of Aristophanes (1916)—ran to well over two hundred pages. The choice of texts to be printed was that of a scholar; as well as the many works of piety Dr. Bubb printed translations of many classical works—Anacreon, Euripides, Ausonius; Renaissance Latin verse; Middle English poems—and also of modern Russian and German work.

At the other extreme from Dr. Bubb's press had been Frank Holme's Bandarlog frivolities right at the beginning of the century. While Holme had still been a newspaper artist in Chicago one of his friends had been a young Detroit journalist named Edwin Hill. Hill had gone through the common boyhood stage of hobby printing before becoming a journalist; but unlike most boys he retained his enthusiasm for the craft and continued to print throughout his life. His earliest work was in the form of small amateur journals which were circulated to like-minded fellow members of the National Amateur Press Association, but he also produced a number of small poetry booklets and one very substantial book. This was an anthology of ten articles on the work of Thoreau which he printed a page at a time between 1900 and 1901. All this was in addition to his long hours as News Editor of *The Detroit Journal*, and it ruined his health. In 1901 he was compelled to abandon journalism and to adopt an outdoor life. After seven years in the Michigan woods he entered the U.S. Reclamation Service, and moved to Mesa in Arizona, and subsequently to a small Mexican-Indian township named Ysleta near El Paso in Texas. He remained there until his retirement many years later, all the time printing occasional pamphlets and broad-sheets. He was particularly active in his hobby from about 1920 onwards, and his years at Ysleta saw the circle of his literary correspondence broaden to include E. V. Lucas, Vincent Starrett, Herbert F. West, Frank Dobie and many others. Hill was no ordinary man; in circumstances which could scarcely have been less propitious he became a Lamb scholar and an authority on Thoreau (many of his more than two hundred pamphlets are devoted to these two authors) and an expert on the bibliography of the American South West. For some years he was President of the Frank Holme Memorial Group in Tucson, and several of his booklets were devoted to the work of his old friend.

In 1945, some years after his retirement, Hill moved to Tempe, Arizona. Before his printing equipment could be moved to its new home the warehouse in which it was stored was destroyed by fire. There are not many men of seventy-eight who would attempt to start again, but Hill did so. Will Washburn presented him with an old Columbian and with other equipment which he had used at the Palmetto Press, and Hill printed another sixteen pamphlets before his death in 1949. He was by no means a great printer, but his work in the best traditions of those amateurs who print mainly for their own pleasure (none of his publications paid for the paper on which they were printed, and he made no attempt to profit from his work) and almost incidentally publish material which is of value to others. His was a very honest private press, far preferable to many more pretentious undertakings which sprang up in the United States, just as they did in England, in the 1920s.

Another newspaper man who had a very long-lived press was Hal Trovillion, owner and editor of *The Herrin News* in the coalmining area of southern Illinois. Inspired in part by the little bibelot editions of Thomas Bird Mosher, and in part by some keepsakes he had received from a paper importer, in 1908 he decided to produce a booklet for circulation to friends at Christmas. The booklet, *Thoughts from R. L. Stevenson*, was by no means a piece of beautiful typography, and no wonder; it was printed 'in between issues of a small weekly paper in a wild booming mining town, with a cursing foreman and a periodically drunken printer who was always getting his long unanchored, grease-spotted necktie mixed in the fountain of dabby black ink'—a far cry indeed from the serenity of the Doves Press.

For many years the only private productions of Trovillion's press were these annual Christmas booklets, in which the standard of printing steadily improved. But as Mr. Trovillion's printing business grew larger, so did his resources for this private printing, and several books of considerable interest were produced 'At the sign of the silver horse'—anthologies of garden lore, and a number of reprints of rare gardening books. The *First garden book*, an edition of Thomas Hyll's *A most brief and pleasant treatyse, teachynge how to dress, sowe and set a garden*, the earliest book on gardening in English, had never been reprinted before the Trovillions issued it in 1938. There was an immediate demand for the book, and it was partly as a result of this demand that in the same year the Trovillion Press first offered its books for sale—they could no longer afford to give copies to all who requested them. The *First garden book* was reissued in a new edition, as were several of their other books for which there was a steady demand. Of these perhaps the most important was *Delightes for ladies*, a reprint of a recipe book by Sir Hugh Plat originally published in 1602.

From 1940 onwards an annual prospectus-retrospectus entitled 'At the sign of the silver horse' gave news of the work of the Press, which ceased only with the death of the owner in the early 1960s. In its last years much play was made in its advertising of its position as 'America's oldest private press' (a position to which it had succeeded on Edwin's Hill's death in 1949) but in fact it had become more of a publishing concern than a private press. Undoubtedly still conducted with little idea of making a profit, for some time it used the normal resources of Mr. Trovillion's newspaper office, the work being done entirely by his employees, though the last two books were produced elsewhere

—one being printed in London by the John Roberts Press, the other being a photolithographic reprint of an earlier edition. Many of the books were printed in objectionably small sizes of newspaper typefaces, and in many of the books there was a want of taste in the binding materials used and in other details of production. These faults, together with a sort of smug cosiness which pervades a good deal of its editorial work, did not prevent the Trovillion Press from having a good deal of success. Herman Schauinger's fulsomely written *Bibliography* of the Press (1943) shows this clearly enough; and in its physical production reveals the lack of distinction all too common in the Press's work. This is a severe judgement on a press whose work gave pleasure to many readers, but I would not recommend any collector to specialize in its work.

A very much more inspired and inspiring press was that of Joseph Ishill. Of Rumanian descent, Ishill was a printer by trade, and originally turned to printing for pleasure while living in Stelton, New Jersey, in 1916. The hobby rapidly grew to be his real life's work. Working in New York City, and with four hours commuting each day, he somehow managed to find the time to print a considerable number of very substantial books, as well as a flood of slighter pieces. Plenty of amateurs have done as much, and the results of their labours have often been abominable. Ishill's work was very different indeed: he was in the good old tradition of American radicalism and the texts which he printed were often of considerable importance—works by Stephan Zweig, Elie Faure, Havelock Ellis, Anne Cobden-Sanderson, Peter Kropotkin and others. But it was not only in the choice of his texts that Ishill was outstanding; typographically it was also exciting—'sufficiently unusual and unusually efficient' as Will Ransom put it. In layout, choice of paper, types, colour of ink and illustrations the Oriole Press (as Ishill named it in 1926) revealed its owner's very individual ability. In some of his smaller pieces there is a charm and delicacy in the conception which is reminiscent of Pissarro's work at the Eragny Press. But he was no mere imitator. Nor did his work depend purely on his layout for its success; his illustrators included Frans Masereel, Louis Moreau and John Buckland-Wright.

All the Oriole Press books were printed on a hand press from hand-set type. Few of them were placed on sale; instead they were distributed free of charge despite the financial hardships that this decision caused Ishill. It was not a decision forced on him by circumstances; by the mid-1930s his work was widely known and admired, and he could have sold it with ease had he not believed it would better support his aims to give his books away.

Probably the most important of his publications, as representing Ishill's own philosophy as well as his typography, are the two volumes of *Free vistas: an anthology of life and letters* which he published in 1933 and 1937. But his later books, like the *Collected works* of his wife Rose Freeman-Ishill (ten pamphlets, each of twenty to fifty pages, enclosed in a slipcase) which he published in 1962, show his consistency and his application equally well. At the time of his death in the spring of 1966 he was at work on *A calendar for Dinah* by Marney Pomeroy, and the book was completed by another New Jersey amateur, Ralph Babcock. With the passing of the Oriole Press went one of the finest of all amateur printers, which in the modesty and probity of its work is unlikely to be equalled.

Another private press which flourished in the early 1920s was that operated by the scholar and librarian George Parker Winship, working 'At the sign of the George'. From the 1890s onwards Winship had from time to time produced small limited editions of books of historical, literary or bibliographical interest; doing this in the belief (so he said) that since his professional life was devoted to removing rare books from the market it was his duty to replace them by others 'which might not be just as good, but which might supply future collectors with something to talk about'. In this he certainly succeeded, and many of his private publications—more than a few printed for him by Updike at the Merrymount Press—have become very much sought after. It was not until 1920, however, that Winship turned printer himself. A friend had given his young son a hand press and some type (with the result that when the son went to school, he had never heard of 'capital letters' but knew all about 'upper case') and with this press Winship produced some pieces to demonstrate deceptive cataloguing and the dangers inherent in manufactured rarities to the class he was teaching at Harvard. Several pieces of a sort to appeal to collectors were produced, the largest being Robert Louis Stevenson's *Confessions of a unionist* which had not previously been published. Indeed, in order to test his own mastery of the tricks of the trade, Winship issued two versions of this, one on handmade paper at $10, and another very much smaller impression on ordinary paper which he offered at $1.50 'for libraries . . . of no collector's value'. The ten dollar issue sold very well; of the latter only two or three copies were sold . . .

Though a few pieces were printed on the premises it was not Winship's usual practice. His children were so much better at distributing the ink on their clothes than on the formes of type that he decided it was wiser to limit their work to composition; the presswork was normally farmed out to a commercial printer in Cambridge.

Winship's press was deliberately light hearted in its approach to books for collectors and the mystique of Fine Printing. There were several other private presses in the United States in the 1920s which had a similarly light-hearted approach, and a disregard for whether their work sold or not. Some of these ventures were busmen's holidays; amateur printing by professional printers or typographers. Carl Purington Rollins's printing at 'The sign of the Chorobates', L. A. Braverman's Fleuron Press in Cincinnati, and the Holiday Press (a private press within the works of the giant Lakeside Press of R. R. Donnelley & Sons, which was set up 'to promote more virile and original expression of design and craftsmanship in American printing') were examples of the zest for their craft which more than a few printers retained after their day's work was done. Some of these amateur affairs were very amusing in their irreverence, like Earl H. Emmons's long-lived Maverick Press, which published such pieces as *The saga of BRnacle BRuce the sailor* and the *Ballad of Mae West's bust*, many of them with very skilfully executed type pictures.

Probably the finest of these presses was Arthur K. Rushmore's Golden Hind Press, originally set up in 1927 as an aid in producing experimental layouts for books published by Harper & Brothers, where Mr. Rushmore was in charge of production. This is by no means an uncommon practice; even today when Letraset and other modern aids have made it easier to produce life-like mock-ups of pages plenty of typographers still turn occasionally to a small hand press for such work. But in Rushmore's case the pleasure of printing took over and turned the Golden Hind into far more than an experimental proofing press. Early in its career a chance came to print a definitive edition of a well-known poet's works. It was to be a massive undertaking; seven folio volumes printed on handmade paper, with no expense spared to make it right. Type was ordered from Enschedé in Holland, some trial pages were set and printed, and then the project fell through—perhaps fortunately, since so huge a task would have weighed heavily indeed on part-time printers. But the type was to prove useful on many occasions, for the Golden Hind Press composed (although it did not itself print) many of the volumes of poetry of Edna St. Vincent Millay which were published by Harper. Though private, the Rushmores did accept commissions if the books concerned were books they wanted to produce, and if they were allowed to take whatever time they found necessary to do the work properly. But although their printing was always interesting, it is those which they published themselves which have most appeal. Some of these were placed on sale, although the majority were given away.

One of the most intriguing of these was a book which they produced for presentation to friends at Christmas 1940. In that year there was a rash of exhibitions, lectures, pamphlets and articles about Gutenberg to celebrate the five hundredth anniversary of printing. Rushmore was something of a sceptic about this, so as his own contribution to the celebrations he 'discovered' in a Mainz garret the private diary of Gutenberg's wife, his quotations from which established conclusively that the real credit for the invention of printing belonged to her. *The Mainz diary: new light on the invention of printing* was published with reproductions of the bindings and of a page of the manuscript of the diary. There were plenty of people in the joke; the librarian who had supplied suitable bindings, Otto Fuhrmann who had translated the text *into* German and written out the page of manuscript, W. A. Dwiggins who, as Dr. Herman Püterschein, wrote the Foreword. But when the two hundred copies were sent out letters began to pour in which showed that it was being taken at face value. Rushmore had a difficult time for a while, though his comment that his story had as much truth in it as most of the stuff he had been forced to listen to during the year was not unjustified.

After his retirement in 1950 Rushmore was able to devote himself entirely to the Press ('Being in business always was a nuisance') and by 1955, when work ceased, the Golden Hind Press had produced nearly two hundred books and pamphlets, many of which had been included in the 'Fifty best books of the year' shows. On the lighter side, the Press had produced a lot of interesting ephemera (including some fine nature prints made in the 1940s) and the Rushmore children and grandchildren had enjoyed many hours of playing with type.

Another even longer-lived printer's press was the Stratford Press of Elmer F. Gleason. On a very much humbler scale than the Golden Hind, it had its origins in the demise of Gleason's commercial printing firm of the same name in Worcester, Mass. in 1913. For a few years he printed only amateur journals and ephemera; but from 1922 (when it was re-established in Cincinnati) until the mid-1960s Gleason produced a considerable number of books, of which the most important was probably his *The Rowfant Club: a history*, published in 1955. Without the panache of the Rushmores, the Stratford Press was nevertheless an excellent example of the sound work of which the amateur is capable.

Just as in the years after William Morris's typographical adventure it was the commercial printers in America who really comprehended his purpose and were to follow his teaching, so in the 1920s the production of 'fine books' was to be dominated by the commercially run presses. As reference to Will

Ransom's *Private presses and their books* shows very clearly, far better and more substantial work was being done by many commercial undertakings—firms like Pynson Printers, W. E. Rudge or the Grabhorn brothers—than was being produced by any amateur. More than a few of these undertakings were very close indeed to the private press in spirit and in practice: the Grabhorns in particular, and others like Hawthorn House, the Peter Pauper Press or the Georgian Press were certainly hardly less private than Nonesuch. But there was also a host of other quasi-private presses and publishing imprints which sprang up in the boom in book collecting in the late 1920s about which little is worth saying. With the slump, the bubble burst; the pity is that several of the honest workmanlike enterprises were dragged down with these imitators.

The American private and semi-private presses in Paris were a microcosm (if an unusually literary one) of the whole fine book production scene. Among the 'pure' private presses was William Bird's Three Mountains Press. Bird had been told by another expatriate American writer in Paris of a hand press which was going very cheaply; he purchased it, installed it in a diminutive shop in the Ile St. Louis and used it to print small editions of work by Ezra Pound, Hemingway, Ford Madox Ford and others, all being printed by Bird himself. So small were his premises, in fact, that Sylvia Beach has recorded that when she went to call on him they had to converse on the pavement outside; there was no room for more than one in the printing office. When Bird eventually lost interest in his press, the equipment was sold to Nancy Cunard who used it at her Hours Press in Normandy.

Bird was a partner with Robert McAlmon in Contact Editions, a publishing imprint used on small editions of *avant-garde* works by James Joyce, William Carlos Williams, Hemingway and other writers. These were printed commercially, but had much of the spirit of private presses about them. 'Contact Editions', the partners wrote, 'are not concerned with what the "public" wants. There are commercial publishers who *know* the public and its taste. If books seem to us to have something of individuality, intelligence, talent, a live sense of literature, and a quality which has the odour and timbre of authenticity, we publish them.'

Other expatriate printers were less single minded in their devotion to literature, and wanted to make fine books. At the Black Sun Press which they set up in 1927, Harry and Caresse Crosby produced some fine volumes with the help of a master printer, Roger Lescaret. Their books included Archibald MacLeish's *Einstein* and Joyce's *Tales told of Shem and Shaun* as well as some of the more usual stand-bys of the printers of Fine Books: Poe, Oscar Wilde,

Sterne. After Harry Crosby's death in 1929 his widow carried on the Press, but it became far less private and more of a publishing imprint. At 'Harrison of Paris' Monroe Wheeler, financed by Barbara Harrison, designed a series of thirteen books which were, in the Nonesuch manner, printed elsewhere by such firms as Enschedé—many of them the usual range of classics of which there were already more than enough satisfactory editions (Aesop, Merimée's *Carmen*, Shakespeare's *Sonnets*) but with a sprinkling of young contemporary authors, and a splendid display of fireworks in their *Typographical commonplace book* (1932). Harrison of Paris was in fact a very good press of the sort producing de luxe editions, but the 1930s did not provide a place for such presses as the 1920s had done.

Only in California, it seemed, was it possible for excellent work in the private press tradition to continue, even to flourish. California is the only one of the states in the union to have developed a strong regional character in its printing. Perhaps because of its relative lack of the large printing houses which dominate the trade in other parts of the country, perhaps because of its distance from the traditional publishing centres of Boston and New York, or perhaps because of the presence of wealthy patrons and societies and bookshops who commission local work—or probably as a result of all these factors, California has proved an ideal locale for many small and highly individual presses working in the private press tradition.

The earliest of these was John Henry Nash, who, starting in 1916, produced many books of merit (if rather heavily influenced by William Morris) for the Book Club of California, for William Andrews Clark, and for other clients as well as many produced on his own account. But infinitely more attractive and original has been the work of the Grabhorns. Born in Indiana, the two brothers Edwin and Robert set up their press in San Francisco in 1919; two years later they started on book work with Emma Frances Dawson's *A gracious visitation*, which was commissioned by the Book Club of California. Their lively and virile work, in the best traditions of the private press movement (and very far removed from the pseudo-presses with their cult of the deckle-edge et cetera), quickly earned them a high reputation. Though, like every other printer, they were hit badly by the Depression they weathered it successfully, and have continued ever since to produce books of the highest quality. Many Grabhorn books have been produced on commission, but a good many were purely private publications. In addition, Jane Grabhorn, wife of Robert, has produced some splendid pieces from her Jumbo Press and Colt Press, and some of the later private printers—Adrian Wilson, Sherwood

Grover, Jack W. Stauffacher—have received more than a little inspiration and encouragement from their association with the Grabhorns. *Life & hard times, or Sherwood Grover's twenty-five years with the Grabhorn Press*, produced for the Roxburghe and Zamorano Clubs in 1968, is an excellent brief account of their working methods.

Fine printing in the Kelmscott-Doves tradition was not to flourish only in the San Francisco Bay area. In Los Angeles Saul and Lillian Marks's Plantin Press, established in 1931, produces some of the best and most classical printing in the United States. The firm has deliberately been kept small in order to retain personal control of quality, and work of a very high standard indeed has been printed for such clients as the Huntington Library and Dawson's Book Shop. Another equally fine, though more prolific and bolder undertaking, is the Ward Ritchie Press. While Ward Ritchie was reading law without much enthusiasm at college, he came across a copy of T. J. Cobden-Sanderson's *Journals*, and was filled with enthusiasm for printing. He went to San Francisco to ask advice of the Grabhorns and of Nash, and in 1928 entered a trade school in order to learn the rudiments of the craft. There followed a period in which he worked during the day in Vroman's bookstore in Pasadena, and spent the evenings with Lawrence Clark Powell (later to become Librarian of the University of California, Los Angeles) printing in the Abbey of San Encino. They produced a good number of small pamphlets of poetry by such writers as Archibald MacLeish and Robinson Jeffers, which they gave away to any friends who seemed interested. In 1930 Ritchie took himself to Paris to work in the atelier of Francois-Louis Schmied, who had written in *The fleuron* on the books of the future. While in Paris Ritchie printed a small edition of Jeffer's *Apology for bad dreams*, and after his return to California in the following year continued with some other privately printed pieces. But in 1932, when the Ward Ritchie Press really started, the emphasis moved steadily towards more commissioned work. From 1935 onwards—especially when Gregg Anderson (who had previously operated the Grey Bow Press with Roland Baughman) joined up with him—the Press grew apace, producing some very powerful typographic work for the Huntington Library, the Limited Editions Club and other outside publishers. But like the Grabhorn Press the Ward Ritchie Press continued to publish many books in its own right; some of these, like *XV poems for the heath broom* by 'Peter Lum Quince' (i.e. Ritchie himself), of which fifty copies were printed in 1934, were without doubt private press work. During the difficult years of the Second World War the Press contracted; with Ritchie working for the Douglas Aircraft Company and Gregg Anderson in the army (he was killed in Normandy in 1944) it was continued by Joe Simon, brother of Lillian Marks of the Plantin Press. After the war, under the style of Anderson Ritchie and Simon the Press has grown very considerably, adding lithographic and bindery sections. The survey of its work, *The Ward Ritchie Press and Anderson Ritchie & Simon*, published in 1961, gives an excellent picture of the vigour of good Californian printing, too little of which finds its way to England.

In the completely private field much of the most interesting printing of the 1930s was also produced in California. Wilder Bentley, who had worked for three years with Porter Garnett at the Laboratory Press at Carnegie Institute of Technology in Pittsburgh, printed a range of handsome pamphlets and books (some commissioned by the Book Club of California, again) on his hand press in Berkeley. Another was Thomas Perry Stricker, a self-taught printer of Los Angeles who between 1930 and 1940 produced some interesting books with meticulous craftsmanship. Some of his contributions to the Typophiles keepsakes are particularly successful.

It was not in California, however, but on the eastern seaboard that the greatest of all private presses of the 1930s was to be established: the Overbrook Press of Stamford, Connecticut. In the scale of its work, and in its record of many volumes given away, and few sold, it is not unlike Strawberry Hill; in its quest for technical excellence regardless of cost the work of Count Kessler at the Cranach Press is a truer parallel.

Frank Altschul, its wealthy owner, had been tempted by printing as a child. He has recorded how he was given a press one Christmas, but that it did not remain in his possession for long: his mother finding smears of ink all over the house it was soon confiscated. After his marriage in 1913 Altschul set up a small press in his New York apartment, printing a few pieces of ephemera on it until the demands of a growing family requisitioned his printing room. Once more his interest in printing had to be suppressed, and it was not until 1934 that it was revived in practical form. About that time August Heckscher who had been running the Ashlar Press as a hobby decided to bring its activities to an end. (Heckscher, too, was to find the love of printing too much to resist; small pieces from his Uphill Press still appear occasionally.) Margaret B. Evans, who had been the guiding spirit of the Ashlar Press, approached Altschul to find out whether he would be interested in continuing the venture. He responded enthusiastically: some outbuildings at his home Overbrook Farm in Stamford were adapted, a second-hand Colt's Armory press and other necessary equipment installed, and Miss Evans engaged to act as designer and compositor. The pressman was John MacNamara. Altschul was a good deal more successful in the staff he engaged than many owners of private presses: Miss Evans remained at the Press until 1944, when John Logan succeeded her as designer; MacNamara continued as pressman until his early death in 1955, after which the printing was done by Frederick Warns.

The lavish scale on which the Overbrook Press was set up was fully equalled by the ambitious books which it has produced. But not only books; during the more than thirty years that the Overbrook Press has been active it has printed a considerable number of ephemeral pieces—awards, certificates, programmes and the like—for many organizations in which Mr. Altschul is interested; bodies like the English-Speaking Union, the Woodrow Wilson Foundation, the Committee for the Marshall Plan and the American Institute of Graphic Arts. Many of its pamphlets and smaller books have a seriousness of purpose not frequently encountered in private press work, and an excellence of typography and presentation not often to be seen in political or social publications. Such productions as the *Adverse report of the [Senate] Committee on the Judiciary on a Bill to reorganise the judicial branch of the government* (1937) or Senator Fulbright's *Towards a more creative foreign policy* (1959) are not the sort in which one would expect to find much typographical merit, yet the Overbrook Press's care and success in the printing of works of this sort is far better than that of the majority of private presses working in far easier fields. On the many occasions that Overbrook itself has produced books in the more conventional areas for a private press, its work has been of a quality which places it in the very highest class of those concerned with the art of the book. Many artists have been commissioned to work for the Press: Valenti Angelo, Anna Simons, Bruce Rogers, W. A. Dwiggins, Rudolph Ruzicka and others produced decorations for many books. Of the early work of the Press the most ambitious book was the edition of Robert Louis Stevenson's *An inland voyage* published in 1938. For this the French artist Jean Hugo was engaged to follow Stevenson's route along the canals of France and the Low Countries, the gouaches he produced being printed in Paris by the firm of Jean Saudé, using the pochoir process, while the text was printed at Overbrook.

One area of book production in which the Overbrook Press published some outstandingly well-designed books during the 1940s was that of books on chess. As a devotee of the two-move chess problem, Altschul had noticed how poorly produced were most of the books on the subject. Starting with *A century of two-movers* (1941) the Press produced a series of half a dozen books of chess problems which demonstrated superbly how attractively such work could be presented, using the ordinary chess type in conjunction with good type and superlative presswork.

In these volumes, in the political pamphlets and in the 'fine books' the design and the choice of types (mainly hand-set Caslon, Centaur and Lutetia, though machine-setting in such faces as Electra, Bembo and Janson has also been used) without exception produced books which one feels impelled to read. Even the largest and most sumptuous of Overbrook volumes are books designed for reading; one never has the impression that they are museum pieces to be looked at and admired but not read.

Without doubt much of the credit for this must go to Margaret Adams, who masterminded the production of most of them. But beside hers the name with which some of the best of the Overbrook books are most closely associated is that of the artist T. M. Cleland. Starting with Richard Aldington's *A dream in the Luxembourg* (1935) Cleland later illustrated Sterne's *Sentimental journey* (1936) and some minor pieces for the press. In the 1950s he was responsible for the production of the Press's most ambitious book, Prévost's *Manon Lescaut*. Published in 1958, the volume had been six years in the making. The many illustrations were produced by the artist using the silk-screen process, himself printing every sheet (and many of the illustrations called for eight or ten different workings) before returning them to the Press for the text to be printed in conformity with a layout he had previously designed. The expense of the production was enormous, but the delicacy of colouring could not have been achieved by any commercially viable process. As an example of the luxurious book at its most magnificent, at its furthest remove from commercial printing, the Overbrook *Manon Lescaut* is unequalled among modern private press books, and has few peers among the books of earlier presses.

18

World War Two and the aftermath in Britain

———

In the years after the Depression had killed most of the presses catering for the luxury market in England, few private presses of importance to anyone except their owners were set up. Nonesuch and Golden Cockerel continued, but there were few others. One exception to the general rule was the Perpetua Press in Bristol where two young men, David Bland and Vivian Ridler, had started experimenting with an Adana. This was soon replaced by an automatic platen, to which a cylinder press of the Miehle sort was later added—for this was not merely a hobby; after Bland finished at University in 1933 they did a good deal of jobbing work operating from the basement in Bland's house. They were not only jobbing printers, however, but also produced a few very interesting books in the mid-1930s: *Old nursery rhymes*, with coloured linocuts by Biddy Darlow was selected as one of the 'Fifty books of the year' in 1935, and in 1936 they produced *The little chimney sweep*, a fascinating book with charming silhouettes by Lotte Reiniger. In 1937, however, both Bland and Ridler left Bristol; Bland to join Faber and Faber, Ridler to go to Oxford University Press (where he is now Printer to the University). They had nobody to operate the Press in their absence, and though they still used it occasionally on visits to Bristol little more work of substance was produced, and at the beginning of the war the plant was sold.

Another private press set up in the mid-1930s was Viscount Carlow's Corvinus Press. Named for Matthias Corvinus, the bibliophile king of Hungary, the Press was to produce a series of small books which are among the handsomest of the period. Distinctly experimental in character, the Press used many different typefaces—from the elegance of Centaur and Arrighi to Graily Hewitt's unhappy calligraphic type Treyford—and many different papers in the books which were all issued in very small editions. The bindings were particularly well done, quarter leather with cloth boards being used very

229

successfully in such books as Walter de la Mare's *Poems* (1937) or *The Rhyme of the ancient mariner* (1944). One of the last books from the Press was Norman Douglas's *Summer islands*. Printed in an edition of forty-five copies in 1942, because of delays in the binding the book was still not issued when Lord Carlow was killed in a plane crash in 1944, while on the way to take up a diplomatic mission in Yugoslavia. Perhaps because much of the Press's best work was produced during the early war years, and it did not survive to continue when more attention could again be paid to such matters, the work of the Corvinus Press has never received the attention it merits.

Almost the only private press to continue working right through the war years was the Golden Cockerel. That the Cockerel should have been able to survive the bombing of its premises, that it should have been able to continue operations throughout the blitz, with its owners both away on active service, seems remarkable; but it was defiance, of a determination to continue as usual despite the difficulties, not unlike the spirit which drove the Dutch in the clandestine production of finely printed books. The difficulties were very considerable indeed, but perhaps less so than for a press working at a less exalted level. At a price the pure rag papers of the sort needed for printing the engravings that were a feature of Golden Cockerel books could be obtained; at a price good leather for binding, and real gold for blocking, were also available in very small quantities—quantities just sufficient for the Cockerel's limited editions.

Undoubtedly the conditions of war did adversely affect the quality of production. Christopher Sandford recorded that some details of design in the first volume of Napoleon's *Memoirs* (1945) were poor because the printers at the Chiswick Press misinterpreted instructions he sent them while On His Majesty's Service, and in more than a few cases—in the second bibliography of the Press's books, *Pertelote* (1943) or in *Together and alone* (1945) the presswork on the engravings was far poorer than in earlier work from the Press. Nevertheless the Press survived these difficulties; it survived the death of one partner, Owen Rutter, in 1944; Christopher Sandford, who had been invalided out of the army, carried on alone. During his convalescence he reconsidered his work as a book-designer, and inspired by the work of Meynell produced a number of books which were considerably more experimental than his earlier work.

The work of the Golden Cockerel Press during the late 1930s and the 1940s has not received nearly so much praise as its earlier publications. In part this was because they were carrying on Gibbings's policy of publishing books finely illustrated with wood-engravings, which was not novel any longer (less newsworthy); in part it was because in the war years there was not a public with leisure to discuss and admire the latest Cockerels—any more than the volumes produced by the Corvinus Press received the attention they deserved. And yet many of the Golden Cockerel books produced during this period were as fine as anything the Press ever published, and many of the texts had a very genuine importance. *The log of the Bounty* (1937), *The voyage of the Challenger* (1938)—which had the author's coloured sketches copied by hand in each copy—and other volumes like *A voyage round the world with Captain James Cook* (1944) published in the Press's 'Sea Series'; *The travels and sufferings of Father Jean de Brebeuf* (1938) or *The first crusade* (1945)—these were all splendid books.

In the austere years of the postwar world Sandford carried on producing books in his old fashion. Some of these, like Keats's *Endymion* (1947), which is perhaps the finest of all the books illustrated by John Buckland-Wright, or John Barclay's *Euphormio's Satyricon* (1954), were fine essays in the traditional Cockerel manner. During the 1950s some attractive books less obviously Cockerels were also produced; such books as *The Ephesian story* by Xenophon of Ephesus (1957) with collotypes of linoleum paintings by Eric Fraser, or Shelley's undergraduate extravaganza *Zastrozzi* (1955), for which Cecil Keeling provided some splendidly Gothick wood-engravings. There were also a few late essays in the grand manner, like the folio *Songs and sonnets of John Dryden*, the last book to be set in the Golden Cockerel type, with hideous illustrations by 'Lavinia Blythe'. But the market for expensive books of this sort had been contracting for years—in the 1940s Sandford had said that 'half a dozen such books was as much as the market could absorb', and by the late 1950s the market had shrunk too far for Sandford to feel it was worth continuing. In 1959 he sold the Press to Thomas Yoseloff, the New York publisher, and although under the new ownership three books already in production were completed, no new work was undertaken. After nearly forty years, and the production of some two hundred books containing among them some of the best wood-engraving of the century, the Golden Cockerel ceased crowing.

Golden Cockerel was not the only private press to attempt work in the grand manner in the postwar years. In 1945 Lord Kemsley took over the plant of the Corvinus Press with the aim of producing fine books of literary merit (how remote it all sounds today). The Dropmore Press, as it was named, was put under the direction of Edward Shanks. At first it promised highly, printing such books as Sir George Sitwell's *On the making of gardens* and *The Holkham Bible picture book*. But its poorer work was very weak indeed;

in such books as the selections from Landor published as *The sculptured garland* or in De Quincey's *The revolt of the tartars* there is all the pretentiousness of fine printing at its worst allied to a reactionary or at the least unadventurous view of 'literary merit'.

Dropmore was not Lord Kemsley's only venture in the private press field; in addition he controlled the Queen Anne Press, which was under the artistic direction of Robert Harling. It promised rather better than Dropmore, but neither survived beyond the middle of the 1950s. Had these presses been at work a quarter of a century earlier, their work would perhaps have been more sympathetically received, although the inferiority of much of their presswork to the earlier presses would have received unfavourable comment. The fault for this presumably lay with the owner; neither of the two artistic directors could be accused of not knowing anything of Nonesuch. But there was little sign of Nonesuch influence in the books, and in the egalitarian society of post-war Britain they were simply an anachronism, and a second-rate anachronism at that.

Other private printers who attempted to carry on in the relatively care-free way of the prewar private presses also found themselves in difficulties. One which represents their beautiful ineffectuality in an exaggerated degree was the Latin Press of Guido Morris. Like Count Potocki Morris was (and is) for private press enthusiasts a character about whom myths have grown to an astonishing degree: a Che Guevara of the amateur printer.

The origins of Morris's press were in the best tradition. While working as a laboratory assistant to Solly Zuckerman in 1934–5, he suddenly became attracted by the idea of printing. With encouragement from Beatrice Warde he started to experiment with type, and in 1935 persuaded the authorities at Bristol Zoo, where he was then working, to allow him leave to produce a magazine, *The Bristol Zoo broadsheet*. This was printed with considerable difficulty in a cottage at Langford. Before the four numbers of the magazine had all been printed, Morris had got to know several important figures in the printing world—John Johnson, Eric Gill, St. John Hornby and others—and decided to abandon a scientific career for what seemed the more congenial field of printing.

His intention was to work mainly as a jobbing printer, but despite work fed him by Beatrice Warde and other friends he was defeated 'because there was time, and no money to combat time'. In 1937 he left Langford, set up his press again in a studio off the Fulham Road in London, and printed a volume of translations of medieval Greek and Latin hymns which was seen through the press by Helen Waddell, a poem sequence by Nigel Heseltine, some catalogues for R. E. A. Wilson and other jobbing work. But London did not suit him, and like some of the less (financially) successful fifteenth-century printers he wandered, setting up his press for a while back in the Mendips, in Oxford, in London again, in Northampton—until in 1940 he joined the army as a private in the RAMC. After five years which seemed 'as though I spent most of my army days scrubbing floors which had to be rescrubbed the next day, and most of my nights compiling a Latin dictionary which, from its sheer size, is unlikely ever to be finished, and is certain never to be published' he was demobilized. In May 1945 he set up his Latin Press once more in London. But to start a business from scratch with no capital, even for a man of Morris's determination, proved impossible in London, and in the following year he moved his press to its final home in St. Ives. Here he was to produce a good deal of ephemera—letterheads, exhibition catalogues, wedding services and similar things—and a number of small books, such as a bibliography for Sir Gavin de Beer, or the 'Crescendo Series' of poetry; most of it extremely well printed from Bembo types. Some larger books were also produced for commercial publishers—translations from Sappho published by the Staples Press; *Letters of Fr Rolfe Baron Corvo to Grant Richards* for the bookseller George Sims; *Treasures of a London Temple*, a study of the plate at Bevis Marks; and a history of Machzike Hadath, *A fortress in Anglo-Jewry* written by his friend Bernard Homa. All these were far too large for Morris to print them on his hand press, and were machined by the firm of Worden in Marazion. Morris would set the type by hand in St. Ives, and take it over, a page at a time, in the saddlebag of his bicycle . . .

Despite the encouragement which he received from many patrons, and the publicity his printing received in John Farleigh's book *The creative craftsman*, Morris did not earn anything like an adequate living wage from his work. He was so much the heedless artist that according to one (perhaps apocryphal) story when he was once commissioned to print a wedding service he became so fascinated by the text of the service for the burial of the dead that he set that up instead. His printing had a splendid monumental quality, seen at its best in some of his broad-sheets and the letters to such friends as Gordon Craig— which he used to set up in type and print a single copy, instead of writing them—but his patrons dropped off one by one. In the middle 1950s he suddenly abandoned printing completely, and became a guard on the London underground railway. Though there have been rumours that he intends to start printing once more, it seems unlikely that the Latin Press imprint will be seen again.

By the time that Guido Morris abandoned printing, it seemed as if the private press movement in England was dead, and that the amateur no longer had a part to play in the production of books. This was not far from the truth where the press in question had to provide its owner with a living (like Golden Cockerel or the Latin Press) or where the standard of its workmanship was mediocre, as Dropmore's often was. But where the profitability of the press was of minor concern it was still perfectly possible in the 1950s to develop a press in the direct Kelmscott-Doves-Golden Cockerel tradition.

One of the presses which blossomed at this time was by no means a new foundation. At Stanbrook Abbey, a Benedictine house near Worcester, a printing press had been installed as early as 1876, at the initiative of Fr. Laurence Shepherd, its Chaplain. Fr. Shepherd was himself an enthusiastic amateur printer, with a table Albion press of his own, and he took personal direction of the Stanbrook Abbey Press. This had not been set up to provide the Nuns with an artistic hobby; its purpose was to serve the needs of the English Benedictine Congregation, and it was to become an integral part of the Nuns' life of dedication and prayer.

In this it was not particularly unusual; there are many such monastic presses which produce work of a respectable mediocrity. Stanbrook was to be very different, and the technical excellence and artistic mastery revealed in its books has been due not only to the skill of its printers but also to their talent for knowing when and from whom to seek advice—and how to follow it. For many years Sir Sydney Cockerell was a close friend of Dame Laurentia McLachlan and he was to play no small part in the affairs of the Press; giving advice, recruiting expert help from his friends (both Emery Walker and St. John Hornby were to visit Stanbrook Abbey at his request) and providing commissions for work to be done. Nor was his influence to be exercised only in the field of printing; in calligraphy the high standards which had been set by Edward Johnston were to grow in the Abbey and be kept flourishing by visits from Katherine Adams and Madelyn Walker. The books from the Press included several of considerable importance—Abbot Gasquet's *Bosworth psalter*, the *Reguli Sancti Benedicti*, the standard English text of St. Teresa of Avila.

During World War Two the quantity and the quality of the Abbey's printing declined very considerably, but in the 1950s a remarkable revival took place. Robert Gibbings, the former owner of the Golden Cockerel Press, recommended the purchase of Eric Gill's Perpetua type to replace the Press's stock of worn-out Caslon and Dolphin types, and suggested that John Dreyfus might be able to give technical advice. Dreyfus, and later John Peters (also of Cambridge University Press), were to give considerable help in improving standards. Through Dreyfus a long correspondence began between Dame Hildelith Cumming at Stanbrook and the eminent Dutch typographer Jan van Krimpen, who through his work at Enschedé had come to know many Benedictine houses in France and North Africa. Several of his own type designs—Spectrum, Romanée, Romulus and Cancellaresca Bastarda—were to be installed at Stanbrook, but van Krimpen's death in 1958 came too soon for him to see the magnificent way in which the Press was to use them, often in conjunction with calligraphic initials by Wendy Westover and Margaret Adams.

TODAY, DEARLY-BELOVED, OUR SAVIOUR IS BORN: LET US REJOICE! Surely there is no place for mourning on the birthday of Very Life, who has swallowed up mortality with all its fear, and brought us the joyful promise of life everlasting. No one is excluded from taking part in our jubilation. All have the same cause for gladness, for as our blessed Lord, slayer of sin and death, found none free from guilt, so has He come to set us all alike at liberty.

Let the saint exult, since he is soon to receive his recompense; let the sinner give praise, since he is welcomed to forgiveness; let the pagan take

1

Fig. 42. St. Leo *On the birthday of Our Lord Jesus Christ*, printed at Stanbrook Abbey, 1958

The first of the new Stanbrook work was *Christmas lyrics*, a collection of twelfth-century Christmas poems of which two (slightly different) editions were printed in 1956 and 1957. Though it was a handsome piece of work, it was to be dwarfed by the splendour of such books as *Magi venerunt* by St. Ambrose of Milan (1959), Siegfried Sassoon's *The path to peace* (1960) or the splendid *Rituale Abbatum*, printed for the use of the English Benedictine Congregation in 1963. Nor is the work of Stanbrook any less assured in its smaller books. In such publications as St. Leo *On the birthday of our Lord Jesus Christ* (1958), or Guigo's *The solitary life*, translated by Thomas Merton (1964) or *The pelican* by Philippe de Thuan, printed for Philip Hofer in 1963, their touch is exquisite.

The only book from the Press that can really be regarded as a failure is Siegfried Sassoon's *Something about myself* (1966) in which the text of this story written by Sassoon in his childhood was written out and decorated by Margaret Adams, and printed from line-blocks. The calligraphy is excellent, the presswork as good as usual, but like all attempts to reproduce the scribe's work by letterpress printing it looks all wrong—but one failure against nearly thirty successes since *Christmas lyrics* is no cause for concern. For a few of the books Monotype setting has been used, the type afterwards being rejustified by hand; but normally all the work of composition, presswork and rubrication is done by a small team of these enclosed Nuns, only the binding being done outside Stanbrook Abbey, usually by George Percival of Leicester.

At about the time that the work at Stanbrook was being revived, two young men on the other side of the country in Huntingdonshire were setting up a press which was to approach the standards of Doves and Ashendene more closely than any other English private press since 1945. Peter Foster was an architect, with a great interest in fine printing, and a close neighbour of John Peters, a typographic designer at Cambridge University Press and designer of the fine Castellar titling type. Both men had noticed the relatively poor quality of presswork in books produced since the war, and the idea gradually developed of seeing what they could do themselves. A Cope & Sherwin Imperial Press, loaned by Cambridge University Press, was installed in an outbuilding of Peter's house in the village of Hemingford Grey, and the Vine Press was born.

Almost a year later, in August 1957, their first work was completed. It was a leisurely start; at first they had little idea of the style of type they should use (they explored the possibility of obtaining some of Graily Hewitt's Treyford type from Oxford University Press; those who care about fine printing and admire the work of the Vine Press are glad that it came to nothing). Into the first book they built as many of the problems of composition and presswork as they thought might have to be faced. Unlike their pre-war models, they had no intention of employing professional pressmen—all the work was to be done by themselves in their spare time, and they had to acquire their skill by the use of printers' grammars, advice from friends in the trade, but most of all by trial and error. No trouble was spared in their quest for perfection; like Morris before them they imported ink from Jaenecke Schneemann (though for later books they used English ink) and all except one of their books was printed on paper made by hand.

The first book, *Vitis vera*, an anthology of passages on the vine taken from the Bible was set by hand, with the Latin text from the Vulgate in 12-point Perpetua Titling, and the parallel English of the Authorised Version in 18-point Perpetua. One hundred copies were planned, but in the course of printing they discovered some of the unforeseen eccentricities of their century-old press, some of which they were able to resolve in later books, but others they had to accept as a natural hazard. In the end forty copies were completed to their satisfaction and distributed to friends, but they had discovered that if they were to manage to produce one book a year handsetting would have to be abandoned.

For their second book, the first to be offered for sale, they secured a short story by Marjorie Sisson, *The cave*, which they thought would respond to lively illustration. Frank Martin was commissioned to provide wood-engravings, the text was machine-set in Perpetua at the Shenval Press (where Peters had worked for some years) and work begun. The presswork still gave some problems, and though the blocks were printed excellently in some cases the type was somewhat patchy in appearance, and the results (though highly satisfactory to most purchasers) were rather disappointing to the printers. Their third book, Constantine Fitzgibbon's *Watcher in Florence* (1959), was more satisfactory, and in fact presented less trouble than any of their other books. A charming little sextodecimo, the type (Blado italic, with a special alternative sort for the *z*) was again set at the Shenval Press.

Inspired by the success of the Fitzgibbon, Peters and Foster embarked on the production of their most ambitious book, Sir Herbert Read's play *The parliament of women*. The idea that they should publish this and three of his plays written for radio had been suggested to Peters by Philip Ward (founding secretary of the Private Libraries Association) in the summer of 1958, and planning of the production of the single play they had decided to print had started then. Experiments with the design of the book started early in 1959, but it was not completed until the end of the following year. The text was set in Monotype Centaur at Cambridge University Press, and Reg Boulton, who had provided a wood-engraving for the title-page of *Watcher in Florence*, executed the large three-colour illustrations, which were produced by a combination of relief-etched plate, linocut and wood-engraving. As each of the sheets containing an illustration also carried at least two pages of backed text and a heading in red, this called for several printings. It also meant that the paper had to be damped twice, with consequent risk of the sheets stretching different amounts, and it is a tribute to their skill that there was not much wastage. There was one near disaster with the black printing of the final sheet: for some reason the ink would not take properly on the second colour. It took a considerable time before they found a solution—sponging the image with a weak solution of household detergent. The book, quarter-bound by Gray of Cambridge in saffron morocco, with the boards covered in marbled paper specially made by Cockerell, was extremely successful, though the printers expressed themselves only 'reasonably satisfied with the presswork . . . the text lacked something in tonal quality'.

The next large work from the Vine Press was also by Sir Herbert Read; his oration to the Society of Industrial Artists on the subject of *Design and tradition* (1962). At the time the new typeface Octavian designed for the Monotype Corporation by Will Carter and David Kindersley was being used in a series of experimental settings at Cambridge University Press, and this typeface was used for Read's book as an extension of the experiments, using generous leading and printing on a coarse mould-made paper. The coarseness of the paper gave considerable trouble in the printing of the fine-line engraving by Peter Reddick, and this was overcome only by plate-sinking the paper before printing the engraving.

There was to be one more book from the Press: *Twenty-five poems* by Evelyn Ansell, with wood-engravings by Diana Bloomfield. Again set in Monotype Centaur at the University Press, it was printed on some Kelmscott paper which Batchelors had made sixty years earlier, and which through the good offices of Sir Sydney Cockerell had come into the possession of Cambridge University Press. The preparation and printing went smoothly enough, but the book was nearly ruined in the binding. Despite instructions on this vital point, the trade binder put the sheets into a hydraulic press with obvious and disastrous results. Fortunately Gray and Sons, who had been entrusted with the binding of ten 'special' copies, were able to restore the damaged sheets to near pristine condition, and most of the other ninety copies were retrieved—though a few of them still showed slight traces of set-off. But the ten special copies represented what the two printers, at last satisfied, regarded as 'the limit in presswork of what we felt we could achieve with our archaic equipment'. And having achieved this, they called a halt to their printing venture. Its success proved satisfactorily that the operation of a private press in the grand tradition need not call for substantial private means. The sales of Vine Press books covered the payments to suppliers, artists and authors adequately, leaving enough money over for the two printers to enjoy a bottle of claret with each shift. In this they did better than most other recent private presses, and seldom can the rewards have been as appropriate.

It was not only in the completely non-commercial field of fine printing, in which both Stanbrook Abbey and the Vine Press operated, that the apparently inhospitable postwar world could be overcome. As a jobbing printer cum private press owner Guido Morris failed, but the causes of his failure cannot be put down to an unwillingness on the part of the public to support a small jobbing printer doing fine work—for in Cambridge the Rampant Lions Press, which was to do precisely this, was launched successfully in 1949. Will Carter had been active as an amateur printer ever since he had in 1924 at the age of twelve visited Oxford University Press. His interest in printing was sustained throughout his school days, and on leaving school he went to work in the printing firm of Unwin brothers. Later he moved to Cambridge where for many years he worked for Heffers.

In 1930 he had bought a wooden flatbed press, and in 1936 he replaced it with an Albion, two years later adding a treadle platen press. For as well as his full-time employment at Heffers, Carter was a spare-time printer of the sort so disliked by the trade, producing a good deal of jobbing work for friends and associates as well as a number of small books on his own account. But he was a 'back-bedroom printer' with a difference; his skill and taste were re-markable, and these were to be reinforced by a visit to the workshop of Paul Koch in Frankfurt in 1938.

After the war, which Carter spent in the Royal Navy, he returned to his old employers, and also resumed his old spare-time printing activities. But after three years the call of printing on his own account became so strong that he decided to set up in business. 'I was convinced', he wrote in *The first ten*, an anniversary publication which he issued in 1959, 'that there was a market for fine jobbing printing of the sort that was too small to be handled by the big printing houses and yet was beyond the scope of the small jobbing firm. Being blessed with a useful pair of hands I was by now a fair compositor and press-man and had acquired some ideas of simple typography. With these skills and a small printing plant and any amount of encouragement from wife and friends the wind seemed set fair . . .' And certainly the wind was set fair; by 1959 the pressure of commissions was such that one pair of hands could not

Spring song

So fresh my joy that winter's past,
  Green worlds to find about me now;
Nor yet will burning summer cast
  Dust and sweat upon my brow.

Crown of the year, O heart of spring,
  So fair with birth and ripe with bloom—
Not yet can ageing fancy bring
  Thought of life's autumnal doom.

Fig. 43. Page from Evelyn Ansell's *Twenty-five poems*, the last book from
the Vine Press, 1963. Wood-engraving by Diana Bloomfield

the decision

Spun by the lustful planet,
stung by the waspish rain,
bruised by my body's silence,
I wrote to you again.

Improbably, you answered, and across the paper
words tore their way towards decision:
'I think we ought to end it now.'
What moved you in your equal winter
to battle finally across the snow,
printing these platitudes with such precision?

Lovers drowning in the night
revel in their tidal play,
trusting the pale moon to bless
a love too hot for day.

Stimuli and secrets wane,
essential love is commonplace.
'I think it ought to end today'
your loving nakedness would say.

Cynically forced into grimace,
too conscious of the heart's display,
I burn your letter and destroy your face,
hoping you will, in a compulsive way,
be banished to the brain.

Fig. 44. A page from *Lobsters*, printed by Sebastian Carter, 1961

cope with the demand, and much of the bread-and-butter jobbing work was relinquished to allow him to concentrate on the printing of books.

Many of the books and pamphlets printed at the Rampant Lions Press (the first, Robert Nichols's *A Spanish triptych*, had been published as early as 1936) were printed for outside publication, like the splendid version of *The rime of the ancient mariner*, with David Jones's copper engravings, printed for the Chilmark Press of New York in 1963–4. But like the Officina Bodoni, which it resembles in being closer to an early printing shop than the 'normal' firm, the Press has produced many small books on its own account, like Christopher Smart's *A song to David* (1960) or John Farrow's *Seven poems in pattern* (1955) or William Johnson Cory's *Lucretilis*. Not the least interesting of the work to be printed on the Rampant Lions equipment was in fact the work of a press within a press. Will Carter's own enthusiasm and skill in printing was inherited by his son Sebastian, who started issuing his own books 'from the Junior Branch of the Rampant Lions Press' at the age of thirteen. Later, in vacations from school and university, he produced several books of considerable interest and distinction, such as *Poems from Panmure House* printed for 'The ninth of May' in 1960, or Sir William Jones's *Poems* (1961). Since 1966 he has been working with his father in the 'regular' Rampant Lions printing; with the personnel of the Press doubled, much handsome work in the private press tradition can be expected from Cambridge in the future.

19

The contemporary scene in Britain

———

The Vine Press may have been the last of the amateur presses deliberately set up to operate in the ambitious manner of Doves or Ashendene. But at the time that its first work appeared, a remarkable revival of the parlour printers had also taken place. Amateur printers producing small journals and pamphlets and jobbing printing had continued with their hobbies or part-time businesses right through the inter-war years. They enjoyed themselves at their presses, their productions entertained a few friends; their jobbing activities may have annoyed a few commercial printers, but otherwise they attracted little notice. There was no reason for them to do so; few of them produced work with the quality of a Will Carter—indeed, the whole of the private press movement from William Morris onwards seems to have passed some of them by.

The numbers of these amateurs were growing, and in 1944 the Amateur Printers Association was formed to bring together the users of small printing machines. In 1948 the Association changed its name to the International Small Printers Association—a recognition of the fact that many of its members were not strictly amateurs, but were engaged in business, and that there were many overseas members, particularly in the United States where amateur journalism flourished. The name has subsequently been changed to the British Printing Society, under which name it continues to flourish. As an organization for the enthusiastic amateur who has bought a small press, the Society has done a good deal to spread technical information and to raise the standards of workmanship where they had often been abysmal. It was not however primarily through the British Printing Society, nor through its members, that the development of today's private presses took place. It was rather an entirely independent movement among individuals whose interest in printing had been aroused less by the advertisements for Adana and other small printing

machines than by the work of the great private presses from Kelmscott onwards, and above all by the work of such writers as Stanley Morison and
Beatrice Warde—writers who had made typography into an acceptable subject
for after-dinner conversation.

This interest received a great fillip from John Ryder's *Printing for pleasure*
published by Phoenix House in 1955, and subsequently reissued in the 'Teach
yourself' series. Ryder is a typographer who uses his own press as a tool for
experimental design, and his manual was by far the best practical guide for
amateurs to have appeared; scholarly without being dull, comprehensive
without being too full of detail, stylish without being merely smart, and full of
a most infectious zest for printing. His own Miniature Press has produced
relatively little (though his attractive *Suite of fleurons*, published by Phoenix
House in 1956, grew out of his personal experiments with type ornaments)
but his influence has been very considerable indeed in encouraging the good
typography of many of today's amateur printers.

One of the earliest of these presses was the Signet Press of Greenock.
Thomas Rae, its owner, was the junior partner in an old-established family
firm of jobbing printers. Growing interested in book design, he had in the mid-
1950s produced a small pamphlet of part of *Pickwick papers* as an experiment
in printing Dickens in a pleasanter and more readable form than most editions
of his works. In 1956 he followed this with a slim pamphlet on *Thomas Bewick,
wood-engraver*, which he printed in aid of an appeal for donations to the St.
Bride Printing Library. This was very well received in printing circles. His
Andrew Myllar, a short study which he wrote and printed in 1958 to mark the
450th anniversary of the introduction of printing into Scotland, was a handsomely produced little volume; textually it was less satisfactory, and following
a mauling in the *Scottish historical review* Rae 'decided that the time had come
to end my brief essay into the realms of scholarship'. But not to end the production of small books on the history of printing; in 1962 he published *Some
notes on wood engraving*, selected from Thomas Bewick's *Memoir* and illustrated
with several of Bewick's engravings printed from the original blocks, and in
1963 he published James Watson's *Preface to 'The history of printing' 1713*.
Edited by James Munro, the *Preface* contains the first account of printing in
Scotland.

Before this in 1958 Rae had published *The book of the private press*, a directory of more than 240 amateur printers working in the English-speaking
world. Edited by Rae and Geoffrey Handley-Taylor, the book is one of the
standard works of record in the private press field; a new edition is badly

needed. From 1959 Rae was joint editor (and printer) of *Private press books*, a checklist published annually by the Private Libraries Association, and which attempts to record all substantial work printed by amateurs; work which very

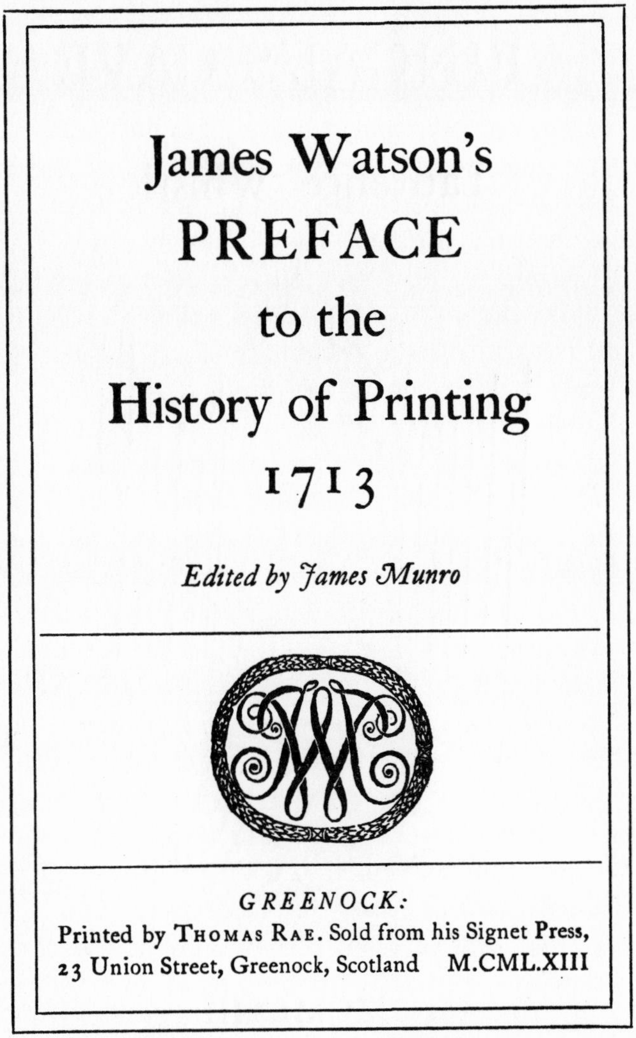

James Watson's

PREFACE

to the

History of Printing

1713

Edited by James Munro

GREENOCK:
Printed by THOMAS RAE. Sold from his Signet Press,
23 Union Street, Greenock, Scotland   M.CML.XIII

Fig. 45. A Signet Press title-page

often never finds its way into the book trade bibliographies, nor sometimes (despite the textual importance of some of the books) into the copyright libraries. After four annual volumes had appeared, however, Rae was compelled by pressure of business commitments to relinquish his share in the undertaking. The same pressures caused a slackening in the output of the Signet Press, though several small books of considerable interest have appeared since, such as Maria Riddell's *Robert Burns, a memoir* (1966).

FINGAL'S CAVE

Laurence Whistler

MCMLXIII

Fig. 46. *Fingal's cave*, printed by F. E. Pardoe, 1963

In 1967 Rae was compelled to change the name of his press, which was thought to be too similar to that of a paperback series, and though the Grian-Aig Press (as it is now called) has since published only one book, *Poems* by

Joan Prince (1969), Rae has also printed William John Stannard's *Anaglyto-graphy* for the Plough Press of Loughborough (1967), and in the following year he produced *The private press: handbook to an exhibition* for Loughborough School of Librarianship. Rae's work is sober, usually without any typographical fireworks (though his *Death of Mary Queen of Scots* which he printed in 1960 in American Uncial types showed how successful he could be in a more florid style) and depending for its effect on the clarity of the traditional layout and the sound presswork—as befits an Elder of the Kirk.

ELIZABETH II

100 copies of this booklet have been printed at the Cuckoo Hill Press, 41 Cuckoo Hill Rd, Pinner, Mx, on Whatman's Bank Note paper, working from the coins themselves.
1964

NUMISMATA

Fig. 47. Title-opening and colophon from *Elizabeth II numismata*, printed by David Chambers at the Cuckoo Hill Press, 1964

Rae was succeeded on *Private press books* by David Chambers, owner of the Cuckoo Hill Press at Pinner. Chambers's press is of a very much less public nature than Signet (Rae, of course, could use the resources of his printing firm for his spare-time printing) and in many ways is typical of many contemporary undertakings, being limited in its typographical resources to a few small founts of type and an Alexandra (Albion) press housed in an outbuilding, and in its human resources to the owner's free time at weekends and in the evenings. Where the Cuckoo Hill Press differs from the mass of presses with similar resources is not in what it prints, nor in the way it prints, but rather in the fastidious care with which all its work is carried out. Chambers is the sort of craftsman who will set quotation marks a hair space into the margin to achieve a nicety of spacing and layout which can be appreciated only by the most discerning reader. Most of his books are small; in his smallest, *Elizabeth II numismata* (1964), he used direct prints from coins, with a success which is marvellous to those who have ever tried such printing. His most substantial book so far is an edition of *The apostles' creed* (1965) with finely executed wood-engravings by Philip Ross.

A similar fastidious taste is to be seen in the work of the Piccolo Press which John Craig operates at Stroud in Gloucestershire. His *These women all* (1966), an early ballad illustrated with lino cuts by Craig, is a splendid essay in the small book.

Fig. 48. Lino cut of an Albion press by Juliet Standing (Daedelus Press)

Another press whose work is of considerable typographic distinction is that of Iain Bain, the Laverock Press at Baldock in Hertfordshire. Closer in style to Rae's work than either of the preceding presses, Bain's books have a solid commonsense quality about their design which accords very well with their subjects—books like John Bell's *Album de Novo Castro*, a description of a commonplace book belonging to an eighteenth-century bookseller and collector published in 1965, *A handlist of western manuscripts from the library of B.S.Cron* (1965), or Christopher Whitfield's *The kinship of Thomas Combe II, William Reynolds and William Shakespeare* (1961). Signet and Laverock are representative of a small group of private presses which are used to produce the fruits of the bibliographical and typographical research of the owner or his friends; another is the Allenholme Press in Northumberland, from which Peter C. G. Isaac has issued occasional numbers of *Bulmer papers, Some Alnwick caricatures, a note and a handlist,* and similar publications.

Something of a whale among sprats is B. Fairfax Hall's Stourton Press. Originally set up in London in 1931, it produced a very substantial *Catalogue of Chinese pottery and porcelain in the collection of Sir Percival David, Bt.* in 1934. This was very much in the grand manner, with a typeface designed specially

Wythin their brest
Their love doth rest
Who lyst to prove shall know
For all their bost
All daye almost
But I will not say so

Fig. 49. *These women all*, printed at the Piccolo Press, 1966. Lino cut by John Craig

by Eric Gill, H. Gage-Cole (of Kelmscott, Doves and Cranach) as pressman, paper made specially for the book . . . After the Second World War, Fairfax Hall moved to South Africa, where he printed a number of books such as Gurdjieff's *The struggle of the magicians* (1957). In the early 1960s he returned to London and set up his press once more. Working single-handed, his first book, three years in the making, was *Paintings and drawings by Harold Gilman and Charles Ginner in the collection of Edward Le Bas* (1965). This was followed in 1966 by *Passing scene: eighteen images of southern Africa* by Rupert Shephard. The quality of the colour-printing in these volumes is unequalled by any other private press; the number of commercial firms who could do as well is few indeed.

Fig. 50. Wood-engraving by Otto Rohse from *Story of the earth*, produced at Kim Taylor's Ark Press, 1960

Among the other private presses at work in England today few attempt to produce work of such high typographical quality in the classical tradition as these. There are those who are interested primarily in the texts which they produce, like Bert Jackson, who at the Lilac Tree Press in Wallasey prints (a page at a time) very small but fastidiously produced volumes of poetry; those by George Lea being particularly attractive. At the Keepsake Press in Hammersmith Roy Lewis and his daughters print 'poems, stories, satires, essays, *jeux d'esprit*, offcuts, marginalia, of our friends, established and unestablished, as keepsakes for them to give their friends'.

Lewis had, like so many, started printing as a boy, though with unusual

E. CLIVE ROUSE

MBE FSA

The Newnham Murals

An account of the recent discovery of
Medieval Wall Paintings
in St Vincent's Church
at Newnham in Hertfordshire

MCMLXIII

NEWNHAM

THE LAVEROCK PRESS

Fig. 51. A Laverock Press title-page

advantages—a father who, having been presented with his first attempt at printing, bought him some type then 'took me aside, presented me with Updike's *Printing types*, and read me a solemn lecture on the iniquities of the Cheltenham family which I have never forgotten'. As Roy Lewis grew up his printing was abandoned for more serious pursuits, and only in the 1950s did

251

TO THE RIGHT WORSHIPFULL,
SIR THOMAS WALSINGHAM, KNIGHT.

*S*IR, *wee thinke not our selves discharged of the dutie wee owe to our friend, when wee have brought the breathlesse bodie to the earth: for albeit the eye there taketh his ever farwell of that beloved object, yet the impression of the man, that hath beene deare unto us, living an after life in our memory, there putteth us in mind of farther obsequies due unto the deceased. And namely of the performance of whatsoever we may judge shal make to his living credit, and to the effecting of his determinations prevented by the stroke of death. By these meditations (as by an intellectuall will) I suppose my selfe executor to the unhappily deceased author of this Poem, upon whom knowing that in his life time you bestowed many kind favors, entertaining the parts of reckoning and woorth which you found in him, with good countenance and liberall affection: I cannot but see so far into the will of him dead, that whatsoever issue of his brain should chance to come abroad, that the first breath it should take might be the gentle aire of your liking: for since his selfe had ben accustomed therunto, it would proove more agreeable and thriving to his right*

3

Fig. 52. A page from *Hero and Leander*, printed in Eric Gill's 'Aries' italic type at the Stourton Press, 1934

he return to his original love. The books that have been printed at the Keepsake Press are often of importance, always of interest: Edward Lowbury's *Metamorphoses* (later republished by a commercial publisher), Charles St. J. Shore's *Reminiscences of a tax inspector*, Gavin Ewart's *Throwaway lines*—these are representative of its work. The production is often less careful than the purist would accept, but Lewis's aim is not the same as theirs. 'I don't know what place there is for a press with such a history as ours', he has written. 'It is not quite a private press: it is an amateur press—it is a retreat. The Freudians (I know them) would recognise it for a symptom of infantilism. Is it not significant (to use the essential Freudian word) that I love very small formats? Was not the use of 18-point Black Letter in the Keepsake Press *Death of God* and *Genesis* an over-compensation? . . . For presses, we have a Model platen and a card Albion. For premises, a shed in a rose-garden. For a philosophy, we grope.' But elsewhere in the same article, he has more seriously stated the purpose of the Keepsake Press: 'if we can see a hole to be filled in the vast output of commercial publishing we will fill it'—and no better reason for having one's own press can be found.

Some of today's private presses exist as vehicles for their owners' artistic expression. The work of Morris Cox at Gogmagog is of this sort. Another is Ben Sands's Shoestring Press at Whitstable, which has produced some memorable little books with exuberant coloured lino cuts—*The walrus and the carpenter* (1958), *The dragon of Wantley*, a burlesque eighteenth-century opera by Henry Carey (1960), and *The tragical death of A apple pie* (1966).

It may be thought that much of this work, however pleasantly produced it may be, and however much pleasure these amateurs gain from undertaking it, is a mere pastime, irrelevant to the needs of society as a whole. There is without question sometimes an air of preciousness about it; the number of readers of these books is strictly limited, not infrequently to other amateur printers. The dearth of original material being published adds weight to the argument often heard that amateur printing is of no more use than composing sonatas in the manner of Scarlatti, or building model railways. With presses like those described above this is to overstate the case; for many others their printing is admittedly little more than escapism, though of an unusually civilized sort for the era of electronic man.

The last few years, however, have seen the development of a new type of private press; the press being used forcefully as a means of 'trying to find new outlets for poetry, or a gesture of defiance directed at the literary establishment'. The so-called 'little press' movement is not in itself a new one; for

ANN TITMUSS

Oxford/London/America

LONDON

The Keepsake Press

1963

Fig. 53. A Keepsake Press title-page

amateur publishers to have their small literary magazine or their pamphlet series of poets is a traditional method of tackling the problems involved in the publication of experimental work. This was the original idea behind the formation of the Golden Cockerel Press; for precisely this reason Laura Riding and Robert Graves started at Seizin; in the early 1930s Cecil Jeffries printed Lawrence Durrell's *Quaint fragment* on a hand press—such instances could be multiplied many times. A good many of such ventures have become recognized and respected in the field of the private press—Seizin, or Erica Marx's Hand and Flower Press, or Guido Morris's Crescendo Series. In the middle 1950s Oscar Mellor's Fantasy Press was particularly important for the first publication in book form of such poets as Thom Gunn, George MacBeth and Donald Davie; together with the Marvell Press it was the chief early supporter of the 'Movement' poets.

During the 1960s more than a few attempts have been made along similar lines. Such magazines as *The review* and *Stand* have produced their own pamphlet series, and publishers like the Fulcrum Press or Edward Lucie-Smith at Turret Books work well in this tradition. Most of them are not however private presses in the sense of using their own equipment to produce small hand-printed editions (Alan Tarling's 'Poet and Printer' is an exception) but are amateur publishing ventures, producing small editions of books of minority interest.

As well as these relatively 'safe' and conservative presses, there are others which are more clearly radical and visibly embattled, like Ian Hamilton Finlay's Wild Hawthorn Press, the principal British stronghold of concrete poetry. Concrete poetry being in a sense 'about' typography, it can in theory produce exciting and highly original effects; occasionally it succeeds in practice. But the work is hardly printing as we would recognize it; a recent *Times literary supplement* review described one such publication as 'a loose collection of items . . . Some of them are duplicated typewriter poems, one is recognizably printed . . . four are cards bearing accidental-looking fricassees of type interspersed with snatches of Letraset and various ink textures.' The use of the typewriter and of the small offset press dominates these ventures, and the alarmed or outraged typographical purist can dismiss them as not really being private press work at all—remarkably little of this work, for example, ever gets recorded in the annual bibliography *Private press books*. It is a pity that there is this distance between these two groups of amateurs, for each has something of value to offer to the other, and both are engaged in building what Edward Lucie-Smith has described as 'a small untidy cairn raised to the spirit of human cussedness'; but it is unlikely that they will ever meet.

a was an
apple pie

Fig. 54. *The tragical death of A apple pie*, printed at the Shoestring Press, 1966.
Lino cut by Ben Sands

One area in England in which there is far more co-operation than usual between these various groups is Leicestershire. And Leicestershire today occupies a very unusual place in the private press world. Just as Hammersmith at the turn of the century was abuzz with private press activity, so today Leicestershire, like the San Francisco Bay area, or Iowa City, has far more private printers than is to be expected for the size and population of the district.

To a great extent this is a postwar development, centred on Leicester College of Art. Before the war there was at least one private press, the Garswood Press, from which Falconer Scott and A. Christopherson printed *The wisdom of Andrew Boorde* in 1936, but the real growth of the movement started with John Mason's work in papermaking, and in the books printed at the College of Art. Mason, who as the son of J. H. Mason and former compositor and binder at the Gregynog Press, was no stranger to private presses when as head of the bookbinding department at Leicester he started experiments in papermaking in 1954. At first his experiments were carried out with improvised equipment at home, but later at the invitation of the Principal his papermaking activities were transferred to the College of Art. Gradually his 'Twelve by Eight' paper became known to those interested in the book crafts, and following the publication of his *Papermaking as an artistic craft* (1959) it became widely sought after. And deservedly so; the papers Mason made were full of variety in colour and texture, and in such publications as the Private Libraries Association's edition of Mason's address to the Double Crown Club, *Twelve by eight* (1959), its charm can be seen very clearly. Since then, Mason has published a number of specimen books of his papers, and other books like Oliver Bayldon's *The papermaker's craft*, a free translation from the seventeenth-century Latin poem *Papyrus* by Fr. Imberdis, which was printed for him by Will Carter in 1964. But Mason's activities are purely those of a papermaker and publisher; unlike Dard Hunter (or today Henry Morris or Walter Hamady) he has not attempted to use his paper for printing himself.

Among the most enthusiastic of John Mason's assistants with his papermaking was Rigby Graham. Some of the most interesting of Mason's experimental papers were those with thread pictures in them which were executed by Graham. So great was the latter's enthusiasm for the craft that he set up his own paper mill, the Holt Mill. Graham was later to become the central figure among the Leicestershire presses, with an influence extending far beyond the confines of the county, but in the late 1950s he was not himself the owner of a private press. His earliest work in this field, apart from his illustrations for *The private press at Gregynog*, which was printed at Leicester College of Art, was as a contributor to the Orpheus Press. Set up in 1958 by Douglas Martin, this 'fugitive private press' as it so aptly described itself, worked at first without premises or equipment of its own, producing occasional pamphlets on borrowed presses. Its first booklet was a preliminary essay of John Mason's on *Papermaking*, of which a very small number of copies were printed on Mason's paper in 1958. The next publication undertaken, by far the finest produced by Orpheus, was Rilke's *Die Sonette an Orpheus* (1959) again printed on Mason's paper and with twelve three-coloured lithographs by Graham. Binding took a considerable time, and before the twenty-five copies were published (from Munich, where Martin had moved with the intention of restarting the press in a much more lavish way) three other pamphlets had been published: *Chidiocke Tichbourne* and Clare's *Lines written in Northampton County Asylum* both illustrated by Graham, and Rimbaud's *Les Corbeaux* with wood cuts by Robert Blythe. The first two were printed in two editions, one on Graham's Holt Mill paper, and the other on good quality machine-made paper. Both editions are now distinctly uncommon: of the Clare, Graham has recorded that 'scores were offered for next to nothing in pubs, used as beer mats, and eventually hurled at sneering crowds in the Market Place one Sunday evening.' An experiment in taking poetry to the people had failed dismally.

After Martin's return from Germany the Press resumed activity. A backer and premises were found, and many ambitious projects started—Herrick's *Hesperides*, Shakespeare's fragment *Sir Thomas More*, Lorca's *Llanto por Ignacio Sanchez Mejias*, a *Life* of the composer Bellini and others. Little ever came of these plans; the only book to be completed as designed was John Best's *Poems and drawings in mud time* (1960) and this was only because the book was printed commercially at the Curwen Press. The Herrick was scrapped when half printed; the type for *Sir Thomas More* was accidentally pied, and Rigby Graham's illustrations used in *Kirby Hall: an uninformative guide* of which fifty copies were printed in an afternoon and then circulated in the way which had become normal for the Press—in the pubs. So chaotic an undertaking could not long survive, and despite the very real promise of its early work the Orpheus Press disappeared from the Leicester scene.

The imprint was revived once, by Rigby Graham, Patricia Green and Toni Savage (who had also assisted with Orpheus Press work), on Thomas Churchyard's *Lovesong to an inconstant lady* in 1961. Once was enough; they found that the name had too many unfortunate associations, and for subsequent books they adopted the name of the Pandora Press. Considering the partners' lack of printing experience and the equipment at their disposal (an Adana flatbed press and two cases of worn and battered type) they managed to produce a considerable number of books rapidly. Most of their publications have been small; such things as Swinburne's *Garden of Proserpine*, Byron's *When we two parted*, Marvell's *Thoughts in a garden*, or *Poems and transations by Count*

WHEN WE TWO PARTED
George Gordon Lord Byron

drawings by Rigby Graham

Toni Savage : Pandora Press
mcmlxii

Fig. 55. A Pandora Press title-page

Potocki. These were produced only because they wanted to print them, regardless of how well they would sell, and the size of the edition is normally 'decided by an aching arm or blistered palm or both'. Only once have they printed for outsiders: a booklet entitled *The living theatre* which was printed and sold in aid of a little professional theatre in Leicester which was threatened with closure for lack of financial support.

Nearly all the books produced have the illustrations in colour, calling for two or three impressions. In the most substantial book of the Pandora Press, Thea Scott's *Fingal's Cave*, the fifty-two pages went through the press eighty times, a total of well over twenty thousand impressions in all as the edition was intended to consist of 250 copies. Disaster struck the project after the seventy-sixth printing: at the time the Pandora Press was operating from the attic of an old rectory at Aylestone, and the sheets had been spread out over the floor to dry. A sudden spell of sunshine hatched out woodworm in the floor, and overnight more than one hundred of the sheets were peppered with holes. As the sheet had a five-colour progressive linocut on it, reprinting was impossible, and the edition was, in consequence, reduced by nearly half.

As well as being a partner in the activities of the Pandora Press, Rigby Graham was also involved in the production of three ambitious books which were printed by the Monks of Mount St. Bernard's Abbey up in Charnwood Forest. Two of these were produced jointly with George Percival, the binder of many of Stanbrook Abbey's publications and John Mason's successor as head of the bookbinding department at Leicester College of Art. The first of these, *Vale*, was printed as a farewell to John Mason on his retirement, and consisted of a humorous account of his career generously sprinkled with wrong founts, phrases upside down and similar tricks printed on Twelve by Eight paper purloined (so they claimed) from Mason. The Chinese-style binding was a real *tour de force*, and the binding of the second book, Wilde's *The nightingale and the rose*, was equally exciting with its use of green metallic boards and pink metallic *doublures* blocked in gold—from the point of view of owners of the book one of the most difficult of bindings to preserve from damage, but a splendid experiment in the use of unusual binding materials.

Graham has also played a considerable part in Trevor Hickman's Brewhouse Press at Wymondham, a little village in the heart of the Cottesmore Hunt country on the borders of Rutland. Another bookbinder, Hickman's association with private press work started through his binding of two of the Pandora Press's books, *Fingal's Cave* and Penelope Holt's *Sicilian memory*. He is, naturally, far more interested in the binding of his books than is usual among today's private presses, and in the past few years Brewhouse has grown up into one of the most substantial of them. A number of its books have been printed outside (*An autumn anthology* was the third of the books printed at Mount St. Bernard's Abbey) but some have been produced on equipment no more sophisticated than a binder's nipping press. And not the least successful of the Brewhouse books by any means: *The Pickworth fragment*, which was selected for the National Book League's exhibition of book design in 1966, is a highly original and successful variation on a Japanese form of binding; a series of pages joined at the fore-edges to make a concertina which when opened out forms a panorama of text and coloured and 'action-tooled' linocuts nearly fourteen feet long. The whole is contained in a quarter-binding of brown suede with gold-tooled and coloured linocuts on the brown paper boards. Other publications have been less startlingly unusual, though nearly all have been original in design, and all are books which have a good reason for existing. They range from a series of broadsides on the history of printing and bookbinding (*The execution of a bookbinder, James Cook*; *The dance of death* and others) through a history of nature-printing, *Typographia naturalis* (which was illustrated with original nineteenth-century nature-prints of seaweeds and ferns, and modern essays in this fascinating technique by Rigby Graham and Morris Cox of the Gogmagog Press), to a substantial history of *The Oakham Canal* by David Tew.

Most amateur printers would be hard-pressed to find the time for the work that Graham has contributed to these activities. But he also inspires the work of the Threoteotha Press, which has produced a number of substantial books of prints by various artists on a single theme—such as *Patterns of brickwork* (1966) and he runs his own press as well. This, the Cog Press, has produced a number of pieces which even the purists regard as private press work, like his splendid *Cogs in transition* (1963), but it has branched out into work of a less traditional sort—such as the catalogue for an exhibition of *Graphic art from the French little magazines* (1966) in which the bulk of the text consists of duplicated sheets, but with the title-page, cover, illustrations and other parts printed on the hand press. Rather similar methods have been used for the production of other exhibition catalogues and for a number of little magazines, such as John Cotton's *Priapus* and Peter Hoy's *In particular*. The results are undeniably better than if duplicating alone were used; Graham's work shows that a shoe-string budget need not result in the dreary unfinished look which far too many little magazines possess.

Graham and Savage and Hoy produced one of the most interesting of these little magazines in *Fishpaste*, a little review of which each issue was printed (by letterpress) on both sides of a postcard. From the point of view of successful combination of text and illustration this was admirable. Despite some frivolities of a sort to drive librarians mad (issues numbered 'Fishpaste four and a half', 'Fishpaste 7 A' and the like—to say nothing of bogus issues circulated by their friends) this publication demonstrates that the worlds of *Private press books* and of Edward Lucie-Smith's little presses need not be mutually exclusive.

Though Rigby Graham dominates the private press scene in Leicestershire, there are plenty of totally independent presses. At Huncote, the Gazebo Press has produced some pleasant little books; in Loughborough the Plough Press is at work; in Leicester the Off-Cut Press prints many little booklets of merit. In the United States there was talk some years ago of amateur printing as a 'new folk art'. Most of these Leicestershire amateurs would laugh you to scorn if you suggested anything of the sort to them. And yet if the type fever is endemic anywhere in the world, it is here in the East Midlands.

20

In America today

The Second World War was to be a much less decisive factor in changing the face of the private press in America than it was in the Old World. Frank Altschul's Overbrook Press was by no means the only press of major importance set up in the 1930s which has continued operations up until the present time.

Carroll Coleman's Prairie Press in Iowa had its origins as a youthful hobby in the early 1920s, when he produced *The golden quill*, an amateur magazine of the sort so often produced by hobby printers. After some time working in commercial printing plants and in newspapers he set up his own press in 1935, since when (with interruptions for his work teaching typographic design at the State University of Iowa, and later as its Director of Publications) he has produced a very considerable number of books. Most of these are of poetry, most are in hand-set type superbly printed on a good-quality machine-made paper, in editions considerably larger than those usual in a private press. For the Prairie Press is by no means an amateur undertaking; it has to pay its way, and it has frequently printed books for sale by commercial publishers. Like Will Carter at the Rampant Lions Press, or Saul Marks, Coleman should properly be regarded as a small commercial firm working well within the traditions of Cobden-Sanderson.

To a lesser extent the same may be said of another press in Iowa City: the Cummington Press of Harry Duncan. This was started in Cummington, Massachusetts, in 1939, as a part of the arts and crafts programme at Cummington School. Subsequently it was moved to Iowa City, where Duncan took over Coleman's old post as director of the work of the Typographical Laboratory at the State University. The Cummington Press has concentrated on printing good editions of modern American literature. More directly within the private press tradition than the Prairie Press, and more restrained in its

263

very severe typographic style (not that the Prairie Press is flamboyant)
Duncan's books have all been printed on a hand-press. In such volumes as
Stephen Berg's *Bearing weapons* (1963) the line of descent from the Doves
Press can be seen very clearly indeed. Not all Cummington books are so

Fig. *56*. Wood-engraving by Roderick Mead from *Brandings* (Cummington Press, 1968)

traditional in appearance: in the same year as *Bearing weapons* Duncan published *Four early stories* by James Agee in which he experimented with the use
of unjustified setting with the text in double columns—to my mind not
altogether successfully, but the execution was again superb.

The excellence of the presswork is a feature of a third, postwar, press in
Iowa City, specializing in the production of small volumes of contemporary

poetry: the Stone Wall Press. Its owner K. K. Merker has been closely associated with Duncan and his methods of production show a similar devotion to hand work. To an English eye, Duncan's books are usually unmistakably the work of an American; books which however classical in design have a vigour about them which few English typographers seem able to achieve without a self-conscious straining for effect. Merker's work is closer to some of the finest Dutch typography, not merely because of his use of such types as Romanée and Spectrum; one feels that Jan van Krimpen, that most severe of critics, would have approved thoroughly of the production of such books as Donald Justice's *A local storm* or Thom Gunn's *A geography* (1966).

These three Iowa presses are an unusual group in producing such good texts in consistently well-designed and executed volumes. But it is their geographical proximity which is unusual, not the work which they produce, for there are several other private presses in the United States which work in much the same vein—sometimes as a part of a wider programme of work—in a manner that far too few English private printers of the traditional sort seem willing to do. One such is Don Drenner's Zauberberg Press at Coffeyville in Kansas, where since 1945 the owner, in the time left over after a working week as a radio engineer, and another sixty or so hours as 'part-time' librarian of the local Carnegie Library, prints small editions of poetry. Entirely self-taught, Drenner's work—as in his own *The graphics of love* (1961) or Joseph Stanley Pennell's *Darksome house* (1959)—shows a rare ability in design as well as a perfectionist approach to production. At present his press is dormant, and its output is understandably small, but his books are among the finest of all contemporary printing.

Another small press which has produced some substantial volumes of poetry is the Rampart Press of John Beecher. A writer in the finest traditions of American radicalism, who has been described in *Time* as 'a product and a proponent of the great unfinished American revolution', Beecher spent many years oscillating between university teaching and social work in New Deal programmes, and after the war in working for the United Nations Relief and Rehabilitation Administration. Following a Ford Fellowship to report on small farming, he became a working rancher on the Morning Star Ranch in northern California. Long a writer, he and his wife started dabbling with printing in the evenings; they were seized with enthusiasm and commenced production of the 'Morning Star Quartos', a handsomely printed series of contemporary poetry. Gradually the sideline ran away with them: following a move to the ghost mining town of Jerome in Arizona, the press was renamed the Rampart Press, and a magnificent series of quarto volumes of Beecher's poetry was produced—*In Egypt land, Phantom City, Report to the stockholders* —as well as a large number of four-page 'Poems for the people' which were given away and were deliberately not copyrighted, so that the poet's message could be spread as widely as possible. It is rare to find a writer of such obvious commitment to a cause who cares enough for the vehicle of his ideas to bother with fine printing, or who can find a typographic style to match the intellectual content, but the strong woodcuts by Barbara Beecher allied to the powerful typography match the forthright expression of the poetry very well. By no means as well known as they should be, the Rampart Press books are among the most harmonious and important of contemporary American work. Following a move from Arizona back to California, and later to Birmingham, Alabama, Beecher's private press has not been used to print any more books, though in his Red Mountain Editions volume *To live and die in Dixie* (1966) some of the pages from his earlier books are reproduced by photolithography, and he has used his type and equipment to set up some of the additional material for reproduction by this method.

As well as these presses which exist mainly for the publication of good poetry in good editions, there are some which are closer to older ideals in private press work—ideals of craftsmanship, derived from the same sources (though expressed in a very different manner) as The Guild of Handicrafts' Essex House Press or the St. Dominic's Press. The first of these to be set up, although not in the United States, was that of Victor Hammer (1882–1967). Viennese by birth, and trained as an architect, Hammer was in the renaissance tradition of artist-craftsmen; a painter, sculptor, carpenter, calligrapher, musician, printer, goldsmith—all these crafts he managed to unify, and to reduce potential complexity to simplicity in a life devoted *ad maiorem Dei gloriam*. His interest in calligraphy dated from Anna Simons's translation of Johnston's *Writing and illuminating and lettering* which was published in 1910; he started printing while he was living in Florence in the early 1920s. As he was a believer in the workshop tradition, his Casa di Boccaccio attracted talented apprentices, and it was with the assistance of Fritz Kredel and Paul Koch (son of Rudolf Koch the type-designer and printer of the 'Rudolfinische Drucke') that a wooden press was built, punches cut and type cast, and the 'Stamperia del Santuccio'—named for a Florentine saint of little interceding power—started work. Its first publication, Milton's *Samson Agonistes*, was published in 1931. Other works followed slowly from Florence and from the Press's later homes in Alsace and in Austria until the Nazi occupation of

TERENCE ❦ DÜRER

sannio: aeschinus, listen to me so you won't pretend to be ignorant of my profession. i am a slave-merchant.

aeschinus: a bawd-master, you mean.

sannio: but one of the most honorable in town. and don't fancy that you shall get off by saying you're sorry for committing this outrage upon me. assure yourself, i will stand up for my lawful rights, and your fine words shall not compensate for the blows you gave me. i know your kind of excuse: 'so sorry about it; will take my oath that you did not deserve such usage.' when the truth is i've been treated like a dog.

aeschinus, to parmeno: run quickly ahead and open the door.

sannio: then you don't pay any attention to what i say?

aeschinus, to the girl: step in quickly with him, my dear rogue.

sannio, stepping between them: but i won't let her go in.

aeschinus: close up on that side, parmeno; you are too far off. keep near to that son of a whore . . . so, that's good! take care to keep your eye full on mine, so when i wink you'll lose no time in giving him a mighty clout on the jaw.

Fig. 57. Text page from *Terence*, printed at the Allen Press, 1968. The illustration by Albrecht Dürer is reproduced by line-block, and printed in blue in the original

Austria. In 1939 Hammer abandoned all his possessions to make a fresh start in the United States. At Wells College in Aurora, New York, he resumed printing, and books continued to be produced under the Stamperia del Santuccio imprint until his death. But these were not his only publications; between 1941 and 1949 some eighteen books were printed with the imprint of Wells College Press, and from 1945 onwards his son Jacob Hammer produced others in similar style from the Hammer Press. Following a move to Lexington, Kentucky, in 1949, another imprint was also used for books produced by Carolyn Reading Hammer and by Jacob: the Anvil Press. Whatever the imprint, all the Hammer publications show a devotion to ideals of craftsmanship equal to those of any other private press. With Hammer's own types and illustration, they have a unity which can hardly be produced by other means; absolutely uncompromising in design and execution, they represent admirably the superb instrument a private press can be in an individual quest for perfection.

Among Hammer's friends in Lexington was a local businessman, Joseph C. Graves, whose own Gravesend Press produced very distinguished work during the 1950s. Very much under the Hammer influence, the Gravesend Press published a distinguished series of books, ranging from Judge Soule Smith's recipe for *The mint julep* (printed as a Christmas keepsake in 1959) to an edition of *Aucassin and Nicolette* with engravings by Fritz Kredel (1957). Not all Gravesend books were printed at the Press; to some extent Graves was less an amateur printer than a very discriminating patron, commissioning work from the Hammers, from Kredel and others. But in what was probably the most successful Gravesend book, Boccaccio's *The three admirable accidents of Andrea de Piero* (1954), all the work was executed in the Gravesend stable.

Much more eclectic in its approach to book design than any of the presses so far considered, the Allen Press of Kentfield, California, is in some ways closer to the French publishers of *beaux livres* than the English and American private printers with their quest for that very different thing: the Book Beautiful. Lewis and Dorothy Allen started their hand press in San Francisco in 1939, and during the 1940s produced a number of books, such as *Heraldry of New Helvetia* (1945) for the Book Club of California, and some for general sale. Following the Press's temporary removal to France, where in 1952 they printed Stevenson's *La Porte de Malétroit*, the Allens became fascinated by the *livres de peintres* in which the French excel, and they made an extensive study of those published since 1945. In their own words, they were 'lured from the strict and all-too-narrow path of straight book-making. It seemed to us that it was about time for American collectors to be exposed to a *livre de peintres*. And so, with high enthusiasm, we cast about for a text which would be in English, and which would be illustrated by one or more of the great artists of our day.'

The first of their essays in this manner was an extremely successful example of the genre: Yvan Goll's *Four poems of the occult* (1962), illustrated with reproductions by line-block and collotype of the line drawings by Fernand Léger, lithographs by Picasso, etchings by Yves Tanguy, and wood engravings by Jean Arp, which had been used in the original separate French editions of each poem. In order to produce some order and consistency in the design, the Californian artist Mallette Dean (who has printed some very handsome books on his own account) was commissioned to design border decorations and initials. The book was not bound; instead the unsewn sections were in the French manner enclosed in a portfolio which was in turn enclosed in a hinged box. Subsequent Allen Press publications have sometimes adopted a similar alternative to binding, like Byron's *A Venetian story* (1963), which was illustrated with offset-lithographic reproductions of eighteenth-century Venetian copper engravings; or Basil Hall's *The great polyglot Bibles* (1966), but for most subsequent books they have reverted to conventional binding—very much to be preferred, in my opinion, if you are attempting to print *books* and not museum pieces. In the scale of their work the Allens are far closer to the standards of Ashendene or of Cranach than almost any other private press still at work, as for instance in *Dialogues of creatures moralised* (1967), an imposing folio reprint of the English edition of 1535 with line-block reproductions of the woodcuts from Gerard Leeu's edition of 1480. In this, as in all the Allen Press work, the old methods of setting type by hand and printing it with loving care on dampened hand-made paper was used to achieve a standard of book production which, for all the missionary work of Nonesuch or the Limited Editions Club, is seldom equalled and never surpassed by more modern mechanical methods.

Other old-established Californian private presses operate on a very much more modest scale. At the Grace Hoper Press Sherwood Grover, for many years a compositor with the Grabhorns, has produced a series of *Typographical commonplace books* (in which quotations are set in a style and types suited to the passage) with amazing virtuosity. In Berkeley James D. Hart has since 1940 issued a small booklet each Christmas which is sent around to friends instead of a Christmas card. These have a strong family likeness—always the same format, the same hand-set Caslon type, the illustrations by Victor Anderson—

and make one regret that the owner does not print other books as well. Another Christmas printer is William P. Barlow, Jr. A fastidious craftsman, his annual productions have included some splendid pastiches of eighteenth-century printing and some amusing playlets for water-skiers. Thomas W. MacDonald's Black Mack is another press which today prints far too little to satisfy the many who admire its work.

The United States is richer than England in amateurs who experiment with papermaking and who also print. Dard Hunter's Mountain House Press is no more, but at the Bird & Bull Press in Pennsylvania, Henry Morris has been making papers of very good quality which he uses in his private printing. His first book was a translation of Fr. Imberdis's *Papyrus*, which he printed in 1961. Several of his subsequent books have also, naturally enough, been concerned with papermaking, and such volumes as *Five on paper* (1963) or *Omnibus* (1967) are interesting and highly accomplished work. Not all his books are so inward-looking, however; they have ranged from *A Babylonian anthology* (1966) to my own favourite, *Three Erfurt tales* (1962), an exceptionally attractive little book with illustrations reproduced by line-block from the woodcuts in the fifteenth-century original—not by any means easy to match with a typeface of the same colour, but very well done by Morris.

Very much less well known than Henry Morris's work in papermaking and printing are the similar activities of Walter S. Hamady of Madison, Wisconsin. His Perishable Press has been at work a relatively short time. Much more literary in its aims than Bird & Bull, the books of the Perishable Press have a family likeness which is agreeable and textually many of them are extremely good. Hamady has experimented with illustration far less than Morris, relying for his effects on the good impression of his Palatino types on papers of unusual textures. On occasion he uses colour in an unexpected and extremely effective manner—the title-page of his *Plumfoot poems* (1967), for instance, is all in black save for a single hyphen in violet. Like many of the better American private presses which do not undertake their own binding, Hamady often has his binding done by Elizabeth Kner of Chicago.

In the fastidious care with which Hamady designs his books he approaches some of the presses which exist in order to provide a means of the owner fulfilling his artistic aims. Leonard Baskin's Gehenna Press at Northampton, Massachusetts, is one of the finest of these. He started printing while an art student at Yale, later working at Worcester, Massachusetts, before moving to Northampton. He works closely with Richard Warren of the Metcalf Printing Company which now produces most of the Gehenna imprints, which have

The rann, the rann, the King of all birds,
St. Stephen's Day she was caught in the furze;
Though she is little, her family's great,
O Luck for me lady, and give us a treat.
Me boots is worn, me clothes is torn,
Following the rann three miles or more,
So up with the kettle and down with the pan,
Give us an answer before we go on;
Put your hand in your pocket,
From that to your purse,
If ye don't give us money, we'll give ye our curse,
If ye don't give us money, if ye don't give us meat,
We'll bury the rann at the pier of the gate:
Up with your kettle, down with your pan,
A penny or tuppence to bury the rann.

THE WREN-BOYS' RHYME *is still sung in Ireland on St. Stephen's Day, December 26th,
by boys who carry a live wren from door to door — unaware that their chant is the survival
of an ancient, ritual king-killing at the winter solstice, meant to ensure the return of the
sun and the beginning of a new year. It is sent to you now with the latter intention by*
JOSEPH LOW *and the* EDEN HILL PRESS *in Newtown, Connecticut.*

Fig. 58. Joseph Low's *The wren boys' rhyme,* printed at his Eden Hill Press

included *Thirteen poems by Wilfred Owen,* with illustrations by Ben Shahn (1956), and a collection of etchings by Baskin on *Horned beetles and other insects* which was printed on a range of handmade papers. Much of his finest work, such as Hart Crane's *Voyages* (1957), which has some very delicate wood-engravings, has been for the Museum of Modern Art in New York. His influence in illustration has been profound; traces of his very personal style can be seen in a great many recent books from American presses.

Baskin's work is, at first sight, full of pessimism; almost Mexican in its obsession with death—even his still-life engravings are full of despair. Joseph Low's work at his Eden Hill Press in Connecticut is the exact opposite, bubbling over with exuberance. Low started to print for the very sound reason that only the artist himself can print his illustrations with the right concern for make-ready, density of ink and other details of production. Another printer could do it easily enough, but no matter how careful and sensitive, he could not anticipate the decisions that the artist would make on these matters; to the extent that *he* has to decide, he comes to share something of the responsibility for the work with the artist. Low wished, as all artists do, to have control over the execution just as over the conception. He is a master of the coarse-textured cut, and has produced some marvellously effective linocuts and rubbercuts— sometimes scraped or etched or sanded down to change the texture. His books, such as *Ten proverbs* (1959) or *The wren boys' rhyme* (1961) are very attractive and understandably sought after.

Another private printer who has made considerable and successful use of linocuts is Bill Jackson of Wichita, Kansas. His 'Printing House at the Sign of the Four Ducks' has produced a number of catalogues and pamphlets for the University of Kansas Library and for other patrons, but has published relatively little on its own account. But the *Four Ducks Press Annual Reports*, a splendid variation on the Christmas booklets or cards produced by so many private presses, are eagerly collected by many.

Jackson is by profession an advertising man. Another such who shares Jackson's enthusiasm for calligraphy is Herbert W. Simpson of Evansville, Indiana. His Feather Vender Press has produced very little, but two of its productions—offset lithographic printings of two of Shakespeare's sonnets and of *Hamlet to the Players*, written out by Raymond DaBoll—are among the most attractive calligraphic work to have been printed by any private press.

Among the presses which have been set up in the past few years the Janus Press, formerly of Philadelphia, and now in Vermont, is one with most consistent excellence in work. While in Philadephia it produced books with a

O Lord, we beseech thee mercifully to hear us; and

grant that we, to whom thou hast given an hearty

desire to pray, may, by thy mighty aid, be defended

and comforted in all dangers and adversities;

through Jesus Christ our Lord. Amen

BOOK OF COMMON PRAYER

Fig. 59. A page from *A Book of prayers*, printed by the Janus Press, 1965.
Wood-engraving by Helen Siegl

variety of illustration processes, such as Kafka's *Parables and paradoxes* (1963) with lithographs by the owner Claire van Vliet. Nowadays although it publishes the occasional book without illustrations, such as *The poetry of Demetrios Capetanakis* (1966), most of its books are illustrated with fine wood-engravings of deceptive simplicity by Helen Siegl; such as Oscar Wilde's *The selfish giant* (1967) and Nancy Willard's *A new herball* (1968). Some of these were printed at the Cypher Press in Philadelphia, which has been responsible for the production of some other fine work, like Edith Kaplan's coloured wood-cuts for *Voices of the revolution*, an anthology edited by Helen Haynes (1967).

The Janus Press books are now distributed by Ferdinand Roten Galleries of Baltimore. Another Press whose work is sometimes distributed by the same galleries is that of Howard John Besnia, the Scarab Press of Sterling Junction, Massachusetts. Still very new, in its typography the Press still does not have the sureness of touch of Eden Hill or Janus, but Besnia's illustrations —his wood-engravings in John McGrail's *Potsherds and palimpsests* (1965) or his relief etchings for McGrail's *Antiphon for the feast of a virgin not a martyr* (1967)—are very successful, and the Press promises very highly.

Just as in England, there are monastic presses at work. One of the most interesting of these is St. Teresa's Press, run by the Carmelite Nuns of Flemington, New Jersey. Calligraphy and illumination were among the crafts practised at the Monastery, and the Press started almost by accident, as a result of a visit by Mrs Herbert Teeple (of the Tudor Press) who showed them Ben Lieberman's *Printing as a hobby*. They thought that a small press would be useful for the community's printing, and despite early disappointments with a small hand press they decided to make printing the work of their community. A second-hand cylinder press was installed (the Nuns soon got to work on this; when the printer who was to show them how to use it arrived, he was amazed—never had he seen so dazzlingly clean a press, even in the showroom). They set to work printing small books about Carmel and its spirit; books with no special typographical merit, but very useful practice, for—having been shown Stanbrook Abbey's *The path to peace*—they decided to attempt work of high quality. In their first fine book, *The prince of peace* (1965), the Stanbrook model was followed closely; in their second, *The dream of the rood* (1966), which was again illuminated, they turned to *The book of Kells* for inspiration. It was a very dangerous model, but the book was carried out with surprising success. With *Psalms of praise* (1967) they succeeded very well in producing printing of Stanbrook quality allied to exquisite illumination of initials. We can look forward to very accomplished work from this Press in the future.

NOS GALAN

NOW the joyful bells a-ringing,
  "All ye mountains praise the Lord."
Lift our hearts, like birds a-winging,
"All ye mountains praise the Lord."
Now our festal season bringing
Kinsmen all, to bide and board,
Sets our cheery voices singing:
"All ye mountains praise the Lord."

Dear our home as dear none other;
"Where the mountains praise the Lord."
Gladly here our care we smother;
"Where the mountains praise the Lord"
Here we know that Christ our brother
(Binds us all as by a cord:
He was born of Mary mother,
"Where the mountains praise the Lord."

Fig. 60. A page from *The prince of peace*, printed by the Nuns of St. Teresa's Press, 1965.
In the original the initial is in gold, outlined in black

Printing for pleasure flourishes in the United States to a far greater degree than it does in England, and the past twenty years have seen many amateur affairs which produce work of value and of typographical distinction among the many more which never attempt book work, but which entertain their owners. Not all these small presses are so new, of course, Emerson G. Wulling's Sumac Press dates back to 1915, and in recent years has produced some very attractive work. Its appeal is mainly to other printers, being concerned largely with niceties of style, as in the various *Press preterite* pamphlets, or in Wulling's attractive little study of *J. Johnson typ.* (1967). Another printer whose work appeals mainly to enthusiasts of amateur printing is James Lamar Weygand of Nappanee, Indiana. His 'Private press of the Indiana Kid' has produced many small books on printing, on the pressmarks used by printers and similar topics, while his regular column on private presses in the *American book collector* has done a great deal to spread knowledge and interest among amateurs. In Detroit, Leonard Bahr's Adagio Press produces a good deal, again material mainly of interest to other printers, though when he breaks out of this into a wider field, as with Ruskin's *The contemptible horse* (1962), his work is of such very high quality that one regrets that he prints so little that is of general interest. Paul Hayden Duensing's work at his private press and typefoundry at Kalamazoo, Michigan, is of the same high technical quality, but it is also restricted in its publishing to material on typography. Some of its books, such as Phil Nuernberger's *Electrolytic matrices* (1966), are models of what such work should be.

Another group of amateurs publishes books on history, particularly local history. The Press of John Cumming, at Mount Pleasant, Michigan, has issued several books, such as George Burges's *Journal of a surveying trip into western Pennsylvania in the year 1795* (1965) or Basil Austin's *The diary of a ninety-eighter* (1968) which have considerable historical value. Yet another Michigan press, Gary L. Granger's Plane Tree Press at Lansing, has printed Sadie Woodward's *Grand River road*, another small book of considerable use to local historians which because of its limited market potential would be unlikely to appear from a commercial publisher.

Other private presses quite often issue books of a similar local historical interest, while not necessarily specializing in them—Roger Levenson's Tamalpais Press in Berkeley, California, for example, with its very handsome *Directory of California wine growers and wine makers in 1860* (1967). Perhaps the most important of all these small presses which are preserving material of local interest in a satisfactory typographical form is the Ashantilly Press at

TWENTY-EIGHT

The Contemptible Horse

dart with it—a bird steers with it—a rattlesnake scolds with it—a monkey can climb with it—and a whale can sink a ship with it—but a horse must have it tied in a knot—or cut off altogether. Seventhly—and in one great count, a horse is the most mischievous of all animals while he is alive and

Fig. 61. A page from *The contemptible horse*, printed at the Adagio Press, 1962. Line drawing by Adele Bichan

KITCHEN SONNETS

BY MINNIE ELMER
AND
JUDITH MOSHER

WOODCUTS BY
SHIRLEY BARKER

Tamalpais Press ◆ *The Friends of Minnie Elmer* ◆ 1966

Fig. 62. A Tamalpais Press title-page

The Journal
of
Samuel Kirkland

NOVEMBER, 1764 - FEBRUARY, 1765

The Alexander Hamilton Private Press
Clinton, New York
1966

Fig. 63. A title-page from the Alexander Hamilton Press

Darien, Georgia, where William G. Haynes Jr. has printed such books as *The field diary of a Confederate soldier* by Draughton Stith Haynes (1963) and *The journal of Anna Wylly Habersham* (1961). Haynes is a very competent typographer and illustrator, and some of his other books, such as Alexander A. Lawrence's *Johny Leber and the Confederate major* (1962) or Margaret McGarvey's *D-Dawn and other poems* (1964), are very satisfying books to handle and read.

Among the smallest hobby presses on the west coast, two in particular are of interest. At the Tenfingers Press in Los Angeles Frank J. Thomas has printed several little books, such as *Proverbis on musyke* (1962) or *Mission cattle brands* (1967) which are among the most attractive work produced by amateurs. Thomas is a professional photographer, and originally started printing in order to produce compliments slips and the like for his business, building his own wooden flatbed press for the purpose. Most of his books have been

Kaʄka saiɒ/
I'ɒ give anything
to be a Benoni
on a Sunday afternoon/
just as the 22 letters
broke into his
threecornered room
and backed him up
against the wall.

Fig. 64. A page from *Aleph, Benoni & Zaddik* (Tenfingers Press, 1968)

printed on an Adana flatbed press—that stand-by of the contemporary printer for pleasure—and most have been illustrated with linocuts or stencilled illustrations by the owner. But occasionally Thomas has used his skills as a photographer: *Mark Twain roughed it here* was illustrated with a number of tipped-in photographs. The other press, the Magpie Press, has also used an Adana flatbed on occasion, although a table Albion press is normally employed. Run by two young ladies, Roberta Nixon and Margaret Gustavson Taylor, the Press is closely connected with the UCLA Library School. Their first publication, Machado de Assis's *What went on at the Baroness'* (1963), was

SIX POEMS

Eugene Vincent Ellis

DRAWINGS BY WILLIAM L. SWENEY

THE TINHORN PRESS ATLANTA GEORGIA MCMLXVII

Fig. 65. A Tinhorn Press title-page

printed on UCLA equipment, while *The Magpie Press typographical cookbook* (1964) contained recipes contributed by the staff of UCLA Library which were set in a typographical style suited to the dish. Most Magpie work is small, but that it still appears at all is astonishing, since all the recent work has been printed with one partner in Hawaii and the other in California. In style it is among the most classical of private presses; its execution is also extremely good. Such books as Eleanor R. Edelstein's *Seven poems* (1967) or *The bequeathing of the Doves types* (1966) are models of the sort of work which can be printed by amateurs with limited spare time and restricted typographical resources.

A commentary on skill and dexterity.
This is the sort of thing that can raise
hell with feeding, sorting and scratching.

Fig. 66. A leaf from *A show of hands*, printed at the Glad Hand Press, 1964.
Wood-engraving by John de Pol

It is in this matter of time and typographical resources that today's amateurs differ most from their wealthier and more leisured precursors. Many of them might wish to print books, substantial books, but if one has only a few hours each week which can be devoted to printing, a hand press on which one can print only a page at a time, and only enough type to set two or three pages at the most, then it is no wonder that many amateurs are not prepared to undertake anything of more than six or eight pages. Even a forty or fifty-page book will take many months, perhaps years to complete; if the amateur undertakes it he often finds that there is little pleasure left in his work. One solution is to abandon hand-setting, as the owners of the Vine Press did—but this is to abandon what many amateurs find the most enjoyable part of printing—another is to abandon the presswork, either handing over the formes to an outside printer, as G. P. Winship did from choice and Guido Morris from necessity, or else limiting the edition to a very short run indeed. For the enthusiast or collector, this can be very frustrating: John S. Fass's Hammer Creek Press in New York is reputed to produce very fine work, but as he keeps the tedium out of presswork by limiting his editions to two (sometimes even a single copy) I have never been able to lay my hands on any of it. But for many amateurs it is not just the composition or the presswork which makes a long-drawn-out project irksome; the time it takes is enough to turn what should be a pleasure into a chore. The obvious solution is to limit themselves to ephemera.

One way in which many of these amateurs have found it possible to produce more extensive work, without its losing its freshness, is through the development of the 'Chappel' movement. In the printing trade, to quote Moxon's words 'Every *Printing-house* is by the Custom of Time out of mind, called a *Chappel*; and all the Workmen that belong to it are *Members of the Chappel*: and the Oldest Freeman is *Father of the Chappel.* . . . There have been formerly Customs and By-Laws made and intended for the well and good Government of the *Chappel*, and for the more Civil and orderly deportment of all its Members while in the *Chappel* . . .' The term was borrowed by Ben Kieberman of the Herity Press as a name for a club of amateur printers living close enough together to meet regularly and to co-operate in printing projects as a group. The advantages were obvious; the companionship of those with like interests, with the chance to talk shop and pool knowledge, the chance to borrow equipment or to buy type, ink or paper in bulk; the opportunity of promoting public interest by organizing lectures, exhibitions and the like. The first Chappel (Dr. Lieberman insists on the spelling) to be formed was the Moxon Chappel on the West Coast, but it was soon followed by the formation of others—the New York Chappel, Westchester, Manhattan, Monks and Friars and others on the East Coast. A London Chappel has also been formed, but the infinitely less clubbable English have not taken up the idea to any extent, preferring to keep their co-operation informal. Without any doubt the

Chappel movement has done a good deal to encourage interest in printing and to improve the standards of workmanship of the tyro. Some of the co-operative projects have been full of verve—the calendars printed by the New York and Westchester Chappels, for example, in which each member Press has responsibility for producing the leaf for one month, the only common factor being the size of the leaf. The New York Chappel has gone further than this, printing some *Uncommonplace books*—in which each signature contains a short piece printed by one of the members—the *New York ABC* (1963) a *Goudy type sampler* (1965) and other pieces. In these, the standard of workmanship is obviously variable, and there is an obvious limit to the amount of co-operative book making which can be done. The most attractive work of the member presses is often that done separately—Fridolf Johnson's Mermaid Press in New York, for example, has never surpassed his *Nasty Nancy and her cat, a horrid ABC book* (1962) which is one of the most charming of all miniature books.

Co-operative work of this nature is not, needless to say, limited to the members of chappels. John Ryder organized a *Miniature Folio of private presses* with considerable success some years ago. Charles Antin, owner of the Serendipity Press in New York, has been responsible for the production of a number of keepsakes, for Alfred A. Knopf (1965) and in memory of Paul A. Bennett of the Typophiles (1968); slipcases containing four-page gatherings printed by distinguished presses (public as well as private) which contain as good a collection of distinguished contemporary printing as one could hope to see. William F. Haywood has for many years now done very much the same thing on a much humbler level with his annual collection of work from different private presses published under the title *It's a small world*. In Canada—which merits a chapter to itself, for its private press work from such competent printers as William Rueter at the Aliquando Press and Peter Dorn at the Heinrich Heine Presse is of very high quality, and quite distinct from the American tradition—the Guild of Hand Printers has for several years produced a portfolio of pieces printed by the members under the title *Wrongfount*. The latest such collection, *Wrongfount 6* (1968), was entitled 'Carl Dair in quotes' and was designed as a memorial volume to Canada's most distinguished typographer.

To attempt to describe the work of all the amateur presses in North America which print interesting work calls for a book in itself. Some further idea of their variety can be obtained if we close with a note on only two more, both in New York. The Peter Kavanagh Hand Press prints books in very limited editions, on a press built by the owner; books such as Lois Byrnes' *Recusant books in America* (1961) or *The John Quinn letters* (printed from the originals which Mr. Kavanagh read and memorized in the New York Public Library—which rapidly obtained an injunction against the publication of the book) or the owner's own dramatic works. These are all produced in very limited editions, and sold only to libraries, and libraries of which Mr. Kavanagh approves at that. At the other extreme is Banter University Press, now alas no longer at work. George Rike's work as Associate Director of this smallest of University presses was distinctly subversive. Far too little of it is available in England, though the quotations from it in Bernard Keelan's *A bold face on it* (privately published by Arborfield in 1964) are very tempting, with such morsels as the colophon 'set by hand, printed by hand, addressed by hand and dropped into the mail box by a giant machine'. Or Banter's application for a grant to the Ford Foundation:

'We are encountering vexing problems in our research in a field that lies largely unexplored—Medieval Printing in the United States. Obtaining the necessary documents, especially, is proving quite costly since in most cases we must manufacture them ourselves. We therefore wish to make application to the Ford Foundation for the sum of $584.17 . . . We understand that foundations look with horror on such relatively small grants. If, however, you feel that the expense of the necessary paperwork would not justify the granting of such a tiny sum, we shall be glad to oblige by revising our request upwards to $1,647,382.31.'

With such presses at work, who can doubt the pleasure and value of amateur printing?

21

School and teaching presses

⎯⎯⎯⎯

I t was not only among the aristocracy that the virtues of the printing press for teaching purposes was realized, and though one may think of the school press as being a twentieth-century phenomenon it is in fact very much older. One of the oldest of teaching presses however was not in a school, nor even on dry land, but on board HMS *Caledonia* while she was blockading Toulon during the Napoleonic wars. Today presses on board liners, and printing at sea, are of everyday occurrence, but they were not at all common in the days of sail. The press on board the *Caledonia* was by no means the earliest—the French fleet which under the command of the Comte d'Estaing assisted the struggling American colonies in their revolutionary war carried a press on which in 1778 a *Déclaration adressée . . . à tous les anciens François de l'Amerique septentrionale* was printed in Boston roads, and a number of other pieces were also printed on this press in Boston and in Newport, Rhode Island. But the press was an official one, 'L'Imprimerie Royale de l'Escadre', whereas the *Caledonia*'s press was supplied for the amusement and instruction of the cadets on board by Admiral Pellew. It was a thoughtful provision; the maintenance of the blockade was a wearisome business, and the opportunity to relieve their enforced idleness must have been particularly welcome to the cadets. Two books were printed; the first a thirty-eight-page octavo entitled *The bloody journal kept by William Davidson on board a Russian pirate in the year 1789* (1812), a horrifying account of cold-blooded slaughter which had first been printed by Sir Walter Scott in the *Edinburgh annual register* for 1810; in the following year the cadets printed a small quarto volume of nearly one hundred pages containing translations (made on board) of Ruiz de Padron's speech *The tribunal of the inquisition* and of Jovellanos's *Bread and Bulls*.

A similar use was to be found for the printing press in whiling away time on some of the Arctic expeditions. While the *Hecla* was icebound during

Captain Parry's voyage of 1819–20 a weekly newspaper entitled *The North Georgia gazette and winter chronicle* was printed on board. Much later, in the expedition of 1850–1 which was sent in search of Sir John Franklin (who had perished in the quest for the North-West Passage), a press which the Admiralty had supplied for printing balloon papers was set to work on printing playbills, songs and other trifles. So great did the enthusiasm for printing become among the officers that they exhausted the stock of paper and turned to chamois leather, shirts, blankets and any other surface that would serve to take printing. The last playbill of the expedition was printed on a piece of leather:

Royal Arctic Theatre
H.M.S. Assistance
Last Night of the Season
Friday 28th February 1851
Historical Drama in two acts of Charles XII
After which, Grand Phantasmagorical Magic Figures
To conclude with the new Pantomime of Zero
Doors open at six o'clock, commence at 6.30
Griffiths Island Printing Office

As well as these sea and Arctic presses, there was to be one in the Antarctic. *Aurora Australis, 1908–1909* 'printed at the sign of the Penguins' was printed on a small Albion press in the winter quarters of the British Antarctic Expedition during the winter months of April to July 1908. Sir Ernest Shackleton's Preface is interesting:

'The reader will understand better the difficulty of producing a book quite up to the mark when he is told that, owing to the low temperature in the hut, the only way to keep the printing-ink in a fit state to use was to have a candle burning under the inking plate; and so, if some pages are printed more lightly than others, it is due to the difficulty of regulating the heat, and, consequently, the thinning or thickening of the ink.

'Again, the printing office was only six feet by seven, and had to accommodate a large sewing machine and bunks for two men, so the lack of room was a disadvantage. The printing was done entirely by Joyce and Wilde, the lithography and etchings by Marston, and the covers, made of provision cases, were manufactured by Day . . .'

These last were not, of course, school presses, but belong on the fringe of the more frivolous group of printers for pleasure. The Victorian teaching presses were by no means frivolous or intended for pleasure; they were set up with the serious and charitable purpose of teaching a trade. One of the earliest of all Trade schools was set up in circumstances which could scarcely have been less encouraging; it was the private venture of a Protestant clergyman in the little village of Bunmahon on the coast of County Waterford in Ireland. The Reverend D. A. Doudney had been a printer in London before he felt a call to the Church. He entered the Church of Ireland, and in 1847 had been ordained Curate of Monksland and Vicar of Kilcash. At the time Bunmahon was a wretchedly poor place, just recovering from the horrors of the great famine, and Dr. Doudney set up industrial and agricultural schools with the laudable intention of providing work for the younger generation in his parish. In 1851 he decided to supplement these with a printing school, inspired by a similar institution which had been set up in the East End of London. He had long wanted to reprint Dr. Gill's *Commentary on the Bible*, and advertised his intention of starting the school and solicited subscribers to the work in the *Gospel magazine* which he edited. The response of readers was encouraging, and Dr. Doudney went off to London to negotiate terms with a publisher, to order the presses and equipment, and to employ some skilled assistants. On his return to Bunmahon, he had much difficulty in finding premises for his new school: there were very few Protestants in the village and the Catholic population was (scarcely surprisingly) opposed to an enterprise which they believed would be used for proselytizing purposes. But the venture got under way, and within two years the boys of the school, who when they started had never seen types or press before, had proved such apt pupils that the six stout quarto volumes of Gill's *Exposition* had been printed in an edition of 2,500 copies. This was no slight undertaking, and had it not been for a providential bequest of £1,000 it would certainly have come to grief—for Dr. Doudney paid his boys from three to twelve shillings a week according to merit after the first month of training, and the cost of materials (twenty-five tons of paper were used) was by no means low. Many other works were undertaken, including a weekly sheet, *Old Jonathan*, and later also the *Gospel magazine*; one of the most interesting of these was *A pictorial outline of the rise and progress of the Bonmahon . . . schools* which Doudney wrote and published in 1856. But the later works were less successful than the first, and the difficulties of selling the press's work were considerable. Doudney's Bishop was unwilling to allow him to spend much time away from his parish in England, the natural market for the Press's work, and in 1858 he was forced to close the Press to avoid running into debt himself. Many of his students later found work in printing houses in

England and America, and Doudney himself resigned his living and left Ireland. He later set up a similar school at Bedminster, which had a much longer life. At Bunmahon he and his schools are now totally forgotten. Visiting the village a year or two ago, I found the Protestant church closed; its windows bricked up and the churchyard a wilderness—while the buildings which had housed the printing school and had been such a hive of activity were in ruins, and silent except for the grunting of a pig rooting in them.

Another charitable press which was concerned largely with the printing of theological works (though of a very different sort from those printed at Bunmahon) was the Holy Rood Press, which was active in Oxford from 1877 to 1882. The press had been set up very much earlier than this: about 1855, Miss Sellon, the Mother Superior of the Devonport Society of Sisterhood, had suggested to E. B. Pusey that printing would be a suitable trade to teach orphan girls. Dr. Pusey welcomed the idea, and assisted in its realization by purchasing the printing equipment of his friend the Rev. Charles Marriott, who wished to give up the press which he had operated at Littlemore since 1848. The new Press was set up at Bristol, and subsequently removed to the headquarters of the Sisterhood in Plymouth.

In 1870 it was thought that it would be more convenient for Dr. Pusey (who provided the bulk, if not indeed all of the material to be printed) to have his printing done in Oxford, where it could be done under his own supervision. Miss Sellon purchased a house named Holy Rood for the purpose, and after her death in 1876 it was purchased by Pusey. Henceforth it was in every sense his own private press. It was no small undertaking: as well as Miss Mary Milner (who took charge of the concern at Pusey's request) there were a housekeeper, a male overseer and eight orphan girls who were apprenticed personally to Pusey and were clothed, housed, fed and educated at his expense. All Pusey's works which he published from 1870 onwards—every book, sermon, or address which he wrote or edited (and they were by no means few in number), was set up by his apprentices, who had to cope with Latin, Greek and Hebrew as well as their benefactor's abominable handwriting. They managed all this with surprising skill and neatness: though the books they produced are in no sense lovely to behold they are quite up to the commercial standards of the day. The cynic could suggest that Holy Rood was in fact just a vanity press, but there seems little doubt that it would have been considerably cheaper and more convenient for Pusey to get his printing done elsewhere by a commercial printer or at the University Press, and that his charitable motives were impeccable.

Most of the work set in type at Holy Rood was not printed there: the presswork was too heavy for Pusey to allow the girls to undertake it, and in any case he had no reason for preferring hand printing to the powered press. It was therefore normal practice only to pull galley-proofs at Holy Rood, the corrected formes being sent over to the Clarendon Press for machining. Very occasionally small editions were printed on the premises, such as *Eleven addresses during a retreat of the Companions of the Love of Jesus*, a duodecimo of 184 pages of which eight copies were printed in 1882. After Pusey died in the same year all printing ceased; the orphanage being transferred to Ascot Priory.

Most school and teaching presses were and are of a very different sort from these charitable undertakings. The commonest sort of all is the press which is maintained as an adjunct to the handicrafts room in a school. There are many hundreds of these, varying in their equipment from a flatbed Adana with a few card founts (like H. G. Dixey's press in its earliest days at the Dragon school) to well-furnished printing offices in which school magazines and the like are printed with the aid of senior boys. On occasion these presses have met with an even sourer reception from the Trade than did the parlour printers of the late nineteenth century: in the 1920s, for instance, William Williams, headmaster of the Council School at Rhostryfan, Caernarvonshire, obtained a small press and type with the idea of teaching the senior boys the principles of the craft by allowing them to set up some small pieces. There was an immediate outcry among local printers, to such effect that Mr. Williams was prevented from carrying on with his plans: he was allowed to demonstrate how it was done, but no more. As a result, all the work of this press—little booklets on Welsh history, in the main—were printed by Mr. Williams's unaided efforts.

Few of the school presses produce much of any interest to outsiders. One very notable exception is the Art Society Press at King's College School, Wimbledon, which since 1951 has been producing a range of books, illustrated with an astonishing number of different processes—wood-engraving, lino-cutting, relief etching and many more—with splendid results. As anybody who has ever attempted to teach printing to amateurs knows, the difficulties of maintaining the interest of the students throughout the production of a book are considerable, and to maintain a proper continuity in every detail when there may be a couple of dozen people involved in the production is almost impossible. At the Art Society Press, which is far more than an art room frill of interest only to those few enthusiasts 'good at art'—its production team is always

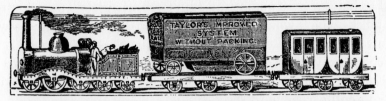

RULES & REGULATIONS.

Every passenger in the second or third class is to be allowed to carry a dark lantern or a penny candle, or a safety lamp into the train with him. The directors have kept the public in the dark quite long enough.

Every tunnel must be illuminated with one candle at least.

No train is to travel slower than an omnibus, let the excursion be ever so cheap, or the occasion ever so joyful.

No stoppage at a railway station is to exceed half an hour.

Cattle are to be separated from the passengers as much as possible, as it has been found from experiments that men and oxen do not mix sociably together.

No fare is to be raised more than at the rate of a pound a week.

No third class carriage is to contain more than a foot deep of water in wet weather, but, to prevent accidents, corks and swimming belts should always be kept in open carriages. The ladies' carriages are to be waited upon by female policemen.

No railway dividend is to exceed 100 p.c. and no bonus to be divided oftener than once a month.

No station should be situated at a distance of more than ten miles from the nearest place of habitation. It is undesirable that passengers expend their energies before boarding the train lest they be no longer capable of walking if and when required to do so on the journey.

Punch's *Suggested Rules and Regulations.*

4

Fig. 67. A page from *Victoriana*, produced by the Art Society Press, 1968

large, and includes a good number of sixth form scientists—they do things with type and blocks which would make a professional printer's hair go white, but they get away with it. Of all the books from this Press, *Victoriana* is probably the most completely successful, and has gone into several editions; to my mind *Graphic methods*, an anthology of the Press's first ten years, published in 1961, represents its enthusiasm most successfully.

The trade printing schools have necessarily a less frivolous approach to the book arts: they cannot afford to use methods which would disrupt a normal printing office. They had their roots deep in the private press movements: in 1905 Professor Lethaby, who as Principal of the London County Council Central School was the St. Paul of the Arts and Crafts Movement, invited J. H. Mason to start part-time classes in printing at the School. At the time Mason was still compositor at the Doves Press, but in 1909 he resigned to take a full-time teaching appointment which Lethaby offered him. At first in temporary premises over a factory in Union Street, and later in Southampton Row, Mason taught the production methods and the modest, simple typographic style of the Hammersmith crusaders. The specimens of the students' work show a quest for perfection which was as characteristic of Mason as it was of the Doves Press.

There were of course critics, who saw in Mason's methods merely a wilful defiance of modern industrial methods. What he was doing, in fact, was precisely the same thing that Edward Johnston was doing in his classes in lettering at 'the Central'—returning to first principles, building up a strong foundation for his students to build upon in their later work. The result, in Sir Francis Meynell's words, 'was to release young minds from those chains of the prison-house with which industrial life too easily shackles those who have been taught *how* to do things before they have any chance to ask why—*why* they are done.'

This concentration on 'fine edition work' was not of course without its dangers: to return to first principles was all very well, but just as it could be (and was) argued against the private presses of the Arts and Crafts Movement that they were producing books for the wealthy so Mason's methods were unsuited to improving run-of-the-mill printing. He turned out fine printers, when there was a greater need for merely good printers. Meynell at the Nonesuch Press was to grapple with this problem in the field of fine book production, and under Leonard Jay the Birmingham School of Printing was to demonstrate the virtues possessed by mechanical printing methods.

Jay had been one of Mason's earliest pupils at 'the Central', and in 1912 joined him as his assistant. While there he had, during Mason's absence at Weimar advising Count Kessler on the Cranach Press, instituted teaching in display setting and in advertising design, and when in 1925 he was appointed head of the new School of Printing in Birmingham he was able to pursue his ideas about the suitability of powered presses and mechanical setting for good work. Despite some opposition within the art school, where some condemned mechanical aids on the grounds that they would promote commercialism and debase standards, Jay persuaded George Davis of Linotype and W. I. Burch of Monotype, and the manufacturers of powered presses, to provide equipment as essential training tools. Soon the first of the long series of books and pamphlets which were set up and printed by the students in the Printing School were to allay the fears of his opponents. The work of the School's Press was to earn an international reputation for excellent work in its charming limited editions, which have deservedly become collected by lovers of fine printing. There was to be no such thing as a 'Birmingham style' (any more than there was a 'Nonesuch style'); each collector has his own favourites, but the series devoted to Baskerville, and the five volumes set by Jay personally, have particular charm.

The other Schools of Printing in Britain as they grew up were also to produce many handsome and collectable books, though none have achieved the output of Birmingham. The quarterly journal *Book design and production* used regularly to include a column on the work of the schools and colleges; work which is too seldom seen outside a very limited circle. Though other printing trade journals sometimes include notes on these books, it has become very much harder to find what is being produced since *Book design and production* ceased publication a few years ago, yet for the typophile many of them are far more interesting than the work of contemporary amateurs—for example, Leicester College of Art's *Slate engraving* (1964), a very accomplished study of the slate-engraved tombstones of Cornwall and Leicestershire, with lithographs from rubbings of the originals.

Most of these presses have moved very far from the methods of the Doves Press or of J. H. Mason, and have followed the Birmingham pattern closely. This is natural enough; the number of printers engaged in book work is very limited and there is far more demand for those with a knowledge of display work. One press which is far closer to the tradition of the private presses (though very far away from Mason in execution) is the Lion and Unicorn Press. This was started as a non-profit-making venture at the Royal College of Art in 1955, with the aim of giving practical training to the book production students by printing books which would be a serious contribution to design and scholarship. It is unlike most other work from the schools, in that it is possible for outsiders to subscribe to the books, several of which have been sufficiently successful to be reissued later by commercial publishers. The books have ranged from *The letters of Gainsborough* to selections from *English as she is spoke*, and are extremely accomplished examples of book making. For the present writer one of the earliest, *The life of John Wilkes gentleman* (1955), has most charm, but all are interesting. The Royal College of Art seems to have had little difficulty in obtaining subscribers to its series; it is a pity that other schools of printing have not followed a similar policy.

In the United States, as might be expected, there is a similarly large number of school presses producing fine work. Of these the most famous, and deservedly so, was the Laboratory Press which was directed by Porter Garnett at Carnegie Institute of Technology in Pittsburgh from 1923 until 1935. The Press was planned as a centre for the study of fine printing where students 'should be encouraged and trained to strive for excellence, dignified originality, and distinction'. With its motto *Nil vulgare/Nil pertriti/Nil inepti* and Garnett's careful concern with type, paper and ink allied to the use of the hand press, the Laboratory Press was to carry the private press message into the market place in very much the same manner that J. H. Mason had done in London. But it was to do so with even more success; less backward-looking than Mason, Garnett showed a typically American flair in his missionary work, and the effect of the Laboratory Press upon commercial printing was to be considerable. Many projects were produced by the students: books by Paul Valery, by Lewis Mumford, by Henri Focillon and others, all of which have become as much collected as the work of the Birmingham School. So successful was the Press in fact that in 1963 Carnegie Tech. revived the venture under the name of the New Laboratory Press, directed by Jack W. Stauffacher. But the revival was not a success: there was a conflict of policies with the university authorities, and after only a few small books had been produced Stauffacher returned to his native state of California.

At the Pratt Institute in New York, the Pratt Adlib Press under the direction of Fritz Eichenberg has been producing a series of annual publications and keepsakes which are available on subscription. Like the work of the Lion and Unicorn Press, its books—of which *Posada's Dance of death* and *A Frasconi family travelogue* are representative—are splendid displays of virtuosity. The student work produced in the Davison Art Center of Wesleyan University, on the other hand, is very much closer to the traditional and contemporary ideas of private press work, and some of the experiments which Russell T. Limbach's students have made with printing Bewick's wood engravings are extremely interesting. The editions are again, though, usually very limited and seldom generally available. The illustrations in *Art Laboratory impressions* (1960) showing some of the work produced since the press was first set up in 1943 are tantalizing indeed.

JAMES RUBY

CREEPY CREATURES

The Art Laboratory
WESLEYAN UNIVERSITY
M C M L X V I

Fig. 68. An Art Laboratory Press title-page

One variety of school press which is not to be found in England flourishes in the United States in some of the Schools of Journalism. Students in the Typographical Laboratory at the School of Journalism in the University of Iowa have the benefit of working under Harry Duncan of the Cummington Press, and their work, in such books as *Leigh Hunt on eight sonnets of Dante* (1965), is very distinguished. And at Syracuse some of the publications of the

Castle Room Press, the imprint of students working in the Goudy Typographical Laboratory, is also very attractive.

A group of teaching presses which remains faithful to the principles of hand setting and the hand press are the bibliographical presses which have grown up in universities and schools of librarianship in the past fifteen or twenty years. Bibliography is by no means a new subject, but the recognition of the importance of bibliography in textual studies is quite recent, despite the fact that R. B. McKerrow presented the case for the establishment of teaching presses as long ago as 1913:

> 'It would, I think, be an excellent thing if all who propose to edit an Elizabethan work from contemporary printed texts could be set to compose a sheet or two in as exact facsimile as possible of some Elizabethan octavo or quarto, and print it on a press constructed on the Elizabethan model. Elementary instruction in the mechanical details of book production need occupy but a very few hours of a University course of literature . . . It would teach students not to regard a book as a collection of separate leaves of paper attached in some mysterious manner to a leather back, nor to think that the pages are printed one after another beginning with the first and proceeding regularly to the last. They would have constantly and clearly before their minds all the processes through which the matter of the work before them has passed, from its first being written down by the pen of its author to its appearance in the finished volume, and would know when and how mistakes are likely to arise; while they would be constantly on the watch for those little pieces of evidence which are supplied by the actual form and "make-up" of a book and which are often of the highest value, in that they can hardly ever be "faked".'

The case for practical bibliographical teaching has never been put better than this, and it is in good measure due to the example and teaching of McKerrow that no modern textual scholar would think of the books he examines as being made up of single leaves 'attached in some mysterious manner to a leather back'. It all seems self-evident now, and the virtues of the hand press in demonstrating such esoteric subjects as skeleton setting or half-sheet imposition need no further justification.

Nevertheless, it was not until 1927 that McKerrow's suggestion was put into practice, when Carl Purington Rollins started the Bibliographic Press in Yale University Library. Others followed slowly: University College London in 1933, Harvard College Library in 1939, Bodley in 1949 (with presses formerly used by Daniel and Ashendene), King's College Cambridge in 1953. From the middle 1950s onwards these presses have multiplied in number very considerably. Some are very grand affairs, using replicas of the old wooden press built according to Moxon's specifications in *Mechanick exercises*; most use Albions or Columbians, a few modern platens. Some are for the instruction of small numbers of postgraduate research students, others for demonstration to much larger groups of potential librarians.

Normally the students will use these presses to print small pamphlets of typographic interest—sometimes, as in Bodley's *Dicta sapientum* (1961), a type facsimile of an early work—in the course of which they will pick up a good general knowledge of printing techniques upon which they may safely build their theories in later research. In particular they are likely to gain a much truer understanding of the problems of setting, and of the textual errors which can result from foul case, pied lines and the like. A very few of these teaching presses produce quite substantial books, but the difficulties of completing books when the courses generally last only for a term or so make most of them limit their output to small pamphlets. Nevertheless, these are often of interest, like *The Glasgow University Printing Office in MDCCCXXVI* (Water Lane Press, Cambridge, 1953) or Dennis Crutch's *Century of annotations to The Lewis Carroll handbook* which was produced by the Northwestern Polytechnic School of Librarianship in 1967.

Many of these presses have a lighter side as well. It does not, as a rule, take the students long to discover that printing can be fun, and in many of these schools the thump of the Albion can often be heard in the evenings, printing letterheads, Christmas cards and other ephemera of the sort produced by the parlour printers. Some of these presses appear in many guises: one such (which shall be nameless) has appeared at different times as 'The Lenin Memorial Press' (printing posters which proclaimed that 'Che lives' or demanding the abolition of the House of Lords), as 'The Pragmatic Press' (*The wit and wisdom of Harold Wilson*, a pamphlet containing a title-page and otherwise blank leaves) and more sinisterly as 'The Cosa Nostra Press'. These activities may not seem likely to turn the students into better bibliographers or librarians; I believe otherwise.

PLATES

TYCHONIS BRAHE

ASTRONOMIÆ

INSTAURATÆ

MECHANICA

SVSPICIENDO

DESPICIO

WANDESBVRGI

ANNO

clɔ. lɔ. IIC.

Cum Cæsaris & Regum quorundam Privilegiis.

Plate 6. Title-page of Tycho Brahe's *Astronomiae instauratae mechanica* (1598)

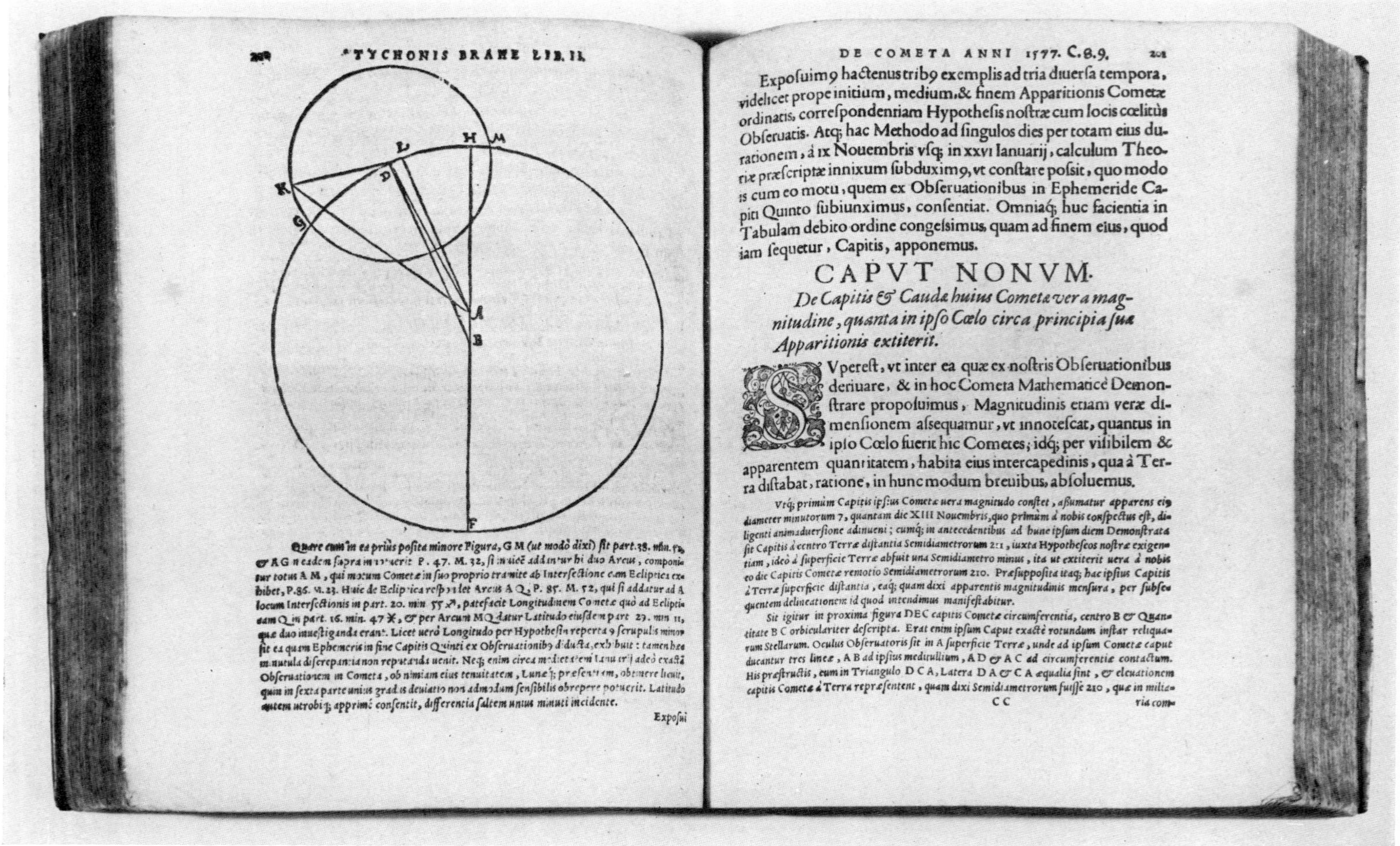

200 TYCHONIS BRAHE LIB. II.

Quare cum in ea priùs posita minore Figura, G M (ut modò dixi) sit part. 38. min. 52, & A G in eadem supra inuenerit P. 47. M. 32, si inuicē addantur hi duo Arcus, componitur totus A M, qui motum Cometæ in suo proprio tramite ab Intersectione cum Ecliptica exhibet, P. 86. M. 23. Huic de Ecliptica respondet Arcus A Q, P. 85. M. 52, qui si addatur ad A locum Intersectionis in part. 20. min. 55 ♐, patefacit Longitudinem Cometæ quò ad Eclipticam Q in part. 16. min. 47 ♓, & per Arcum M Q datur Latitudo eiusdem part. 29. min. 11, quæ duo inuestiganda erant. Licet uerò Longitudo per Hypothesin reperta 9 scrupulis minor sit ea quam Ephemeris in fine Capitis Quinti ex Obseruationib9 deducta, exhibuit: tamen hæc minutula discrepantia non reputanda uenit. Neq; enim circa medietatem Ianuarij adeò exactā Obseruationem in Cometa, ob nimiam eius tenuitatem, Lunæq; præsentiam, obtinere licuit, quin in sexta parte unius gradus deuiatio non admodum sensibilis obrepere potuerit. Latitudo autem utrobiq; apprimè consentit, differentia saltem unius minuti incidente.

Exposui

DE COMETA ANNI 1577. C.8.9. 201

Exposuim9 hactenus trib9 exemplis ad tria diuersa tempora, uidelicet prope initium, medium, & finem Apparitionis Cometæ ordinatis, correspondentiam Hypothesis nostræ cum locis cœlitùs Obseruatis. Atq; hac Methodo ad singulos dies per totam eius durationem, à IX Nouembris usq; in XXVI Ianuarij, calculum Theoriæ præscriptæ innixum subduxim9, ut constare posit, quo modo is cum eo motu, quem ex Obseruationibus in Ephemeride Capiti Quinto subiunximus, consentiat. Omniaq; huc facientia in Tabulam debito ordine congessimus, quam ad finem eius, quod iam sequetur, Capitis, apponemus.

CAPVT NONVM.

De Capitis & Caudæ huius Cometæ vera magnitudine, quanta in ipso Cœlo circa principia suæ Apparitionis extiterit.

SVperest, vt inter ea quæ ex nostris Obseruationibus deriuare, & in hoc Cometa Mathematicè Demonstrare proposuimus, Magnitudinis etiam veræ dimensionem assequamur, vt innotescat, quantus in ipso Cœlo fuerit hic Cometes; idq; per visibilem & apparentem quantitatem, habita eius intercapedinis, qua à Terra distabat, ratione, in hunc modum breuibus absoluemus.

Vtq; primùm Capitis ipsius Cometæ uera magnitudo constet, assumatur apparens eius diameter minutorum 7, quantam die XIII Nouembris, quo primùm à nobis conspectus est, diligenti animaduersione adinueni; cumq; in antecedentibus ad hunc ipsum diem Demonstrata sit Capitis à centro Terræ distantia Semidiametrorum 211, iuxta Hypotheseos nostræ exigentiam, ideò à superficie Terræ abfuit una Semidiametro minus, ita ut extiterit uera à nobis eo die Capitis Cometæ remotio Semidiametrorum 210. Præsupposita itaq; hac ipsius Capitis à Terræ superficie distantia, eaq; quam dixi apparentis magnitudinis mensura, per subsequentem delineationem id quod intendimus manifestabitur.

Sit igitur in proxima figura DEC capitis Cometæ circumferentia, centro B & Quantitate B C orbiculariter descripta. Erat enim ipsum Caput exactè rotundum instar reliquarum Stellarum. Oculus Obseruatoris sit in A superficie Terræ, unde ad ipsum Cometæ caput ducantur tres lineæ, A B ad ipsius meditullium, A D & A C ad circumferentiæ contactum. His præstructis, cum in Triangulo D C A, Latera D A & C A æqualia sint, & eleuationem capitis Cometæ à Terra repræsentent, quam dixi Semidiametrorum fuisse 210, quæ in milia-

CC ria com-

Plate 7. Opening from Tycho Brahe's *De mundi aetheri* (1588) printed at the Uraniburg Press

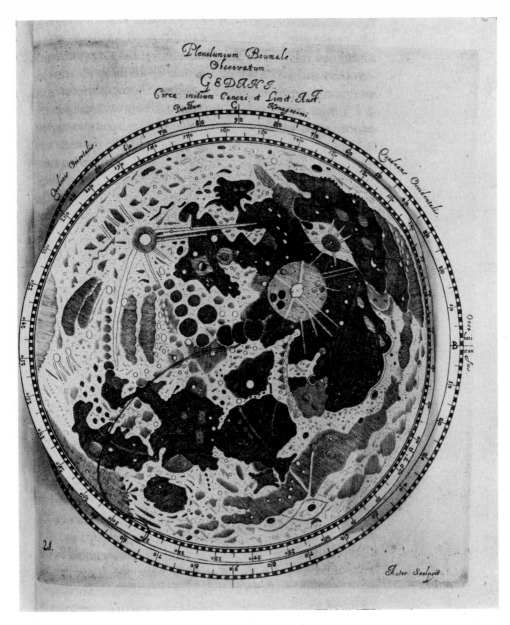

Plate 8. Moving plate from Hevelius' *Selenographia* (1647), printed
at the author's press

TUKSIAUTIT

AKIOREEKSAUTIKSET.

MAKPERSÆGANGOEESA

I

Nöngme. 1793.

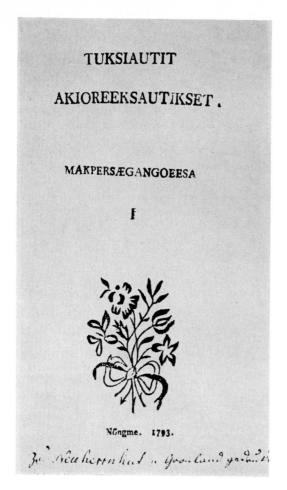

Plate 9. Title-page of Jesper Brodersen's *Choral songs* (1793)

†

HANS EGEDE.

Kalâtdlit palaserкâta pissartagainik suliarissainigdlo, sujugdlitdlo kigdlormôrtumik ilerкокarnerânik.

Iliniarfigssuarme Nûngmitume naкitat.

1857.

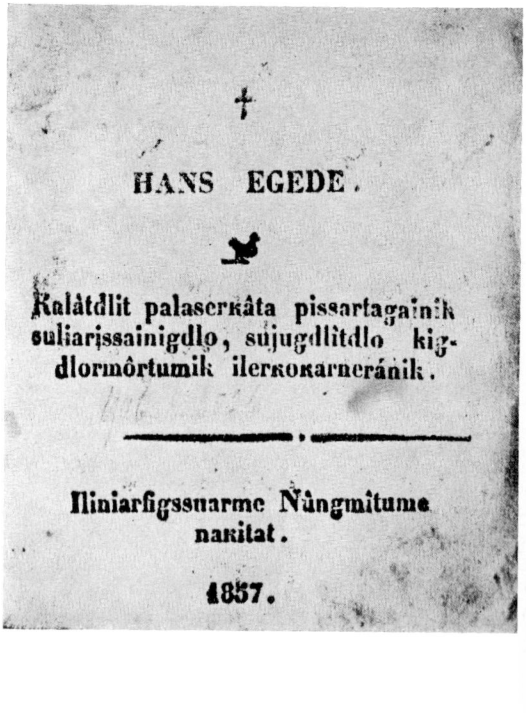

Plate 10. Title-page of a booklet printed in the Godthaab School (1857)

iv

Dessinateurs, ne ferait plus passer annuellement à l'étranger, et sur-tout à l'Italie, des sommes considérables pour en tirer ces sortes de papiers, que l'on pourrait se procurer, des Manufactures de France, à meilleur compte, et au moins d'aussi belle qualité.

Les Papiers-rose & des autres nuances agréables à l'œil, pouraient fournir à la Librairie française, un ornement de plus, pour l'impressions des petits ouvrages de cette Littérature légère, dont notre Nation possède les modèles, et dont elle ne trouve point d'imitateurs chez l'étranger.

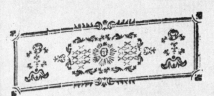

LES LOISIRS
DES BORDS
DU LOING.

COUPLETS
IN-PROMPTUS,

Faits en soupant à l'Hôtel-de-Ville de Montargis, le jour de la Fête aux Anglais, le 5 Septembre.

Air : *De tous les Capucins du monde.*

A notre Cité Montargoise,
Quand les Anglais ont cherché noise,
Pour les punir de leur fureur
Nos Pères ont sçu les détruire.
Buvons, amis, à leur valeur,
Ils étaient Français, c'est tout dire.

A

Plate 11. Opening from Leorier de L'Isle's *Les loisirs des bords du Loing* (1784)

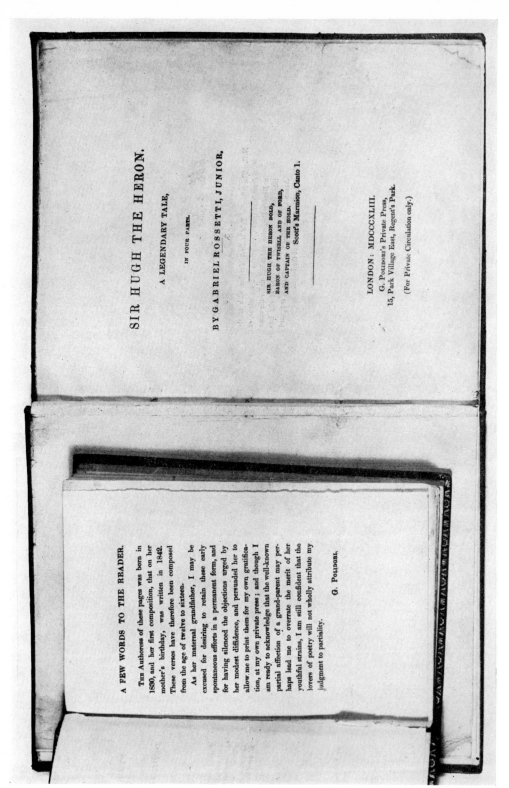

Plate 12. The first books of Dante Gabriel and Christian Rossetti, printed at their grandfather's press

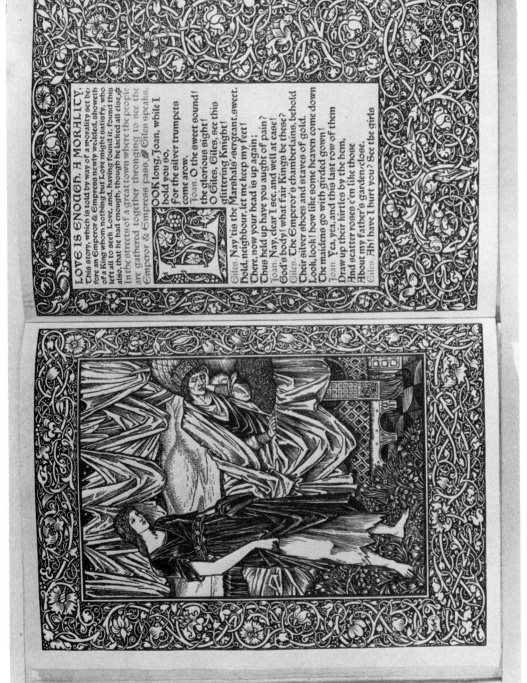

Plate 13. Opening from *Love is enough* (Kelmscott Press, 1897)

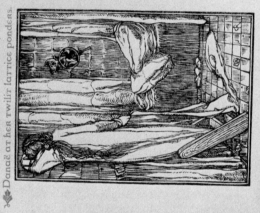

DANAË Glance like bright~parried laughter,
rather's spread; and some
folly. In bravery bend back whence they have
come,
And try their strength with those that
come direct.
With their full genial potency unchecked,
From the god's heart. Oh vanity of pride!
In which a royal miser hopes to hide
His coward purpose, at his child's expense,
Starving her of those benefits immense
Which, to the growing soul, friendship and
love
Yield like boon climates. Is not Zeus
above?
And will he be accomplice to thy fears?
What weapons hast thou 'gainst him, save
thy tears,
If thou dost think to oppose? How! has he
given
His oracle, yet, still out~braving heaven,
Standeth thy coward boast or hollow
brass?
Oh vanity of vanities, alas!

Or how Yet she is loved: Zeus well has weighed her
the love need;
with Although the wealth within her be not
which she freed;
was loved And she know not, as oft it is not known
although To maids whom hearts of worth have
unknown claimed their own.
to her That she is loved. No haunting of her mind
caused a By gaze or voice sets in; still shall she find
brighten.

xxxii

Plate 14. Opening from *Danaë* (Vale Press, 1903)

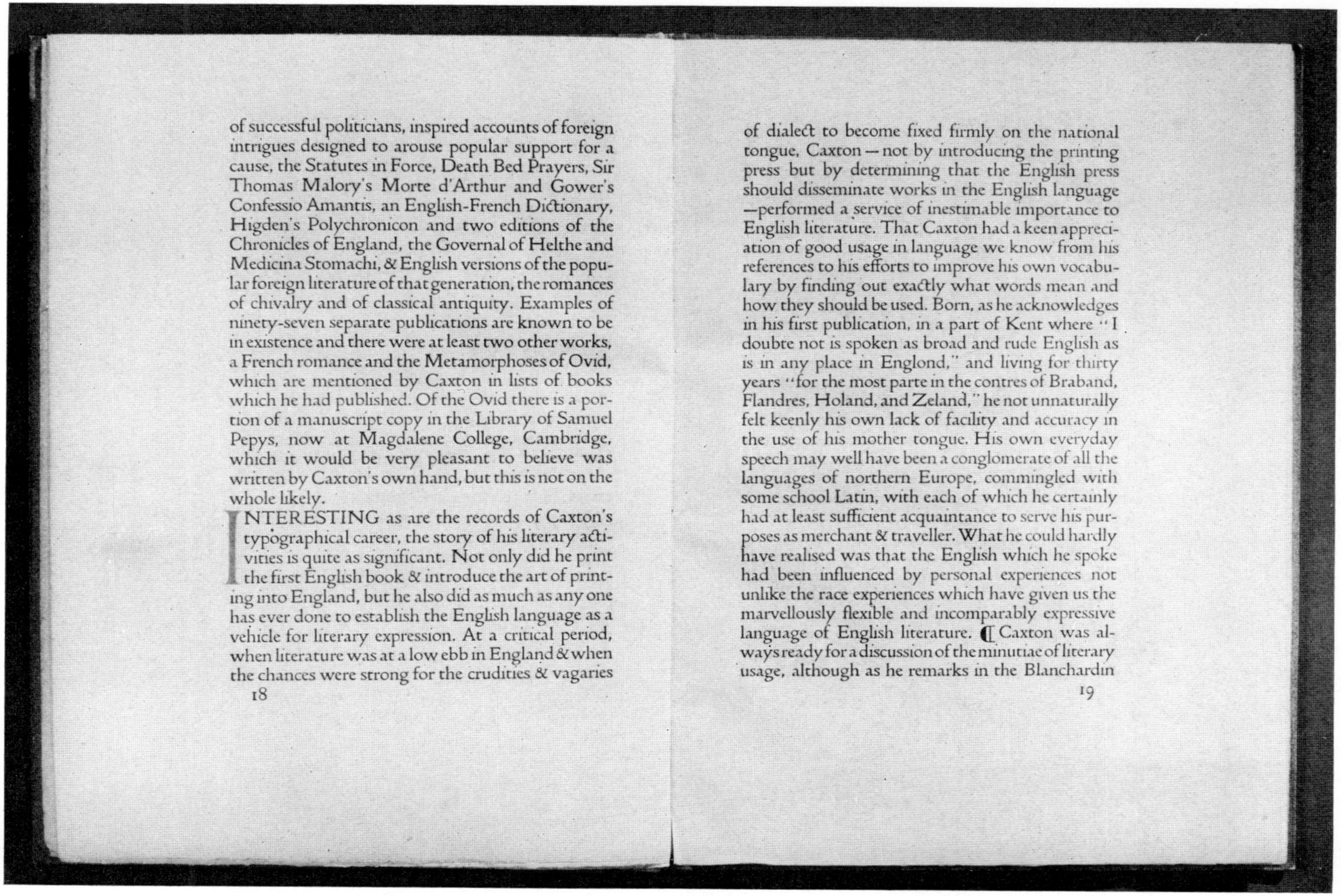

of successful politicians, inspired accounts of foreign intrigues designed to arouse popular support for a cause, the Statutes in Force, Death Bed Prayers, Sir Thomas Malory's Morte d'Arthur and Gower's Confessio Amantis, an English-French Dictionary, Higden's Polychronicon and two editions of the Chronicles of England, the Governal of Helthe and Medicina Stomachi, & English versions of the popular foreign literature of that generation, the romances of chivalry and of classical antiquity. Examples of ninety-seven separate publications are known to be in existence and there were at least two other works, a French romance and the Metamorphoses of Ovid, which are mentioned by Caxton in lists of books which he had published. Of the Ovid there is a portion of a manuscript copy in the Library of Samuel Pepys, now at Magdalene College, Cambridge, which it would be very pleasant to believe was written by Caxton's own hand, but this is not on the whole likely.

INTERESTING as are the records of Caxton's typographical career, the story of his literary activities is quite as significant. Not only did he print the first English book & introduce the art of printing into England, but he also did as much as any one has ever done to establish the English language as a vehicle for literary expression. At a critical period, when literature was at a low ebb in England & when the chances were strong for the crudities & vagaries

of dialect to become fixed firmly on the national tongue, Caxton — not by introducing the printing press but by determining that the English press should disseminate works in the English language —performed a service of inestimable importance to English literature. That Caxton had a keen appreciation of good usage in language we know from his references to his own efforts to improve his own vocabulary by finding out exactly what words mean and how they should be used. Born, as he acknowledges in his first publication, in a part of Kent where "I doubte not is spoken as broad and rude English as is in any place in England," and living for thirty years "for the most parte in the contres of Braband, Flandres, Holand, and Zeland," he not unnaturally felt keenly his own lack of facility and accuracy in the use of his mother tongue. His own everyday speech may well have been a conglomerate of all the languages of northern Europe, commingled with some school Latin, with each of which he certainly had at least sufficient acquaintance to serve his purposes as merchant & traveller. What he could hardly have realised was that the English which he spoke had been influenced by personal experiences not unlike the race experiences which have given us the marvellously flexible and incomparably expressive language of English literature. ¶ Caxton was always ready for a discussion of the minutiae of literary usage, although as he remarks in the Blanchardin

Plate 15. Opening from G. P. Winship's *William Caxton* (Doves Press, 1909)

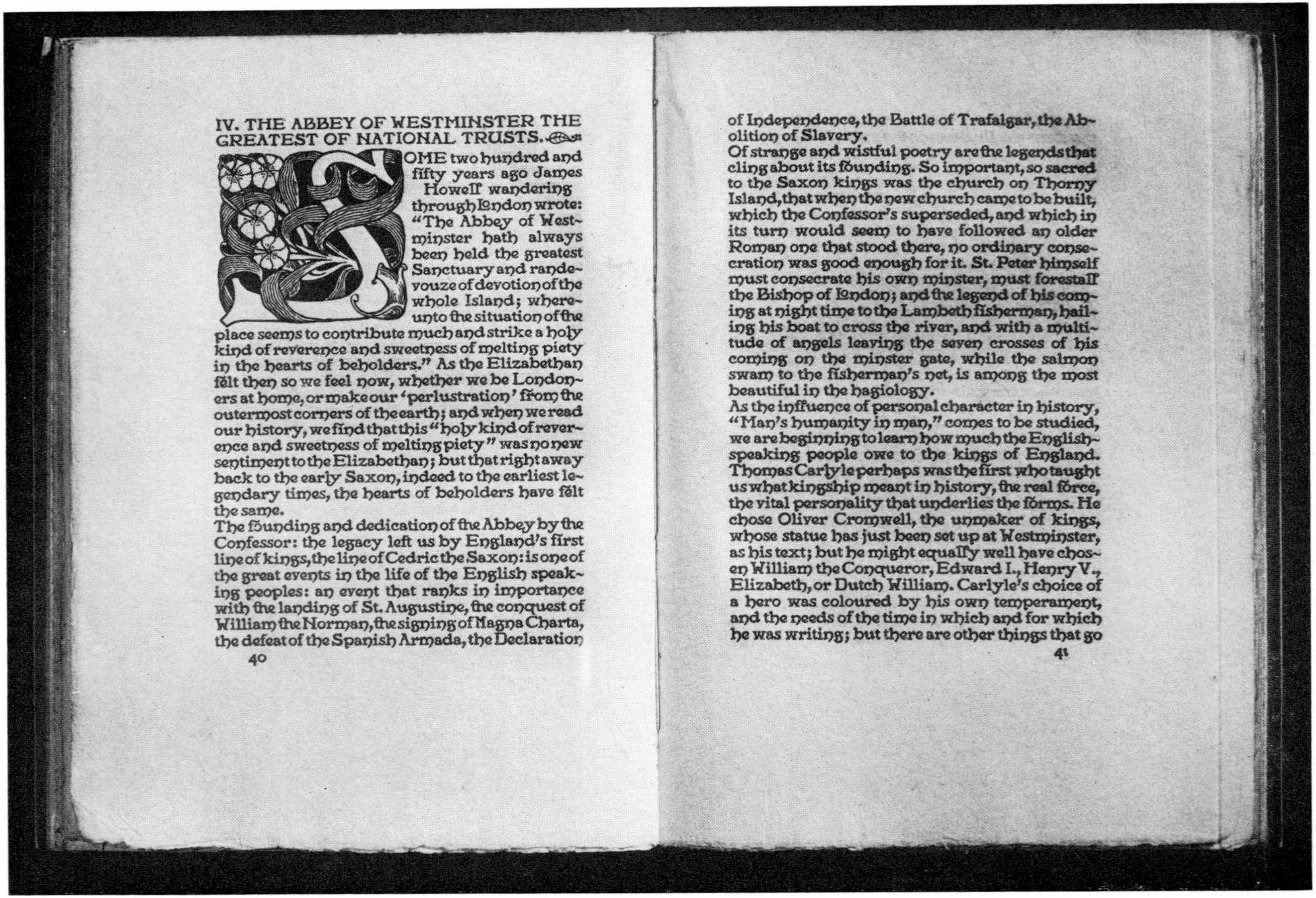

OME two hundred and fifty years ago James Howell wandering through London wrote: "The Abbey of Westminster hath always been held the greatest Sanctuary and rande-vouze of devotion of the whole Island; where-unto the situation of the place seems to contribute much and strike a holy kind of reverence and sweetness of melting piety in the hearts of beholders." As the Elizabethan felt then so we feel now, whether we be Londoners at home, or make our 'perlustration' 'from the outerpost corners of the earth'; and when we read our history, we find that this "holy kind of reverence and sweetness of melting piety" was no new sentiment to the Elizabethan; but that right away back to the early Saxon, indeed to the earliest legendary times, the hearts of beholders have felt the same.

The founding and dedication of the Abbey by the Confessor: the legacy left us by England's first line of kings, the line of Cedric the Saxon: is one of the great events in the life of the English speaking peoples: an event that ranks in importance with the landing of St. Augustine, the conquest of William the Norman, the signing of Magna Charta, the defeat of the Spanish Armada, the Declaration

of Independence, the Battle of Trafalgar, the Abolition of Slavery.

Of strange and wistful poetry are the legends that cling about its founding. So important, so sacred to the Saxon kings was the church on Thorney Island, that when the new church came to be built, which the Confessor's superseded, and which in its turn would seem to have followed an older Roman one that stood there, no ordinary consecration was good enough for it. St. Peter himself must consecrate his own minster, must forestall the Bishop of London; and the legend of his coming at night time to the Lambeth fisherman, bidding his boat to cross the river, and with a multitude of angels leaving the seven crosses of his coming on the minster gate, while the salmon swam to the fisherman's net, is among the most beautiful in the hagiology.

As the influence of personal character in history, "Man's humanity in man," comes to be studied, we are beginning to learn how much the English-speaking people owe to the kings of England. Thomas Carlyle perhaps was the first who taught us what kingship meant in history, the real force, the vital personality that underlies the forms. He chose Oliver Cromwell, the unmaker of kings, whose statue has just been set up at Westminster, as his text; but he might equally well have chosen William the Conqueror, Edward I., Henry V., Elizabeth, or Dutch William. Carlyle's choice of a hero was coloured by his own temperament, and the needs of the time in which and for which he was writing; but there are other things that go

Plate 16. Opening from *American sheaves* (Essex House Press, 1901)

Plate 18. A page from *Riquet à la houppe*
(Eragny Press, 1907)

Plate 17. Page from *The queen of the fishes*
(Eragny Press, 1894)

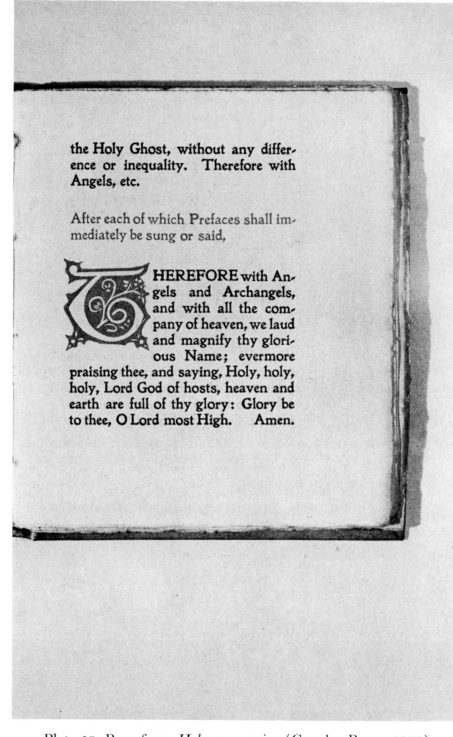

the Holy Ghost, without any difference or inequality. Therefore with Angels, etc.

After each of which Prefaces shall immediately be sung or said,

THEREFORE with Angels and Archangels, and with all the company of heaven, we laud and magnify thy glorious Name; evermore praising thee, and saying, Holy, holy, holy, Lord God of hosts, heaven and earth are full of thy glory: Glory be to thee, O Lord most High.   Amen.

Plate 19. Page from *Holy communion* (Caradoc Press, 1903)

THE NEW
GULLIVER

BY
WENDELL PHILLIPS GARRISON

Vox et præterea nihil

❦

THE MARION PRESS
JAMAICA, QUEENSBOROUGH, NEW-YORK
MDCCCXCVIII

Plate 20. A Marion Press title-page

Wrapt in a gown, for sickness, and for show.
The fair ones feel such maladies as these,
When each new night-dress gives a new disease.
　　A constant Vapour o'er the palace flies:
Strange phantoms rising as the mists arise;
Dreadful, as hermit's dreams in haunted shades,
Or bright, as visions of expiring maids,
Now glaring fiends, and snakes on rolling spires,
Pale spectres, gaping tombs, and purple fires:
Now lakes of liquid gold, Elysian scenes,
And crystal domes, and angels in machines.
　　Unnumber'd throngs on every side are seen,
Of bodies chang'd to various forms by Spleen.
Here living Tea-pots stand, one arm held out,
One bent; the handle this, and that the spout:
A Pipkin there, like Homer's Tripod walks;
Here sighs a Jar, and there a Goose-pie talks;
Men prove with child, as pow'rful fancy works,
And maids turn'd bottles, call aloud for corks.
　　Safe past the Gnome thro' this fantastic band,
A branch of healing Spleenwort in his hand,
Then thus address'd the pow'r: "Hail, wayward Queen!
Who rule the sex to fifty from fifteen:
Parent of vapours and of female wit,
Who give th' hysteric, or poetic fit,
On various tempers act by various ways,
Make some take physic, others scribble plays;
Who cause the proud their visits to delay,
And send the godly in a pet to pray.
A nymph there is, that all thy pow'r disdains,
And thousands more in equal mirth maintains.
But oh! if e'er thy Gnome could spoil a grace,
Or raise a pimple on a beauteous face,
Like Citron-waters matrons cheeks inflame,
Or change complexions at a losing game;
If e'er with airy horns I planted heads,
Or rumpled petticoats, or tumbled beds,
Or caus'd suspicion when no soul was rude,

16

Or discompos'd the head-dress of a Prude,
Or e'er to costive lap-dog gave disease,
Which not the tears of brightest eyes could ease:
Hear me, and touch Belinda with chagrin,
That single act gives half the world the spleen."
　　The Goddess with a discontented air
Seems to reject him, tho' she grants his pray'r.
A wond'rous Bag with both her hands she binds,
Like that where once Ulysses held the winds;
There she collects the force of female lungs,
Sighs, sobs, and passions, and the war of tongues.
A Vial next she fills with fainting fears,
Soft sorrows, melting griefs, and flowing tears.
The Gnome rejoicing bears her gifts away,
Spreads his black wings, and slowly mounts to day.
　　Sunk in Thalestris' arms the nymph he found,
Her eyes dejected and her hair unbound.
Full o'er their heads the swelling bag he rent,
And all the Furies issu'd at the vent.
Belinda burns with more than mortal ire,
And fierce Thalestris fans the rising fire.
"O wretched maid!" she spread her hands, and cry'd,
(While Hampton's echoes, "Wretched maid!' reply'd)
"Was it for this you took such constant care
The bodkin, comb, and essence to prepare?
For this your locks in paper durance bound,
For this with tort'ring irons wreath'd around?
For this with fillets strain'd your tender head,
And bravely bore the double loads of lead?
Gods! shall the ravisher display your hair,
While the Fops envy, and the Ladies stare!
Honour forbid! at whose unrivall'd shrine
Ease, pleasure, virtue, all our sex resign.
Methinks already I your tears survey,
Already hear the horrid things they say,
Already see you a degraded toast,
And all your honour in a whisper lost!
How shall I, then, your helpless fame defend?

17

Plate 21. Opening from *The rape of the lock* (Elston Press, 1902)

Paribus, et toto miscemur ubique vicissim;
Ardoresque novos accendit Numinis ardor.
Sin laudare Deum libeat, nos laudat et ipse,
Concinit Angelicusque chorus, modulamine suavi
Personat et cælum, profiunt et publica nobis
Gaudia, et eduntur passim spectacula læta;
Fitque theatralis quasi Cæli machina tota.
Hinc mundi molem sin vis replicaverit ingens
Numinis, atque novas formas exculpserit inde
Doubus ornatas aliis, magis atque capaces;
Nostras mox etiam formas renovare licebit,
Et dotes sensúsque alios assumere, tandem
Consummata magis quo gaudia nostra resurgant,
Hæc si conjecto mortali corpore fretus
Corpus ut exuerim, Quid ni majora recludam?

And certainly since in my mother's womb this *plastica*, or *formatrix*, which formed my eyes, ears, and other senses, did not intend them for that dark and noisome place, but, as being conscious of a better life, made them as fitting organs to apprehend and perceive those things which should occur in this world: so I believe, since my coming into this world, my soul hath formed or produced certain faculties which are almost as useless for this life, as the above-named senses were for the mother's womb; and these faculties are, hope, faith, love, and joy, since they never rest or fix upon any transitory or perishing object in this world, as extending themselves to something further than can be here given, and indeed acquiesce only in the perfect, eternal, and infinite: I confess they are of some use here; yet I appeal to everybody, whether any worldly felicity did so satisfy their hope here, that they did not wish and hope for something more excellent, or whether they could find on earth, to relieve them in their danger or necessity; whether ever they could place their love on any earthly beauty, that it did not fade and wither, if not frustrate or deceive them, that they did not want much more than it, or indeed this world can afford, to make them happy. The proper objects of these faculties, therefore, though framed, or at least appearing in this world, is God only, upon whom faith, hope, and love, were never placed in vain, or remain long unrequitted. But to leave these discourses, and come to my childhood again.
I remember this defluxion at my ears above-mentioned continued in that

12

violence, that my friends did not think fit to teach me so much as my alphabet until I was seven years old, at which time my defluxion ceased, and left me free of the disease my ancestors were subject unto, being the epilepsy. My schoolmaster in the house of my said lady grandmother began then to teach me the alphabet, and afterwards grammar, and other books commonly read in schools; in which I profited so much, that upon this theme *Audaces fortuna juvat*, I made an oration of a sheet of paper, and fifty or sixty verses in the space of one day. I remember in that time I was corrected sometimes for going to cuffs with two schoolfellows being both elder than myself, but never for telling a lie or any other fault; my natural disposition & inclination being so contrary to all falsehood, that being demanded whether I had committed my fault whereof I might be justly suspected, I did use ever to confess it freely, and thereupon choosing rather to suffer correction than to stain my mind with telling a lie, which I did judge then, no time could ever deface; and I can affirm to all the world truly that, from my first infancy to this hour, I told not willingly anything that was false, my soul naturally having an antipathy to lying and deceit. After I had attained the age of nine, during all which time I lived in my said lady grandmother's house at Eyton, my parents thought fit to send me to some place where I might learn the Welsh tongue, as believing it necessary to enable me to treat with those of my friends & tenants who understood no other language; whereupon I was recommended to Mr. Edward Thelwall, of Plas-y-ward in Denbighshire. This gentleman I must remember

13

Plate 22. Opening from *The autobiography of Lord Herbert of Cherbury* (Gregynog Press, 1928)

IN SEPTEMBER 1927 THE CRANACH PRESS, set up by Count Harry Kessler at Weimar, will publish the Eclogues of Virgil, with an English translation, and woodcuts by Aristide Maillol. The head-line of the title-page was cut on wood by Eric Gill.

The aim of the Press in this book, has been to print an edition of the Eclogues in which the type used for the text, the illustrations, and the paper should be in perfect keeping with one another, and so to emulate the unity of text and illustrations which we see in Carolingian MSS. and in the illustrated incunabula. Three editions have been printed, the first with a German translation in hexameters, by Rudolf Alexander Schröder; the second with a French prose translation, by Marc Lafargue; and the third with a prose translation into English by J. H. Mason.

The paper was made in Count Kessler's own workshop. This workshop was set up in order to experiment in paper-making until a paper was produced which satisfied Count Kessler and his fellow-workers as specially suitable for this edition. The texture and tone, the substance and surface quality, invite, and we believe will sustain, comparison with the best papers made in China, or in Europe during the early days of printing. The paper used for the greater part of the edition is made from hemp fibre, but a paper made from hemp and silk is used for a small special edition. This latter paper has a very closely-knit texture and is delightful both in appearance and handling. Its chief constituent is a special quality of Chinese silk, of which

2

no more can be at present procured owing to the revolution, and consequently no English copies have been printed on this K·M silk paper. For the special English edition a Japanese paper has been used. Both the types used in printing this book were cut for the Cranach Press. The roman type is based on an original type of Nicolas Jenson, used by him in 1473, and was cut under the direction of Emery Walker. It is used in this prospectus. The italic is from designs by Edward Johnston. The unity of the book was the guiding principle in setting the text in type. The text, the illustrations, and initials were conceived architecturally from beginning to end. The arrangement of the Latin text with the facing translation was greatly complicated by the illustrations, but the problems of arrangement were examined exhaustively, until the best solution possible was reached. The woodcuts of Aristide Maillol were designed for the text as set in this edition. From the beginning, he has based his work on the tone of the type in mass and on the proportions of the page, with a view to securing a harmony of line and tone between text and illustrations. Within these limitations he has given his imagination and sense of form the freest play. The Hellenic grace and fertile invention of this great plastic artist is admirably seen in these forty-three woodcuts. The designs may be compared to a series of delicate Hellenistic reliefs decorating the severe typographical architecture. All the woodcuts were cut by the artist himself, and no other hand intervened between his conception and its typographical presentment. The printing was carried

3

Plate 23. Prospectus for the Cranach *Eclogues*

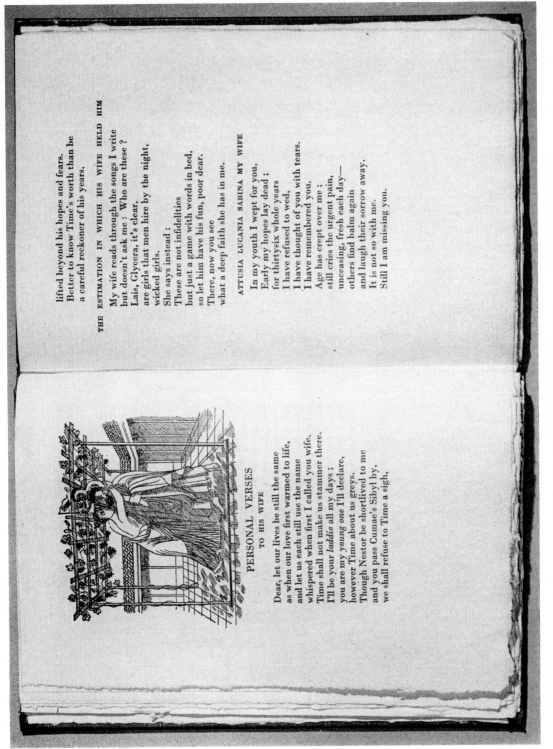

PERSONAL VERSES
TO HIS WIFE

Dear, let our lives be still the same
as when our love first warmed to life,
and let us each still use the name
whispered when first I called you wife.
Time shall not make us stammer there.
I'll be your *laddie* all my days ;
you are my *young one* I'll declare,
however Time about us greys.
Though Nestor be shortlived to me
and you pass Cumae's Sibyl by,
we shall refuse to Time a sigh,

lifted beyond his hopes and fears.
Better to know Time's worth than be
a careful reckoner of his years.

THE ESTIMATION IN WHICH HIS WIFE HELD HIM

My wife reads through the songs I write
but doesn't ask me : Who are these ?
Lais, Glycera, it's clear,
are girls that men hire by the night,
wicked girls.
She says instead :
These are not infidelities
but just a game with words in bed,
so let him have his fun, poor dear.
There, now you see
what a deep faith she has in me.

ATTUSIA LUCANIA SABINA MY WIFE

In my youth I wept for you.
Early my hopes lay dead ;
for thirtysix whole years
I have refused to wed,
I have thought of you with tears.
I have remembered you.
Age has crept over me ;
still cries the urgent pain,
unceasing, fresh each day—
others find balm again
and laugh their sorrow away.
It is not so with me.
Still I am missing you.

Plate 24. Opening from *A patchwork quilt* (Fanfrolico Press, 1929)

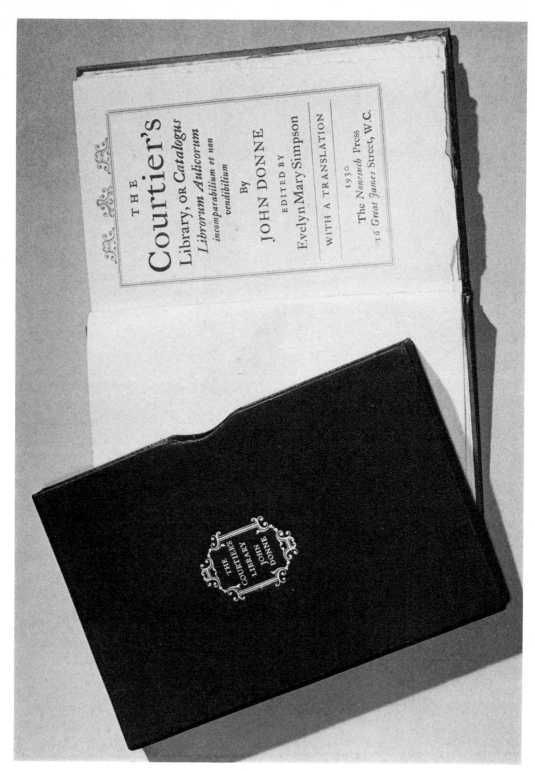

Plate 25. Title-page and slipcase of *The Courtier's library* (Nonesuch Press, 1930)

SPRING

THE ARGUMENT

The Subject proposed. Inscribed to the Countess of HARTFORD. The Season is described as it affects the various Parts of Nature, ascending from the Lower to the Higher; and mixed with Digressions arising from the Subject. Its Influence on inanimate Matter, on Vegetables, on brute Animals, and last on Man; concluding with a Dissuasive from the wild and irregular Passion of Love, opposed to That of a pure and happy Kind.

COME, gentle SPRING, Ethereal Mildness, come,
And from the Bosom of yon dropping Cloud,
While Music wakes around, veil'd in a Shower
Of shadowing Roses, on our Plains descend.

O HARTFORD, fitted, or to shine in Courts
With unaffected Grace, or walk the Plain
With Innocence and Meditation join'd
In soft Assemblage, listen to my Song,
Which thy own Season paints; when Nature all
Is blooming, and benevolent, like thee.

AND see where surly WINTER passes off,
Far to the North, and calls his ruffian Blasts:
His Blasts obey, and quit the howling Hill,
The shatter'd Forest, and the ravag'd Vale;

3

Plate 26. Opening from Thomson's *Seasons* (Nonesuch Press, 1927)

HEAD OF SAINT JOHN

Tall voluted pillars,
The subtle reek of cloying musk.
Faint, the mocking cadence
Of a warning drum. Staccato,
The clink of metal armlets, as white
Limbs in svelte kaleidoscope, yearn,
Impassioned, for the staring head.
Bright teeth reveal the hidden urge of
Gynaecian posturings.
Anais in shrill delight is there
To watch her acolyte.
O, John, what spell wove
He
That you deny
Me?
Choreographic these effects;
Lust needs no pulsing lights,
Or artifice. What power was held by
The monastic Nazarene,
That these . . . these breasts
For which princes die, mean less
To you even than these
Steps of mine about your
Bloody head?

SALOME BEFORE THE

Plate 27. Opening from *Salome* (Boar's Head Press, 1933)

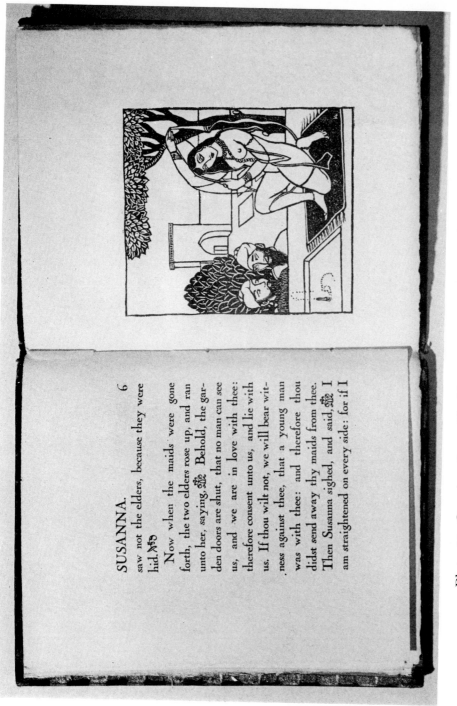

SUSANNA.   6

saw not the elders, because they were hid. ❧

Now when the maids were gone forth, the two elders rose up, and ran unto her, saying, ❧ Behold, the garden doors are shut, that no man can see us, and we are in love with thee: therefore consent unto us, and lie with us. If thou wilt not, we will bear witness against thee, that a young man was with thee: and therefore thou didst send away thy maids from thee.

Then Susanna sighed, and said, ❧ I am straightened on every side: for if I

Plate 28. Opening from *The history of Susanna* (Stanton Press, 1923)

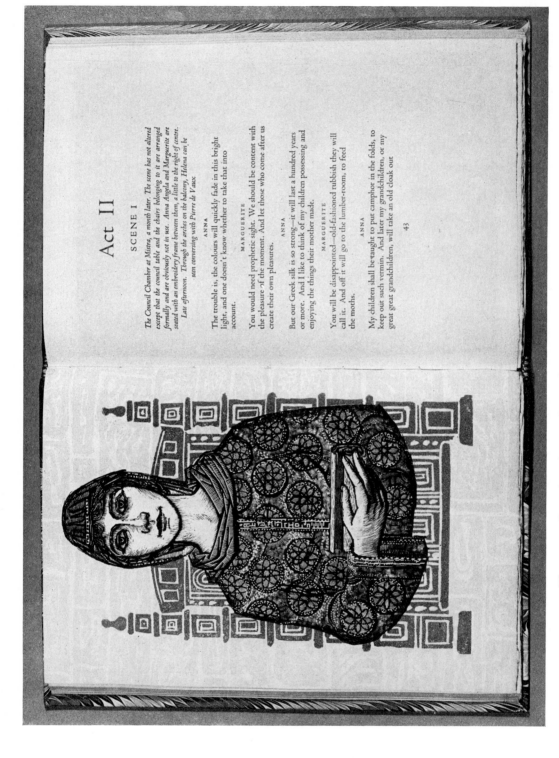

Plate 29. Opening from *The parliament of women* (Vine Press, 1960)

Plate 30. Title-page opening from a postwar Golden Cockerel

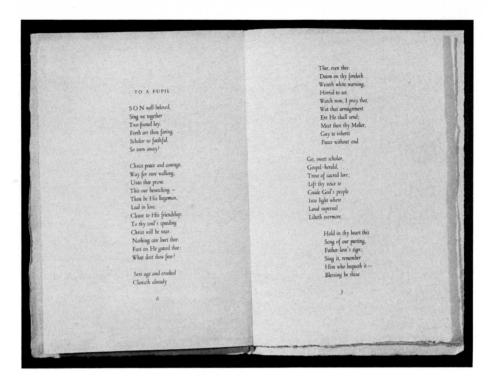

Plate 31. Opening from *Son well-beloved* (Stanbrook Abbey Press, 1967)

Plate 32. A page from *Seven sonnets for Good Friday* (Stanbrook Abbey Press, 1969)

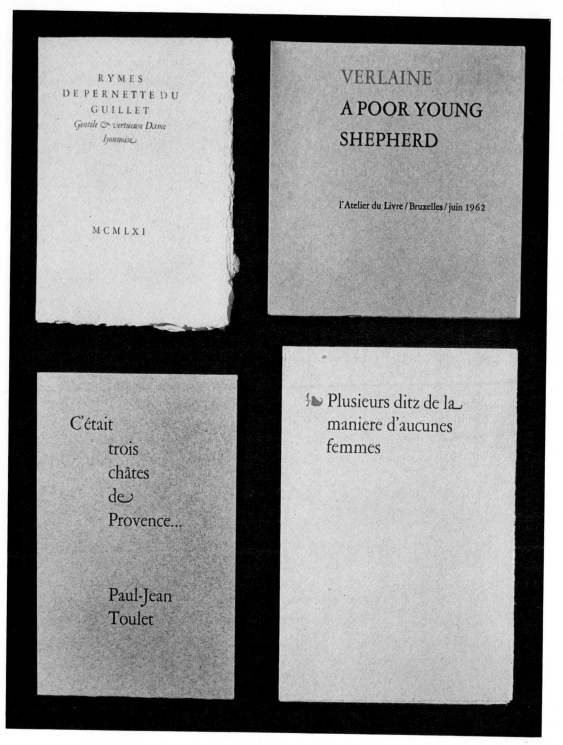

Plate 33. Four pieces from L'Atelier du Livre, a modern Belgian press

Plate 34. Some pieces from *The Miniature folio* (1960)

Plate 35. A group of books from the Signet Press

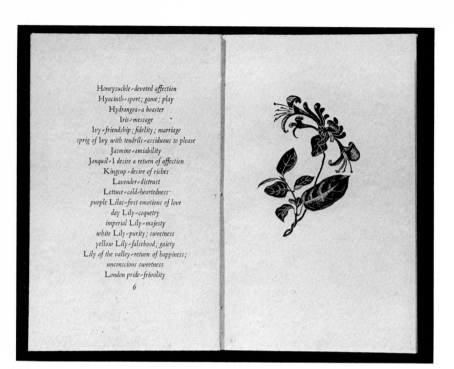

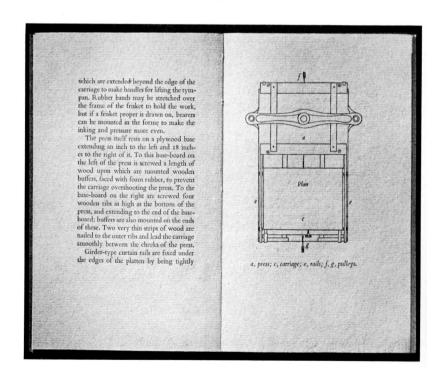

Plate 38. Opening from *The Apostles' creed* (Cuckoo Hill Press, 1966)

BORN OF THE
VIRGIN MARY

SUFFERED UNDER
PONTIUS PILATE

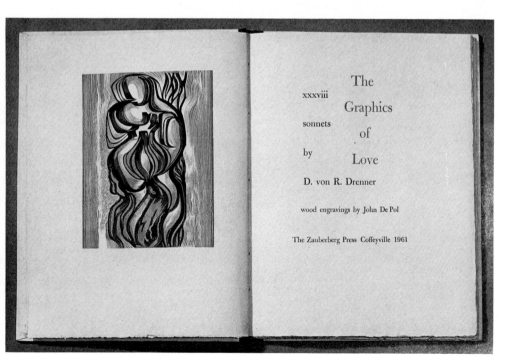

xxxviii

sonnets

by

The

Graphics

of

Love

D. von R. Drenner

wood engravings by John De Pol

The Zauberberg Press Coffeyville 1961

Plate 39. Title-page and frontispiece from *The graphics of love* (Zauberberg Press, 1961)

FISHPASTE *Four & a half*

A letter from PINLEG

Produced by
Rigby Graham, Peter Hoy, & Toni Savage
Published from 32 West Avenue Leicester

FISHPASTE *THREE*

Produced by
Rigby Graham, Peter Hoy, & Toni Savage
Published from 32 West Avenue Leicester

postcard review
of Art & Letters

Fishpaste

Fishpaste Twenty
Rigby Graham, Peter Hoy & Toni Savage
97 Holywell Street Oxford

Dancing Caryatid by Rigby Graham

March 1968

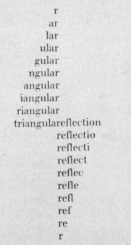

```
       r
      ar
     lar
    ular
   gular
  ngular
 angular
iangular
riangular
triangulareflection
         reflectio
         reflecti
         reflect
         reflec
         refle
         refl
         ref
         re
         r
```

PASTE HAS MOVED
to 97 HOLYWELL ROAD OXFORD

FISHPASTE *EIGHT*   28 June 1967

On the Heights

Wait until I come
To cleave the cold which holds us back.

Cloud, as menaced in your life as I in mine.

(There was a cliff in our house.
Which is why we left and set up here.)

Translated from Char by Peter Hoy

Produced by
Rigby Graham, Peter Hoy & Toni Savage
Published from 32 West Avenue Leicester

Plate 40. Some numbers of *Fishpaste*

The
Nightingale &
The Rose

A Fairy Tale by Oscar Wilde

PERCIVAL & GRAHAM
1961

Io MASONI ET AMICORVM

Plate 41. Three books printed in Mount St. Bernards Abbey

Plate 42. Some Brewhouse Press bindings

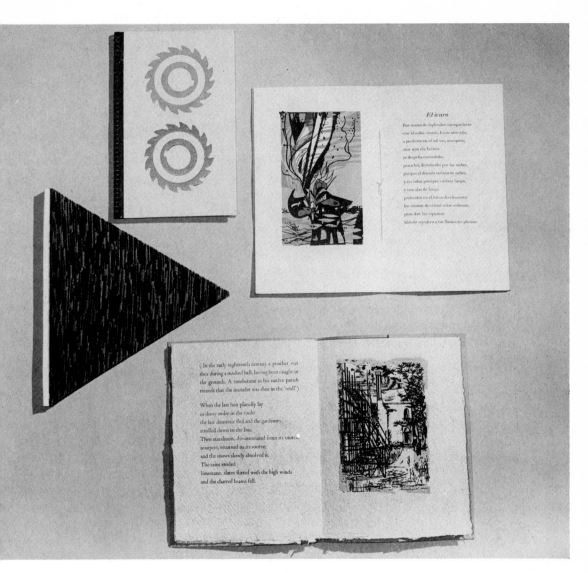

Plate 43. Four books from Leicestershire presses

Plate 44. Four Brewhouse broadsheets

the brickwork and will shortly demolish the culvert which was already settling and sinking. When this happens the rubble will dam the stream and a mechanical digger will be called in to free the stream and will obliterate all remains of this culvert.

Saxby Station and Saxby Junction cover Lock No. 9 and a fair stretch of the canal. It is difficult to imagine when looking at this peaceful line, that a few years ago before Beeching's Axe fell it was such a large and busy area with sidings, warehouses, huts and considerable passenger accommodation and four platforms.

When all this has come and gone it is understandable that there is nothing visible left of the earlier transport system, the Oakham Canal.

When the canal reappears some way beyond the station area the towpath is on the left, and opposite bank. This was because the Fourth Earl of Harborough would not have it on the South bank at any price and made a misery of the lives of those concerned in constructing the canal.

It is mainly marshy here and a small culvert carries an even smaller stream under the canal. Beyond this the canal has been blocked by a mound carrying a field road.

A quarter of a mile or so on from Saxby Station an old railway embankment crosses the canal. This carried the first railway in a sharp sweeping curve because the Sixth Earl of Harborough refused permission for the railway to cross his land. This became known as 'Lord Harborough's Curve'. The railwaymen hated it and many years later it was replaced by the present line because it slowed trains down.

Beyond this embankment the canal, full of water, is both wide and deep. This is the site of Saxby Old Wharf. It is just past here that a fast flowing brook passes under the canal through what was a four-arched culvert. A large proportion of this has fallen in, blocked the stream and has had to be cleared. The stream still runs through the original channels and these are clearly seen between the remaining four arches of the culvert. To the South lies the large embankment of Harborough's Curve. Here the old railway crossed the brook by a pile bridge. Brick piers still stand in the middle, and the wooden piles, now rotten and disappearing, stand out from the grassy banks like blackened teeth. One of these hollow teeth housed a bluetit's nest. Just beyond this half ruined culvert, an old road crossed the canal and the signs are clearly visible particularly when viewed from the top of Harborough's Curve. This was the site of most of the Battles of Saxby. The canal swings southwards again, the banks here are low, and the left of the towpath is lined with overgrown hawthorn bushes. Here stands the first of the cast iron mileposts (see page 37). Melton is 5 and Oakham 10 miles away by canal. Of the five posts which exist this is by far the best preserved, having been polished clean by cattle and sheep, and the oil from these has largely prevented rusting.

Three railway embankments next cross the canal, one dead, (Lord Harborough's Curve), one dying — the old Bourne to Spalding Line, and one still very much alive. This is the line which carries trains from Leicester to Peterborough. Between the first two embankments are the remains of Lock No. 11. This had a rise of nearly six feet and the lock itself is still full of water although all masonry and brickwork has long since disappeared. The canal between the second and third embankment is so marshy and overgrown with hawthorn, nettles, reeds and briar as to be quite impassable.

The embankment of the London line runs along the present boundary of

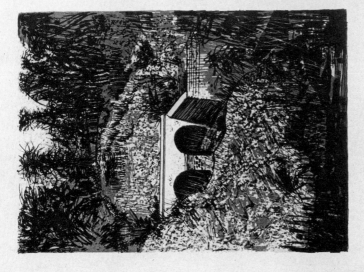

PLATE 18   Two arched culvert carrying Wymondham water.

Plate 45. Opening from *The Oakham Canal* (Brewhouse Press, 1968)

JOHN BEECHER

Report to the Stockholders & Other Poems

1932 - 1962

PHOENIX
MCMLXII

Plate 46. Title-opening from a Rampart Press book

YOU, ANDREW VOLSTEAD

want to make trouble or anything & if you say so, why of course I can get it fixed all right and we'll be just the way we were before, or dear we could be married secretly, but I've got to tell you, dear, I couldn't write it but I've got to tell you that I think I'm going to have—a baby."

"If I have a gin rickey, Jake! Where was I? Oh, yes, friendship. Well I might as well come to the point. No use beating round the bushes. Point is that, darling, God Marian, oh Judas, I hate to make you feel bad, and if there was any way out of it, God knows I wouldn't for the world make you feel bad, but point is, I think we'd better break off our friendship. O. k. Jake. Lime rickey &, what did you say you were going to have?"

"I'm not going to have anything."

"Oh, I thought you were going to have something."

She did not speak.

"Listen, dear. Let's drink to it. I want to drink to your good luck & you drink to mine. What do you say?"

"Do anything you want."

"Two gin rickeys. No. Got any wine? Got any port?"

"We got port."

"Two glasses port. That's stuff to drink hells with, health's with. Well I was saying, Marian, dear, that's the only honest way to do the thing, I mean, as you said, we can't just drag it along this way, Can we? So we'll just finish it off the way a lady & a gentleman ought, ought to. After all, when the thing's died, there's no use keeping it sort of dragging around your neck, like a, like an albatross or something.

"Don't think it doesn't hurt me, darling, I've been thinking it over a long time, only I didn't write, because I decided the honorable thing to do was, come & see you. And honest to God, dear, I did mean to see you more, alone. I wanted to be with you all the time, & see if maybe we couldn't be happy again, I ran into Tom by accident. Entirely by acci-

40

dent. Maybe if we could have just been alone & taken things sort of easy, maybe we could have been happy only now I know there just isn't any use. It would just be painful for both of us. There isn't any sense in that, you know.

"Do you know that sonnet, since there's no help, come, let us kiss & part? Nay I have done, you get no more of me? And I am glad,? with all my heart,? yea I am glad. I can't remember it but, but darling I want you to read that. It's one of Shakespere's, no I guess it isn't Shakespere's, but it's the way I feel, and I want you to feel like that.
"O. k. Jake.

"Now darling, I drink to your good luck, & your happiness. Because darling you will be happy. You know you will. I want to drink to your luck and happiness and you drink to mine. Please, darling. Don't feel bad. Say it, for my sake."

"I drink to your luck and happiness."

"That's great."

They drank. He said "Darling, don't look that way, I didn't mean to hurt you, darling. You're not going to cry, are you?"

"No. I won't cry."

"That's great, darling. Because I wouldn't for the world make you unhappy. I knew you'd be brave about it. You know, that's the only way to be."

He put his hand on her arm, and they sat for a few minutes looking at each other. She said, finally: "What time is it?"

He took out his watch. "Say, my God! Eleven fifteen! Say, I've got to hurry! Just a sec, I want to settle up with Jake."

He left the table, & came back very soon. "Well, dear, we got to be moving. Wish I could take you. Take you to your room. Will you ride on down to Grand Central? Taxi?"

She said: "I guess I'll stay here."
"Oh, gee. You can't do that. You can't—"
"Don't worry about me."

Plate 47. Opening from *Four early stories* by James Agee (Cummington Press, 1964)

du sujet qui m'amène, et par quel rapport j'ai l'avantage de connaître votre nom.

Je la priai de me donner le temps de la lire dans un cabaret voisin. Elle voulut me suivre, et elle me conseilla de demander une chambre à part.

— De qui vient cette lettre? lui dis-je en montant.

Elle me remit à la lecture. Je reconnus la main de Manon. Voici à peu près ce qu'elle me marquait:

G... M... l'avait reçue avec une politesse et une magnificence au delà de toutes ses idées. Il l'avait comblée de présents; il lui faisait envisager un sort de reine. Elle m'assurait néanmoins qu'elle ne m'oubliait pas dans cette nouvelle splendeur; mais que, n'ayant

Plate 48. A page from *Manon Lescaut* (Overbrook Press, 1958)

Sambre and Oise Canal
Canal Boats

NEXT day we made a late start in the rain. The judge politely escorted us to the end of the lock under an umbrella. We had now brought ourselves to a pitch of humility, in the matter of weather, not often attained except in the Scotch Highlands. A rag of blue sky or a glimpse of sunshine set our hearts singing; and when the rain was not heavy we counted the day almost fair.

Long lines of barges lay one after another along the canal, many of them looking mighty spruce and shipshape in their jerkin of Archangel tar picked out with white and green. Some carried gay iron railings and quite a parterre of flower-pots. Children played on the decks, as heedless of the rain as if they had been brought up on Loch Caron side; men fished over the gunwale, some of them under umbrellas; women did their

Plate 49. A page from *An inland voyage* (Overbrook Press, 1938)

Plate 51. Cover of *The Gregynog Press*
(Leicester College of Art, 1964)

Plate 50. Rampart Press binding

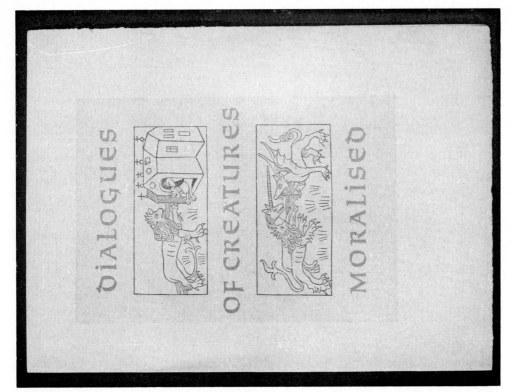

Plate 53. An Allen Press title-page

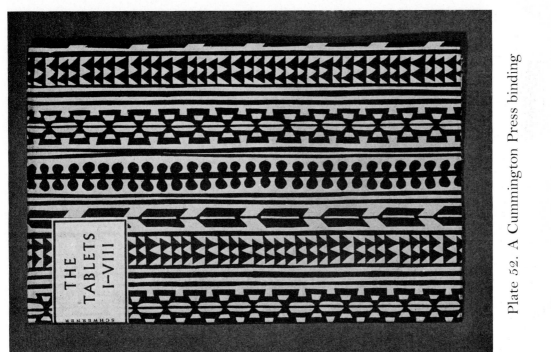

Plate 52. A Cummington Press binding

About the King in the Bath, and How He was Put to Shame.

The First:

Him who in himself does not avoid
Ill-breeding or other pretensions
God punishes either there or here.
Now listen, how it happened here:
A king and also a lord,
Who had great honor
And who was so powerful
That with much might he
Brought under his rule
German and Romance speaking lands,
Both of which were subject to him.
This he wanted to have believed
That nobody could be above him.
This became public knowledge.
That our Lord Jesus Christ
Is a Lord above all princes,
In this he had little faith.
He deemed that he alone
Should be above all princes.

44

Plate 54. Opening from *Three Erfurt tales* (Bird & Bull Press, 1962)

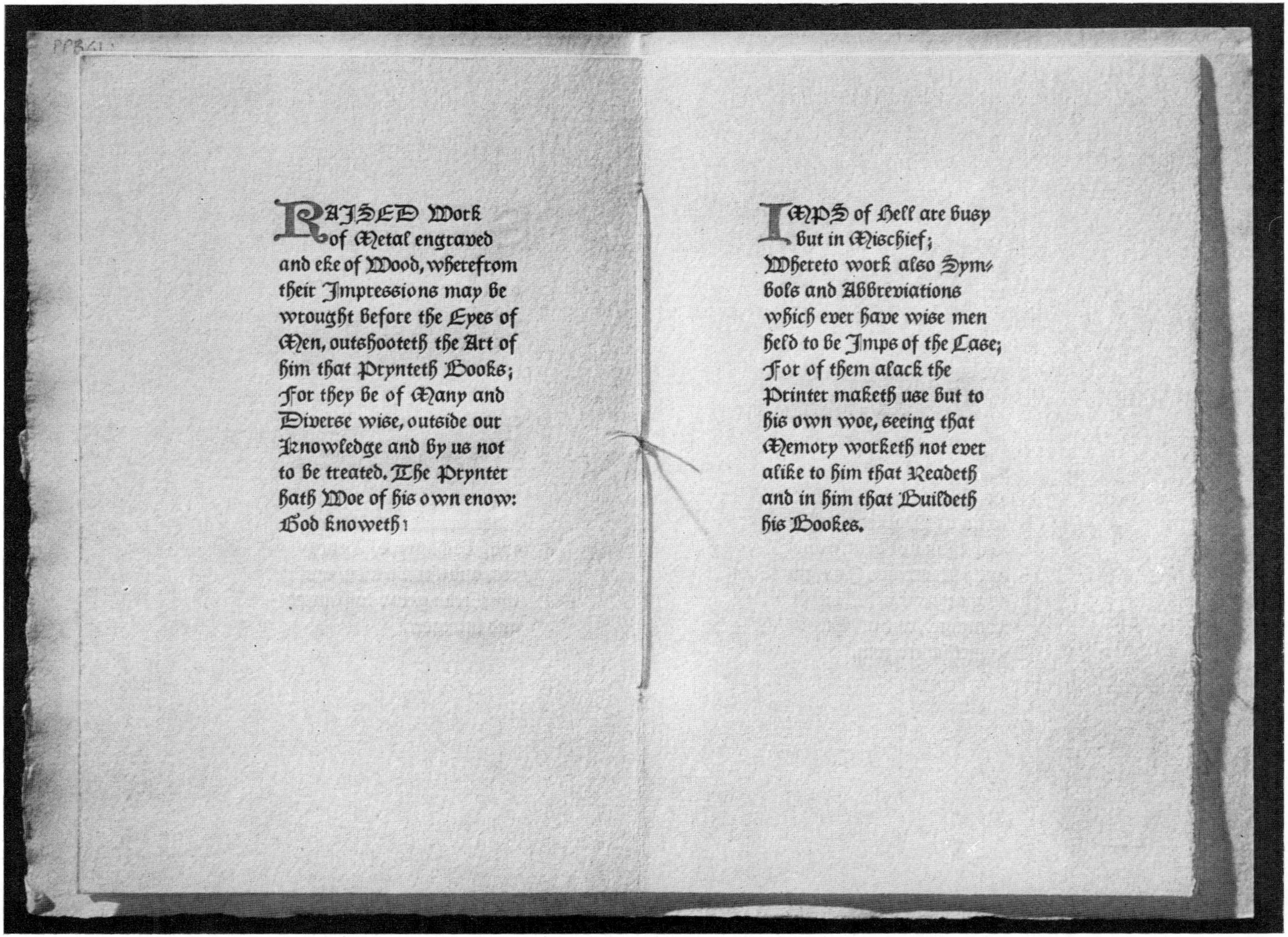

RAISED Work of Metal engraved and eke of Wood, wherefrom their Impressions may be wrought before the Eyes of Men, outshooteth the Art of him that Prynteth Bookes; For they be of Many and Diverse wise, outside our Knowledge and by us not to be treated. The Prynter hath Woe of his own enow: God knoweth!

LEWIS of Hell are busy but in Mischief; Whereto work also Synne-bols and Abbreviations which ever have wise men held to be Imps of the Case; For of them atack the Prynter maketh use but to his own woe, seeing that Memory worketh not ever alike to him that Readeth and in him that Buildeth his Bookes.

Plate 55. Opening from *A mirrour of pryntyng* (Grace Hoper Press, 1960)

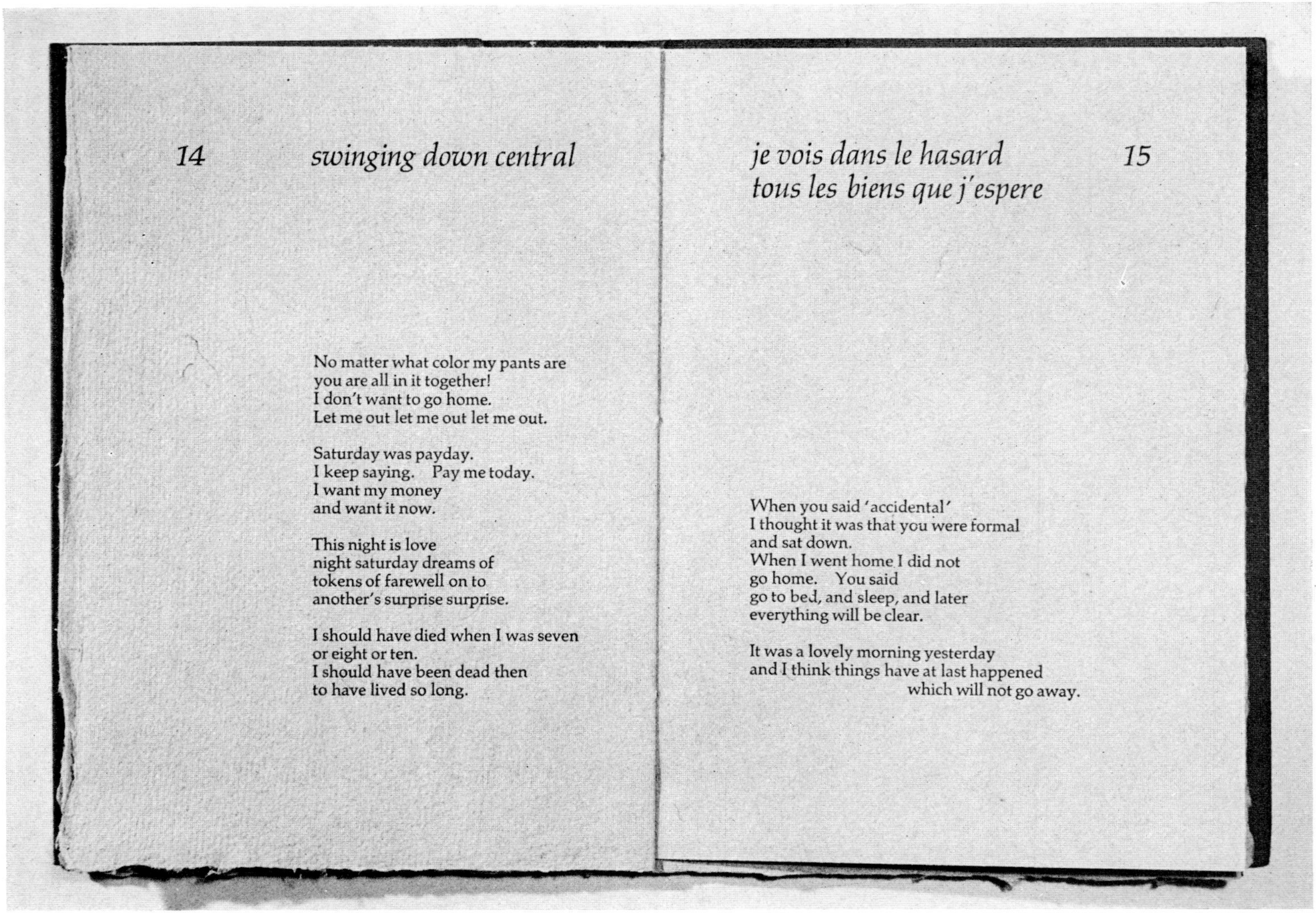

14

swinging down central

No matter what color my pants are
you are all in it together!
I don't want to go home.
Let me out let me out let me out.

Saturday was payday.
I keep saying.   Pay me today.
I want my money
and want it now.

This night is love
night saturday dreams of
tokens of farewell on to
another's surprise surprise.

I should have died when I was seven
or eight or ten.
I should have been dead then
to have lived so long.

15

je vois dans le hasard
tous les biens que j'espere

When you said 'accidental'
I thought it was that you were formal
and sat down.
When I went home I did not
go home.   You said
go to bed, and sleep, and later
everything will be clear.

It was a lovely morning yesterday
and I think things have at last happened
which will not go away.

Plate 56. Opening from Robert Creeley's *Diversions* (Perishable Press, 1968)

"Orders is orders," replied the young sergeant in charge. "A soldier kin have no conscience when it comes to carryin' out his orders. Furthermore, if your grandpappy values his property, he ought to be here to perfect it 'stead of 'skedaddlin'."

He agreed with Johnny, however, on one point. No, they did not have orders to burn the barn, only the cotton. After debating the matter among themselves they rolled the bales out in the yard and burned the cotton there.

A procession of soldiers tracked through the house that morning. The place was ransacked. Storeroom and kitchen were stripped of pots, pans, spoons, meal, molasses, and preserves. A teamster even appropriated a cow-hide seat rocker from the front piazza, claiming that he was entitled to a little comfort in the evenings after driving all day over "these God damn Georgy roads." The soldiers were unashamed in their marauding. When Johnny asked a private what regiment he

belonged to he laughingly replied, "to the Locust Brigade." Worthless as well as useful articles were carried off. A soldier who went away with a file of old newspapers explained that the lies printed in them by rebel editors were his favorite reading.

Johnny learned early in the day that it was a waste of time to protest. The officers gave the men free rein. The first soldier to enter the house carried off several things. Among them were some books. Johnny spotted the private as he walked off with his loot. When his pleas proved useless, he grabbed for the books.

"Why you jg'rent little Secesh beggar, you kain't read. Whatta you want with books?" scoffed the Yankee, shoving him aside.

Johnny followed the soldier down to the road. A company was passing and he appealed to a lieutenant. "Complain to his own officers," was the only satisfaction he got.

Further protests by the boy were drowned out by a headquarters band that now approached. It numbered more musicians than most Confederate companies had riflemen. The band blared forth into the strains of *The Battle Hymn of the Republic*. The men in an infantry company which was behind it joined in with their voices.

The somewhat stolid Salzburger temperament of Jonathan Leber, Jr. had reached the limit of its tolerability. The Yankees had trespassed where the grapes of wrath were stored. A strange scene now took place on the road in front of the house —the spectacle of the angered boy trying to outsing the soldiers with the words of *The Bonnie Blue Flag*.

The sight made an especial impression on a Minnesota soldier. That night he would write in his diary:

DEC. 6th. Broke camp at 6:30. Marched all day, about 17 miles, along sandy roads through poor pineywoods country. Last night saw one of Uncle Billy's bonfires, a big gin mill east of Jacksonborough—the best fire

Plate 57. Opening from *Johnny Leber* (Ashantilly Press, 1962)

Plate 58. Opening of *Slate engraving* (Leicester College of Art, 1964)

Blocked motion

The mysterious life of the statue is an invisible force at rest.

The statue is equilibrium which can be shifted without
losing its balance.

Passion and sculpture don't go together.

Ingenious, impassioned attitudes hardly work in a statue.

Rodin had the controlled passion of the actor. Maillol, with the
simplicity of the great artist, preferred ordinary attitudes.

Sculpture is blocked motion in space; but the living body is like a
waterfall, in constant motion.

Plate 59. Opening from *Mime: the art of Etienne Decroux* (Pratt Adlib Press, 1965)

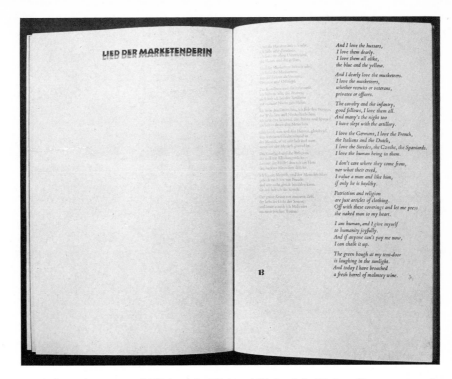

Plate 60. Opening from *Selected poems of Heinrich Heine* (Heinrich Heine Press, 1965)

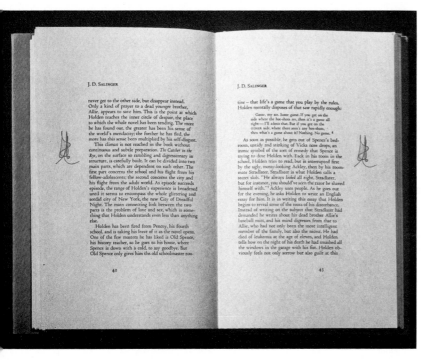

Plate 61. Opening from *Five American moderns* (Roger Ascham Press, 1968)

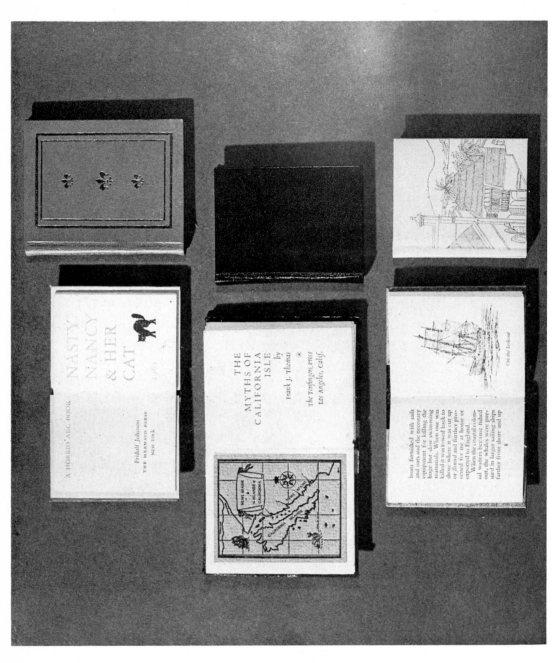

Plate 62. Some miniatures from contemporary American private presses

V

The Party in the Magic Vessel.
To *Guido Cavalcanti.*

GUIDO, I would that Lappo, thou, and I,
  Led by some strong enchantment, might ascend
Fossino presi per incantamento,
A magic ship, whose charmed sails should fly
E messi ad un vascel, ch'ad ogni vento
  With winds at will where'er our thoughts might wend,
Per mare andasse a voler vostro e mio;
And that no change, nor any evil chance,
Sicchè fortuna, ad altro tempo rio,
  Should mar our joyous voyage; but it might be,
Non ci potesse dare impedimento;
That even satiety should still enhance
Anzi vivendo sempre in noi'l talento
  Between our hearts their strict community:
Di stare insieme crescesse'l disio.
And that the bounteous wizard then would place
E Monna Vanna, e Monna Bice poi,
  Vanna and Bice and my gentle love,
Con quella su il numer della trenta,
Companions of our wandering, and would grace
Con noi ponesse il buono incantatore,
  With passionate talk, wherever we might rove,
E quivi ragionar sempre d'amore,
Our time, and each were as content and free
E ciascuna di lor fosse contenta,
  As I believe that thou and I should be.
Siccome io credo che sariamo noi.

14

* There is no pride or resentment here. All is right again with the lover; who seems to have improved his acquaintance with Beatrice, and to think himself warranted, at all events, in mentioning her as one of the three adorables of himself and his two friends.

This sonnet, in one respect, may be said to be the *happiest* of all Dante's effusions. He is young, cheerful, hopeful, full of friendship and of love, and making holiday with both in one of the most charming regions of imagination.

A sail upon the sea of this nature was one of the favourite day-dreams of another loving, intense (I use the word advisedly), and universe-ranging poet,—Shelley,—who in the course of them made a version of the sonnet before us.

Guido Calvalcanti, to whom the sonnet is addressed, was the contemporary poet, whom Dante considered his dearest friend. 'Lappo' or 'Lapo,' was Lapo Gianni, another poet, of whom a laughing little Utopian effusion has been preserved by Crescimbeni; just of a nature to suit the livelier portion of the talk in Dante's fairy ship. The designation of Lapo's mistress by Number Thirty alludes to the place she occupied among the sixty beautiful ladies of

15

Plate 63. Opening from *Leigh Hunt on Dante* (Typographical Laboratory, 1965)

I AM HERE ADJUDGED to die for acting an act never acted, for plotting a plot never plotted. Justice will have her course; accusers must be heard; greatness will have victory; scholars and martialists (though learning and valour should have the preeminence), in England must die like dogs and be hanged. To mislike this were but folly; to dispute it, but time lost; to alter it, impossible; but to endure it, is manly; and to scorn it, is magnanimity: the Queen is displeased, the lawyers injurious & death terrible: but I crave pardon of the Queen; forgive the lawyers and the world; desire to be forgiven and welcome death.

12

Round Robin

A Lift for the Lazy – 1849

13

Plate 64. Opening from one of the Grace Hoper Press's *Typographical commonplace books*

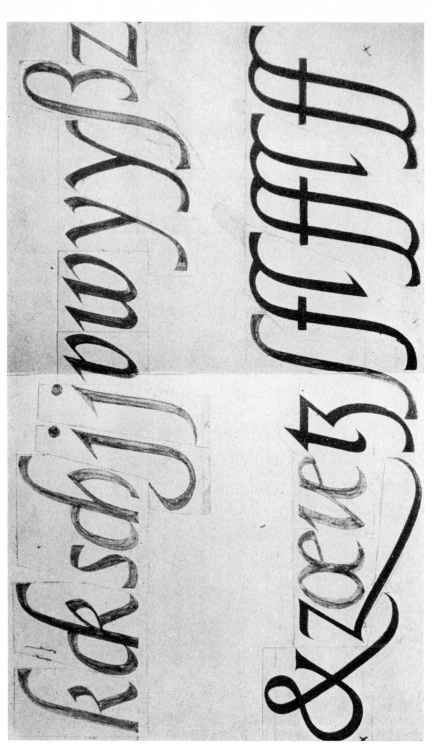

Plate 65. Edward Johnston's drawings for the Cranach italic type

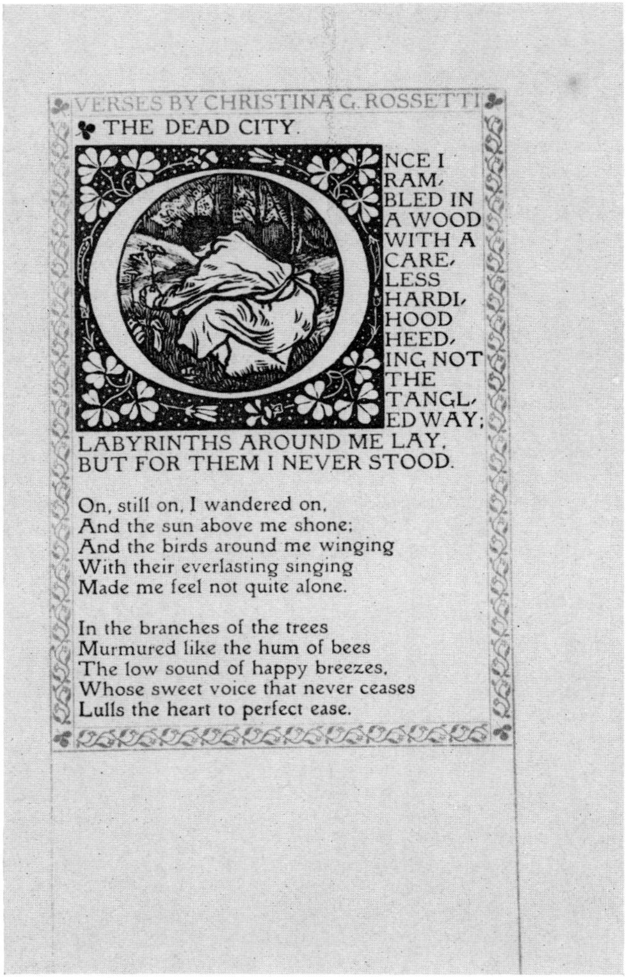
VERSES BY CHRISTINA G. ROSSETTI

THE DEAD CITY.

ONCE I RAMBLED IN A WOOD WITH A CARELESS HARDIHOOD HEEDING NOT THE TANGLED WAY; LABYRINTHS AROUND ME LAY, BUT FOR THEM I NEVER STOOD.

On, still on, I wandered on,
And the sun above me shone;
And the birds around me winging
With their everlasting singing
Made me feel not quite alone.

In the branches of the trees
Murmured like the hum of bees
The low sound of happy breezes,
Whose sweet voice that never ceases
Lulls the heart to perfect ease.

Plate 66. The Eragny 'Brook' type

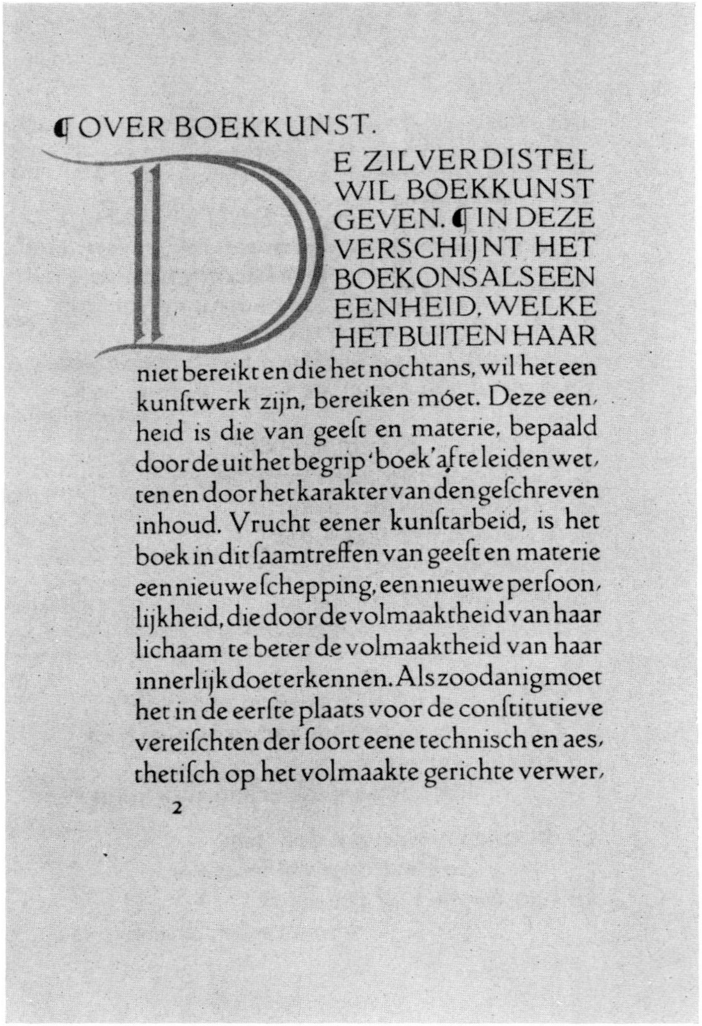
¶ OVER BOEKKUNST.

DE ZILVERDISTEL WIL BOEKKUNST GEVEN. ¶ IN DEZE VERSCHIJNT HET BOEK ONS ALS EEN EENHEID, WELKE HET BUITEN HAAR niet bereikt en die het nochtans, wil het een kunſtwerk zijn, bereiken móet. Deze eenheid is die van geeſt en materie, bepaald door de uit het begrip 'boek' af te leiden wet, ten en door het karakter van den geſchreven inhoud. Vrucht eener kunſtarbeid, is het boek in dit ſaamtreffen van geeſt en materie een nieuwe ſchepping, een nieuwe perſoonlijkheid, die door de volmaaktheid van haar lichaam te beter de volmaaktheid van haar innerlijk doet erkennen. Als zoodanig moet het in de eerſte plaats voor de conſtitutieve vereiſchten der ſoort eene technisch en aesthetiſch op het volmaakte gerichte verwer,

2

Plate 67. A page from *Over boekkunst en De Zilverdistel* (De Zilverdistel, 1916)

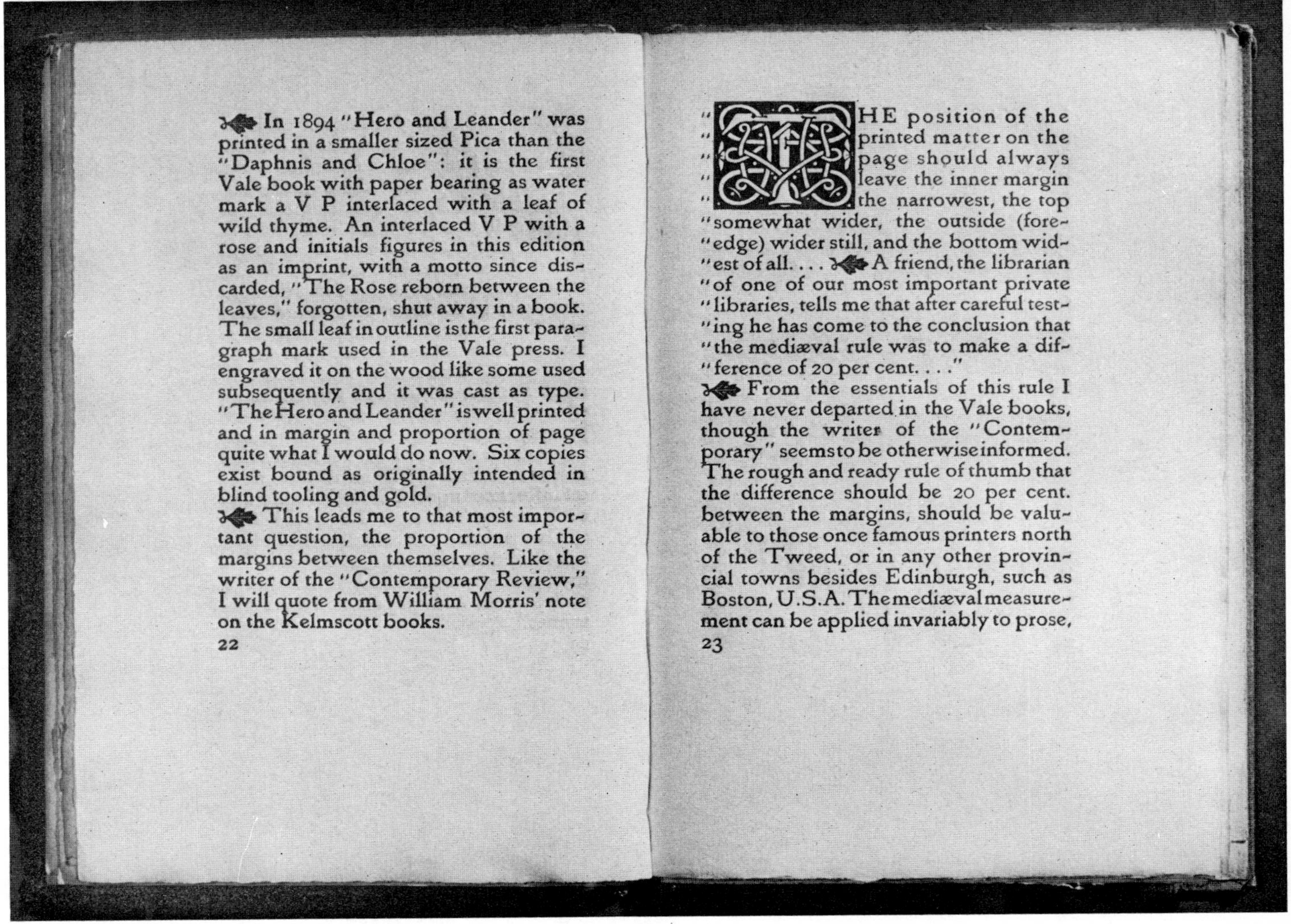

In 1894 "Hero and Leander" was printed in a smaller sized Pica than the "Daphnis and Chloe": it is the first Vale book with paper bearing as water mark a V P interlaced with a leaf of wild thyme. An interlaced V P with a rose and initials figures in this edition as an imprint, with a motto since discarded, "The Rose reborn between the leaves," forgotten, shut away in a book. The small leaf in outline is the first paragraph mark used in the Vale press. I engraved it on the wood like some used subsequently and it was cast as type. "The Hero and Leander" is well printed and in margin and proportion of page quite what I would do now. Six copies exist bound as originally intended in blind tooling and gold.

This leads me to that most important question, the proportion of the margins between themselves. Like the writer of the "Contemporary Review," I will quote from William Morris' note on the Kelmscott books.

22

THE position of the printed matter on the page should always leave the inner margin the narrowest, the top somewhat wider, the outside (fore-edge) wider still, and the bottom widest of all.... A friend, the librarian of one of our most important private libraries, tells me that after careful testing he has come to the conclusion that the mediæval rule was to make a difference of 20 per cent...."

From the essentials of this rule I have never departed in the Vale books, though the writer of the "Contemporary" seems to be otherwise informed. The rough and ready rule of thumb that the difference should be 20 per cent. between the margins, should be valuable to those once famous printers north of the Tweed, or in any other provincial towns besides Edinburgh, such as Boston, U.S.A. The mediæval measurement can be applied invariably to prose,

23

Plate 68. The 'Vale' type

Midgetina

HER lashes lowered to frame his face,
Brown, brave and stern in pride,
With the sad shadowed brows of those
Who see the sunless side.
He would stand silent, being wise,
And yet their eyes would greet
And understand, as when the eyes
Of stars and children meet.

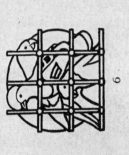

6

Midgetina

THEN he would speak: & for his voice
The things that do not sleep
In musing rhythm gave her choice
Of slender tones and deep,
Pierced by the arrow of a cry,
Distant but dagger-shrill,
Poignant and pitiful and shy
It anguished and was still,

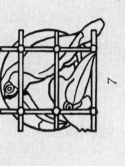

7

Plate 69. The Gregynog 'Paradiso' types as used by Loyd Haberly

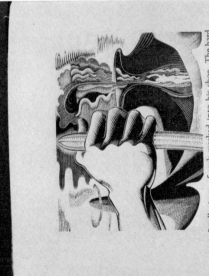

Plate 70. The Golden Cockerel type

Plate 71. Victor Hammer's uncial type

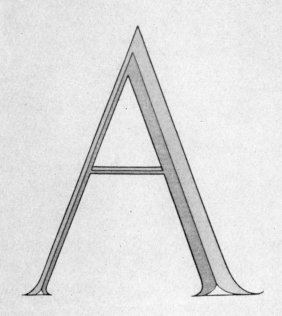

Suole l'usanza antiqua cauare la littera di tondo e quadro, la summa de le qual forme ascende al n. lij, del qual si caua il numero perfecto che è X. E cossì uol esser la tua littera grossa la Xª. parte de l'alteza et per questo modo hauerà tanto del tondo quanto del quadro; et uolsi causare la soprascripta littera doue si tagliano le linie .x. con la circonferentia. Et questo è quanto per misura io, Felice Feliciano, habia nelle antique caractere ritrouato per molte pietre marmoree, cossì ne l'alma Roma quanto negli altri [luoghi].

Plate 72. The Officina Bodoni's 'Dante' type

PART TWO

PRIVATE PRESS TYPEFACES

22

Early presses

―――――

In most cases, those private presses which existed before the nineteenth century used types which were publicly available through the usual trade channels. To distinguish between 'public' and 'private' presses in the fifteenth and sixteenth centuries is very difficult, as we have seen, but although a number of the early printers worked in a way which we may with hindsight regard as being closer in spirit to the private press than to commercial printing, in most of these cases there is little reason to believe that their types were specially designed as part of the aesthetic policy of the printer. Deliberate (and self-conscious) designing of types as one aspect of fine printing certainly came before William Morris and his followers at the end of the nineteenth century, but not typically from the private presses.

One possible exception to this general rule is to be found in the work of the Italian writing masters of the early sixteenth century. Lodovico degli Arrighi da Vicenza, a 'scrittore de' brevo apostolici' as he described himself, produced at Rome in 1522 the first manual on writing to be published, *La Operina*. The first part of this was printed entirely from wood blocks, but the second part, *Il modo di temperare le Penne*, contains several pages printed in a very fine italic typeface modelled upon the 'cancellaresca formata' hand. The type was fairly obviously derived from the hand used by Arrighi himself; it seems very likely that the punches were cut by his partner, who can with reasonable certainty be identified as Lautizio de Bartolomeo dei Rotelli, of whose skill as an engraver of seals Benvenuto Cellini speaks with respect in his *Autobiography*. From 1524 until the sack of Rome in 1527 (in which it is presumed that Arrighi perished) the two partners produced a series of small books printed either in this typeface or in a second chancery italic typeface. If Arrighi's press was not 'private' in that he apparently published for profit, nevertheless the style of his production was more that of a man interested in producing a handsome effect than making much money. His types were large (about 16 point) with very generous ascenders and descenders; he eschewed all ornamentation and favoured a severe style. With the exception of one or two small initials in one of his books he used no decorative material, instead affecting the manner of the manuscript, with blanks for initials to be filled in later by illuminators.

Arrighi's types were used after his death by the printer Tolomeo Janiculo for the works of Trissino. Giovanni Antonio Castellione of Milan used a similar, upright, chancery letter; and the same handsome fount was employed by Gaudentius Merula at his private press at Bergo Lavezzaro, near Novara, in 1542. In the great revival of classical typefaces in the 1920s Arrighi was well served: under the direction of Frederic Warde in 1925 Plumet of Paris recut his faces for a new edition of Arrighi's writing book which was printed by the Officina Bodoni, which had made very distinguished use of the faces in its books. Warde's version of the first Arrighi face needed a good deal of revision for machine composition as a companion face to a roman type, but when issued by the Monotype Corporation married to Bruce Rogers' Centaur type (based upon the Venetian roman used by Jenson in the 1470s) it was an entirely happy marriage. To accompany the very fine recutting of the type used by Aldus Manutius in the *Poliphilus* which the Monotype Corporation undertook in 1923, Arrighi's second italic was used as a model. Named Monotype Blado, after the printer Antonio Blado who used the type in the 1530s, it is one of the handsomest of italic types. The design of Monotype Bembo italic follows it closely.

During the three centuries which followed the invention of printing a good number of typefaces were cut for semi-private use. We can see examples of such in the magnificent Greek face used in printing the New Testament in the Complutensian Polyglot, completed by Arnaõ Guillen de Brocar in 1514; or in the 'Romain du Roi' types cut for the Imprimerie Royale at the turn of the seventeenth and eighteenth centuries. For scholarly printing in particular it was often necessary or desirable to obtain special typefaces: thus Sir Henry Savile (1549–1622), the Provost of Eton, having vainly attempted to obtain a fount of the French 'Grècque du Roi' types for an edition of St. Chrysostom which he was interested in producing, eventually imported a special fount from the firm of Wechel at Frankfurt on Main. This typeface was based fairly closely upon the French Royal Greeks, and became known as the 'silver type' from the legend that it was cast in silver matrices. The preparation of the Chrysostom cost Savile the enormous sum of £8,000, and the book was completed by John Norton in 1612.

Similarly, when the Anglo-Saxon type used by William Bowyer the elder to print the specimen for Elizabeth Elstob's Anglo-Saxon grammar was destroyed in the disastrous fire which devastated Bowyer's printing-house in 1712, Lord Chief Justice Parker undertook to pay the cost of casting a new fount of type with which to print her work. This typeface ought to have been a great success, as the drawings for the new design were (at Lord Parker's request) made by the eminent Saxonist Humfrey Wanley. But Robert Andrews, the punchcutter entrusted with the task of translating the designs into type, failed miserably. 'I did what was required,' commented Wanley, 'in the most exact and able manner that I could . . . But it signified little, for when the alphabet came into the hands of the workman (who was but a blunderer), he could not imitate the fine and regular strokes of the pen; so that the letters are not only clumsy, but unlike those I drew. This appears by Mrs. Elstob's *Saxon Grammar.*' The verdict of history agrees with Wanley; although the type was used by Bowyer and his son occasionally after the appearance of the *Grammar* in 1715, it was not used at Oxford University Press (into whose possession the punches and matrices eventually passed in 1778) until 1910, when with the addition of some extra sorts it was used as a phonetic script by Robert Bridges in his *Tract on the state of English pronunciation.*

An outstanding instance of devotion to scholarship can be seen in the punchcutting undertaken by Charles Wilkins, who was in the Civil Service of the East India Company. Early in the 1770s, William Bolts, judge of the Mayor's Court in Calcutta, provided the London founder Joseph Jackson with designs for a Bengali fount of type with which the East India Company intended to print a grammar. Only a primary alphabet was completed, as the result was too poor to justify continuing. The project might well have languished, had it not been for the fact that Wilkins—then in his twenties—had been experimenting with the cutting and casting of Bengali type as a hobby. It was to remain a hobby for a very short while only. In the words of the Preface to Halhed's *Grammar of the Bengal Language* (1778) 'The advice and even solicitations of the Govenor-general prevailed upon Mr Wilkins . . . to undertake a set of Bengal Types. He did, and his success has exceeded every expectation. In a country so remote from all connection with European artists, he has been obliged to charge himself with all the various occupations of the Metallurgist, the Engraver, the Founder, and the Printer. To the merit of invention he was compelled to add the application of personal labour. With a rapidity unknown in Europe, he surmounted all the obstacles which necessarily clog the first rudiments of a difficult art, as well as the disadvantages of solitary experiment.'

As the father of Bengali typefounding, Wilkins was no longer of course in the position of an amateur, for typefounding became his chief concern. He trained an Indian assistant, Panchanan Karmakar, as punchcutter and founder, and he continued to run the typefoundry which had been set up in Calcutta after Wilkins' return to England in 1786. Subsequently he entered the service of the Mission Press at Serampore, and was responsible for training the other punchcutters whose skill made the work of the Baptist Mission Press so well known in the nineteenth century.

After his return to England, Wilkins continued his linguistic and typographic pursuits, once more at his own initiative and expense. 'At the commencement of the year 1795,' he wrote in the Preface to his *Grammar of the Sanskrita Language*, 'residing in the country and having much leisure, I began to arrange my materials and prepare them for publication. I cut letters in steel, made matrices and moulds, and cast from them a fount of types of the Deva Nagari character, all with my own hands; and with the assistance of such mechanics as a country village [Midhurst] could afford, I very speedily prepared all the other implements of printing in my own dwelling house; for by the second of May in the same year I had taken proofs of 16 pages . . . Till two o'clock on that day everything had succeeded to my expectations; when alas the premises were discovered to be in flames, which, spreading too rapidly to be extinguished, the whole building was presently burned to the ground. . . . I happily saved all my books and manuscripts, and the greatest part of the punches and matrices; but the types themselves . . . were either lost or rendered useless.' Subsequently the East India Company Directors persuaded Wilkins to take up his undertaking again, and his work was published in 1808. It was not from his private press (as he had originally intended) but from that of Bulmer. Specimens of Wilkins' types were shown in Johnson's *Typographia*.

Similar special casting of exotic typefaces was probably commoner on the continent than it was in England. In the New World, typefounding was strictly a normal utilitarian trade, and was to remain one for very much longer; not until the beginning of the twentieth century were special private press faces cut. But there is some evidence to suggest that long before the first commercial typefounding in Mexico (in 1770) type had been specially cast for the Mission Press operated by the Jesuits in Paraguay.

The Jesuit Republic of Paraguay was one of the most remarkable of all European essays in colonialism, though most of us know little more about it than the distorted picture given in *Candide*. The Paraguayan Indians had extraordinary skill in handicrafts; Francisco Xarque writing in 1687 commented that they were able to copy a printed missal with the pen so exactly that only the closest examination enabled one to distinguish the written from the printed text; and in 1711 Father Labbé commented on their skill. 'I have seen,' he wrote, 'lovely paintings from their hands, books very correctly printed, others written with much delicacy. . . .' With such assistants available, one wonders less that the Jesuits were able to establish a press which between 1705 and 1727 produced several of the works used in their own Christianisation. This printing was carried out 'sin gastos, asi de la ejecion, como en los caracteres propios de esta lengua' (without expense in the execution, and in the correct types for the language) and although there is no more circumstantial evidence to suggest that the type was cast by the Indians, the great Latin American bibliographer José Toribio Medina was satisfied that the Mission printers were the first typefounders in the Americas.

When Benjamin Franklin was appointed Sole Minister Plenipotentiary of the United States to the king of France in 1776, and set about equipping himself with a printing press, his press was much more than a hobby. It was as much of an official as a private nature, and it grew to very large proportions. In 1777 he bought a small fount of type from Fournier-le-jeune, much larger amounts in 1778 and 1779, and in May 1780 added typefounding equipment at a cost of 5,000 livres. A foreman and three assistants were employed upon this work, some of the type being cast for American printers cut off from their usual English sources of supply. But it was also employed in casting a special, private, typeface.

In his position as American Minister, Franklin was well aware of the danger of having his official documents (such as passports) forged. He was not unfamiliar with the problem: as printer of much of the paper currency used in the American colonies, he had devised an extremely successful method of nature printing to make the forgers task very much harder. In his passports he does not appear to have resorted to this method (which was continued in America right up to the 1780s) but instead to have relied upon typographical ingenuity and upon the use of a distinctive ornamental script type, perhaps designed by himself, and for which the matrices were cut by Fournier-le-jeune and cast in 1781 in Franklin's Passy foundry.

In few if any of these private or specially commissioned faces, however, can we sense the special aesthetic ideals with which the idea of the private press was to become imbued by the end of the nineteenth century. One notable exception is in the Greek typeface used by Julian Hibbert at his private press at No. 1 Fitzroy Place, Kentish Town, in 1827 and 1828. Hibbert is one of the most shadowy and Peacockian figures of the early nineteenth century. Born in 1800 and educated at Eton and Trinity College, Cambridge, he was a member of the wealthy Hibbert family with estates in Agualta Vale, Jamaica. His uncle Robert Hibbert was the founder of the Hibbert Trust, and George Hibbert the West Indian merchant and book collector was a cousin. Although he read for the law at Lincoln's Inn, he seems never to have practised, and it is fairly clear from what little we know of him that his main concern throughout his short adult life (he died in 1834, reputedly from shock after being abused by a judge before whom he had refused to swear on the Bible) was to further the cause of free-thought and rationalism, in which he was an enthusiastic believer. He did this by lecturing, by generous financial support of Richard Carlile and others when they were imprisoned or otherwise in need, and by his writing and publishing activities. His earliest work was published in Carlile's *Republican*, and we can only guess at his reasons for establishing his own press. He may have had aesthetic reasons, or it may have been pure benevolence. In 1826, however, one of Carlile's assistants, James Watson, who had received training as a compositor in the *Republican* office, fell ill. In his own words 'I was attacked by cholera, which terminated in typhus and brain fever. I owe my life to the late Julian Hibbert. He took me from my lodgings to his own house at Kentish Town, nursed me, and doctored me for eight weeks, and made a man of me again. After my recovery, Mr. Hibbert got a printing press put up in his house, and employed me in composing, *under his directions*, two volumes. . . I was thus employed, from the latter part of 1826, to the end of March 1828.'

The first of the two books on which Watson worked was *ΟΡΦΕΩΣ ΥΜΝΟΙ: The book of the Orphic hymns . . . printed in uncial letters as a typographical experiment. And published for the sum of three shillings and sixpence in the year 1827.* It is a pleasantly printed octavo of 122 pages. In his 'Preface addressed by the printer to Greek scholars' Hibbert stated that the design for the type was 'first composed from the inspection of inscriptions in the Musaeums of London and Paris, and thus it is no wonder, if it still retains more of a *sculptitory* than of a *scriptitory* appearance.' After examining facsimiles of the Herculanean manuscripts and reading Montfaucon's *Palaeographia graeca* he altered the forms of many of the letters: 'If I had adopted the alphabet of any one cele-brated MS., I should have had less trouble . . . As it is, I have taken each letter separately from such MSS. as I thought best represented the beau ideal of an uncial type; . . . yet placed side by side, they look very different from a MS.' It was, Hibbert claimed, 'a Greek type, which at the same time that it is calculated for ordinary use, approaches nearer to old MSS. than types which have

ΠΑΝΤΑ ΓΑΡ ΕΡΓΑCΙΜΟΝ ΒΙΟΤΟΝ ΘΝΗΤΟΙCΙ ΠΟΡΙΖΕΙC .
ΑΛΛΑ . ΜΑΚΑΙΡ . ΛΓΝΗ . ΜΥCΤΑΙC ΙΕΡΟΝ ΦΑΟC ΑΥΞΟΙC .

LXXIX . (78) ΘΕΜΙΔΟC

ΘΥΜΙΑΜΑ , ΛΙΒΑΝΟΝ .

ΟΥΡΑΝΟΠΑΙΔ ΑΓΝΗΝ ΚΑΛΕΩ . ΘΕΜΙΝ ΕΥΠΑΤΕΡΕΙΑΝ .
ΓΑΙΗC ΤΟ ΒΛΑCΤΗΜΑ ΝΕΟΝ . ΚΑΛΥΚΩΠΙΔΑ ΚΟΥΡΗΝ .
Η ΠΡΩΤΗ ΚΑΤΕΔΕΙΞΕ ΒΡΟΤΟΙC ΜΑΝΤΗΙΟΝ ΑΓΝΟΝ
ΔΕΛΦΙΚΩΙ ΕΝ ΚΕΥΘΜΩΝΙ . ΘΕΜΙCΤΕΥΟΥCΑ ΘΕΟΙCΙΝ .
ΠΥΘΙΩΙ ΕΝ ΔΑΠΕΔΩΙ . ΟΤΕ ΠΥΘΟΙ ΕΜΒΑCΙΛΕΥΕΝ :   5
Η ΚΑΙ ΦΟΙΒΟΝ ΑΝΑΚΤΑ ΘΕΜΙCΤΟCΥΝΑC ΕΔΙΔΑΞΕΝ .
ΠΑΝΤΙΜ . ΑΓΛΑΟΜΟΡΦΕ . CΕΒΑCΜΙΕ . ΝΥΚΤΙΠΟΛΕΥΤΕ :
ΠΡΩΤΗ ΓΑΡ ΤΕΛΕΤΑC ΑΓΙΑC ΘΝΗΤΟΙC ΑΝΕΦΗΝΑC .
ΒΑΚΧΙΑΚΑC ΑΝΑ ΝΥΚΤΑC ΕΠΕΥΑΖΟΥCΑ ΑΝΑΚΤΑ :
ΕΚ CΕΟ ΓΑΡ ΤΙΜΑΙ ΜΑΚΑΡΩΝ . ΜΥCΤΗΡΙΑ Θ ΑΓΝΑ .   10
ΑΛΛΑ . ΜΑΚΑΙΡ . ΕΛΘΟΙC ΚΕΧΑΡΗΜΕΝΗ ΕΥΦΡΟΝΙ ΒΟΥΛΗΙ
ΕΥΙΕΡΟΥC ΕΠΙ ΜΥCΤΙΠΟΛΟΥC ΤΕΛΕΤΑC CΕΟ . ΚΟΥΡΗ .

LXXX . (79) ΒΟΡΕΟΥ

ΘΥΜΙΑΜΑ , ΛΙΒΑΝΟΝ .

· ΧΕΙΜΕΡΙΟΙC ΑΥΡΗΙCΙ ΔΟΝΩΝ ΒΑΘΥΝ ΗΕΡΑ ΚΟCΜΟΥ .
ΚΡΥΜΟΠΑΓΗC ΒΟΡΕΑ . ΧΙΟΝΩΔΕΟC ΕΛΘ ΑΠΟ ΘΡΗΙΚΗC :
ΛΥΕ ΤΕ ΠΑΝΝΕΦΕΛΟΝ CΤΑCΙΝ ΗΕΡΟC ΥΓΡΟΚΕΛΕΥΘΟΥ .
ΙΚΜΑCΙ ΡΙΠΙΖΩΝ ΝΟΤΕΡΑΙC ΟΜΒΡΗΓΕΝΕC ΥΔΩΡ .
ΑΙΔΡΙΑ ΠΑΝΤΑ ΤΙΘΕΙC . ΘΑΛΕΡΟΜΜΑΤΟΝ ΑΙΘΕΡΑ ΤΕΥΧΩΝ   5
ΑΚΤΙCΙΝ ΛΑΜΠΟΥCΑΝ ΕΠΙ ΧΘΟΝΟC ΗΕΛΙΟΙΟ .

LXXXI . (80) ΖΕΦΥΡΟΥ

ΘΥΜΙΑΜΑ , ΛΙΒΑΝΟΝ .

ΑΥΡΑΙ ΠΟΝΤΟΓΕΝΕΙC ΖΗΦΥΡΙΤΙΔΕC . ΗΕΡΟΦΟΙΤΟΙ .
ΗΔΥΠΝΟΟΙ . ΨΙΘΥΡΑΙ . ΚΑΜΑΤΟΥ ΑΝΑΠΑΥCΙΝ ΕΧΟΥCΑΙ .

Fig. 69. A page from Julian Hibbert's edition of the *Orphic hymns*, in his Greek type, 1827

hitherto been used', and one which 'represents with tolerable accuracy the forms of the letters used by the Greeks themselves, in the brightest days of their literature . . . I do not mean a type like that used in Bodoni's Callimachus, . . . ornamented (or rather disfigured) by the addition of what, I believe, typefounders call *syrifs* or *cerefs.*'

The second book from Hibbert's private press was *ΠΕΡΙ ΔΕΣΙ-ΔΑΙΜΟΝΙΑΣ*: *Plutarchus, and Theophrastus, on superstition . . .*, an octavo of 280 pages published at a guinea in May 1828. In this strange composite book (which closes with ten pages of the *principal* addenda and corrigenda!) is an entertaining account of the production of the *Orphic hymns*. Evidently, despite Hibbert's wealth, the press operated on a very limited budget. Intending originally to print only in Greek, when Hibbert found he had to print some Latin he had 'to send to London . . . two or three hours being sometimes lost for a single word'. The Preface includes an interesting balance sheet for the production of the *Orphic hymns*, from which we learn that the cost of production was £34 11s 6d, and the income from sales only £3 9s 6d.

Hibbert's typographical experiment was a forerunner of Robert Proctor's revival of the forms used in the Complutensian Polyglot, but it was a total failure. The *Orphic hymns* received no notice whatsoever when they were published, and out of an edition of 258 copies only some twenty seem to have been sold, including '3 copies forced upon H. B. Esq.' Nor have later writers on Greek types often noticed his work with any favour. Updike admitted that his founts 'had considerable charm,' but Scholderer, in his *Greek printing types 1465–1927*, while allowing that his experiment had undoubted possibilities damns it by saying that Hibbert 'seems to have been altogether too much of a dilettante, and his design . . . is for the most part mere wilfulness'.

Reading the prefatory remarks by Hibbert in his two books certainly gives one the impression that Hibbert had approached the design of his type in the manner of a dilettante, but I believe Scholderer did him an injustice to dismiss the face so scathingly. As it was shown in the *Orphic hymns* the design was in a first, experimental, state; and Hibbert expressed himself willing to try to improve it if enough interest was shown. The type, he said, 'is I hope good in theory, altho' I confess the execution of it is detestable.' It is unknown where he had the punches cut. 'I am tired with attempting to produce a better ranging of the characters,' he wrote. 'I cannot afford to employ the best workmen and the successive changes made by indifferent workmen are not improvements but only expences . . . It will easily be perceived that . . . the forms of some of the letters slightly vary in almost every different half sheet. The letter *Γ*, tho' one of the simplest, has given me extraordinary trouble . . .'

Nothing further seems to have come from Hibbert's Press after Watson left him in 1828, although it is possible that some more ephemeral pieces were printed. It is evident that Watson and Hibbert parted amicably, for when Watson set up as a printer on his own account in 1831 Hibbert gave him his press and types, and a further legacy of 450 guineas after his death. It is not known whether Hibbert's Greek type was given to Watson with the rest of his equipment; I have not seen any use of it in Watson's later work. Updike said that it was melted down, and from Hibbert's own account this seems likely.

Other private press typefaces during the first half of the nineteenth century are of less importance, though not without interest. Cotton, in his *Typographical gazetteer*, speaks of one Russell who was said to have printed a duodecimo *Natural history of the bees* at Elgin in 1822, in an edition limited to two copies, using types which he had cut himself. Much more significant was some missionary printing undertaken in Upper Canada in the 1840s by James Evans, a Methodist missionary stationed at Norway House, a trading post between Hudson's Bay and Winnipeg. Evans was noted for his Indian texts, and invented an ingenious syllabic alphabet to aid in scripture reading in his Cree flock. He could not, however, obtain printing equipment because the Hudson's Bay Company—which controlled all transportation—was not inclined to favour the project. Being a man of considerable determination and no small manual dexterity Evans set to work himself in a manner reminiscent of the Jesuits in Paraguay nearly two centuries earlier. He cut moulds in wood, and in these cast his type, using for type-metal the melted-down linings of tea-chests. Lacking paper, he resorted to the bark of the birch (in true Indian fashion), and on this—using a soot solution for ink—he printed a spelling book in 1841. He was not to have to resort to such methods again; shortly afterwards the Hudson's Bay Company consented to take a press to Norway House. Evans's equipment is now in the possession of Victoria University in Toronto.

23

Morris and after

━━━◆━━━

The many private printers of the mid-nineteenth century contented themselves with types which were available commercially. Even for commercial printers, with the exception of such isolated instances as William Howard's cutting of the Basle Roman type for the Chiswick Press in 1854, the idea of having one's own proprietary typeface seemed sunk beyond trace. It was not until the autumn of 1888 that there was to be a revival.

The origins and work of William Morris's Kelmscott Press have already been dealt with in a previous chapter. Morris's earlier experiments with book design in the mid-1860s and again in the early 1870s had been concerned with the book from the point of view of illustration and decoration alone. It did not occur to him—as he later told Sparling—to go beyond what types and other equipment were available. Then, on 15 November 1888, Emery Walker delivered his lecture on printing to the Arts and Crafts Exhibition Society. 'After the lecture, Father was very much excited', wrote May Morris. 'The sight of the finely proportioned letters so enormously enlarged, and gaining rather than losing by the process, the enlargement emphasising all the qualities of the type; his feeling, so characteristic of him, that if such a result had been once obtained it could be done again, stirred in him an overwhelming desire to hazard the experiment at least. Talking to Emery Walker on the way home from the lecture, he said to him, "Let's make a new fount of type." And that is the way the Kelmscott Press came into being—the outcome of many talks between the two men which had needed just this impetus, this spur of excitement, to turn the desirable thing into the thing to be done.'

It would be idle to regard Morris's impulse to produce his own type as the result of an earlier appeal by Kegan Paul who, writing on 'The production and life of books' in 1883 had said that 'there could scarcely be a better thing for the artistic future of books than that which might be done by some master of decorative art, like Mr William Morris, and some great firm of typefounders in conjunction, would they design and produce some new types for our choicer printed books', but it is possible that some faint recollection of this suggestion was influential in Morris's decision.

The aims of the Kelmscott Press, so much more than the mere making of a new fount of type, have been dealt with in Chapter 11. The production of its first typeface, the Golden type, caused Morris a great deal of trouble. Nothing he had ever done, he told Walker, had been as difficult as the designing of this face. What he wanted, he recorded in his *Note on his aims in founding the Kelmscott Press*, was 'letter pure in form; severe, without needless excrescences; solid, without the thickening and thinning of the line, which is the essential fault of the ordinary modern type, and which makes it difficult to read; and not compressed laterally, as all later type has grown to be owing to commercial exigencies. There was only one source from which to take examples of this perfected Roman Type, to wit, the works of the great Venetian printers of the fifteenth century, of whom Nicholas Jenson produced the completest and most Roman characters . . . This type I studied with much care, getting it photographed to a big scale, and drawing it over many times before I began designing my own letter . . .'

Morris's designs were passed to the free-lance punchcutter Edward Philip Prince in the winter of 1889–90. Morris had been introduced to Prince—whose importance in the cutting of private press types has only recently received detailed study—by Emery Walker. It was to be a very successful collaboration between two great craftsmen. Prince's contribution to the type was, however, entirely in the execution of the design; his freedom of action was very limited. A trial cutting of a letter in great primer was rejected by Morris as too large, and it was decided to produce the fount on an English body (approximately 14 point). During 1890 the punchcutting proceeded rapidly if not always smoothly. 'When the design had passed into the expert and sympathetic hands of Mr Prince and was cut, the impression—a smoked proof—was again considered, and the letter sometimes recut,' May Morris recorded. 'My father used to go about with match boxes containing these "smokes" of the types in his pockets, and sometimes, as he sat and talked with us, he would draw out, and thoughtfully eye the small scraps of paper inside. And some of the letters seemed to be diabolically inspired, and would not fall into line for a while.' A surviving smoke-proof of the letter h (now in the possession of Messrs. Sotheby) bears Morris's criticisms and corrections, which show very clearly how little latitude was allowed to Prince in his interpretation of the design. By February 1891 all punches had been cut and the matrices struck; but even at this late stage Morris had second thoughts about the blackness of the g, and had it recut, before the type was cast at Sir Charles Reed & Son's Fann Street Foundry. The types were cast by machine, which may seem surprising in view of Morris's hostility to machinery as being destructive of the craftsman's pride and pleasure in his work, but Morris saw no advantage in the older methods of using hand moulds. 'There wasn't much fun in it for the poor devils who jogged and bumped the mould about,' he observed.

To judge the Golden type dispassionately is not easy. Comparison with its model, Jenson's Venetian roman, is difficult as Morris's face was by no means a slavish copy. Emery Walker's comment that it was 'less elegant' than the original is a considerable understatement. By his deliberate thickening of the strokes, and reduction of the size of the counters (allied to Kelmscott press-work) Morris produced a type far closer to a *fere-humanistica* than Jenson's pure letter. This worried Morris not a whit; in February 1891 Morris told F. S. Ellis that Walter Crane had seen the type and thought it gothic-looking compared with Jenson's: 'This is a fact, and a cheerful one to me.' Some contemporaries were full of admiration: Charles Ricketts considered the capitals an improvement on the Italian originals, and the face was certainly paid the rather doubtful compliment of being imitated commercially in the United States. Modern opinion would agree with Bernard Newdigate when he commented in *The art of the book* (1914), that the face 'lacks the suppleness and grace of the Italian types generally'. Despite its deficiencies when compared with Jenson's fount, however, the Golden type is not without virtues; its lower-case letters compose excellently together, and some, such as the h, are if anything an improvement on their originals. The capitals praised by Ricketts have been abused by nearly all other writers, particularly for the treatment of the serifs ('Brickbat', 'bludgeony', 'singularly graceless'); they certainly do not sit well together and it is difficult to see why so discerning a critic as Ricketts should have admired them.

Morris had scarcely received his Golden type from the Fann Street Foundry before he was at work in designing a black-letter face with which to print his Chaucer. The work went very much more easily than had been the case with the Golden type; as May Morris wrote, it 'was done with no conscious effort, and with little reference to the models by which he was inspired . . . Emery Walker's vivid remembrance is that with practised hand and head full of proportions felt instinctively, he drew the alphabet straight away—

This sayd, he strooke his hand upon his breast,
And kist the fatall knife to end his vow;
And to his protestation urg'd the rest,
Who wond'ring at him, did his words allow:
Then joyntlie to the ground their knees they bow;
And that deepe vow which Brutus made before,
He doth againe repeat, and that they swore.

When they had sworne to this advised doome,
They did conclude to beare dead Lucrece thence,
To show her bleeding bodie thorough Roome,
And so to publish Tarquin's fowle offence:
Which being done with speedie diligence,
The Romaines plausibly did give consent
To Tarquin's everlasting banishment.

Fig. 70. The Kelmscott 'Golden' type

more or less "out of his head".' Once more the cutting of the punches was entrusted to Prince, who had finished cutting the lower-case by the beginning of August 1891. At the end of the year the complete fount had been cut, and cast by Sir Charles Reed & Son on a great primer body.

The type was designed with the avowed intention of redeeming 'the Gothic character from the charge of unreadableness which is commonly brought against it'. Though inspired by Morris's admiration for the types of Peter Schoeffer, of Gunther Zainer and of Anton Koberger, the Troy type (as it came to be known) was very far indeed from its fifteenth-century models; much further than was his departure from Jenson in the Golden type, but the nature of gothic is such that variation of this sort can succeed well, and the type was a splendid success. The lower-case type, though not conforming to the characteristics of any group of black-letter types, avoids the 'unreadable' nature of the compressed and angular northern European forms by resorting to the rounder, looser-fitting and less pointed style of the Italian and Spanish *rotunda* types. As in the Golden type, the capitals are very much less harmoni-

315

ous, some closely resembling Roman inscriptional letters and others being based fairly closely on those used by Koberger about 1480. Though designed with Chaucer in mind, a trial setting in January 1892 persuaded Morris that a great primer fount would be too large for a long work, and the type was therefore first used in *The recuyell of the historyes of Troye* published in October 1892. For the Chaucer itself, Prince was commissioned to cut the same face on a pica body, and comparison of this, the Chaucer type, with the great primer Troy shows how well Prince cut the smaller version: in the various books printed in both founts there is a perfect harmony between the two.

No sooner had Prince completed the cutting of the Chaucer type, in June 1892, than Morris informed him that a fourth type was projected, and that sketches would be available 'in about three months time'. This face was to have been based upon the *fere-humanistica* type used by Sweynheym and Pannartz, the first printers in Italy, at Subiaco in 1464. But the designs which Morris produced for the type did not satisfy him, and he never had the type cut. Though in some ways a pity (one can imagine the exciting Kelmscott work which might have been produced) one cannot help feeling glad that the Subiaco design was still free for the Ashendene Press to use a few years later.

Prince also cut the typefaces for Charles Ricketts's Vale Press. The first, the Vale type, was cut in 13 point in 1896, after brush-drawn designs by Ricketts. Though avowedly inspired by William Morris's work, Ricketts was not completely happy with it. 'I would define the page of a fine Kelmscott book as full of wine, an Italian book as full of light' he wrote in his strange little *Defence of the revival of printing* (1899). The design of the Vale books was very much more Italianate than that of Kelmscott, and his type was obviously intended to be 'full of light' as it was designed with a body 'slightly larger, more open, and the angle of the serifs different again' from either Morris's or Jenson's types. Nevertheless the fount as cut, based very distantly on the faces of Jenson and of Wendelin of Speyer, was if anything blacker and further from the spirit of the renaissance than the Golden type had been. It had some very affected sorts in the lower-case (b, g, u) and an unpleasantly obtrusive set of capitals; but books printed in the type, or in the closely related Avon type, cut in 11 point by Prince in 1902, are by no means unpleasant to read. The same can scarcely be said for the King's fount, cut by Prince to Ricketts's design for use in *The Kingis Quair* in 1903. Ricketts himself was very pleased with it, thinking it looked 'absolutely magnificent in the Latin. It is one of the three founts I like best', but he later admitted that it was 'viewed by all with execration'. And indeed this type, with its very black and fussy mixture of debased roman and pseudo-uncial is very horrid; one of the worst faces ever designed for private press use—about all that one can admire about it is the skill of Prince's punchcutting!

Ricketts had generously made the Vale type available to Lucien Pissarro, to use in the books he was printing at his Eragny Press. But in 1901 or 1902 Ricketts warned him of his intention to close the Press and destroy his types, so long before this happened in 1903 Pissarro set to work on designing his own typeface. This type, named the Brook type after his home at Stamford Brook, might never have come into being; the chronically poor Pissarro could not afford to have Prince cut the punches until his father Camille Pissarro came to his aid. On 15 August 1902 Camille wrote to tell him 'You can get your alphabet made. I have swung a little deal which will bring me exactly the necessary money, two thousand five hundred francs (£100).' The work was put in hand at once: Prince cut the punches, the type was cast by P. M. Shanks & Co., and received its first showing in T. Sturge Moore's *Brief account of the origin of the Eragny Press* in 1903. It was modelled fairly closely on the Vale type, though with shorter ascenders and descenders as it was cast on a 12 point body. A set of capitals was also cut in 9 point. Thomas Balston, in his study of *The Cambridge University Press collection of private press types* (1951), considered that the changes Pissarro made in the design were 'mostly unimportant, and not very satisfactory', drawing attention to the weak g, q, and K in particular. Pissarro was not, essentially, a printer; his concern was to produce a typeface whose colour would harmonize with that of his wood-engravings, and in this he succeeded admirably. Stanley Morison's verdict that the type was 'sophisticated, rather than eccentric' is one in which most authorities would concur. Eventually the Brook type, like the Vale Press founts, found a watery grave; the punches and matrices and types (other than a few specimen sorts, preserved at Cambridge University Press) being cast into the English Channel by Esther Pissarro in the summer of 1947, thirty-three years after the last Eragny Press book had appeared.

These typefaces were by no means the only designs for which E. P. Prince cut the punches in the halcyon years at the turn of the century. Nor were they the most important. In 1900, at the age of fifty-four, he was at the peak of his powers when he cut the most famous of all private press typefaces, the Doves Press roman.

Just as Emery Walker's 1888 lecture had provided Morris with the urge to design his own typeface, so in 1899 Cobden-Sanderson was inspired by Sydney Cockerell's remark that it was strange that nobody had yet had the good sense to reproduce Jenson's typeface, and told Cockerell that he would do so. Although he admired Morris's work at the Kelmscott Press, he did not do so blindly. Some years later, when Cockerell told him plainly that 'had there been no Kelmscott Press, there would have been no Doves Press' Cobden-Sanderson was outraged. 'Candidly I do not think that William Morris himself is a great printer . . . [He] came to printing with a mind set on decoration, and with a mind overscored with tapestry and woven effects, all of which he reproduced where they are not wanted, on the pages of his books. And many of his effects, as I told him at the time, are "typographical impertinences" and utterly destructive of the page as an expression of the author's thought.'

In this reply, one can discern behind the shrewd criticism Cobden-Sanderson's pain and anger at Cockerell's comment, arising from his extraordinary identification of the Doves Press with himself. The production of designs for the recutting of the Jenson roman seems in fact to have been the work of Cobden-Sanderson's partner in the Doves Press, Emery Walker. But not in Cobden-Sanderson's opinion; when Cockerell asked him some years later about Walker's share in the making of the Doves type he was scarcely generous. 'All that E.W. did', he said, 'was at my request to photograph that design from a book in my own possession, and over that design to draw with a brush, by the hand of his employé and under *my* final direction . . . the letters of the Doves Press alphabet.'

Whatever the relative share played by Walker, by his employé Percy Tiffin (who retouched the photographic enlargements) or by Cobden-Sanderson in the production of the designs, the type was certainly an outstanding success. Cut by Prince and cast on a two-line brevier body by Miller & Richard, the result was a type which in the words of A. W. Pollard 'for the first time brought out the full beauty of the Jenson letter'. It was not a type in which Walker had mechanically reproduced Jenson's original, whatever his partner believed. Walker and Prince between them had removed the accidental irregularities resulting from imperfect cutting and casting in the original, and the design was a typeface perhaps too perfect in its regularity. The Doves type is a magnificent type, with near perfect proportions for a Venetian letter, but it is cold and formal for extensive reading. The most successful of the Doves books are those in which the monotony is relieved by the extensive use of colour, as in the *Pervigilium Veneris* (1911) or by the splendid calligraphic initials of Edward Johnston.

In 1911 Cobden-Sanderson had decided to bequeath the type 'to the Bed of

PARADISE LOST
THE AUTHOR
JOHN MILTON

OF

MANS FIRST DISOBEDIENCE,
AND THE FRUIT
OF THAT FORBIDDEN TREE,
WHOSE MORTAL TAST
BROUGHT DEATH INTO THE
WORLD, AND ALL OUR WOE,

With loss of Eden, till one greater Man
Restore us, and regain the blissful Seat,
Sing Heav'nly Muse, that on the secret top
Of Oreb, or of Sinai, didst inspire
That Shepherd, who first taught the chosen Seed,
In the Beginning how the Heav'ns and Earth
Rose out of Chaos: Or if Sion Hill
Delight thee more, and Siloa's Brook that flow'd
Fast by the Oracle of God; I thence
Invoke thy aid to my adventrous Song,
That with no middle flight intends to soar
Above th' Aonian Mount, while it pursues
Things unattempted yet in Prose or Rhime.
And chiefly Thou O Spirit, that dost prefer
Before all Temples th' upright heart and pure,
16

Fig. 71. The Doves type

the River Thames . . . untouched of other use and all else'. Between 1913 and 1917 the punches and matrices and types were destroyed in this way—so, at any rate, the story as given in Cobden-Sanderson's *Journals*, and as accepted by Emery Walker, Sydney Cockerell and others. There is, however, a fascinating alternative story told by one of Cobden-Sanderson's assistants at the Doves Bindery: that when it came to the point, Cobden-Sanderson could not bear to part with the type and instead buried it in the garden of the Doves buildings at Hammersmith . . .

Cobden-Sanderson had deprived his partner Emery Walker of the use of the type long before this. But Walker had the satisfaction of supervising Prince's cutting of yet another version of Jenson's design for Count Kessler's Cranach Press in 1911. These types are remarkably similar to the Doves Roman, and it seems very likely that many of the designs used were in fact those prepared by Walker and Percy Tiffin years earlier for the Doves fount. But Walker had evidently profited from ten years' contemplation of the Doves version, and restored to the Cranach type some of the features of the original Jenson design—in the a, the g, the h and the e—changes which are to my mind improvements. The punches appear to have been cut by the end of 1911; the type was subsequently cast by Shanks.

Already by 1911 Kessler and Walker were discussing the problem of finding a suitable italic face to accompany the roman. Originally they intended to use one of Aldus's italics, but on Walker's advice they changed to a later italic design by the writing master G. A. Tagliente. Once more Percy Tiffin, under Walker's direction, prepared a clean set of drawings from photographic enlargements for E. P. Prince to use as his model. It was by no means a success: neither Tiffin nor Prince appreciated the subtlety of Tagliente's design. As soon as Kessler saw the smoke-proofs he saw the type was wrong, that it needed 'vivifying, brisking up', as he put it. And in the calligrapher Edward Johnston he thought he knew the man to do it.

In his *Italic quartet* (privately published, Cambridge University Press, 1966) John Dreyfus has given a full and amusing account of the efforts of Kessler, Walker, Johnston and Prince in the making of the Cranach italic. It was a splendid example of too many cooks, and when the type was eventually cut and shipped to Kessler in Weimar in December 1915 it was to remain unused for over ten years; and then it was used only briefly in the prospectus for and the colophon of *The eclogues of Virgil* (1926). And by that time Kessler had come to the conclusion that a new series of smaller Roman capitals was needed for the italic fount. Prince was now dead, but another agonizing collaboration was under way. As Johnston wrote to George Friend, who had learned punchcutting from Prince, and had been engaged to cut the new punches, 'We are really engaged on an *extraordinarily difficult experiment*. The problem is to make an Upper Case Type now to a Lower Case Type made some seventeen or eighteen years ago—that is difficult enough in itself, but we have a greater difficulty in our modern (at present unavoidable) division and separation of labour,

> 1st *The Designer* (myself) guessing at an Ideal.
> 2nd *The Punch Cutter* (yourself) giving it material shapes.
> 3rd *The Type Founder* (Shanks) reproducing them in quantity.
> 4th *The Printer* (Cranach Press) applying the types.

Not to mention Assistants, Photographers, etc. We are widely scattered between London and Weimar, and largely ignorant of each other's work and views.'

The new capitals were, however, cut but they were used only in a single book, Rilke's *Duineser Elegien* (1931), before Kessler had to abandon his Press when the Nazis came to power.

The other typefaces which Johnston designed for the Cranach Press were very much more successful. From 1911 or 1912 onwards Johnston was at work on these black-letter faces; said to be based upon the type used by Fust and Schoeffer in the *Mainz Psalter* of 1457, although in fact they bear little resemblance to this, but in the smaller sizes at least seem far closer to Schoeffer's *fere-humanistica* type of 1471. The punches were cut by Prince in 1913, but the type was never cast from them. When Kessler returned to work on his *Hamlet,* for which the types had been designed, he found the punches rusty or lost, and the punchcutting had to be done over again by Friend. Three sizes were cut, 18 point, 12 point and 10 point, with considerable variation between the designs of individual sorts in the three sizes. They married well together, and as shown in the *Hamlet* appeared very handsome and readable. The punches and matrices are now in the Cambridge University Press collection.

At about the same time that E. P. Prince was cutting the punches for the Doves roman, he was commissioned by C. R. Ashbee to cut a face for the Essex House Press, which had taken over the presses and personnel (but not the types) of the Kelmscott Press in 1898. The first type, the Endeavour, was cut on a pica body in 1901. Designed by Ashbee himself, it was without any doubt the worst proprietary type of any cut for private press use in this country. Rightly dismissed by Stanley Morison as an 'inglorious achievement' and by

Updike as 'eccentric, obscure, and dazzling', it added tot he woolliness of the
Golden or Vale types a clumsy serif treatment and a wilfully abnormal design in
many letters. Nor when Prince recut the design in great primer size, the
Prayer Book type, did the design appear any better; the Essex House Press
books are some of the least readable one will meet with.

In 1903, as Sir Sydney Cockerell has recorded, he and St. John Hornby
were discussing the latter's Ashendene Press, which used Caslon and Fell
types.

'At the moment of parting I suddenly exclaimed,
"Why don't you have, like Morris, a special type of your own?"
"I can't afford such a luxury."
"It would cost you £100" I hazarded.
"If that is all" he replied "let us set about it at once."
Morris had died in 1896. In 1892 he had bought a copy of Augustine's
De civitate dei printed in 1467 by Sweynheym and Pannartz in the monastery
of Subiaco, near Rome. The type, never used elsewhere, is a somewhat
compressed one, very elegant, neither roman nor gothic. Morris at once
decided to have a new type based on this model, but it went no further.
Recalling this experiment, I sought out a photograph of Morris's designs.
After consultation with Emery Walker and Robert Proctor, Hornby came
to the conclusion that he could not do better than to take up what Morris had
abandoned; so he instructed the firm of Walker & Cockerell to go ahead.
Well, within a year, the "Subiaco" type was designed and cut. Hornby's
bill for it was exactly £100.'

The typeface, which was cast on a great primer body by Miller & Richard,
is further evidence of Prince's skill as a punchcutter. It was one of the most
successful of all private press typefaces, and was used by Hornby for all the
Ashendene Press books produced over the next twenty-three years. But in
1925 Hornby had a new fount of type prepared. Designed by Emery Walker
once more it was based on the face used by Holle in his edition of Ptolemy's
Cosmographia published at Ulm in 1482. E. P. Prince had died in 1923, still
cutting punches at the age of seventy-seven. There was no other punchcutter
in England to whom they could turn and so they turned to mechanical punchcutting; the types being cast by R. P. Bannerman and Sons (a firm which a few
years later cast some Egyptian hieroglyphic type for Dr. Alan H. Gardiner;
an example of a private face for scholarly purposes). The Ptolemy type was a
curious hybrid *fere-humanistica* with a very uneven set, and it is hard to see

SICCOME DICE IL FILOSOFO NEL PRINCIPIO della Prima Filosofia 'tutti gli uomini naturalmente desiderano di sapere.' La ragione di che puote essere, che ciascuna cosa, da provvidenza di propria natura impinta, è inclinabile alla sua perfezione. Onde, acciocchè la scienza è l'ultima perfezione della nostra anima, nella quale sta la nostra ultima felicità, tutti naturalmente al suo desiderio siamo soggetti. Veramente da questa nobilissima perfezione molti sono privati per diverse cagioni che dentro dall'uomo, e di fuori da esso, lui rimuovono dall'abito di scienza. ⟨ Dentro dall'uomo possono essere due difetti e impedimenti: l'uno dalla parte del corpo, l'altro dalla parte dell'anima. Dalla parte del corpo è, quando le parti sono indebitamente disposte, sicchè nulla ricevere può; siccome sono sordi & muti, e loro simili. Dalla parte dell'anima è, quando la malizia vince in essa, sicchè si fa seguitatrice di viziose dilettazioni, nelle quali riceve tanto inganno, che per quelle ogni cosa tiene a vile. Di fuori dall'uomo possono essere similmente due cagioni intese, l'una delle quali è induttrice di necessità, l'altra di pigrizia. La prima è la cura famigliare & civile, la quale convenevolmente a sè tiene degli uomini il maggior numero, sicchè in ozio di speculazione essere non possono. L'altra è il difetto del luogo ove la persona è nata e nudrita, che talora sarà da ogni studio non solamente privato, ma da gente studiosa lontano. ⟨ Le due prime di queste cagioni, cioè la prima dalla parte di dentro & la prima dalla parte di fuori, non sono da vituperare, ma da scusare & di perdono degne; le due altre, avvegnachè l'una più, sono degne di biasimo e d'abominazione. Manifestamente adunq; può vedere chi bene considera, che pochi rimangono quelli che all'abito da tutti desiderato possano pervenire, & innumerabili quasi sono gl'impediti, che di questo cibo da tutti sempre vivono affamati. O beati que' pochi che seggono a quella mensa ove il pane degli Angeli si mangia, e miseri quelli che colle pecore hanno comune cibo!

Fig. 72. The Ashendene 'Subiaco' type

why Walker and Hornby thought the face worth reviving; they were neither of them addicted to the quaint. The capital letters were extensively remodelled for the Ashendene face, but the lower-case sorts were scarcely changed at all beyond being better spaced.

Several more types of considerable interest were cut by Prince for private use, as well as others which were reserved for the use of individual firms inspired by the Kelmscott-Doves example, such as the Montallegro type for D. B. Updike's Merrymount Press, or the Riccardi type for the Medical Society. Of the private press faces by far the most interesting was the Greek fount known as the Otter type which Prince cut for Robert Proctor in 1903. Proctor was not the dilettante owner of a press with a taste for Greek, as Hibbert had been eighty years earlier; he was not the owner of a private press at all. A brilliant incunabulist at the British Museum, he was also a close friend and admirer of William Morris, having purchased Kelmscott work from the start. Morris's influence, and his own studies of early printing in Greek, inspired him to attempt an improvement in Greek types. The model he chose was that used in the New Testament of the Complutensian Polyglot produced for Cardinal Ximenes in 1514, a face which Proctor regarded as 'undoubtedly the finest Greek fount ever cut, and the only one of which it can be affirmed with certainty that it is based on the writing of a particular manuscript' (a tenth-century manuscript sent by the Pope to Cardinal Ximenes to help him in the preparation of his text, and which—it is said—was used in the eighteenth century to make rockets). Prince's recutting of the lower case was a skilful reproduction of the Complutensian forms; for the capitals there were no models from which to work and Proctor supplied him with fresh designs which match the original lower-case forms admirably. The type was cast by Miller & Richard early in 1903.

After much deliberation Proctor asked C. T. Jacobi of the Chiswick Press to be his printer—much as the Ballantyne Press were the printers of the Vale Press books—and on 12 May 1903 a four-page specimen was produced. The first work, an edition of Aeschylus, was in proof when Proctor went on a climbing holiday in the Alps from which he never returned. The Aeschylus was seen through the press by F. G. Kenyon and was published in 1904. In 1909 an edition of the *Odyssey* was also printed in the type. In his *Greek printing types* (1927) Victor Scholderer described the type as 'the finest Greek face ever cut' while regretting that 'it will not bear reduction to a commercial size'. In the size available, Scholderer considered it 'suitable only for fine printing in the archaistic tradition'. It is to be regretted that the type (now in the posses-

LIVRE I. LES AMOURS PASTORALES

Le combat des deux boucs

grande douleur, celui qui étoit écorné se mit en bramant à fuir, et le victorieux à le poursuivre, sans le vouloir laisser en paix. Daphnis fut marri de voir ce bouc mutilé de sa corne; et, se courrouçant à l'autre, qui encore n'étoit content de l'avoir aussi laidement accoutré, si prend en son poing sa houlette et s'en court après ce poursuivant.

Daphnis et un bouc tombent dans la fosse

De cette façon le bouc fuyant les coups, et lui le poursuivant en courroux, guères ne regardoient devant eux; et tous deux tombèrent dans un de ces piéges, le bouc le premier et Daphnis après, ce qui l'engarda de se faire mal, pour ce que le bouc soutint sa chute. Or au fond de cette fosse, il attendoit si quelqu'un viendroit point l'en retirer et pleuroit.

Chloé appelle au secours un bouvier,

Chloé ayant de loin vu son accident, accourt, et voyant qu'il étoit en vie, s'en va vite appeler au secours un bouvier de là auprès. Le bouvier vint; il eût bien voulu avoir une corde à lui tendre, mais ils n'en trouvèrent brin. Par quoi Chloé déliant le cordon qui entouroit ses cheveux, le donne au bouvier, lequel en dévale un bout à Daphnis, et tenant l'autre avec Chloé, tant

et tous les deux sont retirés de la fosse

firent-ils, eux deux en tirant de dessus le bord de la fosse, et lui en s'aidant et grimpant du mieux qu'il pouvoit, que finablement ils le mirent hors du piége. Puis retirant par le même moyen le

14

Fig. 73. The Ashendene 'Ptolemy' type

ΟΔΥϹϹΕΙΑϹ ΒΙΒΛΟϹ ΤΕϹϹΑΡΑΚΑΙΔΕ
ΚΑΤΗ. ΟΔΥϹϹΕΩϹ ΠΡΟϹ ΕΥΜΑΙΟΝ
ΟΜΙΛΙΑ. ·

Αὐτὰρ ὁ ἐκ λιμένος προσέβη τρηχεῖαν ἀταρπὸν
χῶρον ἀν' ὑλήεντα Δι' ἄκριας, ᾗ οἱ Ἀθήνη
πέφραδε Δῖον ὑφορβόν, ὅ οἱ βιότοιο μάλιστα
κήδετο οἰκήων, οὓς κτήσατο Δῖος Ὀδυσσεύς.

   Τὸν δ' ἄρ' ἐνὶ προδόμῳ εὗρ' ἥμενον, ἔνθα οἱ αὐλὴ
ὑψηλὴ δέδμητο, περισκέπτῳ ἐνὶ χώρῳ,
καλή τε μεγάλη τε, περίδρομος· ἥν ῥα συβώτης
αὐτὸς δείμαθ' ὕεσσιν ἀποιχομένοιο ἄνακτος,
νόσφιν δεσποίνης καὶ Λαέρταο γέροντος,
ῥυτοῖσιν λάεσσι καὶ ἐθρίγκωσεν ἀχέρδῳ.
σταυροὺς δ' ἐκτὸς ἔλασσε διαμπερὲς ἔνθα καὶ ἔνθα,
πυκνοὺς καὶ θαμέας, τὸ μέλαν δρυὸς ἀμφικεάσσας·
ἔντοσθεν δ' αὐλῆς συφεοὺς δυοκαίδεκα ποίει
πλησίον ἀλλήλων, εὐνὰς συσίν· ἐν δὲ ἑκάστῳ
πεντήκοντα σύες χαμαιευνάδες ἐρχατόωντο,
θήλειαι τοκάδες· τοὶ δ' ἄρσενες ἐκτὸς ἴαυον,
πολλὸν παυρότεροι· τοὺς γὰρ μινύθεσκον ἔδοντες
ἀντίθεοι μνηστῆρες, ἐπεὶ προΐαλλε συβώτης
αἰεὶ ζατρεφέων σιάλων τὸν ἄριστον ἁπάντων·
οἱ δὲ τριηκόσιοί τε καὶ ἑξήκοντα πέλοντο.
πὰρ δὲ κύνες θήρεσσιν ἐοικότες αἰὲν ἴαυον
τέσσαρες, οὓς ἔθρεψε συβώτης, ὄρχαμος ἀνδρῶν.
αὐτὸς δ' ἀμφὶ πόδεσσιν ἑοῖς ἀράρισκε πέδιλα,
τάμνων δέρμα βόειον ἐΰχροές· οἱ δὲ δὴ ἄλλοι

11

Fig. 74. Robert Proctor's 'Otter' type

sion of Oxford University Press) has not been used more extensively.

The example of William Morris, of Cobden-Sanderson and above all of Edward Johnston was even more considerable on the continent than in England. As well as the specifically English contributions to the Cranach Press, an English face was produced for the Zilverdistel of Dr. J. F. van Royen in The Hague. In 1914 Prince cut the punches for a face designed by Lucien Pissarro on the basis of the Carolingian minuscule. This type, the Distel type, was a deliberately archaistic fount, very close to manuscript hands and as used by van Royen (who thought very highly of it, and 'wrote some lyrical passages' in its praise) it could look very fine. But by van Krimpen it was regarded as 'an unhappy experiment'. The other proprietary typeface of the Zilverdistel, the Zilver type, was cut in 1915 to designs by S. H. de Roos, and cast by the Amsterdam Typefoundry. A fount which was like the Doves and Cranach romans based on Jenson's designs, it was—particularly in the capitals—less true to its model than they were. The face is a very readable one, with only the serif treatment on some of the capitals standing out at all unpleasantly. Of this face, van Krimpen was less disapproving: 'undoubtedly one of the best modern interpretations [of the Venetian letter]. If the detail had been simpler, the Zilver type would be in many respects a perfect letter.' These two types are now preserved, like the Zilverdistel's other equipment, in the Museum Meermanno-Westreenianum in The Hague.

In the United States also the shadow of Kelmscott lay heavy. Some private printers, like George Booth at the Cranbrook Press in Detroit or Lewis Buddy at his Kirgate Press in Canton, Pennsylvania, had contented themselves with the various imitations of Morris's faces which were available commercially; others with more taste settled for Caslon Old Face. One private printer who showed more initiative was Ralph Fletcher Seymour. The earliest books from his Alderbrink Press in Chicago were written out by hand and reproduced by line-block—a thoroughly unsatisfactory method, as anyone who has tried it knows; the books lose the crispness of the manuscript without gaining the satisfying bite of type into the paper. Seymour was dissatisfied with the results, and after a couple of experiments with Caslon had his own special face cut in 1902. The design was by Seymour himself, with advice from F. W. Goudy; Robert Wiebking cut matrices for it and it was cast by Barnhart Bros. & Spindler. The Alderbrink type had very considerable merit; a Venetian roman, owing (one would suppose) a good deal to the Doves type, the design of some of the individual letters—the kernless f, the high-waisted k—is not altogether happy, though in other sorts, such as the y, there is a distinct improvement on

PRESENTATION DE PARIS A NOTRE DAME

ÉTOILE DE LA MER voici la lourde nef
Où nous ramons tout nuds sous vos
commandements;
Voici notre détresse et nos désarmements;
Voici le quai du Louvre, et l'écluse, et le bief.

Voici notre appareil et voici notre chef.
C'est un gars de chez nous qui siffle par moments.
Il n'a pas son pareil pour les gouvernements.
Il a la tête dure et le geste un peu bref.

Reine qui vous levez sur tous les océans,
Vous penserez à nous quand nous serons au large.
Aujourd'hui c'est le jour d'embarquer notre charge.
Voici l'énorme grue & les longs meuglements.

S'il fallait le charger de nos pauvres vertus,
Ce vaisseau s'en irait vers votre auguste seuil
Plus creux que la noisette après que l'écureuil
L'a laissé retomber de ses ongles pointus.

Nuls ballots n'entreraient par les panneaux béants,
Et nous arriverions dans la mer de sargasse
Traînant cette inutile et grotesque carcasse
Et les Anglais diraient: Ils n'ont rien mis dedans.

6

Fig. 75. The 'Distel' type, designed by Lucien Pissarro for De Zilverdistel

the Doves design. The type had excellent composing qualities, and set in mass it reads very agreeably.

Very much better known than the Alderbrink type was that used by Goudy at the Village Press, a typeface which as has already been said in Chapter 13, was intended originally as an advertising face. Will Ransom has recorded that the type was based loosely on fifteenth-century Venetian designs, and that Robert Wiebking was 'frankly shocked at some of the "liberties" Goudy had taken with certain letters'. Looking at the Village type through prejudiced English eyes, I can see little to recommend it. It is a very wide letter, with some of the sorts—the e, the r, the y—striking the eye particularly unpleasantly, by comparison with, say, the Doves or Alderbrink or Zilver types. But its difference, its eccentricity, was probably useful in its time, just as Morris's distortion of the Jenson roman was in the end justified by the cutting of the Doves type. With Goudy's many later types (he designed over a hundred) we are not here concerned. Several of his types are still popular, particularly with amateur printers in the United States, but most would agree with James M. Wells's opinion that they are 'badly dated. Even his book faces often suffer from mannerisms and eccentricity which call attention to the type rather than the text'.

In 1915 the Chicago Society of Etchers published *The etching of figures* by W. A. Bradley. It had been printed for them at Marlborough-on-Hudson by Dard Hunter, and was the first showing of a new typeface which he had designed. What distinguished this book from all the other private press publications which had appeared since the 1890s was the simple fact that it was *entirely* the work of Dard Hunter. He had made the paper, cut the punches, cast the type as well as composing and printing the pages which was the limit of personal involvement for other amateurs, and for such men as Cobden-Sanderson considerably beyond the limit.

In his fascinating autobiography *My life with paper* (1958) Hunter told the story of the genesis of this type. Following a childhood familiarity with the production of a country newspaper, and an introduction to arts and crafts at the Roycroft Shop, Hunter in 1911–12 moved to London, where he worked at commercial designing. At the same time, through studying at the Science Museum he became fascinated by the traditional methods of producing types by the use of punches and hand moulds. Before he left to return to the United States in 1913 he had determined to have his own personal press. His Roycroft training, followed by his visits to the Doves and Eragny Presses, influenced this decision; but he was determined not to leave any of the stages in the production of a book to others. 'I would return to America and attempt to make books by hand completely by my own labour—paper, type, printing.'

During the next three years Hunter built his small paper mill at Marlborough-on-Hudson, and occupied himself with making paper. In the winter, when the millstream was frozen, and in the summer when the water level was too low for papermaking, he turned to making his fount of type. He had received no training in punchcutting or in casting type, but depended entirely on the instructions given in Moxon's *Mechanick exercises*. One might very well think that a typeface produced under such conditions would be better not discussed. Hunter's type, though, is by no means one to be passed over in silence. It was not a design consciously and deliberately copied or adapted from

IT WAS THE TERRACE OF
God's house
That she was standing on,—
By God built over the sheer depth
In which Space is begun;
So high, that looking downward

Fig. 76. The Village type

the types of Jenson as had been so many private press founts. Hunter did not prepare drawings, but cut the punches direct, without any preliminary outlines, though with pages of fifteenth-century books open before him while he worked. The type, which was cut in 18 point, was one distinctly in the Venetian tradition, with its large capitals, rather heavy serif treatment and diagonal bar to the e. The design of many individual sorts could be faulted, and I find the shortness of the descenders a real weakness, but the types composed well. As printed—and how magnificently they were printed—in the big Mountain House Press folios the types have a sparkle and charm which disarms criticism.

Hunter found a great deal of difficulty in the printing of *The etching of figures* and in a second book which he printed for the Chicago Society of Etchers in 1917. He was so disappointed that he thought seriously of abandoning his enterprise. But he did not do so; the Smithsonian Institution acquired the punches, matrices, moulds and tools with which the type had been made, and Hunter—having previously cast enough type for his own purposes—

carried on with his printing. All the early books produced at his press, which in 1917 moved to Chillicothe, Ohio—*Old papermaking* (1923), *The literature of papermaking 1390–1800* (1925), *Primitive papermaking* (1925) and *Old papermaking in China and Japan* (1925)—were printed in this type, as well as on paper made by the author-printer. For his next few books he turned to other, commercially available, typefaces. But for the last book from the Mountain House Press, *Papermaking by hand in America* (1950), a very different face was again used.

The type for this was a face which had been cut by Hunter's eldest son, Dard Hunter Jr., in 1938–40. He had produced it under the guidance of Otto Egge at Cleveland School of Art, and—like his father—cut it direct in the metal, without any preliminary 'designing'. The first showing of the type was a specimen printed on the hand press in the Paper Museum at MIT in 1940. This was cast in the hand-moulds, but for the type used in *Papermaking by hand in America* the Hunters resorted to mechanical casters, having in the meanwhile acquired a brand-new typefoundry for $300. It is another distinguished face, slightly idiosyncratic but looking very well in mass. It is a pity that it was so little used.

24

After 1918

———

Writing in *Modern book production* in 1927, Bernard Newdigate recalled
that in the special number of *The Studio* devoted to *The art of the book*
which he had edited in 1914 he had 'felt it necessary to be a little apologetic for
making mention of a machine-set type, however excellent, in an article about
fine printing.' Most of the types he had then discussed had been proprietary
faces for hand-setting at private or quasi-private presses. In 1927, however,
though he was writing at the height of the boom in fine printing he did not
show a single new typeface cut for an English private press.

Possessing one's own individual interpretation of Jenson's roman in which
to print one's own version of the *Rubaiyat* no longer had the charm for the
private printer that it had possessed twenty years earlier. Some of the reasons
we have already considered in earlier chapters; without any doubt at all the
most important reason of all was the existence of the Monotype Corporation's
intensive programme of reviving good typefaces commercially. With these
available, why go to the expense of having a special face cut which could well
be inferior to these? Very few of the private presses set up between the wars
ever went so far as to have their own designs cut; of those which did, none
used their proprietary face alone, but resorted to other Monotype or founders'
types on occasion.

As well as reviving good types of the past, the Monotype Corporation was
engaged in cutting new faces. Eric Gill's Perpetua type, which was cut between
1925 and 1929, and was the most important of the new English book faces cut
in the 1920s, was the parent of the next typeface to be designed for a private
press, the Golden Cockerel type. This was commissioned from Gill by Robert
Gibbings, and Gill's designs were cut and cast by the Caslon foundry in 1929.
An italic was added two years later. Gill understood the problems of the
Golden Cockerel Press, in which the harmonious marriage of wood-engravings

The End of Fear

I

The Directors are seated round the boardroom table;
They speak with assurance and very little expression.
The General and his staff at battle headquarters
Betray no emotion as they plan the attack
With an economy of words.
Gentlemen, your masks do not deceive me;
You, I and all of us are full of fear—
Haunted by the terror of an unknown future,
Anxious for the fate of unborn children
To be killed by a secret weapon
In a battle as yet unplanned.

II

Not because they are gallant adventurers
But because they are too much afraid to deal honestly
Do the Directors—with many a sonorous cliché—
Enter into trade agreements
Which can only be ratified with blood.

1

Fig. 77. A page from *Fear and the stranger*, printed at the Stourton Press,
1951, in the Press's 'Aries' roman, designed for it by Eric Gill

to type counted for so much. His solution was to take the basic Perpetua design
and make it rounder and slightly heavier, producing a design which is, in
Robert Harling's words, 'lacking perhaps the dignity of the Monotype fount,
but equally assured and certainly more robust . . . [It] is almost without

equal in its suitability for use with wood-engravings on a printed page.' Any-body who has seen the Golden Cockerel *Four gospels* must surely agree. The italic fount, for which no capitals were cut, is less satisfactory: like all Gill's italics it is a bastard form with 'sloped roman' characteristics in many letters which make it a restless and uncomfortable design. The type was little used in the years of the Golden Cockerel Press's decline after the Second World War, a notable exception being *The songs and poems of Dryden* (1957). It is now owned by Thomas Yoseloff, who bought the Golden Cockerel Press in 1959.

The other purely private press typeface designed by Gill—for his Joanna and Bunyan designs were not private in the strict sense, though they did not become generally available for many years—was the Aries type designed for the Stourton Press in 1932. It is unmistakably a Gill design, but with a number of features which do not appear in any of his other typefaces. Robert Harling has suggested that Gill may have been influenced in his designs by a sight of trial cuttings of Times New Roman, and certainly his fount has several lower-case sorts—a, d, e, h, m—which are very close indeed to some of Morison's experiments. The italic again has sloped roman tendencies, though it is nearer to a true italic than any of his other designs. Cut by the Caslon foundry in three sizes, 18 point, 14 point and 10 point, the type was used originally in a magnificent *Catalogue of Chinese pottery and porcelain in the collection of Sir Percival David, Bt.*, in 1934. In this the type is seen at its best, and its clear forthright design, in the printer's words, 'helps to give unity to what might have been a typographer's nightmare'. The Stourton Press still owns the punches and matrices for the type, which has been cast as needed on the Press's own pivotal caster, in England and in South Africa. A certain amount of the type is possessed by the University of Cape Town, to whom Mr. Fairfax Hall, the owner of the Stourton Press, presented it on his return to England in 1961.

While the Golden Cockerel Press was making use of its own typeface the Nonesuch Press also, in 1931, made its own essay with proprietary material. The idea of a proprietary typeface was scarcely compatible with Nonesuch aims, and it never had a fount of type cut. But for its editions of the *Iliad* and *Odyssey* (1931) the illustration was provided by means of figurines designed by Rudolf Koch and cast as type. Rearranged into appropriate combinations at the head of each double opening, they made extraordinarily effective decoration.

The last of the great triumvirate of the presses between the wars, Gregynog, did not have a special fount of type cast until 1934–5, during Loyd Haberly's directorship of the Press. The typeface was designed by Haberly

A Minos mi portò; e quegli attorse
    otto volte la coda al dosso duro;
    e, poi che per gran rabbia la sì morse,
Disse: ‹Questi è de' rei del fuoco furo›;
    per ch'io là dove vedi son perduto,
    e sì vestito andando mi rancuro.»
Quand'egli ebbe il suo dir così compiuto,
    la fiamma dolorando si partio,
    torcendo e dibattendo il corno acuto.
Noi passammo oltre, ed io e il duca mio,
    su per lo scoglio infino in su l'altr'arco
    che copre il fosso in che si paga il fio
A quei che scommettendo acquistan carco.

Canto ventesimottavo.

CHI PORIA MAI PUR CON
    parole sciolte / dicer del sangue
    e delle piaghe appieno, / ch'i'
    ora vidi, per narrar più volte?
Ogni lingua per certo verria meno
    per lo nostro sermone e per la mente,
    c'hanno a tanto comprender poco seno.
S'ei s'adunasse ancor tutta la gente,
    che già in su la fortunata terra
    di Puglia fu del suo sangue dolente
Per li Troiani, e per la lunga guerra
    che dell'anella fe' sì alte spoglie,
    come Livio scrive, che non erra;
Con quella che sentì di colpi doglie
    per contrastare a Roberto Guiscardo,
    e l'altra, il cui ossame ancor s'accoglie

122

Fig. 78. A page from the Bremer Presse *Dante*, 1921, set in the Press's own roman type.
Initials by Anna Simons

and Graily Hewitt, and was based upon a face originally used by Johann Neumeister for the *editio princeps* of Dante's *Divine comedy* in 1472. The typeface, called by Haberly 'Paradiso' (but shown in *The encyclopaedia of typefaces* as 'Gwendolin'), is fairly close to Neumeister's archaic-looking roman, though Hewitt's influence is unmistakable in such letters as the w. It was a typeface in the same class as Ashendene's Ptolemy: deliberately unusual and unsuited for adaptation to normal commercial printing. In the pages of *Eros and Psyche*, the one Gregynog book in which the type was used, and for which it had been specifically designed, it looks well. But the idea was too backward-looking, too much in the direct Morris tradition to recommend itself to the last director of the Press, and the type was never used again at Gregynog after Haberly resigned his directorship in 1936. The type did not remain unused, however, as the Misses Davies generously presented Haberly with a large fount of it, and he has continued to use the type in the books which he has printed from time to time in Dorset, Massachusetts, Missouri or New Jersey. The punches and matrices for this type are now in the National Library of Wales, Aberystwyth.

On the continent there was quite as much activity as there was in Britain. In Germany in particular many new typefaces were produced by such foundries as Bauer, Stempel and Klingspor; types designed by such men as Rudolf Koch, Walter Tiemann and E. R. Weiss. Most of the private presses used these typefaces which were available commercially, just as the English amateurs used Monotype faces, but rather more of the Germans had proprietary designs for their own use. Several of these private press faces are shown in Rodenberg's *Deutsche Pressen*. Among the more interesting were a fine *fere-humanistica* type used at the Officina Serpentis (a design in some ways similar to the Ashendene Subiaco fount); and the handsome roman and black-letter types used at the Bremer Presse in Munich—types which bear comparison with the best of the English and Dutch type-designs produced under the influence of William Morris.

One Dutch type of considerable merit remains to be described. This was the Meidoorn type designed by S. H. de Roos for his own use at his Heuvelpers. Cut by the Amsterdam Typefoundry in only one size, 14 point, it is a rather heavily modelled venetian roman. As with the other Dutch private press faces, Jan van Krimpen did not think highly of it: 'This face strikes me as indicating at one and the same time a great admiration for the work of Mr. St. John Hornby, and of certain German experiments, leaving me with the impression that the fount was perhaps somewhat hastily conceived,' he commented icily.

Nevertheless, used in the grand manner, as de Roos used it, the type could look very well indeed. It is now in the possession of Messrs. J. F. Duwaer en Zonen of Amsterdam.

It was in Italy that some of the most interesting and beautiful proprietary typefaces were to be produced, although the designers of them came from the other side of the Alps. At the Stamperia del Santuccio in Florence, Victor

second of the three miracles. The third was the healing of Gallienus' daughter, whose body the demon vacated amidst much clamour at the Saint's command. When the grateful Gallienus presented San Zeno with a valuable crown, the Saint at once broke it into small pieces which he distributed among the poor. Nevertheless, a demon who had twice offered resistance could not be allowed to go unpunished; San Zeno therefore compelled him to carry from Rome to Verona a large porphyry basin, another gift of the Emperor. This task the demon accomplished in an instant, but in his fury he scratched the surface of the stone; the

11

Fig. 79. A page from *Bishop San Zeno*, printed in the 'Zeno' type at the Officina Bodoni, 1949

Hammer produced some very fine uncial types, cutting the punches with his own hand. But his first essay in type-design was purely as a designer: about 1924–5 he supervised the cutting (by Schuricht) of a typeface, Hammer-Unziale, which was cast by the Klingspor Foundry. But the type was not a success in Hammer's eyes; obviously he and Schuricht were at variance on the design of various letterforms, and though the fount was by far the best uncial design which had then appeared, he never used the type himself. Very interesting and effective semi-private use of the fount has however been made by Colm O Lochlainn at the Sign of the Three Candles in Dublin. O Lochlainn met Klingspor and Hammer while he was in Offenbach, and persuaded them to cast special sorts for those letters in which Hammer had departed from his Irish models. For these O Lochlainn furnished the designs, and so Baoithin, a Gaelic version of Hammer-Unziale, was evolved. It is interesting to note that in Hammer's subsequent designs he seems to have preferred O Lochlainn's forms to those of Schuricht or himself.

In 1925 Rudolf Koch's son Paul joined Hammer in Florence and taught him punchcutting. Between 1926 and 1928 they produced a new uncial type, used in the *Samson Agonistes* of 1931. After this had been published, both Hammer and Paul Koch cut experimental letters as improvements, which were used in a few trial sheets, then between 1933 and 1935 Hammer cut the punches for the Pindar Uncial, which was cast by Klingspor and used first in Hölderlin's *Fragmente des Pindar* in 1935. More cutting of trial sorts followed, but these had to be abandoned when Hammer left Europe for the United States in 1939. An experimental casting of a new uncial by the American Type Founders Company in 1940 led to nothing, but in 1943 Hammer's work as a type-designer found its culmination in his American Uncial (originally cast by Nussbaumer at his Dearborn Type Foundry in Chicago, and in 1952 made generally available by Klingspor). In its latest form Hammer's uncial is of course no longer a proprietary typeface, though it is doubtful whether any commercial use of it could come into the same class as Hammer's own printing. It is a difficult face to discuss dispassionately; there are those who find the uncial form uncommonly disagreeable, and it is certainly not a type one would ever expect to become popular. But Hammer's quest for the perfect form of the uncial letter has been vindicated in a few special editions, and as a display type the design has considerable virtues.

Far more influential has been the work of the Officina Bodoni in Verona. Mardersteig's first design for a new typeface—after his use of some of Bodoni's types, and of Frederic Warde's revivals of Arrighi's designs—was an adaptation of a letter cut for Aldus Manutius by Francesco Griffo and used in Cardinal Bembo's *De Aetna* in 1495. Under the guidance of Stanley Morison the Monotype Corporation had in 1929 issued a version of this typeface, perhaps the noblest roman of them all, under the name Bembo. It has, deservedly, become the most popular book type in England, but Mardersteig considered that the various modifications in the Monotype fount made it far inferior to its model, and in collaboration with the Paris punchcutter Charles Malin set to work in producing his own interpretation. It was to be ten years before the type came into use, first being employed in *Duo episodi della vita di Felice Feliciano* in the summer of 1939. In many respects Mardersteig's face, named Griffo, is almost indistinguishable from the Monotype version, but for some letters it is a much more faithful recutting of Aldus' face, retaining the almost imperceptible forward slope in such letters as the c, e, and s, and with a rather sharper modelling of the serifs. The result is a very graceful and sophisticated type, perhaps not so immediately agreeable as Monotype Bembo, but certainly with a sparkle which was lacking from earlier private press types based on Jenson's Venetian types which were so long thought to be perfection in roman faces.

Griffo's companion italic is however very different from the Bembo italic. *De Aetna* was printed before Aldus had produced the first italic fount of all, and the Monotype Corporation, having first tried to marry it to Alfred Fairbank's splendid Narrow Bembo Italic (and found it far too strong for a subordinate letter), employed a severely revised version of a letter used by Giovanantonio Tagliente. Mardersteig, on the other hand, settled for a genuine italic cut by Francesco Griffo as his model. Though in its way it is a tolerable design, it is far inferior to the roman with which it is mated; in Hans Schmoller's words 'it is as if a thoroughbred were in harness with a post horse'.

The second new Officina Bodoni type, named Zeno after Verona's patron saint, was used before Griffo, being shown in a book about the saint in 1937. The design was based upon a manuscript *Missale Romanum* written by Arrighi about 1520. It is a delicately modelled rather wide-faced roman with some venetian characteristics, and as one would expect very close to a roman letter written with a broad pen. Its manuscript character makes it unsuitable for extensive use except in a deliberately archaic mode, when it can look quite splendid.

Mardersteig's third type, first used in an edition of Boccaccio's treatise on Dante in 1954, and called Dante, was again cut by Charles Malin. Another old face design, it has a strong resemblance to Bembo. Its companion italic is again

VOILÀ LA MONTAGNE DÉPOUILLÉE
des chœurs qui parcouraient ses sommets; les prêtresses, les flambeaux, les clameurs divines sont retombés dans les vallées; la fête se dissipe, les mystères sont rentrés dans le sein des dieux. Je suis la plus jeune des bacchantes qui se sont élevées sur le mont Cithéron. Les chœurs ne m'avaient pas encore transportée sur les cimes, car les rites sacrés écartaient ma jeunesse et m'ordonnaient de combler la mesure des temps qu'il faut offrir pour entrer dans l'action des solennités. Enfin, les HEURES, ces secrètes nourrices, mais qui emploient tant de durée à nous rendre propres pour les dieux, m'ont placée parmi les bacchantes, et je sors aujourd'hui des premiers mystères qui m'aient enveloppée.

Tandis que je recueillais les années réclamées pour les rites, j'étais semblable aux jeunes pêcheurs qui vivent sur le bord des mers. A la cime d'un rocher, ils paraissent quelque temps, les bras tendus vers les eaux et le corps incliné, comme un dieu prêt à se replonger; mais leur âme balance dans leur

31

Fig. 80. The Officina Bodoni's 'Griffo' type, in Guérin's *Poèmes en prose*, 1954

φαίνεταί μοι κῆνοσ ἴσοσ θέοισιν
ἔμμεν' ὤνηρ, ὄττισ ἐνάντιόσ τοι
ἰσδάνει καὶ πλάσιον ἆδυ φωνεί-
σασ ὐπακούει

καὶ γελαίσασ ἰμέροεν, τό μ' ἦ μὰν
καρδίαν ἐν στήθεσιν ἐπτόαισεν·
ὠσ γὰρ ἔσ σ' ἴδω βρόχε', ὤσ με φώναι-
σ' οὐδ' ἒν ἔτ' εἴκει,

ἀλλ' ἄκαν μὲν γλῶσσα ἔαγε, λέπτον
δ' αὔτικα χρῶι πῦρ ὐπαδεδρόμηκεν,
ὀππάτεσσι δ' οὐδ' ἒν ὄρημμ', ἐπιρρόμ-
βεισι δ' ἄκουαι,

κὰδ δέ μ' ἴδρωσ †ψῦχροσ ἔχει, τρόμοσ δὲ
παῖσαν ἄγρει, χλωροτέρα δὲ ποίασ
ἔμμι, τεθνάκην δ' ὀλίγω 'πιδεύησ
φαίνομαι . . .

Fig. 81. A Greek type designed by F. H. Fobes for his Snail's Pace Press; still used occasionally by Ray Nash at Dartmouth College, New Hampshire

obviously derived from Griffo's italic, but matches the roman far more successfully than was the case with Griffo. Dante has a closely related display type, Pacioli, which is based on the constructed letters used by Luca Pacioli, whose *De Divina proportione* was printed by the Officina Bodoni in 1956.

Dante is perhaps the most successful of all Mardersteig's faces, and certainly more suitable for general work than the others. In 1957 it had the rare distinction for a private press typeface of being cut by the Monotype Corporation for machine composition, and is now generally available for use.

341

25

The contemporary scene

Though there has been a very considerable revival of interest in private printing in the past twenty years, none of the private presses of the present generation—not even those which, like the Vine Press in Huntingdonshire or the Allen Press in California, are closest to the old traditions—have been so ambitious as to have types cut for their own exclusive use. One reason which has been advanced for this is that the cost of having one's own fount cast would be prohibitive today. Undoubtedly this is so for the weekend printer with an Adana in his garage. Yet the cost of having a fount of type cast is in relative terms far cheaper than it was in the past. At about the time that Wilkins cut his Bengali type in the late eighteenth century the Caslon foundry quoted a price of a guinea per punch for similar work. A century later, E. P. Prince's scale of charges to the Kelmscott Press were ten shillings for letters, five shillings for punctuation marks and fifteen shillings for ligatures—in other words £40 to £50 for a complete set of punches. In 1968 Messrs. Stephen Austin quoted the cost of preparing matrices as £2 19s each, or about £240 for a complete fount. When St. John Hornby paid his £100 for the Subiaco type at the beginning of the century he was paying quite a lot more than one would pay today in relation to general monetary values.

Undoubtedly the real reason that there is a dearth of new proprietary faces today lies in the influence of the Nonesuch Press, with its extraordinarily successful use of commercial types, added to the fact that there are so many good typefaces available through the printing trade. Unless the private press owner is a Cobden-Sanderson he has more than enough choice from the types available in his own country. If his desire for individuality, a distinction in the typography of his books from those produced commercially makes him turn away from American Type Founders, from Stephenson Blake or from Monotype faces, he has a similarly wide range of material from Dutch, German,

French or Czech foundries from which to choose. Some private printers, like the Grace Hopers with their *Typographical commonplace books*, have taken full advantage of the riches available to them.

Although the proprietary face may be a thing of the past, a new development has taken place in the United States: the appearance of the amateur typefounder.

These typefounders are not working in the antiquarian tradition of Dard Hunter, cutting punches and casting their type in hand moulds. Their interest is often that of the industrial archaeologist, and they retrieve and preserve the typecasting machines which ousted the hand mould in the nineteenth century only to be made obsolete themselves by the advent of the composing machines. (With the replacement of the hot-metal composing machines by film-setting, no doubt future amateurs will care for these machines as tenderly.) But you cannot be interested in typefounding without also being interested in printing, and you cannot have this double interest without wishing to cast type which is not generally available.

One of the first to be active in this field of having typefaces which had gone out of production reissued was the late Steve Watts of Front Royal, Virginia. His Privateer Press issued one of the most entertaining examples of amateur journalism, *The pastime printer*. Watts was for many years sales manager of American Type Founders, and so was excellently placed for organizing the revival of types of which they held the matrices. Two faces which he had recut which have been used to good effect by private printers were the handsome Oxford face (in which Updike's monumental *Printing types* was printed) and Wayside roman. Wayside is a pleasant scotch roman face, and the reissue had the unusual and useful feature of a set of intermediate capitals, midway between the capitals and small capitals in size. Frederick MacMahon, the 'Yankee Ink Dauber', organized the reissue of Hobo, an ugly art-nouveau letter better left dead, and more usefully Worrell Uncial—a type originally available only on Linotype and therefore not a face which the amateur setting type by hand could have used before.

Paul Hayden Duensing of Kalamazoo, Michigan, is an amateur printer who has made much use of uncommon typefaces in his printing, particularly those of the Czech designer Oldrich Menhart. Duensing has been responsible for some of the most interesting special castings for private press use, including Harlequin (an ornamented titling letter originally cut by Matthias Rosart for Enschedé in 1768) and 'XVI century roman' cast in 1967. This fount was cast from electrolytic matrices made from pieces of the original type, with freshly engraved characters to match the design for a few letters which were missing. The effect of the type, when printed, is of a peculiarly nasty example of seventeenth-century English printing: a *tour de force* certainly, but also a deliberate seeking after quaintness which does not recommend itself. Duensing's

THE PRIVATE PRESS OF PAUL HAYDEN DUENSING was founded in Seattle, Washington on the first day of 1950 [as the Satyr Press] with the residue of some boyhood experiments in printing. In the beginning, the late Mr. Archie J. Little provided patient and generous assistance and the inspiration for the best features in the Credo of the Press. The interruptions of college, military obligations, post-graduate study, and typographic global circumnavigations made the output of the Press very sporadic. During this time however, the desirability of using historic letterforms otherwise unavailable in printing type was keenly felt. This desire to design and produce private types became a reality in 1965 with the acquisition of a pantographic matrix-engraving machine and equipment for punchcutting & electro-depositing matrices. The production of the Private Typefoundry has not been large, nor its operation economically profitable, but it has been æsthetically pleasant & typographically instructive.

Some early efforts of the Private Typefoundry are shown here, along with a selective bibliography of publications from The Private Press of Paul Hayden Duensing.

Set in an experimental 14 pt. Chancery Italic, No. 13001.

Fig. 82. A page set in an experimental chancery italic type, designed by Paul Hayden Duensing, and cast at his private press and typefoundry, 1967

experiments with a completely new typeface, a chancery italic, are very much more promising.

The Harlequin type was cast for Duensing by John S. Carroll, for many years a private printer in Manhattan, and a leading figure in the New York Chappel during its first years. Like so many amateur printers, Carroll was limited by the space at his disposal. One might think that with three presses and one hundred and twenty-five founts of display typefaces, his apartment would have been full, but somehow Carroll managed to fit in a caster as well. On this, as well as Harlequin, he produced some founts of Goudy Medieval (one of Goudy's 'lost' typefaces originally cast in 1930) for the New York Chappel and some interesting revivals of nineteenth-century decorated types, mainly by means of electrolytic matrices made from types in his collection. But Carroll has not limited himself to reproducing older faces. Many years ago Bruce Rogers pointed out that even the most modest private presses could afford their own borders or printers' flowers even though a proprietary typeface might be beyond their means. In several cases Carroll has produced new ornaments for private presses. Perhaps the first of these was one undertaken as an experiment for the present writer in 1960, of which three different forms were cut by different methods. For Peter Isaac's Allenholme Press in Northumberland he cut a 24 point 'Puffing Billy' and for Frederick MacMahon he cast an ink-ball ornament. Since moving from New York to Miami Beach a few years ago Carroll has been less active in producing type, but his experiments with offset printing, using an IBM Selectric Composer, are interesting as pointing another way in which the amateur can work in the future.

As well as the special casting of obsolete faces for private press use, and the occasional casting of new ornamental material, there have been one or two other experiments with type. For *Watcher in Florence*, the Vine Press had a new *z* cut to replace the Blado italic *z* which they disliked; for *Leigh Hunt on eight sonnets of Dante* the Typographical Laboratory used a special casting of Monotype Van Dijck with reduced capitals. But such enterprise is becoming increasingly rare: the amateur printers today are becoming less and less adventurous. The excitement, the experimentation, is nearly all in the offset lithography field, and we shall probably never see another typeface cut for private press use.—Or so I thought when this book was being written, but it has since been announced that a special face for the Crabgrass Press of Prairie Village, Kansas, is being designed by Herman Zapf. Nevertheless, the era of the proprietary typeface is over.

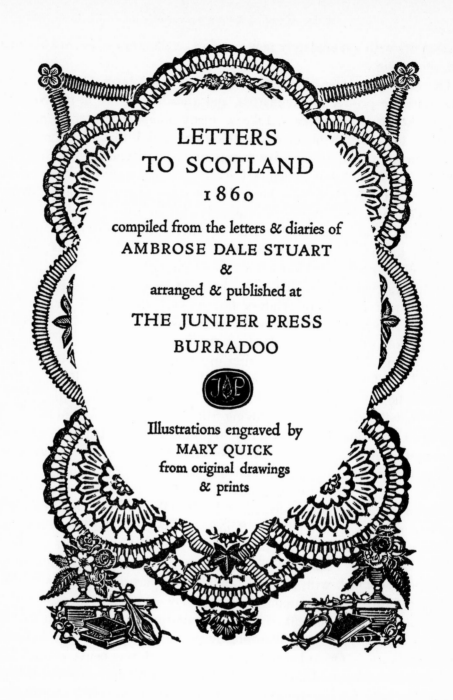

LETTERS
TO SCOTLAND
1860

compiled from the letters & diaries of
AMBROSE DALE STUART
&
arranged & published at

THE JUNIPER PRESS
BURRADOO

Illustrations engraved by
MARY QUICK
from original drawings
& prints

Fig. 83. A Juniper Press title-page; an example of good Australian amateur work

Bibliography

Though relatively few books have been written about private presses, the literature of private printing is extensive. Much of the information is to be found only by chance, in books ranging from Canon Liddon's *Life of Dr Pusey* to Casanova's *Memoirs*. The lack of any agreed definition of a private press makes the use of many reference books particularly frustrating, as it is often impossible to tell without extensive research whether particular books were produced at private presses or merely commissioned from a commercial printer for private circulation. For some private presses, the only accessible information is contained in the Rev. Henry Cotton's *A typographical gazetteer* (2nd edition, Oxford, 1831) and its second series (Oxford, 1866), or in Pierre Deschamps' *Dictionnaire de geographie* (Paris, 1870) published as a supplement to Jacques-Charles Brunet's *Manuel du libraire*. Both however should be used with great caution.

GENERAL

BIBLIOGRAPHIES OF BOOKS AND ARTICLES ABOUT PRIVATE PRESSES

IRVIN HAAS, *A bibliography of materials relating to private presses* (Chicago, 1937).

PRIVATE LIBRARIES ASSOCIATION, *Private press books 1959–* (Pinner, 1960–).
Part III of this annual checklist records 'The literature of private printing'.

BIBLIOGRAPHIES OF BOOKS PRINTED BY PRIVATE PRESSES

JOHN MARTIN, *A bibliographical catalogue of books privately printed* (London, 1834).
The British Museum Department of Manuscripts possesses Martin's own copy, together with his correspondence relating to the book, which is still of very considerable value. The second edition, 1854, omitted the lists of private press books and is much less useful.

BIBLIOGRAPHY

HENRY G. BOHN, *Appendix to The bibliographer's manual of English literature* [by W. T. Lowndes] (London, 1864).
Includes lists of books printed at British private presses.

BERTRAM DOBELL, *Catalogue of books printed for private circulation* (London, 1906).
Includes useful notes on several private presses.

ROBERT STEELE, *The revival of printing; a bibliographical catalogue of works issued by the chief modern English presses* (London, 1912).

G. S. TOMKINSON, *A select bibliography of the principal modern presses, public and private, in Great Britain and Ireland* (London, 1928).
The standard bibliography.

WILL RANSOM, *Private presses and their books* (New York, 1929).
Despite some errors and inaccuracies, this is the most comprehensive general bibliography of presses in Britain and the U.S.A.

WILL RANSOM, *Selective check lists of press books* (New York, 1945–50).
Supplements no. 8. Photolitho reprints of both have been published (New York, 1963).

JULIUS RODENBERG, *Deutsche Pressen: eine Bibliographie* (Zürich, 1925).
The standard bibliography of German private presses; supplemented by his Deutsche Pressen, 1925–30 (Berlin, 1930).

HISTORIES OF PRIVATE PRESSES

ADAM LACKMAN, *Annalium typographicorum* (Hamburg, 1740).
Chapter 8, pp. 28–87, deals with 'Typographea domestica et typi privatorum'. The first book to deal with private presses, it contains a lot of information on early private presses not available elsewhere. But the author's style is abominable, and his Latin villainous.

GABRIEL PEIGNOT, *Recherches historiques et bibliographiques sur les imprimeries particulières et clandestines* (Paris, 18—).
Peignot's Répertoire de bibliographies spéciales *(Paris, 1810) also contains much of the information in this pamphlet.*

AUGUSTE VOISIN, *Notice bibliographique et litteraire sur quelques imprimeries particulières des Pays-Bas* (2nd edition, Ghent, 1840).

PHILOMNESTE *Junior* [*i.e.* PIERRE GUSTAVE BRUNET], *Recherches sur les imprimeries imaginaires, clandestines et particulières* (Brussels, 1879).
The Times Printing number, 10 September 1912.

BIBLIOGRAPHY

THE STUDIO, *The art of the book*, edited by C. G. Holme (London, 1914).
The later volumes in this series, Modern book production (*1927*), *and* The art of the book (*1938*), *both edited by Bernard Newdigate, and* The art of the book (*1951*) *edited by Charles Ede, are also useful.*

DANIEL BERKELEY UPDIKE, *Printing types; their history, forms and use* (2nd edition, Cambridge, Mass., 1937).
Useful for this as for all typographical studies.

WILL RANSOM, *Private presses and their books* (New York, 1929).
Less useful as a history than for its bibliographies, but still good.

PAUL A. BENNETT ed., *Books and printing; a treasury for typophiles* (New York, 1951).
*Reprints many articles and excerpts of particular interest. The paperback edition (*1963*) is particularly good value.*

GILBERT TURNER, *The private press; its achievement and influence* (London, 1954).
An excellent brief history of the English presses.

JAMES MORAN, 'Private presses and the printing industry' in *British printer*, April 1962, pp. 105–20.

KENNETH DAY ed., *Book typography 1815–1965* (London, 1966).
Much wider in scope, but includes a good deal on private and fine presses in several of the chapters.

LOUGHBOROUGH SCHOOL OF LIBRARIANSHIP, *Private presses; handbook to an exhibition* (Loughborough, 1968).
A short introductory history.

COLIN FRANKLIN, *The private presses* (London, 1969).
A very readable account of the aims and achievements of the English private press movement.

PRACTICAL MANUALS FOR THE AMATEUR

JOHN RYDER, *Printing for pleasure* (London, 1955).
A very readable handbook; largely responsible for the current increase in amateur printing.

J. BEN LIEBERMAN, *Printing as a hobby* (New York, 1963).
A useful introduction for the novice.

PERIODICALS

The range of periodicals which sometimes contain articles on private presses is enormous, as the checklists in *Private press books* show. Of periodicals currently published, *The Private Library, The American Book Collector* and the *Quarterly Newsletter of the Book Club of California,* and the German journal *Philobiblon,* most frequently contain private press studies and reviews.

In addition to these publications of general interest, the following books and periodicals are useful for special topics and for individual private presses:

CHAPTERS 1–2: QUASI-OFFICIAL AND PATRONS' PRESSES

G. P. WINSHIP, *From Gutenberg to Plantin; an outline of the history of printing* (Cambridge, Mass., 1926).

ANATOLE CLAUDIN, 'Private printing in France during the fifteenth century' in *Bibliographica,* v. 3, 1897, pp. 344–70.

F. J. NORTON, *Printing in Spain 1501–20* (Cambridge, 1966).

KNUD OLDENOW, 'Printing in Greenland' in *Libri* v. 5, 1958, pp. 223–62.

KNUD OLDENOW, *The spread of printing: Greenland* (Amsterdam, 1969).

CHAPTER 3: THE SCHOLARLY PRESS

JOHN A. GADE, *The life and times of Tycho Brahe* (Princeton, 1947).

LAURITZ NIELSEN, 'Tycho Brahes bogtrykkeri paa Hveen' in *Nordisk tidsscrift for bog- og bibliotekswaesen,* v. 8, 1946.

SVEN ALMQVIST, *Johann Kankel, Pehr Brahes bogtryckare på Visingö* (Stockholm, 1965).

CHARLES NODIER, 'De la plus célèbre des Imprimeries particulières' in his *Mélanges tirés d'une petite bibliothèque* (Paris, 1829) pp. 173–7.

GIULIO NATALI, 'Un marchese teologo e filologo' in his *Idee. costumi, uomini del settecento* (Turin, 1926), pp. 249–54.

EDWARD ROWE MORES, *A dissertation upon English typographical founders and founderies,* edited by Harry Carter and Christopher Ricks (Oxford, 1961).

CHAPTER 4: THE PRESS AS AN EDUCATIONAL TOY

Depositio cornuti typographici, a mirthful play performed at the confirmation of a journeyman, translated from the German by William Blades. New ed. by James Moran (London, 1962).

G. A. CRAPELET, *De la profession de l'imprimeur* (Paris, 1840).

Anon. 'L'imprimerie du Cabinet du Roi au Château des Tuileries sous Louis XV (1718–1730)' in *Bulletin de la Société de l'histoire de Paris,* v. 18, 1891, pp. 35–45.

CHARLES NODIER, 'La revolution prophetisée par Fénelon et par Louis XV' in his *Mélanges tirés d'une petite bibliothèque* (Paris, 1829), pp. 97–100.

JAMES MORAN, 'Printing on the Thames' in *The black art*, v. 2, 1963, pp. 67–70.

JEAN MARCHAND, 'L'imprimerie particulière du Marquis de Bercy' in *Le livre et l'estampe*, no. 22, 1960, pp. 123–30.

CHAPTER 5: THE ARISTOCRATIC PLAYTHING

WILMARTH S. LEWIS, *Horace Walpole* (London, 1961).

HORACE WALPOLE, *Journal of the printing office at Strawberry Hill*, edited by Paget Toynbee (London, 1923).

ALLEN T. HAZEN, *A bibliography of the Strawberry Hill Press* (New Haven, 1942).

CHARLES NODIER, 'De plus rare des Ana' in his *Mélanges tirés d'une petite bibliothèque* (Paris, 1829), pp. 40–3.

LUTHER S. LIVINGSTON, *Franklin and his press at Passy* (New York, 1914).

RANDOLPH G. ADAMS, *The passports printed by Benjamin Franklin at his Passy Press* (Ann Arbor, 1925).

WILLIAM E. LINGELBACH, 'B. Franklin, printer—new source materials' in *Proceedings of the American Philosophical Society*, v. 92, 1948, pp. 79–100.

F. B. ADAMS, Jr., 'Franklin and his press at Passy' in *Yale University Library gazette*, v. 30, 1956, pp. 133–8.

P. VAN DER HAEGHEN, 'Le commerce d'autrefois et l'imprimerie d'une duchesse' in *Le livre*, 1870, pp. 248–53.

Anon, 'Imprimerie de Bel-Oeil' in *Le bibliophile Belge*, v. 1, 1845, pp. 117–21 and v. 9, 1852, pp. 297–300.

BOGDAN KRIEGER, *Friedrich der Grosse und seine Bucher* (Leipzig, 1914).

HANS DROYSEN, 'Friedrichs des Grossen Druckerei im Berliner Schlosse' in *Hohenzollern Jahrbuch*, v. 8, 1904, pp. 83–91.

PAUL SEIDEL, 'Georg Friedrich Schmidt, der erste Illustrator und Drucker Friedrichs des Grossen' in *Hohenzollern Jahrbuch*, v. 5, 1901, pp. 60–7.

CHAPTER 6: PRIVATE PRINTING AND THE BIBLIOMANIA

NICOLAS BARKER, *The publications of the Roxburghe Club* (Cambridge, 1964).

S. I. WICKLEN, 'Thomas Johnes and the Hafod House Press' in *Book design and production*, v. 6, 1963, pp. 30–4.

SIR SAMUEL EGERTON BRYDGES, *The autobiography, times, opinions and contemporaries of Sir Egerton Brydges* (London, 1834).

MICHAEL SADLEIR, *Archdeacon Francis Wrangham 1769–1842* (London, 1937).

Also printed on pp. 201–47 of his Things past (*London, 1944*), *Sadleir's essay includes a good deal that is useful on the Lee Priory Press, and appears to be the only publication which followed the collaboration on a history of the Press which he and Stanley Morison embarked upon in the 1930s.*

A. N. L. MUNBY, *Phillipps studies* (Cambridge, 1951–60).

The material on the Middle Hill Press, scattered in the five volumes, is more conveniently available to the general reader in Nicolas Barker's abridgment of Munby's work, Portrait of an obsession (*London, 1967*).

ALBERT EHRMAN, 'The private press and publishing activities of Prince Louis-Lucien Bonaparte' in *The book collector*, v. 9, 1960, pp. 30–7.

CHAPTER 7: THE AUTHOR AS PUBLISHER

STRICKLAND GIBSON and SIR WILLIAM HOLDSWORTH, 'Charles Viner's *General abridgment of law and equity*' in *Oxford Bibliographical Society proceedings and papers*, v. 2, 1930, pp. 229–43.

A. C. PIPER, 'Private printing presses in Sussex' in *The library*, 3rd series, v. 5, 1914, pp. 70–9.

CARROLL D. COLEMAN, 'The parson-printer of Lustleigh' in *The colophon. New series*, v. 1, 1935, pp. 221–6.

C. DAVY, 'A memoir of the life of the Rev. W. Davy' prefixed to the latter's *Divinity, or discourses on the being of God . . .* (Exeter, 1827).

URSULA RADFORD, 'William Davy, priest and printer' in *Transactions of the Devonshire Association*, v. 63, 1931, pp. 325–39.

SIR GEOFFREY KEYNES, *William Blake: poet, printer, prophet* (London, 1965).

RUTHVEN TODD, 'The techniques of William Blake's illuminated painting' in *Print*, v. 6, 1948, pp. 53–65.

RODERICK CAVE, 'Blake's mantle: a memoir of Ralph Chubb' in *Book design and production*, v. 3, no. 2, 1960, pp. 24–8.

RODERICK CAVE, 'GogMagog: the private press of Morris Cox' in *The American book collector*, v. 12, no. 9, May 1962, pp. 20–3.

DAVID CHAMBERS, 'The GogMagog Press' in *The private library*, v. 5, 1964, pp. 5–10.

CHAPTER 8: CLANDESTINE PRESSES I: MORAL

THOMAS EDWARD STONOR, 'The private printing press at Stonor, 1581' in *Bibliographical and historical miscellanies of the Philobiblon Society*, v. 1, 1854.

THOMAS EDWARD STONOR, 'Description of a copy of *Rationes decem Campiani*' in *Bibliographical and historical miscellanies of the Philobiblon Society*, v. 9, 1865–6.

EVELYN WAUGH, *Edmund Campion* (London, 1935).

A. C. SOUTHERN, *Elizabethan recusant prose 1559–1582* (London, 1950).

J. DOVER WILSON, 'The Marprelate controversy' in *The Cambridge history of English literature*, v. 3 (Cambridge, 1909).

PIARAS BÉASLAÍ, *Michael Collins and the making of a new Ireland* (Dublin, 1926).

JEAM MASSART, *The secret press in Belgium*, trans. by Bernard Miall (London, 1918).

VERCORS, *Voices of silence* (London, 1968).

DIRK DE JONG, *Het vrije boek in onvrije tijd. Bibliografie van illegale en clandestiene bellettrie, 1940–45* (Leiden, 1958).

J. MARTINET, *Catalogue of the 'drucksel' prints . . . by Hendrik Nicolaas Werkman* (Amsterdam, 1963).

L. G. A. SCHLICHTING, 'Dutch underground printing' in *Print*, v. 4, no. 3, 1946, pp. 23–8.

CHAPTER 9: CLANDESTINE PRESSES II: IMMORAL

G. LEGMAN, *The horn book* (New York, 1964).

RAYMOND POSTGATE, *That devil Wilkes* (London, 1956).

ALEC CRAIG, *The banned books of England* (2nd ed., London, 1962).

RIGBY GRAHAM, 'Potocki' in *The private library*, v. 8, 1967, pp. 8–26.

CHAPTER 10: PRINTING FOR PLEASURE: THE GROWTH OF A MIDDLE-CLASS HOBBY

JAMES MOSLEY, 'The press in the parlour: some notes on the amateur printer and his equipment' in *The black art*, v. 2, 1963, pp. 1–16.
An outstandingly good survey, quoting extensively from the amateur printers' manuals of the nineteenth century. Some of these, such as Jabez Francis' Printing at home (1870) or P. E. Raynor's Printing for amateurs (1876), or the journal Amateur printing (1895–1913), are also well worth consulting.

G. A. SNOW, 'Model T's of printing' in *Print*, v. 5, no. 2, 1947, pp. 7–14.
Surveys the American production of presses designed for amateurs.

J. A. FAIRLEY, 'Peter Buchan, printer and ballad collector' in *Transactions of the Buchan Field Club*, v. 7, 1902, pp. 123–58.

A. C. PIPER, 'Private printing presses in Sussex' in *The library*, 3rd series, v. 5, 1914, pp. 70–9.

HENRY R. PLOMER, 'Some private presses of the nineteenth century' in *The library*, 2nd series, v. 1, 1900, pp. 407–28.

E. R. McCLINTOCK DIX, 'The private press at Duncairn, Belfast' in *The Irish book lover*, v. 1, 1909–10, pp. 7–8 and 25–6.

The Daniel Press. Memorials of C. H. O. Daniel with a bibliography of the Press, 1845–1919.

COLIN FRANKLIN, *The private presses* (London, 1969), pp. 19–34.

BRUCE DICKINS, 'Samuel Page Widnall and his press at Grantchester, 1871–1892' in *Transactions of the Cambridge Bibliographical Society*, v. 2, no. 5, 1958, pp. 366–72.
Addenda to this full account were published in v. 3, no. 1, 1959, and v. 3, no. 2, 1960, pp. 176–8, of the Transactions.

CHAPTER 11: WILLIAM MORRIS AND THE KELMSCOTT PRESS

[*The literature on the Kelmscott Press is of course very extensive. This list has deliberately been limited far more than for most other private presses.*]

H. HALLIDAY SPARLING, *The Kelmscott Press and William Morris, master-craftsman* (London, 1924).
Despite its age and over-adulatory approach, still by far the best book.

WILLIAM MORRIS, *A note on his aims in founding the Kelmscott Press; together with a short description of the Press by S. C. Cockerell & an annotated list of the books printed thereat* (Hammersmith, 1898).
The last of the Kelmscott books, reprinted in Sparling and in a photolithographic replica (1969).

WILLIAM MORRIS SOCIETY, *The typographical adventure of William Morris* (London, 1957).
An extremely good exhibition catalogue. The Society's Journal *also often contains material of interest.*

HOLBROOK JACKSON, 'The typography of William Morris' in his *The printing of books* (London, 1938).
A useful corrective to Sparling; originally read to the Double Crown Club's Morris Centenary Dinner, and deliberately provocative.

BROWN UNIVERSITY, *William Morris and the Kelmscott Press; an exhibition* (Providence, R.I., 1960).

WILFRED BLUNT, *Cockerell* (London, 1964).

CHAPTER 12: AFTER KELMSCOTT: THE FINE PRESS IN BRITAIN

RUARI MACLEAN, *Modern book design, from William Morris to the present day* (London, 1958).

COLIN FRANKLIN, *The private presses* (London, 1969).

C. H. ST. JOHN HORNBY and ARUNDEL ESDAILE, *A descriptive bibliography of the books printed at the Ashendene Press, MDCCCCXCV–MCMXXXV* (London, 1935).

B. H. NEWDIGATE, 'Mr C. H. St. John Hornby's Ashendene Press' in *The fleuron*, v. 2, 1924, pp. 77–85.

WILL RANSOM, ed., *Kelmscott, Doves and Ashendene: the private press credos* (New York, 1952).

SIR SYDNEY COCKERELL, *Friends of a lifetime*, edited by Viola Meynell (London, 1940).

PRISCILLA JOHNSTON, *Edward Johnston* (London, 1959).

T. J. COBDEN-SANDERSON, *Catalogue raisonné of books printed at the Doves Press 1900–1916* (Hammersmith, 1916).
The last book from the Press.

T. J. COBDEN-SANDERSON, *Cosmic vision* (London, 1922).

T. J. COBDEN-SANDERSON, *Journals 1879–1922* (London, 1926).

JOHN HENRY NASH, ed., *Cobden-Sanderson and the Doves Press* (San Francisco, 1929).

C. VOLMER NORDLUNDE, *Thomas James Cobden-Sanderson* (Copenhagen, 1957).

J. H. MASON, *A selection from the notebooks of a scholar-printer* (Leicester, 1961).

RUARI MACLEAN, *Cobden-Sanderson and the Doves Press* (Wormerveer, 1964).

CHARLES RICKETTS, *A defence of the revival of printing* (London, 1899).

CHARLES RICKETTS, *A bibliography of the books issued by Hacon and Ricketts, 1896–1903* (London, 1904).

T. STURGE MOORE, *A brief account of the origin of the Eragny Press* (Hammersmith, 1903).

LUCIEN PISSARRO, *Notes on the Eragny Press, and, A letter to J. B. Manson* ed. with a supplement by Alan Fern (Cambridge, 1957).

W. S. MEADMORE, *Lucien Pissarro* (London, 1962).

C. R. ASHBEE, *The private press, a study in idealism; to which is added a bibliography of the Essex House Press* (Chipping Camden, 1909).

C. R. ASHBEE, 'The Essex House Press, and the purpose or meaning of a private press' in *Book collector's quarterly*, no. 11, 1933, pp. 69–86.

CHAPTER 13: MORRIS IN AMERICA

RALPH FLETCHER SEYMOUR, *Some went this way* (Chicago, 1945).

PHILIP JOHN SCHWARZ, 'Will Ransom: the early years' in *Journal of library history*, v. 3, 1968, pp. 138–55.

VREST ORTON, *Goudy; master of letters* (Chicago, 1939).

PETER BEILENSON, *The story of Frederic W. Goudy* (New York, 1939).

BERNARD LEWIS, *Behind the types; the life story of Frederic W. Goudy* (Pittsburgh, 1941).

MELBERT B. CARY, *Bibliography of the Village Press* (New York, 1938).

RUDOLPH GJELSNESS, 'Frank Holme: newspaper artist and designer of books' in *The colophon*, new series, v. 1, 1935, pp. 191–200.

GEORGE G. BOOTH, *The Cranbrook Press* (Detroit, 1902).

PAUL MCPHARLIN, 'The Cranbrook Press' in *The dolphin*, v. 4, 1941, pp. 268–78.

CHAPTER 14: FINE PRINTING ON THE CONTINENT

A. M. HAMMACHER, *Die Welt Henry van de Velde* (Cologne, 1968).

CHARLES VAN HALSBEKE, *L'art typographique dans les Pays-Bas depuis 1892* (Brussels, 1929).

C. REEDIJK, 'The renascence of printing in the Netherlands' in *Bibliotheekleven*, v. 51, 1966, pp. 437–57.

A. A. M. STOLS, *Het werk van S. H. de Roos* (Amsterdam, 1942).

A. M. HAMMACHER, *Jean François van Royen* (The Hague, 1947).

MUSEUM MEERMANNO-WESTREENIANUM, *Jean François van Royen 1878–1942* (The Hague, 1964).

JULIUS RODENBERG, *Deutsche Pressen: eine Bibliographie* (Zurich, 1925).

WILLY WIEGAND, 'German private presses' in *Imprimatur*, v. 1, 1930, pp. 101–7.

JOSEF LEHNACKER, ed., *Die Bremer Presse; Königen der deutschen Privatpressen* (Munich, 1964).

BERNARD ZELLER and WERNER VOLKE, eds., *Buchkunst und Dichtung; Zur Geschichte der Bremer Presse und der Corona* (Munich, 1966).

HANS LOUBIER, 'Die Drucke der Ernst Ludwig Presse' in *Archiv fur Buchgewerbe und Graphik*, v. 50, 1913, pp. 3–23.

ALBERT WINDISCH, 'Friedrich Wilhelm Kleukens, der Buch- und Schriftkünstler' in *Gutenberg Jahrbuch*, 1950, pp. 327–35.

HANS SCHMOLLER, 'Carl Ernst Poeschel' in *Signature*, new series, no. 11, pp. 20–36.

HANS MARDERSTEIG, *The Officina Bodoni: the operation of a hand-press during the first six years of its work* (Paris, 1929).

FRIEDRICH EWALD, 'The Officina Bodoni' in *The fleuron*, no. 7, 1930, pp. 121–31.

HANS SCHMOLLER, 'A gentleman of Verona' in *Penrose annual*, v. 52, 1958, pp. 29–34.

Officina Bodoni Verona MCMXXIII–MCMLXIV (Verona, 1965).
Catalogue (in Dutch) issued for the exhibition of the Press's work in The Hague and Brussels.

JOHN DREYFUS, *Giovanni Mardersteig; an account of his work* (Verona, 1966).

CHAPTER 15: ENGLAND BETWEEN THE WARS 1:
THE GREAT PRESSES

OLIVER SIMON, *Printer and playground* (London, 1956).

The Nonesuch century. An appraisal by A. J. A. Symons, a personal note by Francis Meynell, and a bibliography by Desmond Flower, of the first hundred books issued by the Press, 1923–1934 (London, 1936).

Chanticleer: a bibliography of the Golden Cockerel Press, April 1921–August 1936 (London, 1936).

Pertelote: being a bibliography of the Golden Cockerel Press, October 1936–April 1943 (London, 1943).

Cockalorum: being a bibliography of the Golden Cockerel Press, June 1943–December 1948 (London, 1949).

A. MARY KIRKUS, *Robert Gibbings, a bibliography* (London, 1962).

THOMAS JONES, *The Gregynog Press* (Oxford, 1954).

GWENLLIAN DAVIES, 'Memoirs of Gregynog' in *Manchester Review*, v. 8, 1959, pp. 257–63.

EWART BOWEN, 'Memoirs of Gregynog' in *Manchester Review*, v. 8, 1959, pp. 264–8.

J. MICHAEL DAVIES, *The private press at Gregynog* (Leicester, 1959).

CHAPTER 16: ENGLAND BETWEEN THE WARS II: BACKWATERS AND TRIBUTARIES

WILLIAM MAXWELL, *The Dun Emer Press and the Cuala Press* (London, 1932).

ALLAN WADE, *A bibliography of the writings of W. B. Yeats* (2nd ed. London, 1958).
Appendix I, pp. 399–405, is a checklist of the Cuala Press.

LEONARD WOOLF, *Beginning again; an autobiography of the years 1911–1918* (London, 1964).

LEONARD WOOLF, *Downhill all the way* (London, 1967).

JAMES MORAN, 'The Seizin Press of Laura Riding and Robert Graves' in *The black art*, v. 2, 1963, pp. 34–9.
An 'Additional Note' by Michael Turner was printed on pp. 84–6 of the same volume. Moran's account differs in some matters from that communicated to me by Laura Riding.

ANTHONY ADAMS, 'The Fanfrolico Press: an appreciation' in *The American book collector*, v. 9 no. 8, 1959, pp. 9–14.

PHILIP LINDSAY, *I'd live the same life over* (London, 1940).

JACK LINDSAY, *Fanfrolico and after* (London, 1962).

H. C. D. PEPLER, *The hand press* (Ditchling, 1934).
A reprint was published by the Ditchling Press in 1952.

PAUL JOHNSON, 'St. Dominic's Press' in *The Book Collector's packet*, v. 2, no. 14, 1933, pp. 9–13.

ANN BARRETT, 'The Walpole Press of Old Costessey, Norwich' in *The private library*, v. 8 no. 2, 1967, pp. 38–43.

CYRIL W. BEAUMONT, *The first score; an account of the foundation and development of the Beaumont Press* (London, 1927).

NANCY CUNARD, 'The Hours Press: retrospect-catalogue-commentary' in *The book collector*, v. 13, 1964, pp. 488–96.

PETER C. G. ISAAC, 'H. G. Dixey Press' in *The private library*, v. 6, 1962, pp. 36–9.

CHAPTER 17: BETWEEN THE WARS IN THE U.S.A.

HARRY B. WEISS, 'The miniature books of William Lewis Washburn' in *The book collector's packet*, v. 3, no. 1, 1938, pp. 20–2.

GERTRUDE H. MUIR, 'Edwin Bliss Hill, pioneer private printer of the southwest' in *The American book collector*, v. 18, 1967, pp. 20–7.
Includes an excellent check-list of the press's work, compiled by John M. Myers.

BIBLIOGRAPHY

HERMAN SCHAUINGER, *A bibliography of Trovillion Private Press* (Herrin, Ill., 1943).

JAMES MORAN, 'America's oldest private press' in *Book design and production*, v. 1, 1958–9, pp. 17–19.

BERRKELEY HEIGHTS PUBLIC LIBRARY, *The Oriole Press* (Berkeley Heights, N. J., 1958).

MARIAN C. BROWN, *Joseph Ishill and the Oriole Press* (Berkeley Heights, N. J., 1960).

GEORGE PARKER WINSHIP, 'Recollections of a private printer' in *The colophon*, new series, v. 3, no. 2, 1938, pp. 210–24.

ARTHUR W. RUSHMORE, 'The fun and fury of a private press' in *Bookmaking and kindred amenities* ed. by Earl S. Miers and Richard Ellis (Rutgers, 1942). *Reprinted with a postscript in* Books and printing, *ed. by Paul A. Bennett* (Cleveland, 1951).

JAMES LAMAR WEYGAND, *Elmer F. Gleason and the Stratford Press* (Nappanee, Ind., 1965).

SYLVIA BEACH, *Shakespeare & Co.* (London, 1960).

JOSEPH FAUNTLEROY, *John Henry Nash, printer* (Oakland, 1948).

NELL O'DAY, *Catalog of the John Henry Nash printings* (San Francisco, 1937).

ELINOR RAAS HELLER and DAVID MAGEE, *Bibliography of the Grabhorn Press 1915–1940* (San Francisco, 1940).

STANFORD UNIVERSITY, *Catalogue of an exhibition of the typographic work of Jane Grabhorn* (Stanford, 1956).

WARD RITCHIE, *The Ward Ritchie Press and Anderson, Ritchie & Simon* (Los Angeles, 1961).

HERBERT CAHOON, *The Overbrook Press Bibliography, 1934–1959* (Stamford, 1964).

CHAPTER 18:
WORLD WAR II AND THE AFTERMATH IN BRITAIN

MURIEL HARRIS, 'The Perpetua Press of Bland and Ridler' in *Book design and production* v. 1, 1958, pp. 15–17.

LORD CARLOW, *A list of books printed at the Corvinus Press* (London? 1939?).

CHRISTOPHER SANDFORD, 'Press book production, 1945–52' in *Penrose annual*, v. 47, 1953, pp. 31–4.

ANTHONY BAKER, 'The quest for Guido' in *The private library*, 2nd series, v. 2, 1969, pp. 138–76.
There is a 'tentative checklist' of Morris's work on pp. 180–7 of the same volume.

JOHN FARLEIGH, *The creative craftsman* (London, 1950).
Pp. 231–40 are on the work of Guido Morris.

THE TIMES BOOKSHOP, *Books from Stanbrook Abbey Press and the Vine Press*; with an introduction by John Dreyfus (London, 1965).

JOHN PETERS, 'Notes on the production of Vine Press books' in *The private library*, v. 7, 1966, pp. 42–4.

RAMPANT LIONS PRESS, *Portfolio one* (Cambridge, 1967).

ALAN TARLING, *Will Carter, printer* (London, 1968).

CHAPTER 19: THE CONTEMPORARY SCENE IN BRITAIN

RODERICK CAVE, 'Thomas Rae: a modern Scottish printer' in *The American book collector*, v. 12, no. 2, 1961, pp. 18–21.

THOMAS RAE, 'The Signet Press' in *The black art*, v. 1, 1962, pp. 86–90.

JOHN RYDER, 'A note on the Cuckoo Hill Press' in *Book design and production*, v. 3, no. 2, 1960, p. 15.

DAVID CHAMBERS, 'The Cuckoo Hill Press' in *The private library*, v. 4, 1963, pp. 110–14.

B. FAIRFAX HALL, 'The Stourton Press (from 1930–1935)' in *The private library*, 2nd series, v. 2, 1969, pp. 54–67.

ROY LEWIS, 'The Keepsake Press' in *The private library*, v. 4, 1963, pp. 127–30.

EDWARD LUCIE-SMITH, *The little press movement in England and America* (London, 1968).

JOHN MASON, *Twelve by eight* (Leicester, 1958).

RIGBY GRAHAM, 'The Pandora Press' in *The private library*, v. 7, 1966, pp. 5–10.

RIGBY GRAHAM, 'The Orpheus Press' in *The American book collector*, v. 19, no. 5, 1969, pp. 11–22.

RODERICK CAVE, 'Printing at the Brewhouse' in *The American book collector*, v. 16, no. 9, 1966, pp. 18–24.

CHAPTER 20: IN AMERICA TODAY

L. O. CHEEVER, 'The Prairie Press; a thirty year record' in *Books at Iowa*, no. 3, 1965, pp. 15–33.

MARY L. RICHMOND, 'The Cummington Press' in *Books at Iowa*, no. 7, 1967, pp. 9–31.

BIBLIOGRAPHY

DENNIS C. WENDELL, 'The private press in Iowa' in *Missouri Library Association quarterly*, v. 30, 1969, pp. 4–9.

BILL JACKSON, 'Private presses of Kansas' in *Missouri Library Association quarterly*, v. 30, 1969, pp. 10–15.

RICHARD D. OLSON, 'The private press in Illinois' in *Missouri Library Association quarterly*, v. 30, 1969, pp. 16–22.

LEONARD F. BAHR ed., *Printing in privacy; a review of recent activity among American private presses* (Grosse Pointe Park, Mich., 1960).

WILLIAM M. CHENEY, *A natural history of the typestickers of Los Angeles* (Los Angeles, 1960).

JOSEPH GRAVES, 'Victor Hammer; calligrapher, punch-cutter and printer' in *The amateur book collector*, v. 6, no. 3, 1955, pp. 1–4.

CAROLYN READING HAMMER, 'A Victor Hammer bibliography 1930–1955' in *The amateur book collector* v. 6, no. 4, 1955, pp. 3–12 and v. 6 no. 5, 1956, pp. 6–10.

THOMAS A. SUTHERLAND, 'The Gravesend Press' in *The American book collector*, v. 16, no. 8, 1966, pp. 18–20.

LEWIS ALLEN, 'The evolution of an edition de luxe' in *Quarterly newsletter, Book Club of California*, v. 27, 1962, pp. 29–34.

WILLIAM P. BARLOW Jr. 'The Allen Press; a bibliography' in *Quarterly Newsletter, Book Club of California*, v. 25, 1960, pp. 34–41.

JOHN MASON, 'The Bird & Bull Press of Henry Morris' in *The black art*, v. 1, 1962, pp. 114–18.

HENRY MORRIS ed., *Five on paper* (North Hills, Pa., 1963).

KENNETH NESHEIM, 'Leonard Baskin and the Gehenna Press' in *Yale University Library gazette*, v. 13, 1965, pp. 188–9.

BOWDOIN COLLEGE, *Catalogue of the Leonard Baskin exhibition* (Brunswick, Maine, 1962).

DOROTHY KING, 'Notes on the Gehenna Press' in *Printing and graphic arts*, v. 7, no. 2. 1959, pp. 33–48.

JOSEPH LOW, 'Notes on the Eden Hill Press' in *Printing and graphic arts*, v. 8, no. 2, 1960, pp. 21–30.

EUGENE M. ETTENBERG, 'Paul Hayden Duensing's private type foundry' in *Inland printer*, Sept. 1967, pp. 116–17.

J. BEN LIEBERMAN, *The whys and therefores of a chappel* (White Plains, N.Y., 1961).

BERNARD KEELAN, *A Bold face on it; or three quoins in the fountain of wisdom, being an account of Banter University Press* (London, 1964).

CHAPTER 21: SCHOOL AND TEACHING PRESSES

H. M. CHAPIN, 'Early sea presses' in *Ars typographica*, v. 2, 1925, pp. 39–52.

G. F. BARWICK, 'Books printed at sea' in *The library*, 2nd series, v. 1, 1900, 163–6.

D. A. DOUDNEY, *A pictorial outline of the rise and progress of the Bonmahon schools* (Bonmahon, 1851).

E. R. MCCLINTOCK DIX, 'The Bonmahon Press' in *The Irish book lover*, v. 1, 1909–10, pp. 97–100.

L. J. WALLIS, *Leonard Jay* (London, 1954).

KENNETH DAY, 'The Lion and Unicorn Press' in *Book design and production*, v. 3, no. 4, 1960, pp. 16–24.

J. D. VAN TRUMP, *Porter Garnett and the Laboratory Press; catalogue of an exhibition* . . . (Pittsburgh, 1962).

WALTER LEUBA, 'A Porter Garnett list' in *The black art*, v. 3, 1964–5, pp. 86–93.

PORTER GARNETT, *A documentary account of the beginnings of the Laboratory Press* (Pittsburgh, 1927).

RUSSELL T. LIMBACH, *Art Laboratory impressions* (Middletown, Conn., 1960).

PHILIP GASKELL, 'The first two years of the Water Lane Press' in *Transactions of the Cambridge Bibliographical Society*, v. 2, 1954–8, pp. 170–84.

PHILIP GASKELL, 'The bibliographical press movement' in *Journal of the Printing Historical Society*, no. 1., 1965, pp. 1–13.

CHAPTER 22: EARLY PRESSES

D. B. UPDIKE, *Printing types* (2nd. ed, Cambridge, Mass, 1937).

TALBOT BAINES REED, *A history of the old English letter foundries.* New ed., rev. and enlarged by A. F. Johnson (London, 1952).

M. SIDDIQ KHAN, 'William Carey and the Serampore books (1800–1834)' in *Libri*, v. 11, 1961, pp. 197–280.

J. S. L. GILMOUR, 'Julian Hibbert' [Some uncollected authors, xxvi] in *The book collector*, v. 9, 1960, pp. 446–51.

CHAPTER 23: MORRIS AND AFTER

THOMAS BALSTON, *The Cambridge University Press collection of private press types* (Cambridge, 1951).

BIBLIOGRAPHY

F. C. AVIS, 'Venetian type designs of the English private presses' in *Gutenberg-Jahrbuch*, 1965, pp. 53–7.

F. C. AVIS, *Edward Philip Prince, type punchcutter* (London, 1968).

JOHN DREYFUS, *Italic quartet* (Cambridge, 1966).

ALAN FERN, 'The count and the calligrapher' in *Apollo*, v. 79, 1964, pp. 214–20.

FREDERIC W. GOUDY, *A half-century of type design and typography* (New York, 1946).

DARD HUNTER, *My life with paper* (New York, 1958).

CHAPTER 24: AFTER 1918

ROBERT HARLING, 'The type designs of Eric Gill' in *Alphabet and image*, no. 6, 1948, pp. 55–69.

GWENLLIAN M. DAVIES, 'Lloyd Haberly; a note on his printing' in *Manchester review*, Autumn 1962, pp. 311–20.

CHAPTER 25: THE CONTEMPORARY SCENE

The private press and typefoundry of Paul Hayden Duensing (Kalamazoo, Mich., 1967).

RODERICK CAVE, 'Typefounding for pleasure; a note on the Grimalkin Press' in *Book design and production*, v. 4, no. 3, 1961, p. 184.

ADDENDA TO BIBLIOGRAPHY

LEWIS ALLEN, *Printing with the handpress* (New York, 1969).
A very useful manual from one of the foremost American practitioners.

CHARLES HOLTZAPFFEL, *Printing apparatus for the use of amateurs*. Photolitho reprint of the 3rd ed., 1846, edited by James Mosley & David Chambers. (London, 1971.)
Admirably produced and edited; adds a good deal of information about Victorian amateur printers.

BENEDICTINES OF STANBROOK, *The Stanbrook Abbey Press; ninety-two years of its history*. (Worcester, 1970.)

RATHER, LOIS, *Women as printers* (Oakland, 1970).
Includes a good deal on amateur printing on the distaff side not readily available elsewhere.

Index

(Numbers in italics refer to plates, all other references being to page numbers.)

Date Due

ico 38-297